The Jazz Republic

The Jazz Republic

Music, Race, and American Culture in Weimar Germany

JONATHAN O. WIPPLINGER

UNIVERSITY OF MICHIGAN PRESS
Ann Arbor

Published in the United States of America by the
University of Michigan Press
Manufactured in the United States of America
⊗ Printed on acid-free paper

2020   2019   2018   2017   4   3   2   1

A CIP catalog record for this book is available from the British Library.

Library of Congress Cataloging-in-Publication Data

Names: Wipplinger, Jonathan O., author.
Title: The jazz republic : music, race, and American culture in Weimar Germany / Jonathan O. Wipplinger.
Description: Ann Arbor : University of Michigan Press, [2017] | Series: Social history, popular culture, and politics in Germany | Includes bibliographical references and index.
Identifiers: LCCN 2016046421| ISBN 9780472053407 (pbk. : alk. paper) |
  ISBN 9780472073405 (hardcover : alk. paper) | ISBN 9780472122660 (e-book)
Subjects: LCSH: Jazz—Social aspects—Germany—History—20th century. | Jazz—Germany—1921–1930—History and criticism. | Germany—Civilization—American influences. | Music and race—Germany.
Classification: LCC ML3918.G3 W57 2017 | DDC 306.4/8425094309042—dc23
LC record available at https://lccn.loc.gov/2016046421

And now I have to tell you how it was back then,
when the world, pretty much reaching its goal
on the first try, had become jazz.
—Hans Janowitz

Contents

Acknowledgments

This project has accompanied me now for more than ten years and across four institutions. Over this period, I have had more opportunities than I can recount to converse with scholars and colleagues about the subject of jazz music and popular culture in Germany during the 1920s. Their cumulative effect has helped shape *The Jazz Republic*. Even more so, without the collective support, guidance, and knowledge of friends and colleagues, *The Jazz Republic* simply would not have been completed. Throughout, I've also been financially supported through a number of grants and stipends from the University of Michigan, North Carolina State University, and the University of Wisconsin-Milwaukee.

At both my current and previous institutions, senior colleagues in German have supported me to a degree that went far beyond the call of duty. Fittingly, they each share the first name "Ruth." At North Carolina State, Ruth Gross was my department chair, a scholarly mentor, and simply a wonderful colleague. At Milwaukee, I have had the luck to be helped along and quite often lifted up by Ruth Schwertfeger: our conservations always left me with a smile on my face. I cannot thank each of them enough.

The following is an attempt to list, in no particular order other than alphabetical, some of those who have contributed to the current work over the years. My apologies in advance to anyone I've forgotten: Vanessa Agnew, Kevin Amidon, Don Anderson, Paul Anderson, Naomi André, Kerstin Barndt, Vlad Bilenkin, Viktorija Bilic, Ulrich Biller, Stephen Bourne, Helga Braunbeck, Sylvia Schmitz-Burgard, Peter Cahn, David Choberka, Michael Cowan, Chip Deffaa, Bill Donahue, Andrew Donson, Michelle Eley, Carla Garner, Michael Garval, Karl Gert zur Heide, Daniel Golani, David Gramling, Jürgen Grandt, Jane Hawkins, Gabriele Hayden, Jürgen Heinrichs, Leroy Hopkins, Jochen Hung, Andrew Hurley, Catherine Kirchman, Lutz Kube, Alan Lareau, Priscilla Layne, Rainer Lotz, Jason Miller, Tobias Nagl, Nancy Nenno, Marc Pierce, Arnold

Rampersad, Don Rayno, Marc Reibold, Christian Rogowski, Andreas Schmauder, Michael Schmidt, Barbara Schoenberg, Laurence Senelick, John Sienicki, Meredith Soeder, Werner Sollors, Scott Spector, Noah Strote, Kira Thurman, Louise Toppin, Elisabeth Trautwein-Heymann, Simon Walsh, Silke Weineck, and Michelle Wright.

Special mention, though, is due to two independent researchers of jazz music and African American musicians in Germany and Austria: Hans Pehl and Konrad Nowakowski. Each of them has contributed greatly to the following project through collaboration, joint research, and sharing of their years of knowledge and expertise. They have each greatly enriched the project and their generosity has known no bounds; each read drafts of the manuscript and, in the process, contributed new information and eliminated any number of errors. Needless to say, any mistakes that remain are my own.

My research was also furthered through a number of archives and libraries in the United States and Germany. Generally, I'd like to begin by thanking the interlibrary loan staff at both the University of Wisconsin-Milwaukee and at North Carolina State University for procuring almost every obscure request I've made. In addition, I'd also like to thank specifically: Akademie der Künste (Michael Schwarz), Beinecke Rare Book and Manuscript Library at Yale University, Center for Research Libraries in Chicago, Herzogin Anna Amalia Bibliothek Weimar (Dr. Hans Zimmermann), Hochschule für Musik und darstellende Kunst in Frankfurt am Main (Dr. Andreas Odenkirchen), Institut für Theaterwissenschaft of the Free University Berlin (Dr. Peter Jammerthal), Library of Congress, Moorland-Spingarn Research Center at Howard University, New York Public Library, Paul Whiteman Collection at Williams College, Schomburg Center for Research in Black Culture, Staatsarchiv Ludwigsburg of the Landesarchiv Baden-Württemberg, Staatsbibliothek Berlin, and the Theaterwissenschaftliche Sammlung of the University of Cologne.

To the University of Michigan Press and its entire staff, in particular LeAnn Fields, who has supported the project from the start, I am deeply grateful. I would like to thank the anonymous reviewers of the manuscript as well for their extremely useful comments.

Outside of academia, I have also been supported through my family, my mother and father as well as mother- and father-in-law and my entire extended family.

This book, though, is dedicated to my wife, Katie, and children, Charlotte, Grace, Josephine, and Isabelle. Any words here will not suffice to express what you mean to me, so I'll only say that without you, I would be lost.

Note Regarding Language

Throughout this work, the word "Black" is capitalized when used in reference to people of African descent and the Black African diaspora in all cases except when occurring in direct citation. This usage is common though by no means universal in a variety of fields such as African American Studies and African Diaspora Studies. It is adopted here as a means of signaling these groups' status as communities on par with other nationalities, peoples, etc., yet in a way that also attends to the diversity of Black peoples and cultures in the United States and globally, something especially important given the derogatory and dehumanizing language contained within some of my primary sources. The manuscript also uses "African American" in non-hyphenated form throughout for similar reasons and employs "Black" and "African American" synonymously where appropriate.

Introduction

Sometime in the spring of 1925, a sixteen-year-old Berlin native, Alfred Lion, decided to spend a day at the *Theater im Admiralspalast*. One of the most important entertainment establishments of the German capital, it was well known to Lion from his youth for its renowned skating rink. In 1922, however, the building had been renovated and the rink replaced with a theater hall that could fit an audience of over 2000.[1] In addition to its café and casino, this institution featured performances by musical revues and operettas throughout the 1920s. On that spring day, there was a performance of the African American revue *Chocolate Kiddies*. As Lion recalled much later, in part mixing the establishment's past and present:

> Well, you know I was a young boy and I used to go skating, roller-skating, in a place called the *Admiralspalast*, I think it was. And one day I went there with my skates and they told me there was no skating today, they had a band there and I saw a poster on the wall and it said "Sam Wooding and his Chocolate Dandies" [sic]. And I didn't know anything about it, but it looked strange to me, different, you know. And I went in, checked out my skates, and sat down and there was Sam Wooding. It was the first time I saw colored musicians and heard the music. I was flabbergasted . . .—It was something brand new, but it registered with me right away. . . . I couldn't really put my fingers[sic] on it, but it was the beat, you know. It was the beat. That beat . . .—it got into my bones.[2]

Like so many others who heard jazz during Germany's Weimar Republic, Lion was completely taken by this music from America. Not content with the live experience alone, Lion purchased recordings by Sam Wooding made in Berlin, holding on to them for much of his life.[3] A little more than a year later, in September 1926, Lion undertook a trip to New York City, where, amongst other things, he acquired recordings he could not find in Berlin.[4]

Even in New York, Lion at first found it difficult to find the sort of jazz records he desired, until he discovered so-called "race records." According to Lion, it was only then that he was able to find the work of Duke Ellington, Jelly Roll Morton, and others.[5] Still, New York did not prove to be as enthralled about Lion as he was about jazz. A fight with a dockworker landed him in the hospital, and after convalescing, he returned home to Germany. Back in Berlin, he apparently worked for an import-export company until 1933, when the German-Jewish Lion was forced into exile, first to Chile and then back to New York, this time permanently, in 1936.

While Lion's experience might have remained but an interesting, private aside in interwar history, in 1939, along with Max Margulis, he cofounded *Blue Note Records*, today considered one of the most important record labels in jazz history.[6] Lion was joined in New York later in the year by his friend Francis Wolff, fellow German-Jewish exile and jazz enthusiast from Berlin.[7] The *Blue Note* label became a major driving force behind the recording and dissemination of jazz music and grew from early successes with Sidney Bechet and Albert Ammons and Meade "Lux" Lewis to later working with Thelonious Monk, John Coltrane, Bud Powell, Art Blakey, and Miles Davis. Leaving Harlem for Berlin in 1925, Sam Wooding, the African American performer named in Lion's account, could hardly have imagined the impact his sojourn would have on Lion, jazz history, or, as the present work suggests, on the culture of Weimar Germany itself.

The Jazz Republic argues that encounters between Germans and jazz such as Lion's are emblematic of a broad and unpredictable exchange and dialogue between Germany and America around jazz. From New Orleans to New York, from London to Paris to Moscow, Madrid, and of course Berlin, the 1920s witnessed a global explosion of interest in jazz that found special resonance in Germany. This period in German history was one marked by extremes: in culture, society, and politics. On the one hand, Weimar Germany's culture bristled with the newness and innovation of modernist experimentation in Dadaism and Expressionism, as well as in the films of Fritz Lang and F. W. Murnau. On the other hand, such radical departures from tradition mixed unevenly with repeated crises in politics and the economy: a runaway currency devastated the German middle-class in the early 1920s, followed later by massive unemployment, not to mention a political atmosphere in which murder, rather than debate, often ruled the day. And yet still, in the middle of all this, there stood a new form of music from America called jazz.

From the beginning of the Weimar Republic through the early years of the Nazi regime, American jazz was a constant presence. To speak of the "Golden

Twenties," as the third decade of the twentieth century is often called in Germany, is to evoke images not only of political radicalism and avant-garde artistic experiment but also jazz. More to the point, the Weimar Republic was, in a central way, Germany's own "jazz age." It was an age syncopated by experiences of revolution and betrayal, defeat and "victory" gone awry, hope and despair, progress and reaction. Indeed, because it has become *de rigueur* to refer to jazz's presence within Weimar culture, the music can appear almost omnipresent in scholarly discussions of the period. Yet while there are many individual essays on jazz within German studies scholarship, there are but two monographs devoted to the subject and none in English.[8] More to the point, neither of the existing works investigates the histories of the individual performers to which German commentators responded, nor do they make extensive use of the daily press and the innumerable discussions of jazz that took place there. So though scholars may rarely question jazz's cultural significance, nor do they, as a rule, devote substantive, long-form analysis to showing precisely and concretely how it contributed to, rather than merely reflected, the period's vaunted modernism and modernity. Everywhere and yet nowhere, in many ways jazz figures as a form of cultural background music to Weimar culture proper. Yet jazz and the German interest in it were more than mere passing fancies of a decadent society slipping into the abyss of totalitarianism, more than acoustical accouterment to avant-garde or reaction. Against the implication of jazz as ornament to Weimar culture, *The Jazz Republic* maintains on the contrary that jazz and the German encounter with it must be placed at the center of Weimar culture—of its modernism, modernity, and debates over changing cultural, gender, and racial norms.

Part of the reason for jazz's curious position within contemporary scholarship is the fact that it is a musical, rather than a visual, literary, or otherwise textual, genre. In order to recognize jazz as central to Weimar culture, one must first understand how, as the editors of a collection of writings on music and culture put it, "sound matters"—to culture, subjectivity, and history.[9] While musicologists, in particular via the work of Susan McClary, have for some time convincingly argued for a socially constructed notion of music and sound, scholars within German studies have only more recently begun to ask similar questions. If scholarship in the emerging field of sound studies has begun redefining our understanding of sound in German studies, the exact role this aural realm has played remains much less defined.[10]

For a number of reasons, the case of Germany during the interwar period presents a particularly rich example of crossings between music, sound, culture, and society. As scholars Pamela Potter and Celia Applegate have argued in a variety of contexts, for much of the nineteenth and twentieth centuries, German cultural identity was deeply invested in music.[11] If the equation was neither uniform nor uncontested, the idea of Germans as a "people of music" acted as a powerful framing device within broader debates over German identity. During the interwar period, such debates increased in proportion and intensity. Applegate and Potter summarize: "World War I marked a crisis in German identity that deeply influenced the discourse on German music while condoning attempts to exploit music for political aims."[12] The disruption of society and politics caused by World War I and Germany's ensuing defeat engendered a crisis in national and thus musical identity. Over the course of the Weimar Republic and the Third Reich, various attempts were made to rearticulate the fractured relationship between music and German cultural identity. This lent the reception of jazz special significance during the interwar period and guaranteed debate over the music's powerful resonance in this period of upheaval. As a musical form emanating from the United States, one viewed simultaneously as both mechanical and primitive, jazz posed immediate challenges to the ideologies surrounding this musically inflected cultural identity. Yet if discussion of jazz could act, as it indeed often did, as a means of reinforcing boundaries between "German" and "non-German," so, too, could it lead to spectacular breakdowns of such oppositions, to reforming and rearticulating categories of national and cultural belonging, of constructions of Weimar Germany as jazz republic.

Reimagining America, Rethinking German Americanism

In order to do justice to the complexity, unpredictability, and contradictoriness of the meaning of jazz music for Weimar Germany, it is first necessary to change how we approach the encounter between Germany and America as it took place through jazz. During the Weimar Republic an important debate over *Amerikanismus* (Americanism) and *Amerikanisierung* (Americanization) occurred across German culture and society, with jazz being one essential component of this discussion.[13] From conservatives like Adolf Halfeld who railed against the "mechanical life" of America to Bertolt Brecht's satire of an infatuated group of "700 intellectuals praying before an oil tanker," debate over America and American modernity occupied an important position on both ends of the political and cultural spectrum.[14] With the global recognition of the United States as a world power following the First World War, Europeans and Germans in particular paid increasingly public attention to this once upstart nation, elevating its status in the minds of many to the purest instantiation of the present, of the modern; its skyscrapers, monopolistic businesses, films and film stars, and jazz signaling to Weimar commentators simultaneously hope for renewal as well as marking fear over decline.[15]

At the same time, one of the fundamental questions regarding American-ism is the extent to which Germany's image of America compares to the his-torical reality of 1920s America. In accounts of the period, Weimar's America is all-too-often understood primarily as an absence, a projection of a utopian or, as is often the case, a dystopian imaginary, against which German culture could define itself. This line of thinking was by no means foreign to cultural critics at the time. Rudolf Kayser, for example, could already claim in 1925 that Americanism "[c]ertainly . . . has nothing or only little to do with the American," instead, it "is a new European method" for embracing modern life.[16] While there is little question that Weimar Americanism was a cultural war waged on a German field of battle, with German interests largely driving the debate, this does not mean that the encounter and engagement with Ameri-can culture was purely, or even primarily, determined by German interests alone. To paraphrase Marx's methodological challenge from the *18th Bru-maire*, Weimar Germany may have made its image of America, but it did not make it freely, as it pleased. Instead of viewing German Americanism as a mirror image of internal concerns, the present work understands the relation-ship to be more akin to that of a prismatic refraction. While the prism of Ger-man culture and history did indeed shape the output, the resulting image was to no small part informed by the input of American culture itself. In a word, Weimar's America and the debates around it were, I argue, powerfully in-formed by the contradictions and conflicts inherent to American culture itself, most notably of race. One conclusion to draw from this is that in order to better understand the images of jazz circulating in Weimar culture, one must investi-gate the African American and African diasporic presence in the United States and in Germany. As Tobias Nagl writes in his study of race and Blackness in Weimar film, "representations of the 'Other' cannot be conceptualized within a vacuum; they carry traces of real encounters and are symptoms of a repressed history."[17] In addressing and evaluating the impact of America and jazz on Weimar culture, the current work will argue that one must hear this history in stereo, as it were, simultaneously listening to developments on both sides of the Atlantic. Only in this way can one be attentive both to the ways American culture framed and was in turn framed by the German encounter with it.

For this synching of German and American culture to work to its fullest extent, however, each side of the encounter must be reexamined. On the American side, this process begins with acknowledgment of the fraught racial composition of American culture. Scholarship on Americanism in Weimar tends to abide by the unspoken agreement that when one is discussing Americanism in Weimar, it is of a white Germany confronting a white America, with consideration of the impact of African Americans and Blackness generally treated as a separate topic. As long as this remains the implicit framework from which German Americanism is judged, the German encounter with America will itself remain the caricature it has often become. To move away from such separation and from Weimar's own understanding of Americanism as "European method," one of the first steps is to view discussion of white American and African American culture as inseparable. Ralph Ellison's thoughts on African American culture in relation to white American culture have been important to my thinking here. As Ellison writes in "Change the Joke and Slip the Yoke":

> Down at the deep dark bottom of the melting pot, where the private is public and the public private, where black is white and white black, where the immoral becomes moral and the moral is anything that makes one feel good (or that one has the power to sustain), the white man's relish is apt to be the black man's gall.[18]

Ellison's recasting of the well-known metaphor of the American melting pot not only speaks to the foundational importance of African Americans to American culture *writ large*, but also to the unique structure of American cultural identity in the nineteenth and twentieth centuries. Both Manichean dualism and dialectically dirtied stew of cultures, races, and identities, Ellison's take on American identity points towards the necessity to recognize in everything that originates from this nation a duality of inseparably connected "essences." As Ellison argues, however, such interconnectedness has little to do with the equitable distribution of power. Speaking to the painful and often violent implications of the racial ideologies inherent to American culture, he reminds his (white) readers that white enjoyment ("relish") usually means pain and anger ("gall") for African Americans. In terms of conceptualizing the impact of jazz on German culture, Ellison's thoughts suggest the need to examine how all instances of US culture are bound up with this dialectic of race and to investigate in turn how German commentators engage (or do not) with this aspect.

I will define my use of the term "jazz" shortly, but it is important to consider the implications of this idea in relation to American popular music more generally. As the work of Ronald Radano has shown, the late nineteenth and early twentieth century witnessed a fundamental shift in how African American music was constructed and consumed by critics and audiences. Out of an ideological matrix of music and racial difference, Radano argues, a focus on rhythm in Black music emerged and created a code of listening to and defining Black music that erased earlier understandings, in particular in relation to the African American voice. The trope of an ineffable "Black rhythm" pervaded and shaped American popular music, both Black and white, and in so doing created the fraught system out of which American (and German) conceptualizations of jazz emerge. For Radano, this means that:

> Black music's power [is located] not in a segregated racial preserve but in the relational position of a black sound confessing the mulatto truth of a white supremacist nation. If it unseats the authenticity of black presence so does it reveal for African-America something more: it places claim on the totality of the American social experience that has been persistently portrayed to be white.[19]

Following Radano, my conceptualization of American culture is not one that would erase racial difference through a claim of power equity between Black and white as in the non-Ellisonian idea of American culture as "melting pot." Instead, my emphasis on the relational structure of African American and white American identities gestures towards an understanding of American culture that better attends to W. E. B. Du Bois' concept of double consciousness, which amongst many other things, is tied with striving "to make it possible," as Du Bois writes in *The Souls of Black Folks*, "for a man to be both a Negro and an American."[20] On the one hand, this will mean paying attention to how German images of and interactions with African Americans overlap but are not identical to other African diasporic communities. On the other, this means that it is necessary to show how the seemingly most "white" American phenomena carry "Blackness" and how "Black" phenomena like jazz are often structured via white America's image of African Americans.

Through this specific conceptualization of American culture, I hope to unfold an equally complex German encounter with American culture, jazz, and Blackness during the Weimar Republic. For one, it enables a reorientation of Weimar Americanism along transnational vectors that often lead directly towards Germany's own conflicted racial and colonial past. As a modern European (after 1919 former) colonial power, German society during the first half of the last century took part in a global network of exchanges: of peoples, products, cultures, and ideas. Germany's colonial era escalated the encounter and exchange with the rest of the world, including Black Africans. Moreover, and in parallel to my own thoughts, Andrew Zimmerman's *Alabama in Africa* has shown the value of viewing these questions within a transnational context of race, capitalism, and labor. As Zimmerman demonstrates through his discussion of the expedition of members of Booker T. Washington's Tuskegee Institute to the German colony in Togo in 1901, German investments in Africa and Blackness were part of a network linking African, African American, white American, German, and other European actors.[21] In revealing this interweaving of Africa, African America, and Germany, Zimmerman's work hints at what might be gained through the application of a similar model to the study of Americanism and jazz in the Weimar Republic.

The colonial and transnational context discussed by historians like Zimmerman has obvious implications for scholars working in the interdisciplinary field of German studies. As Sara Lennox argues in "From Postcolonial to Transnational Approaches in German Studies," while many German historians since the work of Sebastian Conrad and Jürgen Osterhammel have come to adopt a transnational approach in the broadest sense, the field of German studies has much more unevenly adopted the transnational perspective.[22] Intervening into this state of affairs, Lennox offers at the end of her essay a series of important methodological challenges to guide German studies scholarship in a transnational direction. She writes:

> How are cultural representations affected by impulses external to the nation state . . . and how does the cultural product position itself vis-à-vis those impulses? To what degree does the text directly thematize these questions, and how must we read differently to find the answers? How and why do German-language texts respond differently to the same transnational phenomena from texts with other linguistic origins? How are the national and the transnational explicitly or implicitly represented in the text?[23]

Given the global reach of jazz in the 1920s, such questions will be crucial for thinking through Germany's encounter with the music. While I address these questions in more detail below, for the moment, the framework offered by Lennox suggests that when thinking through jazz on the global stage, it is necessary to consider the global, transnational context of the jazz's dissemination and reception alongside the music's African American origins.

There were three primary means by which the transnational space of the late nineteenth and early twentieth century inflected Weimar Germany's encounter with jazz. To begin with, this period witnessed a proliferation of racial thinking along social Darwinist lines. As Fatima El-Tayeb argues, during the period leading up to the First World War, Blackness and Blacks became a central component of the ideology of race within German biological, as well as philosophical, sciences.[24] Across a wide range of thinkers, Africans, or rather Blackness, as a socially constructed identity, emerged as the ultimate category of otherness for white European identity. Yet colonialism and its inherently global nature also meant that, in practice, the separation of white and Black, as in the case of America, was a difficult proposition, to say the least. Within Germany's colonies themselves, crucial questions had to be asked about "race mixing" between Black and white, for example regarding the citizenship of offspring between white Germans and Black Africans.[25] While in Germany proper, a Black community was in the process of formation from the 1880s onward.[26] Though the history of the African diasporic presence in Germany stretches much further back in history, German colonialism of the nineteenth and twentieth centuries fundamentally changed how, where, and under what circumstances white Germans and members of African diaspora confronted each other. Further, because such traffic between Germany and Africa did not take place in isolation, but within the broader Western European colonialist project, port cities like Hamburg and financial capitals like Berlin and Frankfurt witnessed significant numbers of African migrant workers.[27] One of the arenas through which this presence entered into German consciousness was popular culture.[28] Beyond well-known associations of Blackness with chocolate as in the advertising figure of the "Sarotti Mohr," commercial advertisements of the period for tobacco, soap, and numerous other commodities were suffused with images of Blackness.[29] Additionally, the entertainment industry in the form of *Völkerschauen*, or "ethnographic shows," such as those of Carl Hagenbeck, not to mention the variety theaters and music halls regularly employed Black performers, as has been documented in works by Eric Ames and Rainer Lotz for example.[30]

To turn back to the topic at hand, how did these phenomena inform and how in turn were they informed by the German engagement with American culture during the period roughly between 1890 and 1945? For one, around the same time as the African diasporic presence was garnering greater visibility within Germany, one witnesses an initial entry of American and African American popular culture that in many ways presages much of Weimar's initial encounter with jazz, as is discussed in chapter 1.[31] Central here were new technologies of mechanical reproduction like the phonograph, in addition to an unprecedented influx of mass-produced sheet music. These developments exponentially increased the number and modalities of German contacts with American music and culture. Simultaneous to this expansion of American mass culture, African American artists, with the incumbent complexities of cultural production under Jim Crow, were gaining greater visibility within the United States and abroad, in Europe and Germany, for example. This meant that Germany's first significant exposure to American popular music (cakewalk and ragtime) was one in which the distinction between white and Black music was both on display and very much up for grabs. It is therefore unsurprising that within the German reception of these phenomena, one witnesses some of the same tropes regarding Blackness, rhythm, and capitalist commodification that can be found within the early debate on jazz during the 1920s. While Astrid Kusser has produced an important monograph on cakewalk dancing from a transnational perspective, with my conclusions generally echoing her own, the relative sparseness of scholarly discussion of cakewalk and other forms of American culture during Wilhelmine Germany, even compared to the literature on jazz during the Weimar Republic, let alone Nazi-era jazz, is striking.[32] That these earlier encounters have until very recently largely been ignored has much to do with the prevailing mythology regarding jazz in Weimar Germany.[33]

Mythologies of Weimar Jazz Culture

As I suggested earlier, the idea that jazz is important to Weimar culture is by no means new and hardly anyone writing a cultural history of the period would fail to refer to jazz's presence or general significance. Yet at the level of the actual history of jazz in Germany, such discussions for the most part remain at the level of superficial glosses—a few names of jazz bands or African American performers are mentioned before turning to other matters—or, alternatively, look at jazz in isolation from the issues addressed above. Most significantly, scholarly analyses have all too often depended on outdated secondary literature, for example, Horst Lange's *Jazz in Deutschland* (*Jazz in Germany*), for details regarding jazz bands in Germany.[34] One result of this is the persistence of a very specific mythology regarding jazz in 1920s Germany. This mythology approaches jazz anachronistically and with the hindsight of around one hundred years of writing on jazz, rather than investigating what jazz meant to Germans, Americans, and members of the Black diaspora in 1920, 1925, or 1930. More specifically, I would like to suggest that most discussions of jazz in Weimar Germany have remained embedded in what Scott DeVeaux has called the "jazz tradition."[35] By this term, he means to indicate the broad consensus regarding jazz as a metacategory for the variety of African American musical styles and genres that emerged in the twentieth century. As DeVeaux writes: "The idea of the 'jazz tradition' is an idea of relatively recent vintage, an overarching narrative that has crowded out other possible interpretations of the complicated and variegated cultural phenomena that we cluster under the umbrella jazz."[36] From Dixieland to big band, swing, bebop and beyond, the "jazz tradition" narrates the history of jazz in a progression of genius musicians like Louis Armstrong, Duke Ellington, Dizzy Gillespie, Miles Davis, and John Coltrane. While this narrative has a great many advantages, it is nonetheless a specific historical narrative, one long in the making and certainly not available to writers, German or otherwise, during the 1920s. Furthermore, while the "jazz tradition" does an excellent job of explaining the history of recorded jazz in the United States, it is less useful at explaining the developments at the margins, such as the case of Germany, where many practitioners were neither African American nor white American, but rather German, Afro-German, Afro-European, African, and other identities, or for that matter where no recorded documentation exists.

While accounts of jazz's historical, cultural, or literary presence within Germany tend to approach the music from the "jazz tradition," they differ in terms of how they view German jazz's relationship to it. At times, references to jazz by Weimar commentators are contextualized with missing information from the "jazz tradition." Though this was particularly prevalent in earlier scholarship, it continues on today and has led to any number of errors about which types of jazz musicians Germans knew or heard in Berlin, Frankfurt, Dresden, and elsewhere. One typical error in this regard is the repeated references to Duke Ellington's presence in Weimar Berlin, and to this day, one can find erroneous claims of Ellington having toured Germany during the Weimar Republic.[37] While errors are inevitable and the present work is by no means excluded, the focus on Ellington and the overall approach to Weimar jazz through the contemporary narrative of the "jazz tradition" has had the effect of obscuring the role played by other African American jazz musicians, like Sam Wooding or members of the *Southern Syncopated Orchestra,* who did in fact perform in Germany. Just as significantly, the work of Afro-Europeans and other non-American members of the Black diaspora was long ignored for similar reasons.

Another manner of responding to Weimar jazz culture, currently much more prevalent, is to dismiss early German jazz and jazz culture as inauthentic precisely because it does not correspond to the "jazz tradition" and its developmental narrative. In other words, a common thread of contemporary scholarship is to suggest that Weimar jazz is largely or even wholly of German origin, sharing little in common with the "jazz tradition." The work of J. Bradford Robinson, in particular his "Jazz Reception in Weimar Germany: In Search of a Shimmy Figure" is perhaps the best example of this mode of analysis.[38] Robinson's conclusion in this influential essay is that "two misconceptions haunt all discussions of the impact of jazz on the musicians of Weimar Germany. One is that the music they confronted was legitimate jazz; the other, that it was specifically American."[39] Based on an analysis of jazz-inflected German and Austrian art music, Robinson argues that the jazz of composers such as Ernst Krenek and Kurt Weill was a German invention, owing to the specific historical-economic situation of the early years of the republic.[40] As Robinson suggestively writes: "Legitimate black-American jazz, as apart from its diluted commercial imitations, was unknown in Germany as a concept until 1930," citing a single review in the music journal *Melos* of recordings by Louis Armstrong and Duke Ellington as evidence of this claim.[41] While Robinson's work was pathbreaking insofar as it challenged naïve assumptions regarding jazz in 1920s Germany, his analytical framework, as is clear from the above, remains that of the "jazz tradition," rather than the more complicated situation in both Germany and the United States. Even more so, Robinson's claim that Weimar musicians and the German public encountered no "legitimate" African American jazz until 1930 is deeply problematic as this work will show. So though his work does indeed push back at the mythologies of jazz in Germany, it is only the beginning of grasping the function of jazz for Weimar culture, hardly the end. For as DeVeaux has argued elsewhere, the "jazz tradition," this narrative upon which jazz history is constructed, is a shifting thing. Those who belong to the "core" and those who are excluded from it (and why and how) is ever changing. As DeVeaux writes in a passage highly relevant for the case of jazz during the Weimar Republic: "It's time to acknowledge that the history of global jazz cannot be reduced to a single story, no matter how 'American' the century in which it developed may have been."[42] The *Jazz Republic* aspires to make one, albeit very specific, contribution to this global history of jazz.

In this reorientation towards the transatlantic and global history of jazz, as well as much else in the following, my thinking is deeply indebted to Paul Gilroy and his seminal work *The Black Atlantic*. Specifically, it attempts to heed Gilroy's call to understand Black diasporic cultural production in all its variation:

How are we to think critically about artistic products and aesthetic codes which, though they may be traceable back to one distinct location, have been changed either by the passage of time or by their displacement, relocation, or dissemination through networks of communication and cultural exchange?[43]

This statement has particular force in terms of the global transmission of cultural forms like jazz under capitalism and colonialism. *The Jazz Republic* as a whole is an attempt to work through these insights by Gilroy, to acknowledge the messiness of cultural transfer, as well as to remain attuned to jazz's cultural and historical specificity as a multiply determined art form of American popular music emerging from and within African American culture and aesthetic practices.

The stakes involved in the application of the term "jazz" for Weimar culture are obviously high. In point of fact, many German commentators have long shown a preference for alternate terms like *Tanzmusik* (dance music), *Unterhaltungsmusik* (entertainment music), or *Schlager* (hit songs), despite the fact that the word "jazz" litters their source material.[44] While from a certain point of view these terms may be more technically precise, I find the disavowal of the term "jazz" conceptually limiting. In many ways, it is an *a priori* negation of the question of whether American jazz influenced German culture and music. Taking this conceptual slippage and Robinson's argument to one logical conclusion, Thomas J. Saunders argues that jazz's

> falsely implied ubiquity, on the basis of very limited exposure to the original American music or bands, can be taken as evidence of just how German, and impervious to America, popular culture remained. Here, as elsewhere, the longing among certain intellectuals for cultural renewal valorized an otherwise marginal cultural phenomenon.[45]

If, as Damon J. Philips has shown, the notion of Germany's "limited exposure" to jazz, at least in comparison to other European nations, can be called into question,[46] there is a broader and more important point to be made here. Though scholars like Robinson and Saunders may be correct to question haphazard and anachronistic assumptions regarding jazz, i.e., those that fill in missing details from German jazz history with information from the jazz tradition, it nonetheless remains counterproductive to close off German culture in an age so replete with international translation, transmission, and cultural exchange. It also means closing oneself off to so many of the encounters with jazz detailed in the present work.

Instead of attempting to delineate a stable notion of jazz against which

German knowledge might be judged, the present work proceeds from a different conceptualization. It is one that seeks to provide sufficient space for moments of volatility and unpredictability, as well as dialogue between white Americans, African Americans, other members of the African Diaspora, Europeans, and Weimar Germans, both Black and white. Under the term "jazz," it understands a shifting set of positions emerging from a specific cultural constellation through which "jazz," or better, jazz effects were produced. By jazz effects, I mean to indicate moments of intersection and interpenetration of discourses of music, race, and American culture. Fundamentally, such jazz effects are the result of interaction and engagement with cultural products originating from America. In other words, a jazz effect emerges when the three cultural coordinates, music, race, and American culture, combine in or after an encounter with a form of American culture. In focusing on such moments of cultural contact and dialogue, I hope to show that jazz was not only a metaphor but also material for Weimar culture.

While naturally the points of departure for my analysis will remain primarily musical and/or auditory (visiting jazz bands, listening to jazz recordings, the training of jazz musicians), this usage carries a number of advantages over the narrower definition of the "jazz tradition." For one, the cultural terrain comprised by these elements is much larger and more complex and is better capable of encompassing the wide variability of cultural documents from the period that were indebted to jazz—music, both popular and serious; poetry; literature; visual arts; criticism; philosophy; advertising; etc. This definition also allows me to discuss under the rubric of "jazz" matters that, from the perspective of the "jazz tradition," would seem only tangentially related to the music, yet because of their intersectional position were caught up within Weimar's jazz culture. Through the idea of the "jazz effect," in other words, I endeavor to reconstruct the broad landscape of German knowledge about American culture and jazz, which could be extremely specific and detailed, if, in the manner of a prismatic refraction, also highly selective. This use of jazz and the idea of a jazz effect are obviously much more than definitions; they act as an interpretive model and seek to build a framework for demonstrating the centrality of jazz to Weimar culture.

While my ultimate aim is to better explain the origins and development of Weimar jazz culture, this can often only be achieved via a more thoroughgoing engagement with matters outside of Weimar's geographical boundaries. At various places within the following work, I devote substantial space to detailing the histories of white and African Americans, various peoples of African descent, members of the Jewish diaspora, Austrians, Russians, and Hungarians. Through the attention paid to the individual histories of figures like Evandale Roberts, Sam Wooding, Paul Whiteman, Sonny "Fernandes" Jones, Mátyás Seiber, and Anna Nussbaum, I endeavor to open up Weimar cultural history and Weimar jazz culture more fully to these "foreign" voices that played such significant roles, yet have not found a central place within scholarship. To identify one extreme case, where does Ossip Dymow's musical comedy *Schatten über Harlem* (*Shadows over Harlem*) belong within Weimar culture, jazz and otherwise? This 1930 work may have premiered in Stuttgart, but it was written by a Russian-Jewish-American author, set to music by a Hungarian composer, and was based upon translations of works by African American and Afro-Caribbean poets done by Austrian and German writers. Unless one looks both within and beyond Germany's geographical and cultural boundaries, this and less extreme examples will remain without a place. For me, then, reading jazz in Germany demands that we look as much at what was going on inside Weimar Germany as at how this inside connected with the outside. Indeed, what else sums up better the promise of Weimar culture than, to cite Peter Gay, the idea of the "outsider as insider"? This history, however, can only be reconstructed at this culture's edges in interstitial spaces that exist between and often beyond America and Germany. In sum, *The Jazz Republic* aspires to reorient current understanding of jazz in Germany as formed by intercultural and, indeed, transnational exchange to provide a new sense of this culture that, like Alfred Lion, was once so thoroughly invested in and enthralled by jazz.

Overview

After the introduction, seven substantive chapters follow. While they are roughly organized chronologically, each also represents an instantiation of Weimar Germany as "jazz republic"; that is to say, each acts as a specific example of how music, race, and American culture collided to produce a "jazz effect" and, in the process, pushed jazz to the center of Weimar culture. It is important to note that while they cover a broad range of political, cultural, and aesthetic issues, they are by no means exhaustive. They have been selected in part on the basis of their representativeness for the broader German discussion of jazz, such as because they belong to a specific cultural arena, e.g., visual culture; but always they were selected because they reveal how the experience of American culture directly shaped the context and contour of Weimar jazz culture. These range from the avant-garde, to social constructions of the jazz experience in relation to critical theory, literary and theatrical modernism, representations of the New Woman and gender on stage and in film, the crisis of high culture, transnational modernism, and Adorno's aesthetic theory. Still, there are many more examples and histories than can be recounted in any single work. So if some better-known figures like Josephine Baker, Kurt Weill, and Ernst Krenek do not receive extensive treatment, this should not be read as an indication of their insignificance, to my argument or otherwise. Instead, these, along with many other lesser-known yet no less important examples, cede their position in order to present the following selection of Weimar Germany as jazz republic.

Chapter 1, "Jazz Occupies Germany: Weimar Jazz Culture between the Rhine and Berlin," looks at the initial responses to jazz after the First World War. It shows how German exposure to jazz from 1919 to 1923 proceeded in an uneven and geographically differentiated manner. In Berlin, new social dances like the foxtrot and "jazz" appeared in the winter and spring of 1919, though with little relation to jazz music. For the next two years, however, Berlin's nascent jazz culture was supported through the activities of modern artists who featured jazz dancing and American popular culture across a spectrum of works that can be read as belonging to the transnational debate surrounding jazz amongst European-American modernists. During the same period, yet within the zones of foreign occupation along the Rhine, jazz bands and jazz music began emerging much earlier than in Berlin and in much closer dialogue with American, British, and French developments in popular music. Along with these jazz bands, the occupation also brought with it debate over the presence of French colonial African soldiers, the so-called scandal of the "*Schwarze Schmach am Rhein*" ("Black Shame" or "Black Horror on the Rhine"). As I show, between 1920 and 1922, both this debate as well as jazz bands, white and Black, German and non-German, moved from the occupation zones along the Rhine to Berlin and elsewhere in Germany. Through analysis of early German jazz criticism, as well as visual representations of the music, I suggest the development of German jazz culture was, from the beginning, both involved in a broad network of European-American jazz criticism and, more importantly, decidedly influenced by the contact and conflict along the Rhine.

The relative stabilization of the economy and society in 1924 ushered in a new era of cultural vitality, the so-called "Golden Twenties." During this period, jazz and its effects were felt most strongly and across a broad swath of Weimar culture. To begin with, Germany welcomed African American jazz musicians like Sam Wooding in greater numbers. These jazz artists, as well as their white counterparts, began to exert an influence that remained strong for the next nine years and beyond. Because of the wide-ranging and long-standing impact of jazz from the mid-1920s onward, each of the next five chapters presents a cross-section of Weimar culture's jazz impulse as it expanded and contracted between the years 1924 and 1933.

The second chapter, "The Aural Shock of Modernity: Sam Wooding and Weimar Germany's Experience of Jazz," considers the 1925 Berlin performances of the African American jazz band of Sam Wooding. It seeks to explain the distinctive impression made by jazz bands, Wooding's in particular, on German audience members like Alfred Lion through development of the concept of the aural shock. Indeed, to many a reviewer, Wooding's jazz seemed to differ from prior experiences with jazz, necessitating within critical writings a renegotiation of the understanding of jazz in the years following his initial appearance. Drawing on the writings of Theodor W. Adorno and Walter Benjamin, it argues that jazz music and Weimar Germany's experience of it were bound up with specific transformations of sound and music under modernity. Through reconstruction of the original performance context, along with analysis of initial reviews and subsequent mediations of the event, it seeks to rethink and retheorize Weimar culture's encounter with jazz as a conceptual space in which questions relating to the individual's experience of modernity were refracted through discussion of jazz.

Just one year after Sam Wooding performed in Berlin, the white American bandleader Paul Whiteman visited the capital. Chapter 3, "Writing Symphonies in Jazz: Paul Whiteman and German Literature," explores a set of literary mediations of Whiteman's "symphonic jazz," which celebrated its Berlin premiere at the *Grosses Schauspielhaus* in June 1926. While the reaction to this less raucous and more "refined" version of the music was divided between music critics who by and large rejected it and the audience and popular musicians who tended to embrace it, Whiteman's controversial pairing of jazz and the symphony found resonance with a number of modernist authors. This chapter explores Hans Janowitz's *Jazz. Roman* (*Jazz: A Novel*), Rene Schickele's *Symphonie für Jazz* (*Symphony for Jazz*), and Gustav Renker's *Symphonie und Jazz* (*Symphony and Jazz*) as literary experiments structured by the German encounter with Whiteman and symphonic jazz. Read as reactions to Whiteman's experimental combination of high and low culture, such works, I argue, are no longer "merely" novels about jazz, but rather literary meditations on the breakdown of traditional form in art and society.

While the previous two chapters considered the significance of visiting American jazz musicians for Weimar culture, how Whiteman and Wooding shaped and were shaped by their German interlocutors, the next chapter focuses on German cultural responses to shifts in gender hierarchies vis-à-vis jazz productions of their own. Chapter 4, "Syncopating the Mass Ornament: Race and *Girlkultur*," investigates the relationship between jazz, gender, Blackness, and visual culture on the Weimar revue stage. Specifically, I'm interested in how jazz and the African and African American performers associated with it collided with the debate over the white American chorus girl or "Tiller Girl." Towards this end, I read the construction of *Girlkultur* by Weimar theorists and artists as having been produced out of fear over racial contamination between Black and white. This chapter shows how such discussion of the white American chorus girl bore directly on the figuration of Weimar's New Woman, as not only a threat to gender but also to racial hierarchies. As is suggested in this chapter's conclusion, Siegfried Kracauer's well-known work on revue culture, portrayed most famously in his 1927 essay "The Mass Ornament," reveals itself to contain traces of these very same tensions around gender and race. In re-reading Kracauer via jazz, in syncopating his mass ornament, I want to show how jazz had a hand not only in the construction of Weimar culture but Weimar theory as well.

Adding further geographical balance and much more, the fifth chapter, "Bridging the Great Divides: Jazz at the Conservatory," transitions away from the city of Berlin to interrogate the scandal of the *Jazzklasse*, or jazz program, at Hoch's Conservatory in Frankfurt am Main. That this was the first example of postsecondary academic training in jazz in Europe indicates the special importance accorded to jazz in 1920s Germany. Composer and conservatory director Bernhard Sekles announced the program in late 1927 and a predictable, if no less vitriolic, debate ensued. Beginning with an explanation of the structural and institutional reasons for this unlikely announcement, I next look at the terms of the debate over the *Jazzklasse* from the perspective of its supporters. My analysis shows how, in their defenses of the program, liberal music critics such as Heinrich Strobel and Alfred Baresel rewrote jazz's origins as ultimately European, rather than American or African American. Yet this debate is but one aspect of the program's broader significance. In this chapter, I also explore the jazz pedagogy of the program's Hungarian-born director Mátyás Seiber as an example of the uneven jazzing up of German culture. Examining the jazz practices at Hoch's Conservatory allows me to reveal the much deeper and more complicated exchange that took place between Germans and their American and African American models than consideration of the debate alone might otherwise suggest.

While the previous chapters deal more or less directly with the issue of jazz music and its place within Weimar culture, the next two seek to show how jazz impacted cultural production even when the music seemingly played no role. The translation of the Harlem Renaissance poet Langston Hughes into German and Theodor W. Adorno's incomplete *Singspiel* based on Mark Twain's *The Adventures of Tom Sawyer* each show how the German discussion and engagement with jazz came to impact cultural production more broadly. Indeed, if African American figures often play a muted role in debates about jazz, such as the *Jazzklasse*, chapter 6, "Singing the Harlem Renaissance: Langston Hughes, Translation, and the Diasporic Blues," demonstrates that African American voices were by no means silent during the era. In the reception and translation of Hughes from 1922 onward, I show how the poetic and musical translation of his work acted as a pivot point for international and transnational exchange between African Americans, Jewish Germans and Jewish Austrians, and other marginalized groups. Reaching beyond Weimar Germany's geographical borders, I identify in the more than sixty translations of Hughes by seventeen different translators a fertile exchange between German and African American modernist cultural production that grew out of and alongside Weimar culture's fascination with jazz and America. Together with the direct, personal encounters of Hughes himself with three of his translators, important works like Anna Nussbaum's 1929 collection of Harlem Renaissance poetry or the 1930 operetta *Shadows over Harlem* demonstrate that cultural exchange between African Americans and German-speaking Europe was hardly one-sided.

At the same time and in the wake of the economic collapse of 1929 and the renewed radicalization of German politics, jazz's position within Weimar culture became ever more precarious. An increasingly loud chorus of voices across the political spectrum proclaimed jazz's relevance for German culture to be at an end. Chapter 7, "Jazz's Silence: Adorno, Opera, and the Decomposition of Weimar Culture," looks anew at Theodor W. Adorno's controversial rejection of jazz. Against the common reading of Adorno as ultimate antipode to jazz, I interpret Adorno's work of the early 1930s as belonging to the very same complex of music, race, and American culture traced throughout the present work. Specifically, I read Adorno's neglected opera fragment *Der Schatz des Indianer Joe. Singspiel nach Mark Twain* (*The Treasure of Indian Joe. Singspiel after Mark Twain*) as an, albeit indirect, engagement with the legacy of Americanism and jazz reception during the Weimar Republic. My discussion of Adorno further serves to demonstrate how Weimar culture was continually defined and redefined through jazz, even at this, its moment of dissolution.

Of course, the construction of Weimar Germany as jazz republic did not proceed smoothly, let alone uniformly. Between jazz's entrance after the war, Alfred Lion's seemingly chance encounter with Sam Wooding, and Theodor Adorno's unfinished opera much changed. Yet one thing held fast throughout the period: jazz's association with the modernism and political travails of the new German democracy born in 1919 out of military defeat and revolution following World War I.

CHAPTER I

Jazz Occupies Germany: Weimar Jazz Culture between the Rhine and Berlin

> The German schoolmaster cannot dance it. The Prussian reserve officer cannot dance it. If only all ministers and councilors and professors and politicians were obliged to dance jazz, even now and again publicly! In what a joyous way would they be stripped of their entire honor (*Würde*)! How human, how nice, how comical would they have to become! No atmosphere of stupidity, vanity, and grandeur (*Würde*) could form. If the Kaiser had danced jazz—all that would never have happened! But no! He could never have learned it. Being German Kaiser is easier than dancing jazz.
> —Hans Siemsen (1921)

In what has become one of the most cited early commentaries on jazz in Germany,[1] Hans Siemsen, cultural critic and early proponent of popular culture, sums up much of the hope placed in jazz by German leftists in the period following war.[2] Offering the absurd counterfactual history of Kaiser Wilhelm II dancing jazz, he suggests jazz could have changed the course of German history. While the comedy of this image ensures its effectiveness, both then and today, Siemsen's words raise more questions than they offer answers. Though jazz for Siemsen clearly has the effect of removing dignity from those who practice it, what exactly would not have happened had the Kaiser danced jazz: the war? Germany's defeat? For another, why does he not ask us to imagine the German Kaiser playing, rather than dancing jazz?

The goal of this opening chapter is to investigate the broader context of Siemsen's statement in order to understand more precisely how jazz entered and eventually spread across Germany's cultural and geographical landscape in the first years of the Weimar Republic, roughly the period between 1919 and 1923. For while Siemsen's report takes jazz's presence for granted, the road leading from the end of the First World War in November 1918 to this text from early 1921 was not only circuitous but filled with developmental cul-de-sacs.

Indeed, any attempt at reconstructing jazz's presence in this early period is faced with a number of difficult, hitherto only vaguely answered questions. How did Germans first encounter jazz? Where and under what circumstances? How did jazz in Germany develop in contrast to the United States, England, France, or elsewhere? And was there something unique to its use and spread in Germany? Such questions are all the more compelling due to the seemingly eccentric place Germany holds within broader jazz history itself, what Damon J. Phillips has called the "puzzle of German jazz."[3]

This chapter will attempt to answer some of these questions by broadly tracing the earliest exposure of Germans to jazz and related musical styles and dances through a comparative framework. On the one hand, I will pay attention to the development of jazz and jazz criticism within the United States and Western Europe, in particular France and England, in order to evaluate the issue of German jazz's uniqueness. In addressing this early history of jazz in Germany, I argue that it is essential to distinguish, at least for the years 1919 through 1921, between the situation in Berlin and that within the zones of occupation and occupied cities along the Rhine like Bonn, Coblenz, Cologne, and Wiesbaden. Though the word "jazz" enters roughly simultaneously in Berlin and in the zones of occupation, Weimar jazz culture proceeds, initially at least, along slightly different paths within these two spaces, with the greater contact with foreign citizens, soldiers, and musicians more quickly producing encounters with jazz music and jazz bands than in Berlin. More substantively, I want to suggest that just as jazz spread across America, Europe, and indeed the globe at different rates and along different paths, there is not one singular genealogy of jazz in the Weimar Republic, but many.

Taking Jazz Seriously in Postwar Germany

As mentioned in the introduction, jazz in Germany, and even more so German critical writing and musical compositions related to jazz, have for at least the past twenty-plus years taken on a reputation of being characterized by misunderstanding and ignorance, due both to Germany's separation from developments in American popular music during the war and then, later, to the political and economic instability of the early Weimar Republic. At the same time, there is general consensus that by 1921, there existed a demand amongst younger, metropolitan Germans for "jazz," also known by variants such as "Yazz," "Dschatz," "Schesbend" (jazz band), and others. What remains in question is whether such a thing has anything to do with what one today would call jazz.

In a retrospective account of his introduction to the music, entitled "Meine Jagd nach der 'Tschetzpend'" ("My Hunt for the 'Tschetzpend'" [i.e., jazz band]), musician Henry Ernst offers a comic glimpse into the apparent ignorance of early Weimar-era musicians and audiences regarding jazz.[4] Ernst's 1926 article is not only a unique firsthand narrative of German musicians' exposure to jazz, it, like Siemsen's image of the dancing Kaiser, has also become a centerpiece of various arguments for German jazz's uniqueness and abberation.[5] Though Ernst's text offers us much in terms of better understanding early jazz culture in Germany, it begs many questions as well. First amongst them is who exactly "Henry Ernst" was and what his relationship to jazz was. This question is especially pressing when one considers that he was described as an opponent of modern trends in music in his obituary.[6]

Born Ernst Ratkowsky in Austria, "Henry Ernst" studied piano and, under Antonín Dvořak, cello in the period before the First World War. In 1903, he became a *Kapellmeister* and worked in Munich, Hamburg, Bremen, and Dortmund as well as touring neighboring countries like Holland, Sweden, and Denmark. After serving in the Austro-Hungarian army during the First World War, he took up residence in Dortmund after the war but also toured within Germany's neighboring countries.[7] It was one such foreign booking that set off the famous "hunt" for the jazz band. Ernst and his Original Wiener Meistersalonorchester were hired to perform in a hotel in St. Moritz in Switzerland in 1920, which became the setting for his 1926 article. Ernst had brought along with him the latest German foxtrots, mostly now-forgotten pieces like Ernst Tompa's foxtrot "Mariposa" and an unnamed piece by another popular composer Wilm Wilm (Wilhelm Wieninger).[8] All seemed to be going as planned, he related, until one evening, an English audience member requested that Ernst play a foxtrot, in other words, the type of music Ernst assumed he had been playing all along. When Ernst replied that he was indeed playing foxtrots and questioned whether the gentlemen had been listening closely, the guest "responded for his part that he had paid close attention to our playing. Though he could not say what we had played, he could say with certainty that there was not a single foxtrot amongst them."[9] Determined to rid his repertoire of such pseudo-foxtrots, Ernst reestablished his subscription to a London music publisher in order to acquire dance music from England and America. This apparently improved his standing with the English and other foreign guests, as Ernst reports no further uncomfortable requests. However, the hotel's director then made his own uncomfortable request. He said that he would like to hire Ernst for the next season, but first the director needed to know if he could play what Ernst initially hears as *Tschetzpend* ("jazz band"), later explaining that last season an English group at the hotel across the street had quite the success with this music. Despite his utter ignorance and inability to parse the word, Ernst claims to know how to play this music, whatever *Tschetzpend* may be, so that he can secure the contract.

The ensuing hunt for the "jazz band" begins, understandably enough, with him excluding musicians in the area as potential sources of information for fear that his ignorance will be exposed and he will lose the potential contract. While from Ernst's perspective this may indeed be a necessary strategy, it is the first of two moves that will isolate him from any international artists in his midst. Avoiding the local musicians, Ernst writes back to Germany and *Der Artist*. Published in Düsseldorf from 1882 onward, this was the most important trade periodical for practicing musicians and popular entertainers in Germany. From there he learns "that the general view is that jazz band is an American Negro music," a claim that, while interesting, does not help him very much.[10] He also writes to the *Kapellmeister-Verband Deutschland* and receives word from his colleagues that jazz is not music, but a "new Negro dance, so a sort of new edition of the cake walk."[11] The organization does, however, provide him with the address of a foreign band in Wiesbaden said to play jazz music, one that had apparently been brought there by the English officers stationed there. Though Ernst follows up on this lead and writes a letter (in English) to the bandleader, he will never receive a response. Within Ernst's "hunt," this is but one dead end of many, and he hardly pauses before turning elsewhere. Yet, the reference to a foreign jazz band in the city of Wiesbaden is more significant than it may at first glance appear.

Following the First World War, German territories west of the Rhine were occupied and divided into four zones of occupation by the American, Belgian, British, and French. I will speak to the debate sparked by the French use of African colonial soldiers and its relation to German jazz reception a bit later. For now, however, I want to think about the occupied territories as a whole in terms of their function as an incubator for German encounters with jazz bands and Weimar jazz culture more generally. First, as in Berlin, there existed within occupied cities like Wiesbaden, Cologne, Coblenz, and Bonn a demand for new dances such as the foxtrot and "jazz," but with the additional element of large numbers of foreign soldiers.[12] Numbering just over 100,000 in early 1919, American soldiers brought with them a variety of entertainment typical in US society. In June of that year, journalist Harry A. Franck noted that the Americans "commandeered the poor man's drinking-places and transferred them into enlisted men's barracks. We shooed the rich man out of his sumptuous club and turned it over to our officers. We allotted the pompous *Festhalle* and many other important buildings to the Y.M.C.A., and 'jazz' and ragtime and burnt-cork jokes took the place of *Lieder* and *Männerchor*."[13] Yet after a severe reduction in forces, by September, the American influence had been limited to the city Coblenz and the immediate area surrounding it.[14] Even still, there are isolated accounts in the German press and in later memoirs of musicians having both heard and learned jazz from American troops.[15] If not the American zone directly, then the neighboring cities of British-occupied Bonn and Cologne and the French-occupied Wiesbaden would prove to have a more lasting influence on the development and spread of jazz within Germany.

This idea is partially substantiated by the fact that the first extended discussion of jazz music in German is published in the city of Cologne in June 1919. The author of this first German-language essay on jazz music was George Barthelme, long-time Washington correspondent for the *Kölnische Zeitung*. Barthelme, to be sure, had a unique perspective insofar as he had experienced firsthand the music's entry into New York during the First World War. Indeed, he is one of the only German commentators to mention the early African American jazz great James Reese Europe, whom Barthelme refers to as New York's great "jazz master" (*Jazzmeister*).[16] Despite this, his politicized, anti-modernist reading of the music shares striking similarities with later Berlin writers. As with Siemsen and his use of the jazz-dancing Kaiser in possible reference to the war, Barthelme uses James Reese Europe's transformation from army lieutenant into American jazz king to argue for jazz as a cultural continuation of the war. Throughout this article, which was reprinted in the American press as well, Barthelme's take on jazz oscillates between ironizing the claims made on the music's behalf and, given the British occupation of the city of Bonn, taking them more seriously.[17] In part satirizing the language of early American jazz modernists, Barthelme invests the music with grandiose aesthetic claims, transforming jazz from music into worldview, jazz into jazzism. "Now listen!" he writes:

> Jazz is a worldview and therefore to be taken seriously. Jazz is the expression of a cultural epoch, the victorious battle of the elementary forces of the soul over the redemptive form. [. . .] Jazz is thus . . . a musical revelation, a religion, a worldview, like Expressionism and Impressionism. But these two are only partial. Jazzism by contrast is total, is the higher unity, the Hegelian synthesis. But its synthesis lies ultimately in the negation of any synthesis. It doesn't bring together, it disperses, isn't solution but dissolution. It is analysis driven to the extreme. In Jazzism form cedes to chaos, law to anarchy, the rule to incidence or coincidence. Jazzism is

amorphous music. It is the negation of all musical syntax and stylistics, likely also of musical notation, which, however, can't be heard. It is the transvaluation of all values of tone and tempo. It is anti-, anti-, anti-: Anti-Wagner, Anti-Strauss, Anti-Reger, even Anti-Debussy. As such musical Bolshevism. Or a big joke to find out what you all can offer an audience of the 20th century while still getting paid.[18]

Despite the article's hyperbolic tone, it is clear that for Barthelme, jazz was to be taken seriously, at the very least as a musical and cultural sign of Germany's precarious present. Linking the war, jazz, and the question of Germany's future, he notes in conclusion: "In the right jazz mood, anyone will pledge anything. Even the introduction of a soviet system or the creation of the Rhine republic! Dschatz [jazz]! Dschatz!"[19]

If Barthelme's experience of American jazz was certainly unique, the presence of jazz bands along the Rhine was not. For one, beginning in December 1919, a French jazz band, Marcel's Jazz Band, performed in Wiesbaden, with many more to follow.[20] Indeed, many of the first jazz formations advertised in *Der Artist*, the same publication in which Ernst's article later appeared, can be geographically located within Germany's occupation zones on its western border. The very first jazz band, Jackson's Jazz Band,[21] that advertised in *Der Artist* (and later examples William's Jazz-Band,[22] The Harlington-"Jazz-Band"[23] Original-Jazz Band,[24] and Jimmy's Jazz-Band[25]) originated in Wiesbaden, while those like the Jazz Band Duet[26] and Harry Johnson's Orig. Amerik. Jazz-Band[27] originated in Bonn. The Original Jazz-Band from Wiesbaden is one early example of the Black diasporic presence in the German jazz scene. The advertisement was placed by Joseph (Joe) Sewonu, a multilingual artist and Togolese migrant active in the zones of occupation and Wiesbaden in particular.[28] It was also in Wiesbaden that an advertisement for a very large group of African American musicians could be found in late 1921. This group, a "Negro Orchestra" from New York featuring 35 performers, potentially represents the largest single group of African American musicians in Germany until 1925.[29] Though very little is known about this group and no reviews of the performance have surfaced, it was potentially a spin-off of Will Marion Cook's *Southern Syncopated Orchestra* (*SSO*), which left New York in 1919 for England and is today considered one of the most important examples of the African American musical presence in Europe during the early 1920s.[30] Cook's group featured an almost ever-changing personnel that amounted to more than one hundred participants and whose repertoire encompassed a variety of African American music, including, but by no means limited to, jazz. Throughout its history, various iterations of Cook's group played in London, Paris, Vienna, and elsewhere, famously inspiring one of the most significant early European commentaries on jazz, the Swiss conductor Ernest Ansermet's tribute to Sidney Bechet in October 1919.[31] Though it is impossible to know with certainty, the group that was advertised in Wiesbaden in October 1921 was potentially similar to the one headed by African American composer Harry M. Wellmon[32] that had performed in Paris in the summer of 1921 and would perform in Vienna from May through October 1922.[33]

So while Henry Ernst was not able to connect with any jazz bands or jazz musicians, Black or white, they were present in Germany and from at least December 1919 onward in Wiesbaden. Indeed, in counterpoint to Ernst, whose relevance to German jazz history is based solely upon this article, the popular German bandleader Bernhard Etté, who recorded prolifically during the 1920s, reported that his jazz career began after he was inspired by listening to a visiting English jazz band in Wiesbaden.[34] As the case of Etté and others indicate, rather than developing in isolation from France, the UK, and America, jazz bands and German jazz culture along the Rhine, both foreign and domestic, emerged precisely at the closest points of contact with American, British, and French soldiers. As should be clear, however, it is important to avoid overgeneralizing the situation of early German knowledge and experience of jazz based upon any individual account. Instead, the situation of jazz in Germany in 1919/1920 was at once isolated from and connected to developments elsewhere, with personal connections and one's individual geography being the most salient factors.

Moreover, not only does Ernst's missed lead in Wiesbaden exclude this avenue of jazz's dispersion in Germany, it impacts the direction his "hunt" next takes him, namely towards Berlin. As he explains: "Berlin has everything, Berlin knows everything, so it will be able to clear up the mysteries of the *Tschetzpend* for me."[35] From an unnamed source in Berlin, Ernst received word that jazz is a new dance, a three step, and that they had been dancing it for months. His Berlin colleagues send him the "Dolores Jazz" by Byjacco, a pseudonym for the popular composer Fritz Jacoby.[36] Like other early German popular songs featuring the word "jazz," the music was labeled a "three step" and was named after a dance pair, in this case Bella Chitta and Arthur Dolores.[37] Still, the reference is telling insofar as it can be connected to perhaps the earliest usage of the word "jazz" in the Berlin press (figure 1). Defined as "the newest fashionable dance," their jazz dancing was a major drawing point for the duo's April 1919 appearance at the *Simplicissimus*, a cabaret and dance club located on *Potsdamerplatz*.[38]

Figure 1: Advertisement for jazz, "the newest fashionable dance" (1919) by Chitta and Arthur Dolores.

This definition of jazz as a new dance, rather than music, was utterly common in 1919, and the jazz dance can be found across Europe in the late 1910s and early 1920s.[39] As Jed Rasula writes in his treatment of jazz's place within the European and American avant-garde: "In both Europe and America jazz is often taken to mean dancing, not a kind of music. The dance audience being considerably larger than the listening audience, recordings are meant for dancing—a point made conspicuous on their labels, in which jazz releases bear a generic indicator: 'Fox trot.'"[40] Still, while jazz dance may have been common elsewhere, Berlin's adoption of the dance had some unique consequences owing to the fact that, unlike in cities like Wiesbaden, let alone Paris or London, there were no corresponding jazz *bands*. Most significantly, the German recording industry's concentration in this city meant that there is a disjuncture in the discographical record between jazz recorded in Germany, i.e., in Berlin, and the jazz bands present in the occupation zones. What this means concretely is that the first German recordings to feature the word "jazz" unsurprisingly refer to the dance, and not the music.[41] While Germany is hardly alone in producing recordings that sought to capitalize on the dance craze by featuring the word "jazz" in their title, the geographical divide between the Berlin recording industry and the jazz musicians in the occupation zones impeded the recording of such groups in Germany until early 1921.

Back in St. Moritz and now outfitted with "Dolores Jazz," Ernst began playing this latest jazz dance music from Berlin. Yet he is again confronted with "puzzled looks" from the audience, confirming for him that he has failed to find the *Tschetzpend*.[42] His confusion only increases as yet another foreigner, this time a Parisian woman, requests a shimmy, also a new dance from America. Confronted with another instance of his failure and frustrated by the answers he has thus far received from Germany and especially Berlin, the next morning Ernst goes to a local Swiss bookstore, where he finds a stack of sheet music containing dance music from France and England. Leafing through them, he discovers a foxtrot with a photograph of a famous jazz band from London. He notes: "Then I finally saw what a jazz band is. Seven little men (*Männeckens*) dressed in sporty clothing: piano, violin, two banjos, saxophone, trumpet, and percussion instruments."[43] Having finally found out what *Tschetzpend* was, Ernst returned to Germany confident in his knowledge. Indeed, in 1921, he even advertised for his group in *Der Artist* as possessing "recognized success as a jazz band."[44] In a final twist, however, Ernst reports that once back in Germany, the audience was less than welcoming of his "real" jazz. He says they still preferred the jazz dance, and in the end, he returned to playing just as he had before his discovery of the *Tschetzpend*.

While Ernst's account of jazz's entry into Germany is generally substantiated by evidence from *Der Artist*, it is clearly also a well-crafted tale, hitting all the right notes of a humorous anecdote. So for as much as it tells us about the encounter with jazz in the early years of the Weimar Republic, it also speaks to the changing conception of jazz in the mid-twenties. To a certain degree, Ernst is laughing at himself, his colleagues, and the Berlin audience in this story, indulging in a bit of self-effacing humor at a moment when he could claim to understand jazz music fully. Recalling the photograph of the jazz band, he notes: "All that which is today considered by every musician to be self-evident regarding jazz, but what was at the time still unclear and mysterious, became evident to me."[45] So if Ernst's individual story contains much about how musicians dealt with the introduction of jazz to Europe and Germany and Switzerland, its status as indicative of the early German experience of jazz writ large needs a degree of contextualization.

Indeed, Ernst's report serves as a reminder of the fact that overreliance on the dissemination of jazz via recordings and the Berlin press to the exclusion of other cities and areas can have a distorting effect on what was an extremely complex process. While Berlin will no doubt remain the focal point for the study of Weimar jazz culture, one cannot lose sight of the fact that jazz in Berlin is also very much a local story. It is, however, one with great implications for the rest of Weimar Germany and one that remains fundamental to understanding how jazz culture in the Weimar Republic develops.

Berlin Dances to Dada's Jazz

The jazz dance's entry into Berlin at the latest by April 1919 was itself part of the broader dance mania that followed the war. An individual example of the European and American dance craze of the time, Berlin's embrace of social dancing, in particular the foxtrot and jazz, was also partially unique.[46] During the war, such dancing had been controlled by the German authorities and there had been a ban on dancing in Berlin. Even before the war, German officers had been prohibited from publically dancing in uniform or associating with people who danced the tango, one-step, or two-step.[47] Of course, the fact that jazz and foxtrot were not just new, but American dances, lent them even more resonance. When the dance prohibition was lifted on New Year's Eve 1918, the *Berliner Tageblatt* wrote the following morning: "Music plays in hundreds of locales, dance after dance: waltz, foxtrot, one-step, two-step. Legs race across the floor as if bewitched, skirts fly, hearts jump [. . .] and new year's greetings resound in the exact same streets where the steps of demonstrators had just echoed."[48] If such frenzied dancing certainly had much to do with the pent up desires of four years of corporeal and psychic deprivation, foxtrot and, later, jazz dances were not only fashionable, they were foreign and racially suspect. In his impressionistic account of the same New Year's eve dancing, writer Karlernst Knaatz wrote in description of two foxtrot dancers that "the couple raised their feet in a negroid manner," continuing: "How it would lose its attractiveness, this joke treated so very seriously, if it were simply called '*Fuchstrab*' [i.e., foxtrot]."[49] Like the critic in the *Berliner Tageblatt*, Knaatz also linked such dancing to the revolution, noting: "The rage with which our contemporaries disjoint themselves at the first partial-peace balls [*Halbfriedensbälle*] ultimately originates from the same source from which the tidal wave of the revolution sprang. It is but the other end of the same current."[50]

In broadly similar fashion to the situation in Britain and France, jazz enters the Berlin public sphere as a dance in 1919, though with the crucial difference that there are no jazz bands in Berlin until 1921 at the latest, whereas in Britain, France (and Wiesbaden), jazz bands emerged, in part, from direct contact with American forces.[51] In addition, such dancing, be it foxtrot, jazz, or any of the other fads of the period, was initially linked to the upper echelon of Berlin society, a fashionable pastime for the city's middle-class and wealthy youth to satisfy their need for the new. The cycle of dance fashions, foxtrot, jazz, *maxixe brésilienne*, fish walk, and others, meant that "jazz" as a word rarely surfaced in isolation. Instead, its fashionable origins as a social dance opened it to conservative, moralistic, as well as leftist, political attacks.

Already in January 1919, one could observe around Berlin the now well-known image of a woman dancing with Death,[52] on which the caption read: "Berlin, stop! Come to your senses. Your dance partner is Death."[53] The poster combines lines from author Paul Zech's "Berlin, halt ein" ("Berlin, stop") with a wartime illustration, "German Tango," by the Belgian artist Louis Raemaekers.[54] Though the original image had referenced the tango, by 1919 the foxtrot and jazz now became implied targets of its message. Indeed, leftist cabaret artists like Walter Mehring connected this specific image with foxtrot and jazz dancing in works from the period. Mehring's "Dada-Prologue 1919," for example, contains the lines: "Berlin, your dance partner is Death—/ Foxtrot and jazz—/ The republic is amusing itself royally / Forget me not on the first of May."[55] Further examples, most notably the "foxtrot epidemic" featured in Ernst Lubitsch's *Die Austernprinzessin* (*The Oyster Princess*), demonstrate the cultural resonance of social dancing and American dancing in particular. Filmed in Berlin in May 1919, i.e., during the initial wave of the jazz dance craze, Lubitsch's depiction of the foxtrot features an absurdist caricature of popular dance and the bands that accompany them. A large orchestra plays to the tune of a conductor wildly flailing about and accentuating his posterior. Equally significant here are the strange percussive instruments depicted, e.g., a saw cuts through wood, a pistol is fired, and a man is slapped in intervals indicated by musical notation, etc. The jazz dance as part of the post-war dance fad and the eccentric conductors and percussionists who provide the musical accompaniment will largely hold sway in Berlin for the first two years of the Weimar Republic. Still, it will produce at least one spectacular example of early exchange between artists in Germany and American jazz, namely the British musician and eccentric arranger Frank Groundsell's recording of the Original Dixieland Jazz Band's classic "Tiger Rag" in 1919 in Berlin.[56]

Yet if Berlin's embrace of the "Dolores Jazz" and eccentric jazz dancing point generally towards the city's isolation in terms of jazz music, the important modernist movement of Dada helped bridge the pre-war history of African American music and dancing with the newfound jazz dance fad. The place of popular culture and Blackness within Dada Berlin, whose activities peak in the period 1918–20, is a reminder of the longer history of modernist engagement with these essential elements of Weimar jazz reception. More than this, Dada's interest in African American music and Blackness is itself embedded within the modernist network of Europe that had similarly embraced precursors of jazz like the cakewalk and ragtime.[57] In considering Dada Berlin's use of jazz, it is therefore important to understand how, during this initial period, their works draw as much on the newness of jazz and foxtrot dancing as on their experience of American popular music and culture from during and before the war.

The significance of African American popular music to Dadaist George Grosz's work in the years 1917 through 1920 is hard to overestimate. More than any other artist, Grosz's works from this period, poetic, performance, and visual, reveal a long-standing engagement with American popular culture and a particular interest in music characterized as African American. Grosz collected ragtime records, and in his letters to fellow artist Otto Schmalhausen, he references ragtime song titles and describes debauched nights spent drinking, dancing, and listening to them.[58] During the dance mania of winter 1919, furthermore, he advertised for "Foxtrot and Ragtime Records" in the short-lived Dadaist periodical *Jedermann sein eigner Fussball* (*Everyone his Own Football*).[59] In addition, at Dada events, he performed American step dances and jigs under the rubric "sincopations"[60] and likely performed in blackface during at least one such event.[61]

Significantly, all of the musical works referenced by Grosz in this period date from the period between 1890 and 1914. While obviously his dependence on these works shows the more or less culturally isolated position of Grosz during the war and afterward, the history of these works' production and their reception in Germany is also noteworthy. It was during this period that American popular music and culture entered the German and European market on a wide scale. This occurred both in the form of African American performers like Elmer Spyglass, Louis Douglas, and Arabella Fields, as well as in the form of blackface minstrel iconography and American racial stereotypes.[62] Further complicating the field was the introduction of ragtime. While piano ragtime music from African American composers like Scott Joplin enjoyed some popularity in Germany, a greater influence was exercised on the German listening public (Grosz included) by related, though distinct, musical forms like the ragtime song and so-called "coon songs." As Fred Ritzel notes, during Wilhelmine Germany, popular music about, influenced, or performed by African Americans became a staple of the German music publishing industry's repertoire.[63] It is thus no accident that Grosz returns, again and again, to songs of this era during the war or that he portrays the same Black performers in three separate drawings between 1915 and 1920.[64] Both through Dada Berlin's resurrection of the prewar encounter with Blackness and American popular music and culture, as well as the foxtrot and jazz dance mania of 1919, Berlin, its artists and dancing public, were thus well prepared for the initial wave of jazz bands that arrive in early 1921.

Berlin Occupied

If jazz bands nonetheless remained largely outside of Berlin in 1919 and 1920, the debate over the occupation did not. In April 1920, the scandal over the use of French African colonial troops along the Rhine, catalyzed by an altercation in Frankfurt, reached its boiling point.[65] France was not only the largest occupying force in the region, it also made the greatest use of colonial, non-white troops. Out of 85,000 troops, in the summers of 1920 and 1921, there were between 30,000 and 40,000 African troops, primarily from Morocco, though troops from West Africa (Senegal) and Madagascar were also present at various times and in significant numbers.[66] As Christian Koller has shown, the propaganda campaign against the so-called "*Schwarze Schmach am Rhein*" ("Black Shame" or "Black Horror[67] on the Rhine") was carried out by official government channels as well as unofficial groups like the *Rheinische Frauen-*

liga (Rhenish League of Women).[68] Apart from claims of "inverse colonialism," the stationing of black troops within German borders brought with it a threat of large-scale encounter between Africans and Germans. In particular, the propagandistic claim that Black troops were raping German women became a major rallying cry for opposition to the occupation. While much has been written on the campaign,[69] even in relation to its use within German jazz discourse,[70] it is important to think through how discussion of the Black presence in the occupation zone functioned in the context of Berlin's modernist interest in Blackness and American popular culture.

Significantly, it is also in 1920 that Black performers, initially unrelated to jazz bands, once again appear in significant numbers in the Berlin entertainment district. Apart from isolated Black performers in cabarets who used pseudonyms like the dancer Tom Black in May 1920,[71] a large group of Black performers and stars were featured in the October 1920 production *Harems-nächte (Harem Nights)* at director James Klein's *Apollo-Theater.*[72] The cast included twenty Cameroonian performers and thirty Bayadere dancers. Most significantly, two of the lead roles were occupied by Black performers: Myriam Barka, a "Sudanese actress," and Louis Brody, the "Negro film star."[73] Barka, about whom little is known, apparently spoke fluent German and had been active as a performer in Berlin as early as September 1919,[74] while Brody, born (Ludwig) M'bebe Mpessa in Duala, Cameroon, was amongst the first Black German artists to be recognized during the period for his work in films such as Joe May's *Die Herrin der Welt (The Mistress of the World)* (1919–20), Robert Wiene's *Genuine* (1920), and Fritz Lang's *Der müde Tod (Destiny)* (1921).[75]

Harem Nights ran during October and November 1920 and was by all accounts a success, if clearly a provocative one. Though details regarding the plot are few, it was described in an official police report as involving "a [. . .] sultan kidnap[ping] the favorite wife of a Negro chieftain. As revenge, the Negro's tribe attacks the sultan's harem and kidnaps its inmates."[76] According to historian Jared Poley, in spite of the regular press reports on the occupation, *Harem Nights* was generally well-received by the Berlin audience, which is said to have been composed primarily of members of the lower middle-class, in addition to foreign visitors.[77] British officer J. H. Morgan, then part of the Inter-Allied Military Commission of Control in Germany, later noted: "By a curious irony, at the very time that all Berlin was flocking to 'Harem Nights' the whole German Press was launching the vast campaign of propaganda . . . against the 'infamy' of 'black troops on the Rhine.'"[78] Though unlike later performances featuring Black men on stage with naked women, *Harem Nights* did not result in police intervention;[79] it did provoke critique from the *Rhenish League of Women*, one of the main groups associated with the "Black Horror" campaign.[80] Indeed, almost two years later, nationalist DNVP representative Reinhard Mumm criticized the piece for featuring "partially-clothed women kowtowing before their black master every evening for weeks on end," continuing: "How can we in the Reichstag act effectively against the Black Horror, when such a shameful act is not forcefully prohibited in the capital?"[81] The timing of Mumm's speech was anything but coincidental; it was delivered during the same month as the Lola-Bach Ballet was performing its own, apparently unrelated *Haremsnächte*, featuring the Liberian artist Peter Johnson.[82]

More typical than Klein's *Harem Nights* in terms of the use of Blackness and American popular music was the newly resurrected *Schall und Rauch (Sound and Smoke)*. Originally created by Max Reinhardt in 1901, this famous cabaret reopened in 1919 and featured performers like Paul Graetz and Gussy Holl, in addition to key modernist writers like Walter Mehring and Klabund (Alfred Henschke), as well as, of course, composers such as Friedrich Hollaender and Mischa Spoliansky.[83] *Sound and Smoke* took part in both the foxtrot and jazz dance craze during this period and was closely aligned with Dada artists, including George Grosz.[84] In terms of jazz, *Sound and Smoke* is important not only of early German jazz criticism but also as a site of jazz performance. In spring 1921, for example, at least two separate jazz bands are featured there.[85] The cabaret also included the participation of two of the authors discussed below in relation to early writings on jazz music, Kurt Tucholsky and Jaap Kool.[86] Already during the 1920 season, one finds Klabund's "Rag 1920," yet another variation of the motif from "Berlin, Your Dance Partner is Death,"[87] while the May 1920 "Dada-Issue" presents three images of the foxtrot-inspired "Dada-Trot" by "Music Dada" Gerhard Preiss.[88]

The impact of the new configuration of race, music, and politics following the "Black Horror" debate can be felt here as well. Two important, early compositions by Friedrich Hollaender reflect the changing circumstances of Blackness and American popular music. The first is his "Fox macabre (Totentanz)" (Dance of Death). Though like Klabund's "Rag 1920" and Mehring's "Dada-Prologue 1919," the primary frame of reference remains the foxtrot and jazz dance with death, Hollaender's lyrics may also be read as offering commentary on the occupation debate. "Berlin, you're dancing with Death! Berlin, you're reveling in filth! Stop, relent, and think about it a moment! You can't dance away your disgrace (*Schmach*), for you're dancing and jazzing and foxing on the powder keg."[89] In including the word *Schmach* in this piece published in December 1920, Hollaender adds a further layer to the idea of decadent jazz dancing as escapism not only from politics but from the continuation of the occupation of Germany.[90] Issued alongside the "fox macabre" was Hollaender's "Jonny (fox erotic)."[91] Though the word "jazz" is absent from Hollaender's 1920 song, its status as a foxtrot places it clearly within the context of jazz's development in Berlin as dance and then in 1921 as jazz band music.[92] Originally performed by Blandine Ebinger at the *Café Größenwahn*, Hollaender's Jonny, as cabaret scholar Alan Lareau has discussed, was issued in two versions, one in which Jonny is a white American and one in which he is a Black African.[93] In both, however, Jonny is a foreign violinist at a local bar, where he attracts the attention of a German girl and impregnates her, only to leave shortly thereafter. Read in tandem, the "fox erotic" and "fox macabre," the American with the African Jonny, suggest an important moment of confluence between jazz and foxtrot dancing, the debate over race, and the presence of Black artists inside and outside the capital city Berlin.

At the same time, as Lareau has also shown, Hollaender is neither the first, nor the last Central European composer to deploy the figure of Jonny or to produce a song revolving around a Black man and white woman.[94] One further example of how cultural production involving American popular music changed through the debate surrounding the "Black Horror" is Walter Mehring's "If the man in the moon were a coon."[95] Mehring, part of the Dada circle around the *Sound and Smoke*, authored a variety of politically inspired cabaret songs at the beginning of the 1920s.[96] Here, one sees not only the continuation of pre-war traditions in this work's citation of the 1905 Fred Fischer song of the same name but a melding of pre-jazz vocabulary and the "Black Horror" debate. This element is most clearly present in the song's refrain, which asks listeners to imagine what would happen if this Black man in the moon: "Gave all white *ladies* / Black babies / Black boys."[97] Postulating the reality of the very worst fears of the scandalized members of the German public, Mehring ironizes, rather than soothes, their anxieties. He achieves this effect, however, not by directly commenting on the "Black Horror" campaign but by borrowing from foreign, here American traditions, with the distance between Germany and America functioning as a buffer for his critique.

Jazz music's relationship to Blackness will be considered in detail below, but it is important to note how Berlin artists and the Berlin public in 1920 were already engaging with these crucial elements of the Weimar jazz discourse prior to the large-scale introduction of jazz bands in the winter of 1921. Dances like the foxtrot and jazz, modernist movements like Dada, and theatrical spaces like *Sound and Smoke,* as well as, of course, the presence of Black performers on stage and screen meant that the city was never far removed from the jazz band's music that soon enough reached Berlin as well.

Enter the Jazz Band

Though the first documented occurrences of the word "jazz" in the Berlin press occur in 1919 and then only in reference to this three-step dance,[98] it was only in the first half of 1921 that one finds a large number of musical groups calling themselves "jazz bands" in the city.[99] If scattered use of the word "jazz" had been made in 1919/1920, early 1921 brought wide-scale use of a new term, the "jazz band," to the press. This term could refer either to a new form of music, closely associated with the latest dance, the shimmy, or simply the trap drum. In this, German usage of the term closely matches that of the French, English, and indeed Australian.[100] What distinguishes this moment from the earlier one is that jazz's presence in Berlin did not dissipate as it had in 1919—it intensified. Not coincidentally, this was also the moment at which jazz bands and musicians from the occupied zones came to the capital in significant numbers.

Beginning in January, but peaking in March and April of that year, jazz and jazz bands seemed to be everywhere in Berlin.[101] There was the Cosmo Jazz Band,[102] Jimmi Jazz Band,[103] Kapelle (or Ballorchester) Boesing mit Original Jazz Band,[104] High Life Jazz-Band,[105] Jazz-Band Max de Groot,[106] and others. If some of these examples refer to the presence of a trap drum alone, there are nonetheless at least two highly significant jazz bands and German jazz pioneers playing in Berlin. The first of all these, appearing in January 1921 at the recently opened *Scala-Casino*, was the four-man formation of the Original Piccadilly Four Jazz Band. While a photograph of this early jazz band exists (figure 2), little certain is known about this group or its history.

It is, however, now clear that the group was not from Berlin, as had been long assumed, but in all likelihood from London. It can also be stated that the group did not come directly to Berlin, but rather reached Berlin via Wiesbaden, where it had performed at the *Apollo* starting in October 1920.[107] After Berlin, the group likely played the north-German resort town Binz auf Rügen and, after a return stint in Berlin in the fall of 1921, traveled to Switzerland, performing in Geneva and Zurich in 1922, and, potentially, Lausanne in 1923.[108] After this date, however, it has not been possible to trace these "famous syncopated Entertainers of London" as they were advertised in Zurich. Of course, had they not performed in Berlin, with its proximity to the German recording

Figure 2: The Original Piccadilly Four Jazz Band at the Berlin Scala in early 1921. From F. W. Koebner, *Jazz und Shimmy* **(Berlin: Eysler, 1921).**

industry, they might have been entirely forgotten. Yet as it was, this group released more than twenty recordings from Berlin in the first half of 1921 on the labels Parlophon, Beka, and Anker. These recordings remain early highlights of early jazz recorded in Germany.[109] The instrumentation features banjo, drums, violin, and piano, which, with slight variations, was typical of the jazz bands active in Germany (and elsewhere) in this period, such as the previously mentioned Marcel's Jazz Band.

In addition to the Original Piccadilly Four, another important jazz band, the Original American Jazz Band was present at the *Scala-Casino* from February 1921 onward.[110] This band was quite probably formed by German jazz pioneer Eric(h) Borchard(t). Born in 1886 in Berlin, little is known about Borchard's life before the First World War, though he likely spent some time in the United States before 1914.[111] While Borchard has long stood out as an early German jazz pioneer and it was assumed he spent at least some time in the

United States, it now appears that between 1914 and 1918 he lived not in Germany, but in America, specifically New York, where he was active as a vaudeville artist.[112] The duration and timing of his stay in the United States are important because, like Barthelme's wartime experiences that resulted in the first German jazz essay, Borchard's stay took place during the beginnings of the New York jazz scene, for example, the arrival of the Original Dixieland Jazz Band. While details of Borchard's exact path from New York in late 1918 to Berlin in early 1921 remain unknown, this information lends credence to Borchard's later claims to the press that he had played jazz in German cities around the Rhine following the war.[113] None of this work, like that of the Original Piccadilly Four, was recorded until his move to Berlin, when in May of 1921 and under the name Eric Concerto's Yankee Jazz Band, Borchard and his band recorded major American hits from 1920, such as "Whispering," "Japanese Sandman," "Everybody Shimmies Now," "After You Get What You Want, You Don't Want It," and "Swanee."[114] In other words, in the cases of the Original Piccadilly Four Jazz Band and Erich Borchard's jazz band, we have clear examples of Weimar jazz culture developing via direct and prolonged contact with foreign musicians and environments, rather than a simple dressing up of German music in the new foreign vocabulary of "jazz" as Ernst's "hunt" may make it appear.

The Original Piccadilly Four and Borchard's band are white jazz formations, yet, from other sources, we know that members of the Black diaspora were also involved in the move of the jazz band from the Rhine to Berlin. This fact is substantiated by the presence of yet another early jazz pioneer in Berlin in July 1921, Evandale Roberts. Potentially the first example of a jazz musician of African descent to perform in Berlin, Roberts, who at times went by the name as the "Original Jazz-King," came to the *Scala-Casino* in the summer of 1921 via Wiesbaden.[115] Another example is Phillips Original amerikanische Neger Jazz Band, which performed in Cologne in September 1921,[116] before appearing in Berlin in November at the *Scala-Casino*, yet again repeating the path from the Rhine to Berlin.[117] A third example from this period, one discussed further in the next chapter, is Pete Zabriskie's jazz band, which performed in Berlin in 1922. As is clear, by 1921 at the latest, multiple artists of African descent were active in the Berlin jazz, music, and entertainment industry. Though like many of these early jazz bands, one can debate whether the music they played was likely to have been jazz in the narrow sense of the jazz tradition, it is important that they and their groups were marketed and indeed marketed themselves via the terminology of jazz and the jazz band.

The Jazz Band Drums

In response to the numerous jazz bands, German writing on jazz increased exponentially as different authors with varying degrees of interest and knowledge of popular music produced newspaper and journal articles, illustrations, and caricatures about the jazz band. Aside from further jazz-inspired works for the cabaret by Walter Mehring and Hans Erich Winckler for example,[118] the presence of jazz bands in Berlin can be tied to an extremely early German-language book: *Jazz und Shimmy. Brevier der neuesten Tänze* (*Jazz and Shimmy: Brevier of the Newest Dances*).[119] To a large extent, this unique work is but a collection of early German-language texts and images related to the jazz dance, rather than the music. *Jazz and Shimmy* was edited by Franz Wolfgang Koebner, author of a series of dance manuals (to which *Jazz and Shimmy* clearly belongs) and fictional works, as well as cofounder and editor of the important journals *Die elegante Welt* and *Das Magazin*. Beyond its noteworthy title, *Jazz and Shimmy* contains selections by modernist writers like Hans Siemsen and Kurt Tucholsky, drawings and texts by the artist and designer Robert L. Leonard, and an essay on dance music by the Dutch ethnomusicologist Jaap Kool.[120] At the same time, it is important to recall that *Jazz und Shimmy* remains a work interested in jazz almost solely from the perspective of modern social dancing. The fact that "jazz" shares the title with the shimmy, the latest of the American dance trends to hit Germany, is an obvious indication of this focus.[121]

In the following analysis of the Berlin and German reception of the "jazz band" in early 1921, attention will be paid both to selections from Koebner's collection, as well as works that fall outside of it, yet are clearly part of the Berlin discussion. While the following selection is by no means exhaustive, it offers a cross-section of responses from Weimar mass media; the music trade press; modernist journals; voices of liberal, socialist, and conservative writers; and German-speaking modernist authors. As a whole, these documents suggest the emergence, through competing claims, of a set of ideas about the jazz band's origins, practices, and place within contemporary society. For example, on March 11, 1921, the *Berliner Tageblatt* publishes an initial report on the jazz band and shimmy as the latest "Berlin hype," only to be corrected and expanded upon two days later.[122] Written by the Berlin music publisher, Curt Max Roehr, the correction later appears in *Der Artist* as well as in Koebner's *Jazz and Shimmy*, yet Roehr's name is included only in the publication in *Der Artist*.[123] Further, in at least one early report, Americans present in Berlin are used to critique the inauthenticity of the Berlin vision of jazz.[124] As this brief excursion suggests, unless early German jazz criticism is considered from such a multi-perspectival approach, its interconnectedness, as well as the different audiences it reached, can all too easily become lost in the focus on any one publication such as *Jazz and Shimmy*.

Aside from the fact that the jazz band was new to these writers, a remarkable trait of almost all of these documents is that names of specific jazz bands, let alone individual musicians, are rarely if ever mentioned, making it all but impossible to align individual accounts with specific groups like the Original Piccadilly Four. Rather, individual names generally remain a distinction reserved for the music's composers. Even in exceptional cases, such as art critic Herwarth Walden's reference to recordings by the Original Piccadilly Four, the author does not praise the group's performers but instead remarks: "The composer doesn't even have a name, but he can certainly compose. An unknown master."[125] In another variation on this theme, Hans Siemsen proclaims of one jazz drummer: "The fat man—a musical genius!"[126]

Like Siemsen, who uses a descriptive adjective in line with the image of the American "doughboy,"[127] most writers functionalize individual members of the jazz band, distinguishing between, without, however, naming the musicians or their groups. It is only later, from around 1924 onward, that reference to the names of individual jazz bands becomes standard, rather than exceptional within German jazz reception. While authors vary in terms of their descriptions of instrumentalists, the most space in these accounts is devoted to the percussionist, or trap drummer, as "the most important person of the jazz band" (figure 3).[128]

Descriptions of the jazz band tend to begin by noting the presence of the piano, violin, and banjo, as well as further instruments like the saxophone, clarinet, bassoon, guitar, trumpet, and harmonica. When writers reach the trap drum and the percussion instruments, however, they often produce a dizzying list of exotic and everyday objects. "Four nice fellows sit and make the noise of a regiment," begins Robert L. Leonard, continuing:

A banjo rattles and causes your bones to shake, a violinist fiddles syncopes, a pianist races across the keys, a fourth man . . . sure, what does he do? What is he? What is he playing?

A fourth man has constructed an instrument for himself, no, not an instrument, an orchestrion of instruments that strike, clap, hammer, torture. He plays everything at once: the small xylophone box, the tambourine, the cymbal, the drum . . . temteremtem, tem—tem—tem.[129]

Figure 3: A Jazz Drummer in Berlin in early 1921. From F. W. Koebner, *Jazz und Shimmy* (Berlin: Eysler, 1921).

Other writers use similar imagery to describe the trap drum of the jazz band as consisting of "an eight-headed instrument,"[130] "a number of extremely interesting objects,"[131] "a number of nameless, extremely fantastical instruments, that don't exactly make music, but a form of musical noise (*Geräusch*),"[132] or, finally, as a "mystical instrument."[133]

Of course, not all commentators respond in this manner. Those more accustomed to describing musical instruments and popular dance orchestras like aforementioned Jaap Kool, Poldi Schmidl, or Richard Effner are less ecstatic in their descriptions. Effner, a Berlin manufacturer of music instruments, seeks to correct readers of *Der Artist* about jazz and its most characteristic instruments: the trap drum and the banjo. On the one hand, he notes that "jazz band" is often incorrectly taken to be synonymous with the trap drum; on the other hand, he insists that "'jazz' is, as we know, a dance."[134] Arguably more successful interventions are those by Poldi Schmidl, Berlin music critic for *Der Artist*, and Jaap Kool, an ethnomusicologist. Though by no means supportive of the jazz band, in his first discussion of jazz from February 1921, Schmidl points not at the centrality of any particular instrument, but at the unique timbre of the jazz band, its rhythm, and, most notably, its use of syncopation.[135] Kool, by contrast, focuses on historical precedents of the jazz band and the technology of the trap drum specifically. He claims that it was around 1900, with John Phillip Sousa and the introduction of ragtime to Europe, that instrument makers began developing a "mechanical apparatus (*Maschinerie*)" that would enable control of the drum and cymbal through the feet so that the hands would be free to use other instruments.[136] Kool's argument here lines up with that of American expatriate composer George Antheil and his 1922 call for composers to take up the drum: "Let our youngest composers buy a drum or two and limit themselves to one or two lines of rhythm for a year. Let them work with a pencil and learn dynamic draughtsmanship. Let them experiment with space and create new musical dimensions."[137] As becomes clear in these early treatments and descriptions of the jazz band, it was the trap drum that carried much of the interpretive weight for these writers. It is also, as I want to suggest in this chapter's concluding section, in such depictions of the jazz band's drum that one most clearly finds the intersection of music, race, and American culture.

Blackness and the Machine, or Jazz Band Modernism

If Cornelius Partsch and others are certainly correct to point towards the strong correlation between Expressionism and jazz, in addition to its equally strong correlation with Dadaism,[138] within early accounts, the jazz band is also related to Futurism[139] and Cubism,[140] with reference to Picasso, Joyce, Klee, Schoenberg, and even Einstein's theory of relativity.[141] So while critics like Herwarth Walden and Hermann Wedderkop may intellectually spar over whether the shimmy and jazz band belong to Expressionism or an as yet unnamed post-Expressionism,[142] there was no overarching consensus regarding the jazz band's specific brand of modernism, other than that it was obviously, fundamentally modern. The three elements of the jazz bands' modernism and modernity that attract the most attention are: the jazz band's connection to machines and mechanization, the music's ability to destroy individual free will, and the music's relation to Blackness.

The effect of the rhythm of the jazz band, of the trap drum and its arsenal of percussion, was interpreted along a variety of axes, commonly invoking the mechanization of war, capitalism, and industrial production. Alice Gerstel writes, for example, that the jazz band has the "rat-a-tat (*Geratter*) of the cannons they have been firing at the 'enemy' for five long years."[143] Kurt Tucholsky links jazz and shimmy to the dance around the golden calf and contends further that "the jazz band is the continuation of business by other means."[144] He continues that its music "clacks to the beat like the typewriters, which the audience left two hours ago," while its rhythm "jerks and its counter-rhythm works against it, firmly and intricately, as a softly tapping motor."[145] For dance critic Heinz Pollack, meanwhile, the rhythm of jazz doesn't sound like it is coming from "four humans, but [from] an electrically-driven band."[146] The jazz band can also serve as but a symptom for the broader mechanization of humanity. "Humans have become mechanical," writes Hermann Wedderkop, "firmly ruled by a rigidly rhythmic, onward-rushing present that calls itself jazz band."[147] Indeed, for some writers, it was the mechanization of labor that stood behind much of jazz's popularity. Of the men dancing to the jazz band, Gerstel writes: "Nothing can dissuade them from the secret of which they are certain: how dreadful is the wretchedness of this time, how there remains nothing for them to do but dance and the market runs itself and [Karel] Čapek's robots make the sewing needles and roll their cigarettes into ready-mades."[148]

The materialism and mechanization authors viewed in the jazz band, its audience, and the age for which it stood, could seem overpowering. In a manner similar to the reaction of critics to the jazz of African American bandleader Sam Wooding discussed in chapter 2, writers report being overwhelmed at the experience of the jazz band. Be it hypnosis,[149] the madness of an insane asylum,[150] or the ecstasy of intoxication,[151] the jazz band overtakes their rational, mental faculties. Dancers, for example, are said to be "under the spell of these rhythms, these colors and sounds."[152] Wedderkop would note that under the influence of the jazz band: "Intellect no longer controls the leg, rather the leg at best controls the intellect, were this not so completely suspended (*ausgeschlossen*) that it no longer sees the consequences for itself."[153] Berlin theater critic Oscar Bie wrote of his experience of another jazz band: "The drummer drummed beyond all measure. It had been paid for. Everything had been paid for. The jazz band, the champagne, the ornaments, and my intellectual faculties (*Geistigkeit*)."[154] One notices this sense of shock in visual representations as well. Visual artist Otto Schmalhausen, previously encountered as correspondent of George Grosz, provided an image to accompany a 1924 essay by Jaap Kool in the journal *Uhu*. Schmalhausen's "Jazz Band Music: What I Felt the First Time I Heard It" (1924) can be read as a visual representation of the chaos of the experience of the jazz band, melding technology, alcoholic excess, and dancing with distortions and screams to visually represent the psychological state of confusion so common to all these representations of the first experience of jazz.[155]

In its depiction of three caricatured Black dancers, Schmalhausen's image also brings to the fore another important element of numerous early jazz discussions, namely race and the function of Blackness within these accounts. Though authors disagreed as to whether jazz in its present form was a Black or white music, they were all but unanimous in attributing a Black, at times African, origin to the music.[156] In this way, German commentators partook in a reading of jazz similar to what Jeremy F. Lane has called the trope of the "techno-primitive hybrid," something he finds within a wide array of French modernist thought, in particular in relation to jazz.[157] While certainly not originating with jazz, this fusion of Blackness and the machine was present at the beginning of white American jazz criticism. This occurs most notably in American critic Walter Kingsley's reference to jazz as "an attempt to reproduce the marvelous syncopation of the African jungle" and as an "opera of ultra modernity" in his article "Whence Comes Jass" from 1917.[158] Long before the "red count" Harry Kessler would connect "ultramodern" and "ultraprimitive" with jazz after seeing Josephine Baker in Berlin,[159] writers in the United States and Europe were already at work linking jazz with Africa, primitive Blackness and urban, industrial capitalism. Not least of them was Austrian novelist Joseph Roth, then working as a journalist for the *Berliner Börsen-Courier*. In a May 1921 article, he wrote in reaction to this idea: "A funny punch line (*Pointe*) of cultural history is that the machine becomes negroid."[160] While Roth's and others' deployment of this idea partake in a broader European and American discourse, unique to the German case is its presence in light of the debate over the occupation on the Rhine.

The Black presence within Germany's borders, on the Rhine and in Berlin, complicated the embrace of jazz and its Blackness by early writers. For example, though claiming a Black origin to the jazz band, Kurt Tucholsky still sought to differentiate between jazz's Blackness and that of the occupation. He writes:

> [Enrico] Caruso is old and fat and meanwhile that which the Nigger sang has gone into the people's blood. (It is very difficult to speak the word Negro in Germany, without one being cut off with the cry "Black Horror." But the black horror, as far as it exists, appears to me to be much more a French one, and Abyssinian rapists do not repudiate [*desavouieren*] the rhythm of Nigger songs.). / The new troubadour is not a Nigger anyway.[161]

This distinction between jazz's white present and its Black past was one whose "nuance" was often ignored by those who opposed the music and its modernism. Indeed, given the centrality of the trap drum to early modernist readings, the issue of the jazz band's Blackness was one not easily pushed aside.[162] It is a point that was caricatured within the pages of the *Berliner Volkszeitung* already in April 1921. In a drawing entitled "The Jimmy" (here meaning shimmy), artist Theodor Leisser depicts a bustling Berlin dance hall with a four-man white jazz band on the left-hand side. In the foreground of this image, however, two caricatured French African soldiers comment: "The Germans are really a curious bunch (*wunderliche Leute*). In the occupied territories they get excited about the 'black horror,' but in their ballrooms they dance to our nigger dances with passion and devotion."[163]

Yet if readings like this from early 1921 still assume jazz's black origins and white present, texts from a bit later, in particular from 1922 onward, hint at the shifting ground of jazz performance in relation to race. For from the summer of 1921 onward, members of the Black diaspora, like Evandale Roberts, Joseph (Joe) Sewonu, and others, were becoming more visible and audible within the Berlin jazz scene. In September 1921, the Berlin correspondent for the Austrian *Neues Wiener Journal*, Albert Held, wrote that, in Berlin, Black performers and jazz bands were all over, noting: "the audience only loves the variety theater stars and the Negroes with their terrible music."[164] In his comments from January 1922, Poldi Schmidl discusses the increasing preference of Berlin entertainment establishments for Black performers over their white

Figure 4: *To Beauty (An die Schönheit)*. **1922. Dix, Otto (1891–1969) ©
ARS, NY. Oil on canvas, 140 x 122 cm. Von-der-Heydt-Museum. Photo
Credit: Erich Lessing/Art Resource, NY.**

counterparts. For him, the "many music-making Negroes in Berlin" are not
musicians but film actors and dancers masquerading as such because they
could not find any roles.[165] In part echoing earlier comments regarding the success of *Harem Nights* despite the "Black Horror" debate, his problem, he insists, is not with the Black musicians but with the public "that runs to the Negroes."[166] Schmidl's thoughts on Black musicians and the "Black Horror"

debate thus act both as a sign of the resistance to jazz's Black origins as well as an indication of the very real existence of Black jazz musicians in Germany in 1921 and 1922.[167]

The jazz band, the trap drum, and the Black presence in Germany find a synthesis of sorts in Otto Dix's *An die Schönheit* (*To Beauty*), from 1922 (figure 4). Like other modernist writers and artists analyzed here, Dix was an early adopter of jazz, both dance and music.[168] Tellingly, Dix's representation of the trap drum in this painting features a large image of a Native American figure in headdress, as well as the words "Tom Boston," an oblique reference to this pseudonym of another Black jazz performer of the period. As with other jazz musicians from these early years, little definitive is known about Tom Boston, a musician and dancer who also went by the names Tom(m)i and Tommy Boston and appeared in Wiesbaden (1920), Frankfurt (1921), Chemnitz (1924), and Erfurt (1928).[169] Like the other jazz artists of the Black diaspora and otherwise, Tom Boston's path seems to have taken him from the occupied zones to the east and Dresden, where Dix and fellow visual artist Friedrich Karl Gotsch encountered him as a drummer in a jazz band in 1922.[170] As one moves away from the Berlin explosion in early 1921, there is less and less a concentration of voices from this city, indicating that the jazz band expanded its impact to other metropolitan areas in Germany like Dresden or the unidentified jazz band that appeared in Danzig around this time (figure 5), not to mention other Central European metropoles like Prague, Vienna, and Budapest.[171]

While Dix's painting is in some ways typical of the space of the encounter with the jazz band in the postwar period, the work also figures its meaning through a contrast between the self-portrait of the artist and the Black drummer. They share identical suits, torso positions, and each engages the viewer with an askew glance. Furthermore, from Dix's sketchbooks, which contain various versions of the Black musician and numerous sketches of his instrument, the highly caricatured presentation of the Black drummer was one Dix came to only gradually.[172] Though the physical and visual proximity between the artist's self-representation and the drummer produce a connection between the two figures, Dix's use of contrasting technologies in the work also act to create distance between the two. Whereas the Black drummer relies on his physicality to communicate via the drum, Dix's persona deploys modern technology to overcome any corporeal limitations. For one, the drummer is the only figure in the work whose mouth is not closed, with his wide grin acting to suggest an oral, rather than technological, mode of communication. Dix, by contrast, presents his white German persona as not only capable of reaching beyond these limitations but via the telephone in his hand of both sending and

Figure 5: A Jazz band in the Winter Garden at Danzig (today Gdansk, Poland). Ca. 1920. Anonymous, 20th century. Photo Credit: Adoc-photos/Art Resource, NY.

receiving information. One might say that Dix uses the telephone within this work to affect an image of himself as the passionless transmitter of information via direct, immediate, and modern technology. While one must be careful not to draw too many conclusions based upon Dix's work in isolation, it is also evident from Tucholsky's and Schmidl's remarks that the Black presence in the German jazz scene impacted the framework for representing jazz in this period, even as the use of the trap drum and technology remained equally significant points of interest.

If initial reactions to the jazz band had generally emphasized the music's Black origins and its white present, Black jazz musicians, whether by choice or by circumstance, complicated this developmental narrative. Indeed, questions surrounding jazz's Blackness as a thing of the past, present, or future, continue throughout the period, with various responses given at different times.[173] Here, as elsewhere, the turn towards jazz between 1919 and 1923 proceeded in fits and starts as jazz expanded across the cultural and physical landscape of Germany. From the embrace of American dancing following the war through the incubation of the jazz band in the occupation zones, by 1922, jazz and jazz bands had become part of Weimar modernists' vocabulary, works, and personal experience. As the debate over the "Black Horror" and a short while later the jazz band travelled east to Berlin, Dresden, Danzig, and beyond, commentators constructed a chaotic vision of the contemporary moment and its disruption, or rather representation, in the jazz band's drum. Finally, reacting to greater numbers of Black performers in Germany, critical reactions to jazz in visual and textual form offered competing interpretations of the music and its meaning, in particular in relation to race.

Still, in 1923, the jazz band momentarily seemed to retreat into the background. Both for musicians and the public, confronting the economic misery and political violence of the early republic outweighed discussion of jazz and, of course, lowered the rates for foreign musicians. In point of fact, as Konrad Nowakowski has documented, the premiere German jazz musicians of the period, like Fred Ross and Eric Borchard, fled the German capital and headed to Vienna, further weakening the resonance of jazz in the capital,[174] while the Original Piccadilly Four had already left for Switzerland in 1922. Yet, after the stabilization of German currency in 1924, Weimar Germans and their jazz musicians continued their consideration of the role of jazz in their republic. This time, however, Black musicians and African Americans in particular moved from the periphery to the center of Weimar Germany's experience of jazz. This change is nowhere more clearly expressed than in the case of Sam Wooding and his jazz band from Harlem.

CHAPTER 2

The Aural Shock of Modernity: Sam Wooding and Weimar Germany's Experience of Jazz

> Sam Wooding's masterful jazz orchestra was the real highlight (*Clou*), the true sensation of the "Chocolate Kiddies."
> —H. H. Stuckenschmidt (1925)

May 1925 bore witness to arguably the most important performance of an African American jazz band during the Weimar Republic. As part of the *Chocolate Kiddies* revue at the *Admiralspalast*, Sam Wooding's eleven-man orchestra introduced the capital to their brand of New York jazz in a series of more than seventy performances occurring over a two-month period. As noted theater critic Oscar Bie wrote following the premiere: "Everything else has been mere preparation, the bands in the bars, the American operetta at the [*Theater am*] *Zoo*, the presentation of exotic poetry with jazz—here you have the final word (*das Endgültige*)."[1] Bie's words begin to register the impact of Wooding's performances on German jazz discourse and indicate that, for those who heard it, the group's arrival represented more than just another evening in Berlin's already crowded entertainment district on *Friedrichstrasse*.

As the first large-scale African American revue to perform in the capital, famously followed six months later by Josephine Baker and *La Revue nègre*, reactions to the revue were often rooted within received racial discourses and their appearance prompted reactions connecting the African American performers to the "Black Horror."[2] What amazed the Berlin public, however, was not just the visual attraction of an African American performance troupe; it was also, and even primarily, the jazz music played by Sam Wooding and his jazz orchestra. So that what was initially received as an African American revue, to a certain degree became even more a jazz show.[3] As Hans Heinz Stuckenschmidt wrote in praise of the revue somewhat later: "Sam Wooding's masterful jazz orchestra was the real highlight, the true sensation of the 'Chocolate Kiddies.'" Stuckenschmidt's, and indeed many reviewers', focus on the novelty of the music has served to amplify the notion that Berlin and Germany had been isolated from live African American performances prior to Wooding's performances. Yet, African American and other Black performers and jazz musicians, as well as white American and European jazz bands, were by no means absent from Berlin before May 1925.

Aside from those groups already referenced in chapter 1, a number of vocal groups, singers, and jazz bands and musicians had already played the German capital. In December 1924, the African American artist and impresario Will Garland and a group of more than ten singers perform and record in Berlin.[4] More immediately, the world-famous Fisk Jubilee Singers appeared in Berlin at the *Beethovensaal* on May 15, 1925, just ten days prior to the *Chocolate Kiddies'* premiere.[5] If these are not jazz bands, then they nonetheless show the range of African American performance styles presented to Berliners. Of course, African American jazz artists were active in the period as well.[6] Jacob Pete Zabriskie performed in Berlin during 1922. He appeared first at the *Esplanade* in September 1922 and then, along with drummer George "Bobo" Hines, at the *Fiametta* from October through December 1922, with Hines alone returning there in January 1923.[7] Further, during the same month in 1924 as African American tenor Roland Hayes performs in Berlin at the *Beethovensaal*,[8] George Clapham's jazz band was appearing at another Berlin locale, the *Alhambra*.[9] Clapham's band also appears to have recorded in Berlin as well, producing two songs "Nothin' But" and "Runnin' Wild" for Vox in the summer of 1924.[10] Perhaps most striking within the context of Bie's words, jazz drummer Buddy Gilmore will perform with his wife Mattie as "Buddie and Buddie" at the *Scala* in April 1925, just one month before the premiere of the *Chocolate Kiddies*. The presence of George Clapham and the Gilmores in Berlin, along with Black musician James Boucher who played with Julian Fuhs (see below) in Berlin from December 1924 through early 1925, is noteworthy as all three had performed with the *Southern Syncopated Orchestra*, once again linking German jazz history with that of European and African American jazz history.[11] In addition, white European jazz bands and bandleaders, in particular from New York, had been performing in Germany since at least 1924. Amongst these can be included the German-Americans Julian Fuhs[12] and Alex Hyde,[13] as well as the British dance band, the London Sonora Band.[14] Finally, two white American jazz groups with no apparent biographical connection to Germany arrived in Berlin—the Kentucky Serenaders under Eddie Woods, who had first performed in Munich in April 1924, came to Berlin in October 1924, in each case appearing as part of the show *Wien gib acht!* (*Vienna Watch Out!*),[15] and the Ohio Lido Venice Band led by Harl Smith, which arrived in Berlin during the winter season of 1924/25, playing at the *Palais Heinroth.*[16]

That in May 1925 reviewers tended not to refer to these performers can be in part attributed to one important novelty of the *Chocolate Kiddies*, namely where prior Black and/or jazz performers had played and where Wooding and the *Chocolate Kiddies* premiered.[17] While earlier Black jazz performers had appeared in entertainment locales, ones typically ignored by the mainstream bourgeois press (bars, cafés, hotels, variety theater houses like the *Wintergarten* or *Scala*), Wooding performed in Hermann Haller's *Admiralspalast*, a large and relatively well-known establishment catering to a middle-class crowd. The other, perhaps even more unique attribute, was, as is discussed below, the advertising campaign that accompanied their debut. This meant, amongst other things, that for the first time, across a wide spectrum of news outlets, an African American jazz band received broad discussion in the Berlin press. So while other African American performers and jazz musicians had preceded the *Chocolate Kiddies* and Sam Wooding, this chapter will argue that their Berlin performances became central to the German critical understanding of jazz throughout the 1920s and into the early 1930s.[18] A partial list of those who discussed or heard them would include cultural critics Fritz Giese, Siegfried Kracauer, Kurt Pinthus, Alfred Polgar, Herwarth Walden, Frank Warschauer, and Hermann von Wedderkop; ethnomusicologists Erich Moritz von Hornbostel and Jaap Kool; and music critics Max Butting and Hans Heinz Stuckenschmidt, as well as composers Ernst Krenek, Klaus Pringsheim, Franz Schreker, Karol Rathaus, Kurt Weill, and others. In a word, much of Weimar critics' conceptualization and experience with African American jazz can be traced back to Sam Wooding and his jazz band (figure 6).

Before proceeding to a discussion of the history of the revue and the reactions to the premiere, it is important to understand the cultural and musical context of Wooding's band, as these elements, too, will play a role on that May evening in Berlin. Born in Philadelphia and schooled in ragtime and jazz in Atlantic City and later Harlem, Sam Wooding (1895–1985) has emerged as a crucial figure in the history of jazz and its global reception. In World War I, Wooding played in the 807th Pioneer Infantry Band, a formation similar to James Reese Europe's referenced in the previous chapter. During this time, Wooding came to know other important jazz pioneers, such as Will H. Vodery and Earl Granstaff, and even performed for the first time in France in January 1919.[19] After returning to the United States, the pianist and arranger eventually made his way to New York and Harlem. As he later wrote:

Figure 6: Jazz Musician Sam Wooding in Berlin. (Photograph Courtesy of Chip Deffaa and Mrs. Sam Wooding.)

"I found Harlem to be everything a young Negro would look forward to and desire, to give the necessary push to his hungry ambitious spirit for culture and musical aspirations."[20] Yet, Wooding most indelibly left his mark not on the New York jazz scene but on the European one. Wooding and his band traveled to Berlin, Budapest, Copenhagen, London, Moscow, Paris, Prague, Vienna, and beyond. Having introduced so many across the world to jazz, Wooding came to view himself "as the Christopher Columbus of jazz," as "having brought big band jazz to a new world."[21] Beginning with the *Chocolate Kiddies* revue, Wooding toured Germany and Europe between 1925 and 1931.[22] His first stint included over seventy performances in Berlin alone. Wooding not only toured the capital, however, but across Germany, traveling, amongst others, to Danzig, Hamburg, Hannover, Leipzig, Dortmund, Mannheim, Magdeburg, Breslau, and Frankfurt am Main. He also, unlike other American jazz bands, both Black and white, returned repeatedly to the capital. After their May premiere, the *Chocolate Kiddies* made a return trip to Berlin in December 1925, appearing at the *Neues Theater am Zoo*, though without the fanfare of their initial arrival.[23] After the show disbanded, Wooding next returned to Berlin to perform at the *Faun des Westens* in June and July 1926 and, in a sign of his growing fame, was part of a panel of jazz experts invited to weigh in on jazz's meaning in the *Berliner Tageblatt*, where he published a short text, "The Transfiguration of Jazz," which is discussed below.[24] Wooding was back in Berlin in October 1926, performing at the *Ufa-Palast am Zoo*.[25] After a return trip to the United States in 1927, Wooding returned to Berlin in 1928 for a new African American show, *Die schwarze Revue (The Black Revue)*, which premiered in Berlin on June 15.[26] A final appearance in Berlin occurred during his April 1930 stint at the *Dachgarten Café*.[27] So while Wooding's Berlin performances were neither the first experience Germans had with live jazz, nor with African American music in general, the duration and geographical variety of his engagements in Germany, in addition to the sheer critical mass of German-language writings about him, are further reasons why his jazz music became one of the most cited examples of African American jazz during the period.

Finally, one must consider Wooding's own understanding of the genre of music that he aspired to play. It was not only the sound of Black jazz artists that Wooding admired, but also Paul Whiteman and symphonic jazz, a style which other African American artists like Fletcher Henderson were also involved in. It was not for nothing that the section of the *Chocolate Kiddies* revue in which his band played was designated in programs as a symphonic jazz concert.[28] Indeed, in a 1930 retrospective of his impact, a reporter from the African American newspaper the *Chicago Defender* noted: "Mr. Wooding's orchestra was the first symphonic jazz unit ever to play in Germany."[29] Yet, Wooding also sought to distinguish himself from Whiteman's vision of "massive jazz (*Massenjazz*)" as he termed it and in the aforementioned "Transfiguration of Jazz" he argued for the refinement of jazz by drawing upon African American musical traditions, not only of rhythm but of melody.[30] He concluded his short comments on the question of jazz and artistic production by writing:

> Against all prognostications, the future of this improvisatory music consists not in further development of breadth, but in an internal purification and clarification, one might say, of chamber-musical refinement. Jazz and art music enrich each other. How long will it be, ten, twenty years before one will no longer refer to the pariah "jazz"—because it has become the expression of a refined feeling (*eines geläuterten Gefühls*).[31]

So like Fletcher Henderson and other African American musicians, Wooding can be considered part of the symphonic jazz movement, without this impacting the originality or authenticity of his music. As one scholar has recently argued, many African American and white jazz bands and musicians of the period produced music that transcended current distinctions between jazz and jazzy popular music, creating "an overlapping family of syncopated musics in dialogue with one another."[32] Indeed, while Wooding could be hailed as a symphonic jazz pioneer in the *Chicago Defender* in 1930, in January 1925, he and his orchestra were described in the *Baltimore Afro-American* as "far and away the hottest and jazziest combination of colored musicians . . . in many a day."[33] Aligning Wooding's jazz with symphonic jazz therefore in no way diminishes his achievements; instead, it enriches our understanding of how jazz was practiced by African American musicians in the 1920s.

The *Chocolate Kiddies* between New York, Moscow, and Berlin

The first published reference to the show that would become the *Chocolate Kiddies* was released in mid-April 1925, a little more than one month away from the premiere.[34] Indicative of the personalities at stake in its creation, a short notice was placed on the front page of the American publication *The Billboard* on April 18. Under the heading "To Offer Colored Revue in Europe," the release frames the show that will become the *Chocolate Kiddies* as a collaboration between Morris Gest and Arthur Lyons.[35] If Lyons' name as producer of the revue has long been known within scholarship on the *Chocolate Kiddies*, Gest's name has been largely absent. According to this early report, however, the show was to be performed under the title "Morris Gest presents . . ." and after an initial stint in Berlin, it would go on to Paris, Vienna, and then Moscow, where it would be featured at the Moscow Art Theatre (MAT), famously founded by Constantin Stanislavski and Vladimir Nemirovich-Danchenko. Though much in this early report is inconsistent with the show as it would premiere in Berlin, the references to Morris Gest and the MAT represent lost traces of the transatlantic connection between Russian and African American diasporic communities that played a major role in producing this important moment in early German jazz history.

Though not named in the release, at the center of the relationship was the Russian-Jewish impresario Leonid Davydovich Leonidoff-Bermann.[36]

Leonidoff, born in Kharkov (Charkow) to a merchant family, became involved with the MAT in the 1890s and enjoyed a particularly close relationship with the theater's cofounder Nemirovich-Danchenko. He left Russia during the civil war, taking part in a famous theater troupe around the actor Vasily Kachalov. With this group, he performed across southern and central Europe, including a prolonged stint in Vienna in the early 1920s.[37] Yet like other Russian émigrés, he eventually settled in Berlin, where he became chief negotiating agent of the MAT for Europe and North America. Leonidoff was part of the vast community of the Russian diaspora in Berlin, a population that peaked in 1923 at around 360,000.[38] Berlin's location and the size of its Russian émigré community made it an important pivot point for Russian exiles and Soviet artists alike, as they traveled back and forth between Moscow and New York and places in between. Morris Gest, of Russian-Jewish extraction, travelled regularly to Berlin, and his brother Simeon ("Sam") resided there during the period, acting as a local representative for his brother. In the New York theater scene, Russians, and Jewish Russians in particular, played an equally pivotal role in the early 1920s. It was through Morris Gest that the MAT became a sensation in New York. Beginning in 1922 with Balieff's "Chauve Souris" ("Bat Theater"), Gest orchestrated a series of successes. As one of its representatives, Leonidoff negotiated between the MAT and Gest, both in Berlin and New York, and worked with world famous artists from the singer Chaliapin to dancer Pavlova and, of course, Balieff. If today Russian theater and the MAT in particular are generally held in high regard, as Valerie Hoffmann argues, Gest's promotion of Russian art and artists led to this shift in their perception, catapulting them from the variety theater to paragons of high art in Europe and America.[39] It is a shift that resonates with developments in the African American theater scene from which the cast for the *Chocolate Kiddies* was drawn. Through his involvement with the success of MAT in New York, Leonidoff had had ample opportunity to learn from Gest's strategy, which combined massive press campaigns with high salaries to top entertainers.

As Leonidoff related in an interview given on the occasion of the *Chocolate Kiddies* premiere in Vienna, he first hit upon the idea of bringing an African American revue to Berlin and Europe after visiting a cabaret in Harlem. In all likelihood, this took place during 1924 when Leonidoff visited the newly established *Club Alabam*.[40] At the time, pioneering African American musician Fletcher Henderson was performing there. Henderson and his band left the *Club Alabam* in July 1924, and they were replaced by Sam Wooding's band. So that when Leonidoff returned to New York in March 1925 with plans to bring an African American revue to Berlin, it was to the *Club Alabam* that he headed, and there he encountered not only Sam Wooding but the agent and producer Alfred S. Lyons.

Like Leonidoff and Gest, Lyons was of Russian-Jewish extraction. Later in his career, he became an important agent in Hollywood, representing over the course of his career artists like Jack Benny, Cole Porter, Ida Lupino, Heddy Lamar, and Lucille Ball. During the 1920s, Lyons represented a number of African American artists, including Wooding and the famous comedian Johnny Hudgins. In the fall of 1924, Lyons became the producer of a new musical revue at the *Club Alabam* called *Alabam Fantasies*. Though it premiered in the fall, the most important performance of *Alabam Fantasies* took place at the *Lafayette Theatre* in January 1925. This was to be a springboard for the show's move to Broadway and beyond. Indeed, advertisements in The *New York Times* announced that the *Alabam Fantasies* were booked for a European tour in London, Paris, and Berlin, inverting the order that would accompany the initial report of the *Chocolate Kiddies* in April.[41] For reasons to be discussed below, shortly after the Lafayette premiere, the planned European tour of *Alabam Fantasies* fell apart. Yet Lyons' intention to bring the *Club Alabam* show to Europe represents an important precondition of the curious origins of the *Chocolate Kiddies*.

The January 1925 performances at the *Lafayette Theatre* were by all accounts a success, though they were initially marred by controversy. First, the prima donna of the show, African American singer and actress Abbie Mitchell, bowed out of the show on the first night. Mitchell's name will resurface in a subsequent chapter, and so it is important to detail here her connections to African American performance in Europe and the New York theater scene. Mitchell had first appeared on the European stage in the first decade of the twentieth century as part of her then husband and composer Will Marion Cook's London production of *In Dahomey* (1903). Equally importantly, she would again tour Europe as part of Cook's *Southern Syncopated Orchestra*, which, as is mentioned in chapter 1, toured London, Paris, and Vienna amongst other European cities. After returning from Europe in 1923, she gave a number of concert performances and, in the fall of 1924, joined the *Club Alabam*. In her unpublished memoirs from 1938, Mitchell remembers the club fondly, noting that the management was "gracious, unprejudiced, and endeavored to keep every-thing pleasant."[42] Like other clubs in Harlem at the time, the *Club Alabam* was frequented by an elite, primarily white New York audience. Though alongside Johnny Hudgins and Eddie Rector she received top billing in advertisements, on the opening night, Mitchell performed but one song. According to Mitchell this was because the numbers of the show had not been rehearsed and because they included things, which, as she told a reporter at the time, "should be allowed to remain buried in the past."[43] Though her allusion is oblique, one aspect of the show to which she may have objected was the blackface act of African American comedian Johnny Hudgins. Mitchell's status as singer, whose concert repertoire regularly featured European art songs, was potentially at odds with the more populist tradition represented by Hudgins.

Yet if Mitchell was a major draw for the show, Hudgins was its star. His career trajectory had been rising steadily since the fall of 1924 when the Baltimore native received widespread attention from his performance in Noble Sissle and Eubie Blake's *Chocolate Dandies*. It was in this show that he debuted his signature "Silent Hudgins" act. While a trumpeter played, Hudgins mouthed the sounds, seemingly transforming the human body into brass instrument. If the performative brilliance of his act is clear, contemporary viewers are nonetheless equally likely to notice the minstrel iconography through which Hudgins voiced his modernist act. This is equally the case of the *Chocolate Kiddies* trio "Three Eddies:" Shakey (Clarence) Beasley, Chick (Layburn) Horsey, and Tiny (Earle) Ray.[44] They too will perform in blackface makeup, but for Berlin, rather than New York, audiences. Further connecting the trio with Hudgins is the fact that Chick Horsey, first with Arthur Bryson and then with Willie Robins, did a version of "Silent Hudgins" with trumpeter Bobby Martin as part of the *Chocolate Kiddies* revue in Europe. The disconcerting images of blackface performers that abound in European advertisements and stage design therefore must not only be placed within the context of the German history of representations of Blackness but also within the context of American and African American performance history. More to the point, the fact that Hudgins was one of the most successful acts in New York in the mid-1920s points towards a high degree of similarity rather than dissimilarity between the proclivities of (white) German and North American audiences. Needless to say, the entire matter of Blacks in blackface and the response of the African American community to this practice is a highly complicated matter, to which Mitchell's objections in 1925 may attest.[45]

While Mitchell bowed out after the first performance of *Alabam Fantasies*, Lyons, too, made a less than gracious exit, though not of his own volition—he was fired after the first week by the management of the *Club Alabam*. Lyons quickly turned to the courts and sued the management for monies owed him.[46] While Lyons' case was still being adjudicated in the New York Supreme Court, Leonidoff returned to New York on March 24, 1925. The primary reason for his visit was to negotiate with Gest for the next season of New York performances by the MAT. Whether Lyons initiated contact with Leonidoff or vice versa remains unclear, but very shortly after Leonidoff's arrival he came to the *Club Alabam* to hear Sam Wooding. As Wooding later recalled: "And then one day, Lyons came in and said to me: 'How would you like to go to Europe?' I looked at him as if to say, 'Are you kidding?' He said, 'No, I got a man coming in from Europe, an impresario, a fellow named Leonidoff.'"[47] According to Wooding, the contracts were signed the next day at 4:00 a.m. Leonidoff, however, needed more than a jazz band; he needed a show and with the fate of *Alabam Fantasies* revue locked in court, Lyons turned to the outside to recruit new talent. If the show's top stars like Johnny Hudgins, Eddie Rector, and Abbie Mitchell could not be convinced to go to Europe, Lyons and Leonidoff had many things working in their favor. For one, Lyons was a known figure within the Black theater scene, while Leonidoff could offer intimate knowledge of the European theater scene and, equally importantly, could trade on Gest's and the MAT's international fame and reputation.[48]

Lyons and Leonidoff filled the cast of the *Chocolate Kiddies* with performers who were all well-known figures of the Black theater scene. These included singers Arthur "Strut" Payne and Lottie Gee, like Hudgins, formerly of the *Chocolate Dandies*. In addition, performers George Statson, Charlie Davis, Bobby and Babe Goins, and Adelaide Hall all became part of the show. Yet other than Wooding's band, the stars of the show were Thaddeus Greenlee and Arthur Drayton.[49] The duo was one of the premiere acts of the period, starring in Broadway and at the Cotton Club in the 1920s. They had also performed in Europe before the First World War and incorporated a number of foreign languages into their act, something that proved to be of great value during their stint with the *Chocolate Kiddies*. Unlike their contemporaries, "The Three Eddies," or Johnny Hudgins, Greenlee and Drayton did not perform in blackface. Instead, through their immaculate dress and linguistic proficiency, they positioned themselves as an international and sophisticated "class act." This latter term designates in the narrow sense an act of multiple dancers performing alongside in unison and correspondingly demanding precise execution; yet it also is meant to stake out a new space beyond minstrelsy for African American artists. Like *Alabam Fantasies*, then, the *Chocolate Kiddies* was composed of various elements of contemporary African American entertainment. So though it may never have been performed in America, neither its stars nor their acts would likely have struck a Broadway audience of the period as particularly out of place.

Lyons also commissioned original music for the show. For this, he turned not to Wooding, but to the songwriting duo of Joe Trent and future jazz great

Duke Ellington. Ellington had moved to New York from his native Washington D.C. a few years earlier, and aside from playing in the city and touring with his band in the northeast, he also made ends meet through "Tin Pan Alley" compositions.[50] The songs he composed for the show were a big break for Ellington, and he vividly describes in his memoirs how he had to write the music for the show in just one night.[51] Though obviously exaggerated (in fact, one song, "Deacon Jazz," had already been written the year before), Ellington did deliver at least four original songs in a very short amount of time: "With You," "Jig Walk," "Love Is Just a Wish," and "Jim Dandy." These songs, as Ellington scholar Mark Tucker has suggested, both follow and break with standard harmonies and rhythms of popular music of the time and are demonstrations of Ellington's early compositional techniques and point forward towards his later work of the 1930s.[52] Well-known German bandleaders and composers, amongst others Dajos Béla, Mischa Spoliansky, and Bernhard Etté, took note and produced recordings of Ellington's songs from the *Chocolate Kiddies* between August and September 1925. Ellington's impact through these songs was felt as late as 1928 when the famous vocal group the Comedian Harmonists recorded a test version of "Jig Walk" for *Deutsche Grammophon*.[53] So though Ellington himself never made it to Weimar Berlin, his music via the *Chocolate Kiddies* and Sam Wooding was heard and performed by Weimar-era musicians.

Given the personalities involved and the size of the group, news of the *Chocolate Kiddies* was reported on regularly in the African American press. In a short notice on the show, the *Baltimore Afro-American* claimed that this would be the first large group of African American performers to tour Europe since Cook's *In Dahomey*, though this claim ignores the slightly earlier *SSO*.[54] Within the African American press, the *Chocolate Kiddies* was more than just another Broadway show to African Americans at home: it was an opportunity to demonstrate abroad and at home their importance to American cultural life. On May 3, 1925, a farewell party was organized for the departing members of the troupe. Featuring performances by cast members as well as Florence Mills and Fletcher Henderson, this grand send-off from Harlem also received coverage in the African American press.[55] Two days later, the cast of the *Chocolate Kiddies*, thirty-two singers and dancers and Sam Wooding's eleven-man band, embarked for Hamburg aboard the *SS Arabic* of the American White Star Line.[56]

After arriving in Berlin via Hamburg, the *Chocolate Kiddies* revue opened at the *Admiralspalast* on May 25, 1925. The timing of the revue's premiere, however, was less than opportune. The prime season for Berlin's great revues was in late August and early September, and spring shows often struggled to fill the house. It was for this reason that the large revues often left the capital in the spring to go on tour. Indeed, the departure of the prior year's show was the reason for the *Chocolate Kiddies*' booking at the *Admiralspalast*. According to a report in *The Billboard*, Haller's show was leaving the capital as of April 1, and he needed something to fill the space until the beginning of the new season.[57] According to cabaret historian Peter Jelavich, Haller's annual revues between 1923 and 1929 "epitomized the genre [of the revue] in the minds of contemporary observers."[58] Performing in such a venue was obviously a significant factor in the troupe's ability to garner critical recognition for the revue in the German press.

Broadly following the strategy of Gest and Leonidoff with the MAT in New York, the revue was widely publicized, apparently under the direction of Fritz Jacobsohn.[59] The *Chocolate Kiddies* advertised in major dailies like the *Berliner Tageblatt, Berliner Montagspost, 8 Uhr Abendblatt, Berliner Lokal-Anzeiger, Vossische Zeitung*, and elsewhere; and from photographs the band took of themselves while in Berlin, there is evidence to suggest that scattered throughout the city were posters on kiosks and elsewhere announcing the troupe's arrival. In an advertisement from the 27th of May, the *Chocolate Kiddies* were cited as containing the "most famous colored artists of America,"[60] while an advertisement from June 6 heralded the group as the "latest sensation of Berlin."[61] In addition, at least four articles appeared before the revue's premiere discussing the rehearsals.[62] In these advertisements, illustrations, and in the many newspaper accounts that followed the premiere are further indications of the event's significance and of its highly effective marketing, which included, like Paul Whiteman's symphonic jazz concerts just over a year later, inviting members of the press and celebrities to the special premiere performance on May 25. All this is another indication of why, though other African American artists were present in Weimar Germany both before and after, the *Chocolate Kiddies* was the first jazz performance widely visible to the Berlin public and widely reviewed by the Berlin press.

From the program for the show's Berlin premiere, one can reconstruct not only the scenes, dances, and music the audience experienced, but also the manner by which the audience's experience was framed (figures 7 and 8).[63] Interestingly, the first page of the program, unlike the advertisements, merely describes the revue as a "Negro Production with a Prologue and Two Acts."[64] It lists Arthur Lyons as writer and director, along with choreographer Charles Davis, music by Joe Trent and Duke Ellington, orchestrated by Arthur S. Johnson, and scenery by Willi Poggany.[65] After a cataloging of the performers' names, their home New York theater, and their specialties, there follows a synopsis of the show.[66]

> 1000 words English[67] are hardly required of the visitors to the "Chocolate Kiddies" to understand what the following scenes, songs, and dances are about. The language of music, rhythm, and—legs is international.
>
> Beginning on the "plantation" of the American South, where the black farmers dance and sing their peaceful songs, where they pray at sunset, laugh and joke around during sunlight; from there it goes out into the world, to the north, to the city of millions that lures and draws everyone: New York. The duo of Greenlee and Drayton plays the role of tour guide through the different stations: new types of dances, comic appearances, eccentrics, lyric and religious songs, the New York Negro quarter of "Harlem" is mirrored in its life and goings on. The Symphonic Concert of the Sam Wooding Jazz Band opens act two, and the extensive program of the Negro Cabaret in the Harlem quarter forms the conclusion.[68]

The first words of the above quote, "1000 words English," appear in large, bold letters. Should the description at first arouse a sense of anxiety in those viewers who do not understand English, it then allays this fear by emphasizing the extra-linguistic, in part sexual, aspects of the show: music, rhythm, and legs. Another reason for this emphasis on the performers' legs is to frame it as belonging to the chorus-line genre of the American Tiller Girls. Accordingly, jazz music plays little or no role in this description of the show. Indeed, aside from the reference to the symphonic concert in "The Sam Wooding Jazz-Band," the word jazz appears only once more in the program.

Instead, most of the space in the opening acts is devoted to the "Old South," which is then replaced by the modernity of New York and Harlem, a city whose poets were already being translated into German as is discussed in chapter 6. The prologue begins with the sketch "Plantation at Sundown," a scene depicting an imagined return to the antebellum South. "Gone are the days when my heart was young and gay, / Gone are my friends from the cotton fields away," Arthur "Strut" Payne sang in his performance of Stephen Foster's "Old Black Joe," the first song of the show.[69] During all this, Sam Wooding and his band accompanied the cast from the pit.[70] The first act also featured the star singer Lottie Gee performing Stephen Foster's "Old Folks at Home" under the more popular title "Swanee River."

The two concluding numbers of the prologue, "Farewell to the Plantation"

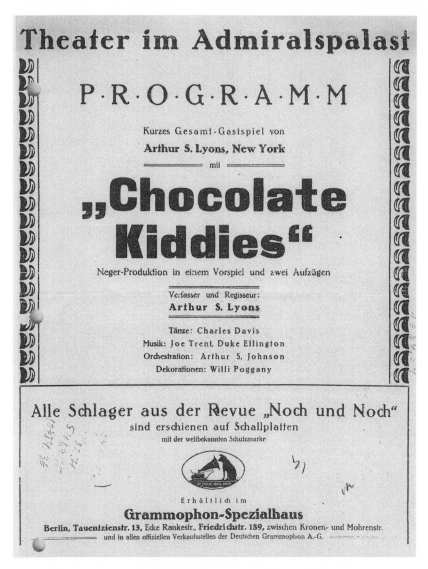

Figure 7: Cover of the Berlin Program for *Chocolate Kiddies Revue* at the *Theater am Admiralspalast*, 1925. Courtesy Institut für Theaterwissenschaft der Freien Universität Berlin and Dr. Peter Jammerthal.

Stiftung
Fritz E. Croner
Berlin-Zehlendorf
1962

Figure 8: Performers and Summary from the Berlin Program for *Chocolate Kiddies*, 1925. Courtesy Institut für Theaterwissenschaft der Freien Universität Berlin and Dr. Peter Jammerthal.

and "Grab Your Girl," transition the show to the first act, which was made up of a peculiar assemblage of milieus and genres. For example, after a dance by Bobby and Babe Goins, the scene opened into a "'Zulu Forest,'" during which singer and dancer Adelaide Hall performed "Jungle Nights in Dixie," donning only a white wig, grass skirt, and brassiere.[71] As Garvin Bushell, a musician with Wooding's jazz band, later recalled: "There was always a jungle number in the Negro shows. In New York Florence Mills used to do one called 'Hawaiian Night in Dixieland'. . . . In *Chocolate Kiddies* we had 'Jungle Night in Dixieland.' They'd always give the same reason to have some jungle music: tom-toms and hoochie-coochie."[72] The sixth scene of the first act, "Harlem in New York—The New York Negro Quarter and Its Life and Goings On," shifted the scene to the contemporary. It consisted of eight separate skits, one of which, the Ellington song "With You," with its subtitle "Four Generations of Love," revolved around a story of sexual infidelity between cast members playing mother, postman, a messenger boy, and children. The depiction of Harlem concluded with the entire cast performing the "Rabbit Hop" across the stage.[73] Contributing to the mélange of old and new, nestled between "With You" and the "Rabbit Hop" and framed by a thick-lined border, was an announcement of the cast's performance of the Charleston, "America's latest dance rhythm."

After intermission, the Sam Wooding Orchestra made its way onto the stage to perform the second act of the show. The personnel of the Sam Wooding Band at the time of their performance in Berlin was as follows: Bobby Martin, Maceo Edwards, and Tommy Ladnier, trumpets; Herb Flemming, trombone; Johnny Mitchell, banjo; Garvin Bushell, Willie Lewis, and Gene Sedric, saxes/clarinets; Sam Wooding, piano; John Warren, bass; and George Howe, drums. Wooding's contribution here was truly original. In the midst of this revue on a plantation and in a Harlem cabaret, Wooding and his orchestra gave a jazz concert to which no one danced and that was not accompanied by any visual stimulus other than eleven African American musicians performing jazz music. This bold move, as becomes clear from the song selection, was in dialogue with Paul Whiteman's earlier "Experiment in Modern Music" from 1924, the impact of which will be discussed in the following chapter. The concert opened with a medley of popular songs. According to Wooding, this medley included an arrangement of "By the Waters of Minnetonka," a claim substantiated by the fact that it was amongst those recorded in Berlin's *Vox* studios a short while later.[74] "By the Waters of Minnetonka" was especially important in the development of symphonic jazz; it had been famously recorded by Whiteman in 1924 and received extended discussion in Charles Osgood's 1926 *So This Is Jazz*, one of the first book-length studies of jazz written in America.[75] The second song, "I Want to Be Happy," was from Broadway composer Vincent Youmans with words by Irving Caesar and had appeared in the 1925 musical *No, No, Nanette*. This was followed by two versions of Rudolf Firml's "Indian Love Call," the original and a jazz version arranged by Wooding. This is yet another possible homage to Whiteman, whose 1924 concert had featured the same contrastive method to demonstrate the specificity of jazz. Next, Wooding's band performed "O Katharina," which is followed in the program by the words: "how it is heard by Negro musicians!" "O Katharina," written by L. Wolfe Gilbert with music by Richard Fall, was a popular song from the previous year in both America and Germany. Their concert ended with two jazz standards, W. C. Handy's "St. Louis Blues" and "Limehouse Blues" with music by Philip Braham.

The *Chocolate Kiddies* revue was thus palimpsest of contemporary African American performance. Simultaneously behind and ahead of its time, the revue gave Berliners and later Hamburgers, Frankfurters, and other Weimar Germans, a composite view of African American culture and its representation within American popular culture. This included both "class acts" like Greenlee and Drayton and the Black symphonic jazz of Wooding, as well as stereotypes associated with slavery and blackface minstrelsy.

Experiencing Jazz, Experiencing Modernity

If it is clear that for very complex reasons Wooding and his 1925 performances occupy a privileged position within Weimar jazz culture, this status owes as much to the music and performance venue as to German cultural history. In an attempt to explain the distinctive quality ascribed to Wooding's jazz and to explore the broader function of the German experience of jazz during this period, I want to develop the concept of aural shock as an analytical model to explain Wooding's unique status specifically, as well as the power of the jazz experience to represent modernity more broadly. Nora M. Alter and Lutz Koepnick write that "the arrival of modern sound can best be described through the figure of the shock. Industrial noises and mechanically reproduced sounds disrupted the working of the subject's perceptual apparatus. They often elicited fear, pain, or horror, and prompted the development of sensory protection shields that could cushion or even parry traumatic intrusions."[76] Alter and Koepnick argue that the transformation of the lived environment through industrialization and industrialized culture created qualitatively new sounds and that these sounds in turn necessitated new modes of experiencing sound.

While their discussion of the modernization of sound can be applied to a number of examples during the Weimar Republic, the syncopated and seemingly cacophonous sounds of jazz resonate strongly with the aural experience of the metropolis described by Koepnick and Alter. Thus if film is often seen as registering the shock of the visual in this period, jazz was equally powerful in registering the shock of the aural, in being experienced as an aesthetic mediation of the danger and exhilaration of the sounds of the street and the machine. As author Fritz Giese argued in the same year as Wooding's Berlin performances, jazz is capable of expressing the sounds and experiences of:

> being run over, electric shock, the clap of the mail box, the whistle of the locomotive, the whetting of the razor blade [. . .] the rolling of the elevated train, the workings of vending machines, the flapping of the revolving door of a café, stumbling up and down a subway stairway, the calls of newspaper sellers, the pounding of jackhammers at the construction of a high rise building, the grinding of cranes, howling of factory sirens.[77]

Jazz signifies here both the inescapability of modern sound and the ever-increasing danger it represents to the individual. The noise of modernity permeates the air and fills the listener with sounds of friction and anguish. Giese's description of jazz resounds with a disjointed and discomfiting modernity and implicitly locates in jazz's syncopations and improvisations the unexpectedness and horror, as well as exhilaration, of daily metropolitan life.

However, the experience of jazz did more to German listeners than merely reflect back to them *a priori* notions of modernity. Jazz also directly impacted and concretely transformed them. The experience of jazz, like the sounds of the street, was at first confounding and confusing, understood as noise rather than as music. Yet precisely because of this, German listeners found in it a means of accessing, and thereby reflecting upon, the aural component of the everyday shocks of modernity. It is for this reflective mode of the jazz experience that I want to use Benjamin's and Adorno's ambiguous employment of shock as a category of aesthetic experience. Before proceeding to an analysis of the German experience of the *Chocolate Kiddies* revue and Wooding's jazz, it is therefore first necessary to explore the ideas of shock and experience in relation to music in order to develop a theoretical apparatus capable of more meaningfully exploring the significance of jazz to German culture and of Wooding to the German jazz experience. In putting Wooding's jazz into conversation with Benjamin and Adorno, I not only want to lend theoretical weight to the German experience of jazz but also suggest Weimar jazz reception as a part of the impetus of this period's theorization of modernity.

At its core, Benjamin views the concept of experience as one divided within itself, split, in his famous distinction, between the fragmentary and isolated form of *Erlebnis* and a deeper, diachronic mode of *Erfahrung*. As Miriam Hansen's and Margaret Cohen's respective analyses of these terms have shown, Benjamin's understanding of experience underwent significant change from its initial iteration in pieces like *One-Way Street* to its fullest expression in the 1939 "On Some Motifs in Baudelaire."[78] Constant to his understanding, however, was his anchoring of the dialectic of these two types of experience through the key third term of shock.

Following Freud, Benjamin maintains that the maelstrom of modern urban existence necessitates the cultivation of a protective shield of consciousness. Here, one might think as well of Simmel's discussion of the *blasé* attitude of city dwellers in "The Metropolis and Mental Life." By preventing or, rather, by deflecting the impact of the shock, this protective shield saves consciousness from experiencing the everyday of modernity as one unrelenting trauma. This necessary parrying of shock by consciousness carries a heavy cost according to Benjamin. In order for the defense against shock to work properly, potentially traumatic experiences must be emptied of their content and transformed into less meaningful events. Benjamin describes this process in the following passage: "The greater the share of the shock factor in particular impressions, the more constantly consciousness has to be alert as a screen against stimuli; the more efficiently it does so, the less do these impressions enter experience (*Erfahrung*), tending to remain in the sphere of a certain hour in one's life (*Erlebnis*)."[79] What distinguishes successful from unsuccessful parrying of shock, *Erlebnis* from *Erfahrung*, is the presence or lack of an accompanying *Schreck*, or fright, horror, terror, to the impression. Horror is to be distinguished in this context from fear (*Angst* or *Furcht*). Fear steadies the subject before impact, serving to deflect the full extent of a potentially traumatic impression. As Benjamin continues, it is only in the absence of such reflection that "the joyous or (usually) joyless horror sets in which . . . confirms the failure of the shock defense."[80] Benjamin's focus is indeed upon such failures. They form the foundation of his aesthetic theory of the experience of modernity because they are experienced directly, as it were, rather than mediated by waking consciousness. Through a short-circuit of the psyche, the *Schreck cum* shock is able to inscribe itself in the unconscious, making possible, but not guaranteeing, a retroactive revealing of the horrifying truth of the subject's position. The paradox is that because this experience occurs without the knowledge of the subject, such liberating truth remains largely inaccessible to the conscious mind and the attempt to access it directly remains fraught with difficulty and, perhaps, impossibility.

Benjamin worked to expose examples of these unlikely successes in the poetry of Baudelaire, Proust's *mémoire involuntaire*, and in film and film practices like montage. Of course, Benjamin devotes little space in his analysis to questions concerning sound, noise, and music. Yet if he ultimately fails to take the aural mode of experience into account, Theodor Adorno, someone as accustomed to thinking with his ears as with his eyes, did gesture on numerous occasions towards the shock of musical experience.[81] While at first glance placing Adornian theory at the forefront of an analysis of the experience of jazz in the Weimar Republic may appear as an incongruous move, particularly in the face of his caustic criticism of jazz and the justifiable skepticism regarding the validity of his claims regarding jazz, its purpose reflects a genuine desire to read Adorno against the grain. To do so carries the inherent threat of circuitously "defending" critical theory through critical theory. I hope to avoid this trap by reading Adorno much as he reads music, i.e., as fragmentary and incomplete. In other words, I want to read Adorno's writings on music, experience, and shock not so much as a theory to be applied to jazz but as a means of opening up the question of jazz in Weimar culture to the aesthetic experience of modernity through the figure of shock.

Adorno's concern for musical experience is especially evident in the 1934 text, "Music in the Background," a short *feuilleton* article on the fate of music in the café.[82] Taking as its object the non-object of background music, it asks how music is experienced when it is no longer heard; music in the background is defined for Adorno by the fact that "you don't have to listen to it."[83] Driven into the margins of society by the sound film, recorded music, and the radio, the live music of the café carries on with a meager existence in much the same way as the once-glorious arcades of the nineteenth century lingered on in the early twentieth. Adorno writes:

> Nowhere has music become so wholly appearance as in the café. But in appearance, it is preserved. It must, or so it seems, be thus emancipated from all human seriousness and all genuineness of artistic form if it is still to be tolerated by human beings amidst their daily affairs without frightening [*erschrecken*] them. But it is its appearance that lights up for them. No—that lights them up. They do not change in it, but their image changes. It is brighter, sharper, more clearly defined. When café music falls silent,

it sounds as if a miserly waiter is turning off a couple of electric bulbs. Background music is an acoustic light source.[84]

What Adorno argues for in this passage is the unconscious power of such music, not only as object in the background, but as source of knowledge, of experience qua *Erfahrung*. If it does not (yet) do so in the sense of a Benjaminian shock, then one nevertheless recognizes in it remnants of experience in the strong sense. Music in the background has become appearance, has been protected against and removed from the everyday so that it will no longer terrify the subject. Yet such distance, its separation from the seriousness and genuineness of the concert hall, marks but one determinant of this music's transformation into appearance and light. The music that resounds here is constructed from the remnants of the past: potpourris of works by Puccini, Grieg, and Tchaikovsky. Described by Adorno as "dissolved works, by those once-famous, then forgotten masters," such compositions are proper for the background because their unconscious familiarity makes no demands on the listener.[85] These works continue to exist only as musical ruins stitched together for the moment of performance. And yet: "The joints between the brittle sounds into which they are layered are not firmly bonded. Through them shimmers the mysterious allegorical appearance that arises whenever fragments of the past come together in an uncertain surface."[86] What interests Adorno in the music of the café are these tears and rough edges. For him, these imperfections imbue café music with an enigmatic luminescence. Their light puzzles, much like *Vexierbilder*, or puzzle pictures, those objects of fascination for Adorno and Benjamin, in that it can be read two ways: manifestly as a sign of decay and demise or allegorically as an illumination of the dreams of the past. "However dimly," the musical ruins of the café illuminate for Adorno, as Richard Leppert puts it, "what might have been."[87] Unlike filmic shock in Benjamin, such illumination, pointing not towards the present, let alone the future, can only exist as otherworldly, or, more precisely, as netherworldly. "But it is not a black shadow," Adorno continues, "rather a bright one, like milk glass."[88] The shadow of history cast by such music is bright because these are soothing spirits of the past and do not disrupt the spell of the present. The moment of fright and thus shock is therefore missing here and the musical fragments listeners hear are "quoted from the unconscious memory of the listeners, not introduced to them."[89]

Yet music in the background is not always so easily absorbed or parried. At times, it can unexpectedly inspire moments of horror, particularly when the listener becomes aware of the absence present within it. This takes place when the music travels, via the background, beyond the protection of consciousness to strike the listener. The means by which music may do so remains unclear. As Albrecht Riethmüller suggests, much of Adorno's writing on music and experience during this period remains largely gestural.[90] Such a moment is, however, described by Adorno in the conclusion to "Music in the Background." He writes: "Anyone who, moved, yet startled [*aufschreckt*] out of his conversation or thoughts, and who looks in that direction [i.e., of the performers], is transformed into Georg Heym's suburban dwarf: 'he looks up to the great green bell of heaven, where silent meteors cross far away.'"[91] Here is presaged the distracted viewing of Benjamin's cinema viewer, yet with a difference. It is not the content of the music that frightens the listener, but the absence it signifies. True, the music may continue, but it has activated a gaze which looks in vain for the object of its desire, for an origin that no longer, if ever, existed. Surely, the poor musicians performing in the café towards whom the gaze is directed will not quench the listener's desire. And this is Adorno's point. Such moments transform the listener's perception of the world from the oceanic calm of nonexistence into a melancholic awareness of lack. But it is an awareness that can be rendered into a form of knowledge about the present. The meteors of the past are silent only from a distance, that is to say, the present, and in remembering, the listener can re-experience that which once was not but might have been.

Perhaps it is all too understandable that Adorno remains silent about contemporary music in this Nazi-era piece about the silencing of music. Yet near the end, he remarks: "Strange that the new dances don't want to fit in, either. Their function is too fresh for them to allow themselves to be used as background yet."[92] Implicit within this statement is that the new dance music, a common code word for jazz at the time, was not yet fully incorporated into the protective shield of consciousness, and that it was still, if only slightly so for Adorno, shocking in a more immediate way. The remnant of shock contained within the new dances could be furthered, by ripping them from their context and placing them into a new constellation through the principle of montage construction. In his 1932 "On the Social Situation of Music," Adorno discusses at length the role of montage in contemporary music and elucidates his thoughts through analysis of the music of Kurt Weill. Musical montage for Adorno results from the interpolation and transformation of both popular and classical compositional practices and clichés through which new relationships within the music and of the music to the audience can be created. Though Adorno is ultimately critical of this technique, his criticism is directed not against its immediate impact but its sustainability. The type of musical montage created through Weill's style:

abrogates the "organic" surface structure of neo-classicism and moves together rubble and fragment or constructs actual compositions out of falsehood and illusion, as which the harmony of the nineteenth century has today been revealed, through the addition of intentionally false notes. The shock with which Weill's compositional practices overexposes common compositional means, presenting them as ghosts, becomes horror [*Schrecken*] about the society within which they have their origin and, at the same time, it becomes a negation of the possibility of a positive communal music, which collapses in the laughter of the devilish vulgar music as which true music is exposed.[93]

As with the music of the café, Weill's music is constructed from the ruins of the musical past. At the same time, Weill's music differs qualitatively from the music of the café in that it is suffused with the very modernity disavowed by the latter. While the performers in the café seek to soothe through immediate quotation from the listener's musical unconscious, Weill's music intends the opposite: namely, to awaken the audience to its own unconscious by showing them "their own 'use' music in the distorting mirror of his artistic method."[94]

Such conscious application of shock, however, transforms the nature of its experience for Adorno. While in the café the moment of horror is accidental, perhaps unlikely, here it is built into the very structure of the music itself. Adorno distinguishes this form of shock through the concept of overexposure, which serves to indicate that the glow of Weill's music is an artificial form of the netherworldly glow possessed by the music of the café. Rather than critiquing him, Adorno praises Weill for this achievement, writing: "It is beyond question that Weill's music is today the only music of genuine social-polemic impact; which it will remain as long as it resides at the height of its negativity."[95] Yet in order for the artificial shock to retain the power of its punch, it must remain unrelentingly negative, dealing blow after blow lest it succumb to the deadening effects of repetition and the power of presence.

Indeed, the punch, as it were, of art is something Adorno took quite literarily. In the aphorism "Special Edition" from *Minima Moralia*, where Adorno returns to the complex of shock and experience, he writes: "Baudelaire's poetry is filled with the type of flash that is seen by a closed eye when it is struck. The idea of the new is itself as phantasmagorical as this light."[96] Adorno's metaphor reveals the pain that often lies implicit in discussions of shock: with little protection other than a thin layer of equally fragile skin, the blow to the eye is a particularly debilitating experience. Equally central here is that the light, or knowledge, produced by both Baudelaire's and Weill's works is of a phantasmagorical nature, an unreal, if still powerful, afterimage of the suffering of the individual. Maintaining this effect obviously requires tremendous energies, and it is the endurance of Weill's montages that Adorno doubts most. Thus it is that the critique of the popular (and classical) achieved in the Weill's *Dreigroschenoper* (*Threepenny Opera*) metamorphoses into its opposite at the precise moment the audience "peacefully consumes the songs . . . as hit tunes."[97] Intentioned shock, then, easily falls victim to its own success, its shock effect eventually becoming as unpredictable and unlikely as the ghostly music of the café.

Adorno's theory of sonic experience and aural shock, though obviously indebted to Benjamin, possesses some distinct advantages in terms of the analysis of the jazz experience during Weimar. For one, his thoughts shed greater light on the corporeal dimension of these experiences. Second, as Riethmüller correctly notes, Adorno is not so much interested in the issue of the artist's or composer's shock as he is in the reception of such music, i.e., its impact on the listener.[98] As we will see, this emphasis on the experience of the listener, on the pain that music can inflict, is especially germane to comprehending the German experience of jazz and Wooding's jazz in particular. In addition, Adorno's atmospheric description of music's impact on the listener speaks to the indirect and diffuse effects of the music felt by its listeners. This diffusion of effect will be especially important in dealing with the afterlife of shock. By remaining sensitive both to the immediate light of recognition and to the ghostly, phantasmagorical afterlife of aural shock, Adorno's understanding opens up new interpretive possibilities for reading the lasting image of Wooding's music in Weimar culture.

Hearing Sam Wooding in May 1925

Given jazz's function within broader German cultural discourse and its association with modernity's dangers and dreams, let us now turn to the critics' and audience's reaction to Wooding's music. Reviews of the performance appeared in the socialist, liberal, conservative, and even Russian-language press in Berlin.[99] As might be imagined, reviewers reacted differently to the show, depending upon their political and aesthetic leanings, as well as their professional focus, be it theater, entertainment, or music. While some focused on the dancers and the show's effectiveness as a theatrical production, others discussed the group in relation to racial difference and, in the socialist press, racial and class solidarity.[100] Even with these differences in focus and quality, taken as a whole these many reviews represent a unique moment in the public discussion of and encounter with jazz and African American jazz in Weimar Germany. Still, before coming to the German reaction to Wooding and the *Chocolate Kiddies*, mention must be made of Wooding's reaction to the German audience. Long after the premiere, Wooding recounted his impression of the initial moments after "By the Waters of Minnetonka," this standard of the symphonic jazz repertoire and, by today's standards, a relatively sedate offering.

> The last notes of the overture faded away into silence. Silence, stark silence. [. . .] Then . . . the silence was shattered as, like a clap of thunder, the audience erupted into a wild demonstration of foot-stamping and shouting: 'Bis! Bis! Nochmal! Hoch! Bravo! Bis! Bis!' over and over again, sounding like the roaring of a large pack of angry and hungry lions. The musicians didn't understand a word of German and knew even less about local customs. The conglomeration of sound was so great that the word 'Bis!'—a way of showing approval in German—sounded like 'beast' to them and they thought the audience was shouting: 'beast! beast!' and were out for blood. [. . .] But after the foot-stamping and shouting continued for nearly five minutes and nobody has attacked us physically or thrown anything at us, we then realized that the audience was giving us an ovation. Our fright turned to confidence.[101]

This anecdote gives a sense of both the performers' and audience's state of unpreparedness and the difficulties of intercultural communication between African American performers and their German and European audiences. The few beats of silence that followed the end of the first song suggest that many in the audience were simply unsure how to react, how they were supposed to react to this music, in this setting. The applause that followed, however, functioned as a release of anxiety and enabled audience and performers to coalesce in their communal experience and enjoyment of jazz.

Such collective experience recalls the work of music critic Paul Bekker on the *gesellschaftsbildende Kraft* ("socially-creative power") of symphonic music. If the connection at first seems far fetched, it is important to remember that Wooding was performing a symphonic jazz concert. Bekker writes in his 1918 *Die Sinfonie von Beethoven bis Mahler* (*The Symphony from Beethoven to Mahler*) that the symphony possesses the faculty "to create a unified, distinctly individual being from the chaotic mass of the public, when in the moment of listening, of aesthetic experience, it recognizes itself moving towards an indivisible unity with identical impressions and identical goals. It is this community forming capacity of the work of art that first determines its significance and its value."[102] In its jubilant response, Wooding's audience opened itself up to the experience of jazz and, in so doing, ceased to be mere spectator and, at least to one reviewer, became part of the performance itself. "Here the people's applause is no longer a response to the stage," wrote Oscar Bie, "rather it has already become a part of the ubiquitous noise that belongs to all of this and which strengthens the sensation."[103] As Fritz Zielesch summarized, audience members left in an exhausted state, as if they had themselves performed, due to the energy expended throughout the performance. "Already within the first few minutes there was applause mid-scene and hurricanes of cheering blew from every corner of the gigantic room. This taxing of our nerves continued for hours through the overabundance of acoustic and optic noise and the overabundance of repetition of similar scenes. Many an audience member staggered away, as if broken (*wie zerschlagen hinauswankte*)."[104] Similarly, in what is likely the last article from Berlin written in response to the show's original run, Artur Michel noted: "Already by the end of the prelude, one is so physically (*körperlich-motorisch*) agitated that one can hardly sit still."[105] The totalizing effect of the audience's response added a synergistic component to the overall experience of the music. For Kurt Pinthus, who described Wooding's band as Berlin's first experience with "a true Negro jazz band that plays for Negroes" and as "the best band that ever played in Berlin," Wooding's jazz was the "binding element of this Negro show."[106] He continued: "Without this music it [the revue] would collapse into many, individual variety and cabaret numbers." Jazz, as element of Wooding's concert and as accompaniment to the show, appeared capable of melding the listener with the music and, at times, even with the world.

That the performance engendered such a sense of community and in the process elicited powerful emotions can be glimpsed in the longevity of the impression it made on audience members. As was noted in the introduction, the experience of Wooding profoundly impacted Alfred Lion, who went on to cofound *Blue Note Records*. Here, I want to return to Lion's later recollection of this experience he had as a teenager in order to analyze Lion's experience of Wooding as typical, rather than exceptional. Lion recalled of his initial impression:

> It was the first time I saw colored musicians and heard the music. I was flabbergasted . . .—It was something brand new, but it registered with me right away. . . . I couldn't really put my fingers[sic] on it, but it was the beat, you know. It was the beat. That beat . . .—it got into my bones.[107]

This description of the music as affecting the entire body of the listener was an important trope of the reviews at the time as well, even if it could lead, as here, to an implicit denial of the previous presence of Black performers. As it had in 1921, the music seemed to enter into and possess one's body, to get into your bones as Lion puts it. This was often expressed through a deflection of such possession onto the musician, while at other times it remained with the listener, as in the case of Lion. Klaus Pringsheim, who wrote glowingly of the music in *Das Tage-Buch*, remarked: "the world a twitching whirlwind (*zuckender Wirbelsturm*)—the demonic power that grips these people, when their rhythm drives into their limbs: no, we never imagined anything like that."[108] Another reviewer wrote generally of the revue: "you're swept away, lashed (*aufgepeitscht*), fall into rapture and for three hours outside of yourself."[109]

Due to the energy of the music, the frenetic rhythm of the show, the dancers, and the combined effect on the audience, a sense of overstimulation and eventual exhaustion can be found in response to Wooding and the *Chocolate Kiddies*. Indeed, many, though hardly all, reviewers felt tortured by the tempo and music of the revue, regardless of whether the overall impression was positive or negative.[110] In the view of conservative critic Adolf Stein, for example, the relentless drive of the show became excruciating: "But to this music that issued torturously forth for two and a half hours, they dance unceasingly."[111] Or in the mixed review from the *Berliner Tageblatt*: "In the long run, it is horrendously exhausting, but it is by no means boring."[112] Finally, Erich Urban, writing in the *BZ am Mittag* recommended the show, but only for those with robust nerves or with a desire to be tortured: "It hammers, bangs, drums as if against the skull!"[113] These various remarks hint at the level of conscious exertion necessitated by the experience of jazz. In the Benjaminian vocabulary of shock, we might say that jazz, here Wooding's jazz, could not be easily parried, swept aside by consciousness. This ascription of mercilessness to the music and show by the reviewers can be read as a reflection of their inability to process the sound of jazz within received categories of musical understanding. The seemingly awkward fit of jazz music to listeners' expectations raised the further question of categorization, that is to say whether jazz should be considered as music at all.

The reviewer to treat this question most directly was Herwarth Walden in *Die Weltbühne*. Walden begins his review cryptically, noting: "The world has seen again and again (*noch und noch*) in the Admirals-Palast."[114] His oblique reference is to the title of the first Tiller Girls revue, *Noch und Noch* (*More and More*) from 1924, and throughout the piece, he will use the Tiller Girls (and their legs) to construct an opposition between their mechanized precision and the "primitive" vitality of the *Chocolate Kiddies*. "Are the people really so blind," he asks further down, "that they see the legs of the female Creoles? Do they really only think about their legs? Do they not see the formed movements, to which the legs merely serve as an artificial body? Whoever only sees legs here is looking for female artists not art."[115] In this passage, Walden frames the focus on the legs of the Tiller Girls as resulting from the fragmenting of the senses under modernity, in particular the separation of sound and vision in European art. By contrast, the legs of the dancers in the *Chocolate Kiddies* cannot be separated from their bodies; according to Walden, they remain integrated and retain meaning only as part of a totality of movement and sound. Walden specifically imagines such a unification of the external world and art occurring in the revue's music.

> And all of the sudden Sam Wooding and his Orchestra are sitting on the stage. Without notes. Through the room swing sounds of whooshing, howling, groaning, quacking, bawling, murmuring, whining, rattling, clanging. Sounds ring out and are joined together to form an organism. Formed movement, thus art. It is not the sound (*Ton*) that makes the music. Where sound is missing, the concept of noise appears. Music, however, is not to be conceptualized, it is to be heard. One does not hear music, when thinking of noise.[116]

Walden here describes the music of jazz not through musical concepts, but by invoking an amalgam of the sounds of modernity. The sound of jazz is for him all encompassing, like the experience of the street, but with the distinction that in it noise has become art. Yet precisely because it remains closer to noise than European art music, jazz is uniquely capable of uniting this cacophony into art for Walden. It swirls and swings through the acoustic space like the howling of the siren or the clanging of the train, unfettered by the restrictions of form. Bie, as well, likened jazz to the noise of the metropolitan street. On that evening in the *Admiralspalast*, one could, he writes, "hear the great noise of the world that otherwise only weakly resounds from the newspapers, the true joy of the world in drumming, screaming, dancing, singing, and jumping, without any content, just like it is on this earth."[117] Obviously, while many reviewers connected jazz to noise, not all connected it with art. In the conservative *Neue Preußische Zeitung*, the show was also described as "overwhelming" and "noisy," but ultimately this was a function of the performers' race "and therefore not art."[118]

  Still, what both Bie and Walden suggest in their accounts is a view of jazz as a method of conceptualizing the sense and non-sense of noise. For Jacques

Attali, noise is both repressive and liberatory, in a word, for Attali "noise is violence."[119] Like shock for Benjamin and Adorno, noise in Attali acts as a disruption of received codes of meaning, which are often experienced as painful. Yet noise for Attali is neither natural nor ahistorical. "Noise," he argues, "does not exist in itself, but only in relation to the system within which it is inscribed: emitter, transmitter, receiver. Information theory uses the concept of noise . . . in a more general way: noise is the term for a signal that interferes with the reception of a message by a receiver, even if the interfering signal itself has a meaning for that receiver."[120] Attali's argument demonstrates that the view of jazz as noise has nothing to do with jazz as unintelligible or chaotic. Jazz could appear as noise only because it seemed indecipherable within the existing system of musical meaning; it was precisely this unintelligibility that made jazz so meaningful in terms of relating it to modernity and modernism. Through the idea of noise, the shock imparted to the listener upon the first hearing of jazz could be made to resonate with the shock of the initial hearing of the mechanical press, car horn, or jackhammer. By making meaning of jazz through the idea of noise, audience members like Lion and reviewers like Bie and Walden were able to reactivate the alienating and painful sounds of the metropolis, leaving them "broken" as we saw earlier. In this way, one can understand the description of jazz as noise as acting to bridge the gap between the audience's system of aesthetic understanding, music, and modernity, to see in this music a possibility of what Attali calls "the symphony of the future."[121]

Yet if the initial experience of jazz shook the consciousness of the German public, breaking through the protective shield of consciousness to form a unifying experience, the ecstatic rapture found in reviews by Bie, Walden, and others did not maintain itself over the course of the next five years, something foretold by critic Fritz Zielesch. He maintained in his review that the success of the *Chocolate Kiddies* was a one-time occurrence and that "a second troupe of this kind will certainly be met with cooler heads."[122] In point of fact, after another African American revue *Black People* premiered in July 1926, one reviewer noted that two years ago the audience would have been taken with the show but continued: "Now, however, after we've seen and heard the 'Chocolate Kiddies' and their incomparable Sam Wooding, the lightning image that chaotically flashes (*chaotisch vorüberzuckende Blitzbild*) before us hardly has any noticeable, unmitigated impact."[123] More generally, shortly after the *Chocolate Kiddies* made a return visit to Berlin in 1926, Kurt Weill wrote:

> Jazz is not created when one mechanically plays a syncopated rhythm in two-two time. The music of Negroes, which forms the basis of the jazz

band, is composed of a complexity of rhythm, of a harmonic care, of a tonal and modulatory wealth that most of our light orchestras simply cannot bring about. Now we have heard for a few weeks a real jazz band nightly on the radio: Ernö Rapée's *Jazz-Symphoniker*.[124] If one measures it against the magisterial jazz bands of the Negro revues, even this organization still lacks the sophistication of the latter. But it nevertheless exhibits that stomping confusion (*stampfendes Durcheinander*) of saxophones, jazz drums, and muted trumpets, that unleashed rhythm, that improvised humor, which the jazz band alone makes tolerable. Everything else offered by the *Funkstunde*[125] in terms of dance music is only a surrogate.[126]

Though Weill like Bie, Walden, and the others draws here upon the vocabulary of the jazz experience, his language is already more precise, more subdued. More importantly, the exhaustion and torture associated with the jazz band has become tolerable in his account. Thus, while Weill's language contains a trace of the first, painful experience of jazz, of noise, and of the street, his description has already slipped past the dialectic of pain and pleasure witnessed within the first reviews and has moved into the realm of more detached observation and description.

Weill's analysis is part of the beginning of a more sober analysis of jazz that fully set in only after Wooding's initial performances and which becomes more pronounced after the visit of the "King of Jazz," Paul Whiteman, to Berlin discussed in the following chapter. This shift in the function of the Weimar experience of jazz is brought into focus in a 1927 essay by composer Karol Rathaus, himself composer of a jazz-influenced opera *Fremde Erde* (*Foreign Soil*).[127] Rathaus explores in this short text whether jazz is in a process of decline, whether a "*Jazzdämmerung*," or "twilight of jazz," as he entitles his article from *Die Musik*, is currently afoot.[128] He begins by asserting the history of jazz is for the most part well known to Germans and later asserts that Europeans know jazz is African American in origin.[129] What interests Rathaus at this point is not primarily how jazz is practiced or what it is. Rather, what he strives to explain are the psychological conditions under which jazz became popular first in the United States and then in Europe.

He begins by rejecting the commercial, "civilized" jazz performed in Germany's café houses, seeing it as a direct byproduct of American civilization, in which the rhythm of production dominates over mental and spiritual work. From America, came (and come) almost all forms of life in finished form, the express culture devours more than it can absorb, hypertrophy of the ability to absorb led already long ago to the *record*, to the victory of achievement perceivable by the senses over the spiritual value to be embraced. With movingly ruthless honesty, with which America professes its faith in *Materie*, it created the most favorable conditions for jazz.[130]

To this static and oppressive version, he counterpoises another type of jazz, one that could combat the very same instrumental rationality now conspiring to create a type out of the individual. He writes: "We only received a correct idea of jazz from the Negroes. *Chocolate Kiddies*, the revue of *Josephine Baker* and *Black People* brought us to the edge of the source. Here, jazz reached a state of perfection as a result of their deep state of rootedness."[131] And: "While America has led to the lifeless Whiteman Orchestra, which is unable to develop, the opposing path of Europe led to the simple 'Negro spirituals.'"[132]

Rathaus' vision of European culture admits jazz into its vocabulary only as an idealized return to an organic primitivity. In this cul-de-sac of European subjectivity, the role of the African American begins to recede behind an impenetrable aura of authenticity. Paradoxically, however, it is the perfect authenticity of African American jazz that now makes it expendable.

Because we are familiar with jazz, because over the course of approximately twelve years jazz has conquered the ground of the entire civilized world, because it is now danced and sung unproblematically (*widerspruchlos*) . . . because we have eavesdropped on all the secrets of its instrumentation and can use them freely, because one must no longer fight over jazz—now one begins to speak of a *twilight of jazz*.[133]

Jazz no longer holds the secrets it once did in 1921, in 1925: African American jazz has been studied and incorporated into European art music, while resistance to the materialist jazz of white America grows. In a word, for Rathaus, the European has listened to jazz's siren song, and now that the European has done all this, has been tempted without falling into temptation, its usefulness has come to an end. As Rathaus concludes on an ambiguous note: "behind all great events, movements, and people stands history. It has already absorbed jazz, now it goes unwaveringly (*unbeirrt*)—onward."[134]

This transformation of jazz from aural shock into cultural background music pervades Hans David's 1930 "Farewell to Jazz," one of a group of departures from jazz written by critics in the early 1930s.[135] Like other documents written during the end phase of the Weimar Republic, David's text takes a critical tack vis-à-vis jazz. Yet it interests here because its point of departure is a return visit to Berlin by Sam Wooding.[136] David begins by suggesting that Wooding's original 1925 performances have stuck within German consciousness as exceptional. He writes,

> Five years ago we heard him for the first time. He led the orchestra of the "Chocolate Kiddies," one of the great Negro revues. The theatrical achievements of the "chocolate children" were not bad, even if the troupe lacked a talented performer of [Josephine] Baker's caliber. More than anything else, there were a few transitional concert pieces in the musical interlude which have adhered to our memory (*im Gedächtnis haften*) as amazing and fascinating. And for a long time memory has likewise busied itself with the achievements of the accompanying orchestra, the form of its leader, an animal-like, fanatical musician.[137]

David's commentary is more than merely demonstrative of the continued importance of Wooding. Cleaving to German cultural and individual memory alike, in 1930, Wooding's performances were still able to draw upon the power of the original experience. This laudatory tone, however, quickly turns into one of memorialization. To David, jazz has lost its novelty and, more importantly, its role in avant-garde art.

> It is not to be feared that jazz as a unique form will diminish in use; but its captivating technique which appeared at first to be of interest to the more intellectual person is presently losing the hint (*Beiklang*) of meaningfulness that was attached to it as long as it contained within it progress and a qualitatively different future. People forget quickly: soon one will see in jazz nothing more than a neutral form of dance composition. Jazz is becoming a musical complex that may be useful and perhaps necessary . . . but it is a complex whose intellectual, artistic power has been extinguished. In this sense it is valid to bid farewell to jazz.[138]

What jazz has lost for David is the capacity to point towards the future through an aestheticization of the experience of the present. The noise that was attached to the original experience of jazz has subsided and the shock of jazz has become a memory, or ghost. Like the performances of the forgotten masters in the café, jazz in general and Wooding's music as well now seems to wash silently over the audience, recalling a distant and subdued past as opposed to the turbulent present. But the critical turn against jazz by David and others ought not be read as but a reflection of the music's failure in Germany. The experience of Wooding's jazz that presented itself to those thousands of Berliners in 1925, not to mention the Frankfurters, Hamburgers, Danzigers, Leipzigers, Dresdeners, could, after all, still be felt in 1930. The general dismissal of jazz as a progressive art form by German modernists might more profitably read as a mourning of the passing of the earth-shattering power of its initial successes. Wooding's final appearance in the capital took place in 1930, yet even when Wooding was not physically present in Germany, he was textually present through repeated references to him within German jazz criticism.[139] It was through these echoes that the aural shock of modernity represented by Wooding's music could still be remembered, long after May 1925.

Yet while Wooding's impact on the German conceptualization of jazz is at least partially due to the duration and geographical variety of his performances in Germany, another American jazz musician had an equally great effect on Weimar jazz culture, yet visited Germany but once. This is Paul Whiteman. Carrying the title of "King of Jazz" for the vast majority of audiences across Europe and North America, Whiteman and his symphonic jazz cast a shadow over German discussions of jazz even larger than that of Wooding. For despite the critical view taken by music critics, Whiteman enjoyed incomparable standing in the popular press at large and with the majority of jazz musicians in in this period and, as I want to suggest in the next chapter, became an unlikely model for Weimar-era novelists as well.

CHAPTER 3

Writing Symphonies in Jazz:
Paul Whiteman and German Literature

> When I put on . . . one of the magnificent records from Paul Whiteman, I immediately become another person. My pulse is elevated . . . , I imagine the most colorful images and a tremendous need for action (*Tatendrang*) overtakes me. I then say to myself: "You have the most magnificent symphonies by Mozart and by Bruckner, works that you would go through fire for. . . . And yet—this fantastical effect the music of the jazz band has, you still haven't felt that with any of them."
> —Jaap Kool (1924)

Symphony and jazz existed at the center of much of the debate about musical culture during the Weimar Republic, in particular through the controversial practice of jazzing the classics, be they Mozart, Beethoven, or Wagner.[1] Together, the pair formed what could often seem like a self-writing script of German jazz criticism—both for the music's proponents as well as its opponents—pitting an almost sacred symphonic tradition against a profane and racially other jazz. Of course, what made the combination of the terms so evocative was that cultural, musical, and aesthetic developments were constantly threatening to bring the two into ever-closer proximity. As the above statement by ethnomusicologist Jaap Kool hints at, symphony and jazz seemed to exist in worlds apart, yet they were also worlds that seemed to be in a constant state of collision. This meant that in many instances, neither jazz nor symphony could be thought of in this period without also invoking its other, and perhaps no greater representation of their collision existed than the musical genre of symphonic jazz. Most closely associated with the white American bandleader Paul Whiteman, from at least 1926 onward, symphonic jazz dominated the German jazz scene while at the same time shaping German musical culture in innumerable ways.

Still, the importance of symphonic jazz to Weimar culture goes far beyond its role in German popular music. Beyond this, symphonic jazz and its promise of unifying tradition with modernity (and vice versa) became especially attractive to Weimar-era novelists. Just as composers like Ernst Krenek attempted jazz operas, novelists tried their hand at producing jazz novels. Czech-born Hans Janowitz's *Jazz. Roman (Jazz. A Novel)* (1927), Alsatian René Schickele's *Symphonie für Jazz (Symphony for Jazz)* (1929), and the Swiss-Austrian Gustav Renker's *Symphonie und Jazz (Symphony and Jazz)* (1931) are each examples of such jazz novels, or more specifically of the symphonic jazz novel.[2] Put differently, I want to suggest that each novel represents an example of a literary response to the challenge of symphonic jazz. In this set of novels, symphony and jazz become organizational figures around which these authors experimented with jazz's aesthetic potential. Significantly and unlike the music's use in much Weimar literature, jazz in these works acts not primarily as a symbol of social disorder, a Dionysian, racialized, sexualized other, but as an experimental aesthetic. In other words, these works explore, with all its attendant contradictions, the idea of symphonic jazz as synthetic melding of modernity and tradition, as an aesthetic capable of structuring and making manageable the foreign and modern.

To be sure, this pairing of jazz music and German literature may at first seem unlikely, yet it serves two very important purposes. The first is to rethink symphonic jazz and its meaning for German jazz culture. While Whiteman's name is by no means unknown, the popularity of the corpulent, white Whiteman during the 1920s regularly serves as proof that Germans did not listen to and/or were unfamiliar with African American jazz. If this argument is an important corrective to anachronistic visions of Weimar Germans listening to Louis Armstrong, James P. Johnson, or Fletcher Henderson, as we saw in the previous chapter, by the mid-1920s, African American jazz was routinely felt to be more representative of authentic jazz than white American jazz, albeit for vastly different reasons than today. Yet, the stakes of Whiteman's symphonic jazz during this period were simultaneously greater and less than was recognized by Weimar critics: greater because symphonic jazz's influence extended beyond popular music and less because Whiteman's jazz was hardly the only way by which Weimar Germans came into contact with the music.

Tellingly, such dismissals of Whiteman stand largely in parallel to current judgment regarding the Weimar-era jazz novels of Janowitz, Schickele, and Renker, which aside from isolated treatments have been for the most part ignored within general accounts of the period's literature.[3] Separately, these works are the isolated endeavor of a one-time novelist (Janowitz), a minor work by a major author (Schickele), or the conservative rant of an author obsessed with racial and cultural purity (Renker). Yet when read together as a set of novels responding to the aesthetic challenge of symphonic jazz, an entirely new sense of their significance emerges. In their common focus on the relationship between symphony and jazz as a means of engaging with modernism, literary and otherwise, they stand as an index not only of the wide-ranging influence of Whiteman but of the profound ways by which jazz affected German culture in the 1920s. In other words, they propel jazz in German literature beyond the superficial and gesture towards the music's presence at a formal and structural level. Or to speak with a language indebted to jazz itself, these authors use symphony and jazz not as a self-writing script but as a jazz standard: a well-known, popular melody, onto which each author sought to produce a new version through improvisation, variation, and addition. Writing symphonies in jazz, each attempted to carve out a space within the center and, in so doing, gave birth to a new literary genre, the symphonic jazz novel.

It is significant here that this literary genre owes its existence not only to the American Whiteman but to three novelists from the margins, geographically and culturally. Because of jazz's transnational and geographically indeterminate position, figures like Janowitz, Schickele, Renker and many others seem to have been particularly attracted to jazz as an object of identification and self-expression. As had Grosz and Dix in the early 1920s, these figures use jazz, their encounters with and representations of the music, as a means of symbolically creating a new German culture into which they not only fit but have a hand in creating.

Paul Whiteman in Berlin

Still, their experiments owe a great debt to the idea and form of Paul Whiteman's symphonic jazz. Before looking at Janowitz, Schickele, and Renker, it is first necessary to examine Whiteman's project as well as the reaction to his music in Germany following his Berlin concerts of June 1926. Born in Denver, Colorado, to a local music teacher, Whiteman's early life was spent far away from traditional centers of early jazz music in New Orleans, Chicago, or New York.[4] It was only in 1918, he notes in *Jazz*, a 1926 work coauthored with Margaret McBride, that he first heard the music: "My whole body began to sit up and take notice. It was like coming out of blackness into bright light. [. . .] I wanted to dance. I wanted to sing. I did them all. Raucous? Yes. Crude—undoubtedly. Unmusical—sure as you live. But rhythmic, catching as the small-pox and spirit-lifting. That was jazz then."[5] Soon thereafter, he quit his work for the symphony and turned to playing popular music and jazz. Despite early setbacks (including being fired for not being able to play jazz correctly), he eventually became a sought-after arranger of popular jazz-influenced music on the American West Coast.[6] Out of this early success, he was offered a job playing at the Ambassador Hotel in Atlantic City, where the Victor Recording Company discovered and signed him. In August 1920, he recorded "Whispering," with its B-side "Japanese Sandman." This recording is said to have sold more than a million copies and made Whiteman a national and international star. As discussed earlier, Whiteman's music had an almost immediate impact on the German jazz scene. His "Japanese Sandman" was not only recorded by early jazz pioneer Eric Borchard in 1921, it was also the subject of an early treatment by the German-speaking Prague author Max Brod in 1922.[7]

Yet quite possibly, Whiteman would have remained one name among many in American popular music had he not attempted his "Experiment in Modern Music" in February 1924. There, Whiteman introduced his peculiar fusion of jazz and symphonic music that came to be known as "symphonic jazz." This concert, held at New York's prestigious Aeolian Hall, attempted to demonstrate to an elite audience that jazz deserved to be recognized as America's classical music. As well as jazzed-up selections of popular music, it was here that Whiteman premiered what was to become George Gershwin's signature piece for the next decade, *Rhapsody in Blue*. With this concert, Whiteman hoped to showcase the music's transformation into something that no longer belonged in the brothels of New Orleans' Storyville district but in the concert hall. This raising up of jazz also had a racial component. "My notion," he wrote in 1926, "is that the chief contribution of the white American to jazz so far has been his recognition of it as legitimate music."[8] Whiteman's attempt to separate jazz qua legitimate art form from its African American roots and transform it into the national music of white America has rightly been criticized.[9] Yet his view of jazz also seeks to rearticulate the relationship of American to European culture, specifically by claiming that jazz belongs amongst the pantheon of great national musics. In seeking to put American jazz music on par and in dialogue with European music, Whiteman's aspirations were shared by many of his contemporaries, including African Americans like Sam Wooding. To quote Paul Allen Anderson, Whiteman was "not alone . . . in fusing vernacular source materials with large-scale and orchestral instrumentation and scored-through compositions. New Negro composers and concert artists were pursing a simultaneous campaign of syncretism, idiomatic formalization and bourgeois vindication."[10] Whiteman's symphonic jazz should thus be understood as both exploiting Black musical traditions as well as part of the broader trend towards greater appreciation of the aesthetic value of American music and culture.

Word of Whiteman's successes with symphonic jazz soon spread to Germany, and by 1925, German musicians were embracing this new style of music. Not merely an idea, Whiteman's model was copied by numerous German musicians and arrangers of the period. Bernhard Etté, Marek Weber, Dajos Béla, Julian Fuhs, Efim Schachmeister, and others became implicit ambassadors for symphonic jazz in Germany through the numerous recordings and performances of their "jazz symphony orchestras" (*Jazz-Symphonie-Orchester*). There were many reasons for the rapid adoption of symphonic jazz. For one, with members numbering between twenty and thirty, symphonic jazz orchestras represent a considerable enlargement over the small group formations of early jazz, common in both America and Germany during the early 1920s. The larger size of the orchestra meant employment for greater numbers of this profession still struggling to cope with losses due to technological innovations like gramophone and radio. Second, symphonic jazz moved the emphasis away from the practice of collective improvisation, something particularly difficult for the conservatory-trained musicians who made up a significant proportion of Germany's popular ensembles. Though in America the exactness and precision characteristic to performances of symphonic jazz was intended to put jazz orchestras on a level approaching that of the symphony orchestra, classically trained German musicians were simply much better suited to this new form. Finally, from the monetary perspective of practicing musicians, a turn towards symphonic jazz was attractive because it was said to earn a great deal more money. Whiteman, for example, was quoted in the German trade journal *Der Artist* as saying: "Musicians who had before earned 30 to a maximum of 60 dollars a week, were paid upwards of 150 dollars a week by first-class jazz bands."[11] For all these reasons, then, Whiteman's brand of symphonic jazz appeared especially attractive to Weimar-era musicians.

Still, a full two years passed before Whiteman personally presented the case for symphonic jazz to German music critics as opposed to musicians. By the time he reached Berlin, there was a great deal of anticipation. In fact, no other jazz concerts of the period were as widely discussed (or publicized) as Whiteman's Berlin concerts. Like Sam Wooding's performance in the *Admiralspalast*, the site of his concerts was also significant, Erik Charell's *Grosses Schauspielhaus*. Designed by Hans Poelzig in 1919 for Max Reinhardt, in the mid-1920s, Charell's theater featured mid-brow entertainment; but with 3,200 seats, this largest theater in Europe was certainly befitting the visiting jazz dignitary.[12] Indeed, the American was feted by the German press throughout the month of June; the *Berliner Zeitung* is even reported as having hired a plane to take Whiteman on an aerial tour of the city.[13] Photographs and caricatures of Whiteman were widely reprinted in the daily newspapers, as were regular reports about the concert. For example, an image of Whiteman playing multiple instruments adorned the cover of *Lustige Blätter*, a popular illustrated magazine.[14] One extreme instance of the attention allotted Whiteman during his stay in Berlin occurred when a reporter submitted an article after happening to cross paths with the jazz king on Potsdamer Platz.[15] Whiteman responded by giving numerous interviews to reporters as well as authoring a text about himself for the *Berliner Tageblatt*.[16] According to Albert Henschel, who reviewed the concerts in *Das Tage-Buch*, Berlin was barraged with publicity in anticipation of Whiteman's arrival: "Placards screamed for weeks: King of Jazz! Jazz Symphony Orchestra!"[17] A report on the Berlin concert from Paul Goldmann for the *Neue Freie Presse* in Vienna noted that Whiteman's face, his thin mustache and upper lip, were all recognizable before he took the stage due to such publicity.[18] Not only placards, however. Like the *Chocolate Kiddies*, Whiteman also held open rehearsals for the press and was visited by academics, as well as by the composers Arnold Schoenberg and Franz Schreker.[19] In addition, a competition was held for the best German foxtrot, with the winning entry receiving its world premiere during Whiteman's final Berlin concert.[20] Based on the rehearsal, the *Vossische Zeitung* published an initial article praising the musical virtuosity of Whiteman's orchestra and the sensation about to happen in Berlin.[21]

By the time Whiteman reached the German capital in June 1926, he had already enjoyed a warm welcome from other European audiences, such as in London. Yet what Whiteman could not know was that Berlin's music establishment would approach his project not with excited anticipation but with skepticism. So that while Berliners sold out his four concerts and heartily applauded the performances, the response by Berlin's music critics remained rather cool. Indeed, according to one Whiteman biographer, it was in Berlin that his music met with harsh criticism for the first time.[22] The origin of such resistance is not to be found in the German musical establishment's rejection of American popular music or even of jazz, as the generally warm response of the press to Sam Wooding and the *Chocolate Kiddies* demonstrates. Nor can the generalized antipathy displayed by reviewers towards symphonic jazz be explained simply by pointing towards jazz's controversial nature in this period. Instead, as I want to argue, the cooler reception of Whiteman's symphonic jazz by Berlin's music critics can best be understood when viewed alongside the question of the perceived decline of the classical European symphony in the first quarter of the twentieth century.

This period witnessed a prolific decline in the number of symphonies produced by European composers. Against the grandiose monumentality of the symphonic form, after 1908 and Schoenberg's "emancipation of dissonance," a new generation of composers turned increasingly towards the musical miniature: suites, quartets, and small ensemble chamber music. The period of progress in symphonic composition that could be located between Beethoven and Mahler seemed to have come to an inglorious end. It was, in fact, the professional music critics, those who were most critical of Whiteman, who, according to Karen Painter, kept the form alive as it were. Through their writings, the symphony was imbued with even greater cultural worth than it had in the nineteenth century, transforming the symphony into a central cultural icon of the early twentieth century. As Painter summarizes: "During periods of crisis in the late nineteenth and early twentieth centuries, writers repeatedly turned to the symphony and symphonic analogies to reconcile an ideal wholeness and unity that stood opposed to the atomizing effects of democracy, industrialization, and urbanization."[23] Out of the musical form of the symphony, these music critics created a cultural trope meant to undergird the German musical establishment against the incursion of modernism and modernity. If the symphony became a sign of tradition threatened, jazz was a primary symptom of that threat. Delivered in raucous, three-minute urban miniatures, it was no less threatening to the idea and ideal of the symphony than an atonal composition by Schoenberg. Perhaps no greater sign of this trend away from the symphony could be found than in the person of Mitja Nikisch. Son of the famed conductor of Bruckner and Beethoven, Arthur Nikisch, the younger Nikisch became one of the Weimar Germany's best-known practitioners of symphonic jazz.[24] The stakes for German music critics were therefore high; jazz seemed to be taking over the world, and, if the word from abroad was to be believed, Whiteman's symphonic jazz threatened the concert hall as well. Indeed, just after his Berlin concerts, the satirical magazine *Simplicissimus* featured a caricature of the jazz king Whiteman holding Beethoven's death mask and commenting "There is one thing I have on him—my music has made a lot people thin" (figure 9).[25] If the threat of jazz to the symphony is clearly lessened through the caption, the image of Whiteman literally holding Beethoven in his hand next to a drum set featuring Native American imagery is suggestive of jazz's potential power over the classical tradition in the contemporary moment.

Of course, not all of Berlin's critics fretted over this possibility; some modernists like Hans Heinz Stuckenschmidt awaited Whiteman's arrival more

Figure 9: Cover of satirical magazine *Simplicissimus* from July 5, 1926, featuring a caricature of Paul Whiteman by Wilhelm Schulz (1865–1952). Courtesy of Dr. Hans Zimmermann of the Herzogin Anna Amalia Bibliothek Weimar.

or less with dispassion, while others like Hans Siemsen embraced the idea. On May 28, 1926, Siemsen reworked his "Jazz-Band" article from 1921 to welcome the news that Whiteman would be appearing in Berlin.[26] Siemsen opens this piece by repeating certain statements from this earlier text but then adds to it by filling in the past five years of German jazz history. Speaking of those from the province who don't know what a jazz band is or think it to be a trap drum, he notes: "they still don't know that a jazz band is nothing more than an orchestra constructed according to new principles, whose tonal possibilities are more complicated, richer, and adaptable (*wandlungsfähiger*) than those of the old . . . orchestra."[27] He mentions Eric Borchard as the first musician who brought real jazz to Germany and names Sam Wooding and Julian Fuhs as further examples of authentic jazz. Rejecting the earlier clown-like performances of drummers from the period around 1921, Siemsen ends by saying about jazz: "There's no more joking around. It creates real music."[28] Much in tune with Whiteman's own presentation to the Berlin press, jazz for Siemsen has become a serious matter, a serious music, rather than the mere parody thereof. As Whiteman explained to the readers of the *Berliner Tageblatt*: "We don't intend to jazz well-known pieces or, as has been done in Germany, execute jazz variations on well-known motifs. Rather, we want to create something new."[29] Distancing himself partially from the entertainment sphere traditionally understood as jazz's rightful home, Whiteman emphasizes that he "did not come to Europe to create a sensation for the Europeans. I've come to pave the way for the development of futuristic music."[30] Whiteman, then, wanted to show how jazz had developed into an art music in the strong sense, how it had developed beyond an initial imitative stage and had begun to create unique musical compositions of its own.

Likewise, Hans Heinz Stuckenschmidt also authored a piece in anticipation of the concerts. Stuckenschmidt was an important liberal music critic and part of the Berlin Dada movement. In the year 1926 alone, he defended "mechanical music," wrote separate paeans to gramophones and revues, and declared Sam Wooding's jazz band the "true highlight" of the *Chocolate Kiddies*. In a word, he was precisely the type of critic for whom Whiteman's music would seem to have been made.[31] Like Siemsen and Whiteman, Stuckenschmidt suggests that jazz has developed into an art form from the clowning and joking present at its origins, but he also sees in this development a danger that "this most joyous expression of contemporary humanity will go to waste as a result of seriousness and compositional method."[32] Equally notably, he outlined how he felt the German audience would receive Whiteman and his attempt to elevate jazz to the concert hall as the music of the future. Analyzing

Whiteman's place within jazz, and, in turn, jazz's position within modern culture, Stuckenschmidt writes:

> Paul Whiteman, King of jazz, accessible to Germans up to now only through gramophone records, has to his merit that he made these principles acceptable for the concert hall.
>
> With his orchestra . . . he deftly and with the clearest of instincts drew symphonic consequences from jazz. In February 1924 he made a triumphal debut at New York's greatest concert hall, the Aeolian Hall.
>
> In June 1926 he will tour Germany.
>
> Snobs will have fits of lust. Spectacles will shatter with fright. Musicians will dedicate scores.
>
> And only some will recognize: here one of the most typical emanations of the *Zeitgeist* of the 20th century's first half has been formed.[33]

Jazz emerges within Stuckenschmidt's positioning of Whiteman and his symphonic variant as a cool, calculated, rational emanation of modern culture. The emotion surrounding Wooding's appearance of but a year prior is absent, replaced by this reading of jazz and Whiteman as but "the most typical emanations" of modern culture and society.

After weeks of preparation by newspaper articles, advertisements, and airplane tours, Whiteman finally presented his concert program to the Berlin public on June 26 with Gershwin's *Rhapsody in Blue* as its centerpiece (figure 10).[34] As with Wooding's performances with the *Chocolate Kiddies*, the concert program allows us to better understand the presentation of Whiteman's symphonic jazz to his audience and contextualize certain idiosyncrasies within the reviews. Most notably, the program contains explanatory notes by noted musicologist Hugo Leichtentritt, who based his remarks in part on Whiteman's recently published coauthored monograph *Jazz*. Over two dense pages, audience members learned of jazz's history and aesthetic developments, and of the virtuosity of Whiteman's band members. Though certain grotesque, i.e., low-cultural, excesses remain, as Leichtentritt writes in summary: "Paul Whiteman views in jazz the first specifically American musical practice (*Betätigung*). He leaves open the question of whether jazz has already been elevated to the level of true art. He is, however, profoundly certain that jazz is doing great service for the matter of art in America."[35] Following the introduction, two separate concert programs are included. The first, which was the subject of almost all critical writings, was performed on Friday, Saturday, and Monday evening, as well as the Sunday matinee, with the second apparently offered only once on

Figure 10: Berlin program of Paul Whiteman's Concerts at the *Grosses Schauspielhaus* (1926).

Sunday evening.[36] As such, I will focus here solely on the first program, a variation of concert programs Whiteman had given previously on his European tour.[37] It began with Ferde Grofé's "Mississippi," which is described as a musical depiction of a trip down the Mississippi river, modulating in style as it takes the listener south towards New Orleans in four movements. The second piece was "Five Popular American Melodies": the jazz standard "Tiger Rag," Fritz Kreisler's "Caprice Viennois," Zez Confrey's "Dizzy Fingers," "Spain," likely by Gus Kahn, and concluding with Ray Henderson's "I am Sitting on Top of the World." The medley was followed by Chester Hazlett's saxophone solo of the song "Nadine" by B. Hinton. Fourth came "Castles in the Air," and the fifth piece was "Meet the Boys," a standard of Whiteman concerts in which individual band members were featured. Also included, though not listed in the program, was Whiteman's smash hit of 1926, "Valencia," which was referred to in many reviews of the concert. The program then indicated that an intermission would take place. However, this intermission, as well as the concluding piece, a number to be picked by audience, was skipped for the premiere concert, something that caused some confusion on the part of reviewers. Instead, the program at the premiere ended with what was to be the highlight of the concert: George Gershwin's *Rhapsody in Blue*, which as the notes for this piece make clear, became famous after Whiteman debuted it as part of his Aeolian Hall concert in 1924.

The premiere began at 10:00 p.m. and continued until after midnight. It was warmly received by the audience, though according to Whiteman's biographer, the jazz king had been particularly nervous about the reaction, given what he perceived as the cold demeanor of the Berliners.[38] Most of the reviews that appeared over the next few days began by discussing the marketing campaign that had now gone on for weeks, as well as referencing that all of Berlin society had been present. Almost all of them praised the virtuosity and technique of the Whiteman orchestra. Equally prevalent in the reviews, however, was their rejection of the idea that the concert demonstrated that Whiteman had created a new art form for the future.[39] Despite, or perhaps because of, the framing of Whiteman's concert by Stuckenschmidt and the coordinated media campaign, Whiteman emerges in the view of Berlin's music critics as a disappointment. "Before one knows what Whiteman is," begins the reviewer of the *Vossische Zeitung*, "the concert was at an end."[40] The reviewer was amazed that at the precise moment he had expected the concert to have an intermission, it was over. Even more negatively, Hans Feld in the *Film-Kurier* maintained that while Whiteman has created perfection in the realm of dance music, "Paul Whiteman is no musician. For this reason, it would be better if he would refrain from giving concerts and playing symphonies."[41] Similarly, Dr. Leopold Schmidt wrote in the *Berliner Tageblatt*:

> When one heard of the triumphs of Paul Whiteman and his "Symphonic Jazz Orchestra," there appeared to threaten danger that the boundaries between art and artistry (*Kunst und Kunstfertigkeit*) could be altered. Now we have been satisfied with our own ears by the results of the *Grosses Schauspielhaus* and can be reassured. Jazz remains jazz, whether one plays it well or poorly . . .[42]

Schmidt's fear of jazz infiltrating high culture receded, as his expectations of jazz as the music of the future were not met. As he writes, the concert "disappointed those who awaited two things: jazz itself and an art developed from jazz that was forward looking."[43] Along a somewhat different vein, the reviewer in the *Berliner Montagspost* noted of the performance: "Whiteman has really separated jazz from dancing and it almost appears as if the public senses the importance of this day for aesthetic production, even if the originators themselves remain stuck in the variety theaters."[44] Referring to the continued presence of African American and Black jazz musicians, who, other than Wooding, could never dream of the press and attention heaped on Whiteman, this comment is an important reminder that Whiteman's jazz, while often the most visible, was not the only example of jazz heard by the German public.

Returning to Whiteman's June 1926 concerts, one can say that *pace* Stuckenschmidt there were no fits of lust and spectacles did not shatter with fright. Instead, reviewers conclude one of two things from Whiteman's concert: first, that what they heard that evening was no threat to the classical tradition, or second, that there was more symphony than jazz in Whiteman's concerts. For example, the reviewer for the *Berliner Lokal-Anzeiger* began his review by noting that "from the perspective of music as art . . . , there is hardly anything serious to be said about that which Mr. Whiteman and his cohort perform."[45] Or, as Klaus Pringsheim more pointedly wrote a short while later: "We are thankful for the visit of *Paul Whiteman* because it has given us clarity about that which our future music has to expect from jazz. It has nothing to expect from jazz."[46] Instead of reeling back in horror or disgust at the grotesque, blasphemous nature of jazz, reviewers repeatedly suggest that Whiteman's symphonic jazz music is banal and backward looking. Indeed, the tone of many of these critiques borders on mockery. "The symphonic attempts . . . point namely in the direction of the past: 'Mississippi' by Ferdy [sic] Grofe towards the area of Grieg; the 'Rhapsody in Blue' by George Gershwin is an extremely banal matter, filled with romantic platitudes."[47] Or, from Schmidt: "the pair of 'symphonic' pieces . . . , the 'Mississippi Suite' or the 'Rhapsody in Blue,'—my God, what kind of feeble (*dürftig*) music is that!"[48] Even Oscar Bie, who had so greatly praised Sam Wooding, said that these pieces were "undeveloped, of thematic and tonal, rather than musical interest."[49] Finally, musicologist Walter Schrenk, writing in the *Deutsche Allgemeine Zeitung*, concluded: "If jazz is to acquire an intellectual and musical meaning apart from a technical one, then it must first create a corpus of significant compositions. What we heard yesterday, the 'Mississippi' by Grofe or 'Rhapsody in Blue' by Gershwin, was insipid and uninspired, lacking any value whatsoever (*ohne irgendeinen diskutablen Wert*)."[50]

Yet if Stuckenschmidt's prophecy that snobs would be appalled at this music did not come to fruition, one assertion did: namely, that a few would see in Whiteman a prototypical example of the modern *Zeitgeist*. Another prevalent theme of the immediate reviews of Whiteman's Berlin appearance was that here the culture of New Objectivity, of Americanism, consumerism, and machine-age modernity could be seen flourishing. Frank Warschauer's article, written seven days in advance of the concerts, typifies this tendency. For Warschauer, jazz, however one may feel about it, is simply, objectively an elemental component of modern society and moralizing about its status or debating whether it is art or commerce, German or American, does little to change this fact.

> The same question always arises: whether it [jazz] is art or could some day become art. Answer: the question either cannot be answered at all or at least not immediately. [. . .] It bears repeating that the method usually applied in Europe is pernicious: to point a pistol at every new phenomenon with the demand that it reveal its ultimate aim and pass the test of whether it can be designated art! [51]

Yet as such calculated acceptance of jazz replaced the subjective moralizing of writers like Schmidt, this often resulted in abstracting jazz from its individual elements and transforming it into a mere vocalization of American society, rationalization, and modernity. In other words, Whiteman's music and persona were often put to the type of trite and predictable uses in the culture war of traditionalists versus modernists that typifies many German discussions of jazz. One example of this is an article in *Der Deutsche* that simulates a discussion between anti- and pro-jazz critics, in part using passages from earlier textual discussions of jazz. The opponents predictably fail to reach a compromise and, in the process, frustrate each other and the reader. As the anonymous author concludes: "In this discussion, two worlds talk across each other. For my part, I'll be buried with jazz."[52] Yet if the "King of Jazz" Whiteman was never accepted by Weimar's music critics, the remainder of this chapter will suggest that Whiteman and his symphonic jazz did exert an influence commensurate with his chosen moniker in another arena, namely in German literature. For it was in the jazz novels of the period that not his music but the structure and idea of symphonic jazz took hold.

Jazz Literature and the German Jazz Novel

Of course, an author didn't have to be familiar with, let alone be a fan of Whiteman, to include jazz in his or her works. Numerous authors of the period used references to jazz within works from the period. From well-known authors like Hermann Hesse and Thomas Mann to lesser known authors like Bruno Frank, Claire Goll, Vicki Baum, Hedwig Hassel, and Klaus Mann, discussions of saxophones, drums, shimmies, foxtrots, Black performers, and other indicators of the jazz milieu abound within Weimar literature.[53] Even in novels featuring the word "jazz" in their title, such as Felix Dörmann's *Jazz. Wiener Roman* (*Viennese Novel*) (1925), the music acts as little more than a surface phenomenon, a mere reference to cultural disorder,[54] rather than gesturing towards the evocative, if still ill-defined, category of jazz literature. Instead, jazz most commonly was deployed within Weimar literature as a reified symbol of modernity.[55] As Marc Weiner summarizes: "Viewed within the cultural vocabulary of the time as fundamentally antithetical to German cultural traditions, [jazz] both acted as an icon of non-German forces and provided an acoustical screen for the projection of fears regarding rapid and violent political change in postwar Germany."[56] For most writers, then, jazz was more often than not used as a ready-made symbol of the present, either to be rejected or embraced.

In order to address the ways in which jazz was transformed from its use as literary *topos* into a literary form in the novels of Janowitz, Schickele, and Renker, it is first necessary to investigate what jazz literature would and could look like to Weimar Germans. Writing in 1927, critic Friedrich Hirth attempted to understand modern French literature as "literary (*literarisierter*) jazz."[57] Searching for commonalities in the post-war French literary scene, Hirth counterintuitively suggests that the work of young French authors tends towards the grand and colossal.[58] He writes: "A generation that has experienced something like the world war, can, at base, do nothing other than to aspire towards the colossal in order not to feel minimized and overwhelmed."[59] Yet, he specifies that these are colossuses with feet of clay: "One might be tempted to compare the newest French writing with a symphony in which new motifs are continually arising. But it is in the essence of the symphony that in the end all motifs and motif beginnings merge with each other. The young French writers do not aspire to any form of merging (*Zusammenfassung*)."[60] Instead of harmoniously uniting individual tones, notes, sounds, and instruments, in this contemporary French jazz literature, the independence of the individual elements is maintained. So that while figures and motifs may sound out simultaneously, they remain fundamentally isolated from each other. For Hirth, this polyphony without harmony is precisely the jazz quality of the new literature. As he writes of his experience reading it: "One almost has the sensation of listening to a gigantic jazz band (*Riesenjazz*) executed by machines."[61]

Hirth's analysis, with its diagnosis of jazz literature as narrative progression without *telos* is strikingly similar to Hans Janowitz's *Jazz. Roman* (*Jazz: A Novel*).[62] To be sure, Janowitz is hardly a figure with whom most would today associate jazz. Instead, he is most famous for his coauthorship with Hans Meyer of the film *Das Cabinet des Dr. Caligari* (1920). Nonetheless, Janowitz's jazz novel is a worthy follow-up to this masterpiece of cinematic history. Like *Caligari*, the novel is richly evocative and resonant with broader modernist impulses and can be said to reveal important undercurrents of German culture and society in its modernist experimentation.[63] Staging the setting in the then distant future of 1999, Janowitz's novel begins with his narrator's attempt to explain the interwar period to contemporary readers living in the "United States of Europe." Opening the novel in clear, stylistic parody of Dickens' *A Tale of Two Cities*, the reader learns of the 1920s: "It was the time of the 'page boy' hair cut, it was the time of the 'short skirt,' 'flesh-colored nylons,' it was the time of prodigal sons and kidnapped daughters" (JR 6). Not only through such grandiose and futuristic evocations does Janowitz's novel follow Hirth's description of literary jazz, his novel also displays narrative dissonance. Interruptions, elliptical thoughts, and elisions fracture the narrative of the novel to such a degree that the reflection of the times promised in the opening is more akin to a cubist's refraction of reality than any form of realism.

The plot begins on a train from London to Paris, where the main character, named Lord Henry, meets Madame Mae R. The two immediately delight in deceiving the other passengers: she pretending to faint and he pretending to be a medical doctor capable of attending to her. After arriving in Paris, Lord Henry responds to an advertisement for musicians and meets the other members of the soon-to-be world famous "Lord Punch's Jazz Band Boys." Instead of chronologically narrating the group's predictable rise to fame and fortune, Janowitz introduces a separate narrative thread surrounding the figure of Arpad, a Hungarian *Eintänzer*, or dancer for hire.[64] As if playing a similarly coquettish game with the reader's expectations, Janowitz's narrator continually veers from the ostensibly principle voice, Lord Henry and his Jazz Band Boys, towards such minor notes. As Jürgen Grandt summarizes: "The narrative voice [in *Jazz: A Novel*], much like the jazz musicians, leaves the basic melody of the story-line behind and improvises to elaborate on anything and everything."[65] In point of fact, while the section on Arpad ends with the narrator's promise to return to jazz, the text instead sheers in yet another direction.[66] Such narrative misfires and misdirection are central to the novel and can be viewed as part of its attempt to recreate jazz in literary form. As the narrator informs the reader in a *mea culpa* to his literary conscience:

> I am aware that I've portrayed the characters a bit superficially and arbitrarily (*eigenwillig*) and thereby violated on numerous occasions the law of the epic: to provide exposition of the characters through the action and not to 'narrate' (*schildern*) the figures of the action. Professional writers aren't likely to forgive me for this. If one grants me the mitigating circumstance that I'm writing a jazz-novel, either as an excuse or apology, this can be used to demonstrate that this book is no typical novel. I believe there are different laws governing it, just as the laws for a work of jazz are different than those for a sonata for piano and violin. (JR 25)

One senses here more than mere bravado, more than the superficial exploitation of jazz as a literary subject, for example in the oblique reference to the literary-musical coupling of Beethoven's and Tolstoy's *Kreutzer Sonata*. Rather, the text gestures towards an understanding of jazz as aesthetic form, something that cannot be incorporated into traditional culture (here, the form of the novel) without consequence. Put differently, one senses that the narrator feels jazz pushing back at him, back at literature.

In a very important way, then, Janowitz's novel is less about jazz than a jazz piece itself. Or as one reviewer put it: "This jazz novel is not so much, as is promised at the beginning, the story of 'Lord Punch's Jazz-Band-Boys,' than it is a story composed and executed in the manner of jazz music."[67] The title, *Jazz: A Novel*, already hints at this productive tension. Here, the generic subtitle "A Novel" is not merely a convention, but exists to connect the two terms "jazz" and "novel." Most explicitly, the terms' seeming separation through the colon is easily erased through the substitution of a different form of punctuation, as the narrator does in the above quotation, to form a "jazz-novel" (*Jazz-Roman*) from *Jazz: A Novel* (*Jazz. Roman*). The significance of the proximity between these two terms is, I would suggest, the very meaning of the work. Through its conscious exploration of the formal rules of the novel, Janowitz is investigating the ability of traditional literature to narrate the new. Whereas most other authors saw little difficulty in this matter, deploying jazz as symbol of anarchy, rebellion, primitivism, etc., the fact that Janowitz bothers to ask this question is significant, even if, as I later show, his response remains ambiguous.

While overall *Jazz: A Novel* suggests that modernity's newness has progressed to a point beyond which traditional narrative form can be relied upon to contain and represent it, Janowitz's rather traditional narrator struggles with this fact—it is, of course, only with a guilty conscience that he has proceeded with the jazz novel. More significantly, jazz is not the only aesthetic form put forward in the novel as a model for representing the new; instead, jazz remains but one, certainly privileged, example amongst many.[68] All these various attempts eventually exhaust themselves, and the novel concludes on a particularly pessimistic note regarding the very possibility of representing the new. As the narrator states to close the novel:

> As one sees, in general our ensemble fared exactly just as well as every living ensemble on the earth has for a few thousand years—with every day they lost a new day of their lives. The old flaw (*Fehler*) that everything living is condemned to live from its capital, rather than only off the interest. This old fundamental flaw of creation is to blame if in this matter we have nothing new to offer, even to the reader of a jazz novel. (JR 122)

As the multiple strands of the plot are finally brought together, the narrator reaches what are, for him, the limits of the jazz-novel: death and ending. While jazz may demand new modes of representation, aesthetic innovation cannot fundamentally alter life and consequently its representation in art. The unexpected entrance of death retroactively undercuts the freedom towards which the narrator seemed to have been striving.

In order to understand why the narrator figures the work as a formal failure, it is necessary to turn the analytical screw once more, to consider the work not only as a jazz-novel but as a novel about jazz, in this case about symphonic jazz. For one, it is important that within the narrative, loose though it may be, Lord Henry and his Jazz-Band-Boys progress from rowdy, anarchic "jazz band boys" in the beginning to members of a jazz symphony orchestra towards the end (JR 111). More than merely reflecting the history of jazz in Germany, when read in the context of the critical rejection by music critics of symphonic jazz as a backward-looking pseudo-revolution, the shift to symphonic jazz also serves to signal the narrator's turn against jazz. Like the critics who came to view in Whiteman's jazz but a dressed-up salon orchestra, Janowitz's narrator slowly but surely gives up on his initial dream of jazz. Most important here is not that he gives up on jazz but how he does so: through a shift in the narrator's own understanding of the project from jazz novel to jazz symphony. Towards the end of the novel, the narrator states: "I don't think we even have to be there when our ensemble slides into a catastrophe. This would perhaps suffice as an exciting climax to a dime novel, but cannot provide the final movement of a *jazz symphony*. It must be said again that different laws are governing the music of these pages than those for a sonata for piano and violin or even a banal finale of an operetta" (JR 111, emphasis added). This is repetition with a difference. The substitution of symphony for novel alters how the references to Tolstoy and operetta function: instead of existing above, or at the very least beside, jazz, they now clearly exist below them.

For if Whiteman took the listener on a journey from "primitive" jazz to "elevated" symphonic jazz, the narrator sees himself taking the reader on an equally important journey through modern literature: mixing the high culture of Dickens and Tolstoy with contemporary, more popular modes like the detective novel. Still, while Whiteman's "Experiment in Modern Music" was in many ways a demonstration of the brilliance and modernism of symphonic jazz, *Jazz: A Novel* ultimately exists as a eulogy of this attempt. Though the incorporation of jazz initially pushes the narrative towards ever-greater crimes against the literature, in the end, the narrator pushes back at jazz and does so by way of symphonic jazz. As he suggests in the novel's conclusion: no matter how daring the escape, no matter how dissonant and syncopated the individual moment, there will always exist a point of ending, a last page, a final word, jazz-novel or not. Still, it is important to remember that though Lord Henry (and the narrative) fails not as jazz band boy, but as part of a jazz symphony orchestra, the narrator refuses to distinguish between the two. Moving from the jazz novel to jazz symphony and then in the final scene back to jazz novel, Janowitz's narrator ultimately conflates the failure of symphonic jazz with the failure of jazz itself.

Symphony for Jazz

While *Jazz: A Novel* struggles to understand jazz's significance for German literature, Janowitz's project of writing the German jazz novel continued in the

works of two other authors, René Schickele and Gustav Renker. Though neither of these later works shares the radical form of *Jazz: A Novel*, their engagement with jazz, symphonic and otherwise, as well as the legacy of Whiteman's
project, combine to form a German jazz literature of its own. Unlike Janowitz
or Renker, René Schickele clearly belongs to the canon of German literature.
Highly praised for his trilogy of novels *Das Erbe am Rhein* (*The Inheritance
on the Rhine*) (1925–31), Schickele's *Symphonie für Jazz* (*Symphony for Jazz*)
appears at first glance to offer relatively little new insight into the meaning of
jazz for Weimar literature.[69] It covers the life of composer and jazz musician
John van Maray, who makes his way across Europe as a successful popular
artist. Early in the novel, van Maray will marry a young woman named Johanna. As the plot progresses, however, their marriage becomes increasingly
strained and, after separating, each seeks out a space of his and her own, his
wife finding a new life in Berlin, while van Maray moves between Lake Constance, Paris, and Southern France. It is the timing of the separation that is of
most interest here. The couple separates just as van Maray sets about composing a jazz symphony, and his progression in the composition inversely mirrors
the state of his relationship with Johanna: the more he succeeds with it, the
further apart the lovers grow. The two will eventually reconcile at the van Maray home on Lake Constance, but only after van Maray has tossed his saxophone into the lake, thereby forsaking American jazz.

Though unlike Janowitz, Schickele authored further novels, he, too, never
returned to the subject of jazz. While the work's manifest subject matter stands
out against his other works, its treatment of Franco-German relationships and,
even more so, the strong similarities between the relationship of the composer
van Maray to his wife Johanna and writer Schickele to his wife Anna Schickele, firmly place it within the broader context of his *oeuvre*.[70] The question
must arise then: Does it matter at all that Schickele wrote about jazz? The first
point to make in this regard is that Schickele's work can be seen as in conversation with Janowitz and the discourse of symphonic jazz. Beyond the obvious
fact that each novel contains a composer who creates a jazz symphony, at the
level of content, both works use the saxophone as an organizing metaphor[71]
and include a Josephine Baker-like character.[72] Equally important are the formal similarities. Like Janowitz, Schickele uses his jazz subject as motivation to
experiment with language and narration. He begins the novel with an onomato-
poetic homage to the sounds and rhythms of jazz, such as in the opening line
of the novel: "Bäbä, tu. Bäbä, tut. Tut! Bäbä."[73] Combining, inverting, defamil-
iarizing, Schickele is playing with these terms and others in the novel's opening as he moves words, ideas, and sounds like so many pieces on a chessboard—

indeed, nowhere in the novel is he as jazzy as in the opening pages. At the same time, there is much more at stake here than mere play. First, his word play eliminates language's representational power, and its reduction to sound, rhythm, and form can be read as an attempt to mimic the non-representational nature of music. Second, and by contrast, the ultimate end of Schickele's opening gambit is not to disregard language's capacity to signify in a turn towards abstraction. Instead, this opening creates a disjuncture of language and meaning in order to create a space of freedom, which Schickele can later fill with new meaning. Indeed, all the terms referenced in the opening four lines, though stripped of context and content, will come to have very specific meanings within the narrative. For example, "bäbä, tu" is associated with the sound of van Maray's saxophone and serves as a leitmotif throughout the novel, while a seemingly random reference to a kangaroo will later appear in a discussion regarding technological progress (SFJ 252–57). The language of the opening section is thus both a play with language, demonstrating Schickele's jazz chops, as well as a straightforward narrative device used to introduce themes from the novel.

At the same time, Schickele's opening is a hard act to follow, and the remainder of the novel proceeds in a much less radical manner. As Kurt Martens notes in his critical review of the work, it isn't clear from the first lines whether Schickele "intends to objectively represent the style of jazz, adapt his writing to it or develop it *ad absurdum*."[74] If Schickele leaves this question in many ways unanswered, the novel nonetheless builds upon the Weimar jazz literature project in significant ways. After van Maray returns from touring abroad to Lake Constance, two central events take place that simultaneously shape the novel's trajectory as well as reveal a potential debt to the debate on Whiteman. The first involves the symphonic work for which the novel is named. Having tired of his life as a popular jazz musician, John van Maray travels to the Alps, where he is inspired to write a "symphony for jazz band" (SFJ 53). Upon his return, he proclaims to Johanna: "Let's go! I'm writing a symphony for jazz, strings (*Streicherkorps*), and organ" (SFJ 54). The specification of "jazz band" and then jazz's serialization with strings and organ transform the significance and meaning of the novel's title, which here cannot mean a symphony dedicated to jazz, but rather only to one written for jazz ensemble, i.e., a specific set of instruments. In other words, instead of placing jazz qua musical form on relatively equal footing with the symphony, jazz is here subsumed under the symphonic form, existing alongside and in apparent harmony with traditional bourgeois string instruments and the religiously coded organ. This constellation, as is hinted at in van Maray's initial description of the piece, can also be read historically as a reversion from contemporary popular music to bourgeois to religious music. As he explains to Johanna, the symphony will tell "the entire history of us bipeds. From our departure from the jungle to . . . nickel-plated instrument cabinets. . . . You'll have nothing to laugh at" (SFJ 54–55). In part following the seriousness of Whiteman's experiment in modern music and in part satirizing the culture of New Objectivity, jazz is ultimately framed in the work as the loveless result of modern progress from which van Maray desires to escape.

Yet if van Maray would seek to control jazz by positioning it underneath the symphony, a jazz experience that evening at a hotel will disrupt his monopolization of the debate. Shortly after he has announced his intention to write a symphony, van Maray and Johanna attend a performance by a jazz band. During the performance, Johanna admits to van Maray that she is in love with the band's drummer. As with other depictions of the drums, race plays an important role here. Though the drummer is white, an "image of a Negro baring his teeth" is painted upon a percussive metallic surface of his drum (*Schlagblech*) (SFJ 57). Schickele's description here generally recalls the paintings on early drum sets such as that seen on the drum of the unidentified jazz band in Danzig or the one in Dix's *To Beauty*. Unlike these examples, however, the image in Schickele has to be continually painted anew as the drummer's daily strikes upon it are constantly erasing it. This inventive detail suggests that jazz's Blackness, its "primitivity," exists in a state of tension with its modernity, here represented by the metallic surface upon which the image is painted. The very next evening, Johanna and van Maray once again attend the nightly concert of the jazz band, during which they bear witness to the following sensational scene involving the drummer:

> At the evening concert the man struck the drum with the mockery of a self-important Roman augur ("gives me the chills," whispered Johanna and timidly edged her knee towards mine under the table)—as planned, the music stopped to let this single drum hit resound. The man gasped (*schnappte*), opened his mouth wide, and blood shot out. The stream of blood formed an arc and landed exactly on the rim of the drum. The painted negro skull snarled its teeth. (SFJ 60)

This scene depicting the gory death of the white jazz drummer and competitor of van Maray raises any number of important questions about the role of Blackness within jazz discourse in the late 1920s. In order to answer these questions, however, it is necessary to investigate the cultural meaning of both the drum and the saxophone, the instrument associated with van Maray and the one he will toss into a lake at the novel's conclusion.

That within German and European discussions of jazz the drums were commonly associated with Blackness is well-known from chapter 1. As an instrument dedicated to rhythm in a culture that coded melody and harmony as intellectually superior, before the introduction of jazz, the drums were generally viewed as an instrument of but minor importance for the future of European music. With the entrance (and popularity) of jazz during the first-half of the 1920s, the instrument takes on exceeding importance and quickly became the primary symbol of this music. As we've seen, the connection between the jazz music and the drums was so strong that drummers were routinely called "jazzers" and a trap drum set simply "jazz" or "jazz band."[75] By the time Schickele was writing in 1929, the importance of the drums to jazz had receded significantly. No longer were they the only or even primary symbol of jazz music. Instead, that honor had shifted to the saxophone, which will see increased popularity and production until the stock market crash in 1929 and continue as a means of connoting jazz and modern, American, and foreign dance music well into the 1930s.[76]

The shift reflected in German jazz culture generally and implied within Schickele's novel specifically can also be connected to the development of symphonic jazz, however. For example, when German jazz critics like Alfred Baresel advised saxophone players to be able to play more than one variant of the saxophone, from bass to soprano, this was due to the practice of doubling within symphonic jazz orchestras, something obviously tied to Whiteman's popularity, though by no means to his alone as this was also practiced by musicians with Sam Wooding.[77] Revealing a similar historicizing look at jazz in Germany is Otto Dix's famous *Großstadt-Tryptychon* (*Metropolis-Triptych*) from 1927. In the background of the center panel of this masterpiece of New Objectivity, one sees a caricatured Black drummer waving a drumstick in the air, while the foreground features a band dominated by the white saxophone player and in front of him stands a gigantic bass saxophone. The number of saxophones in this very famous painting is thus neither coincidental, nor exaggerated, and here again the indirect influence of Whiteman's symphonic jazz on Weimar representations of jazz can be seen. Returning to *Symphony for Jazz*—through the death of the drummer and the almost simultaneous rise of the new jazz composer van Maray and his saxophone, Schickele restages the dominant narrative of jazz's development during the 1920s.

In one sense, the hotel jazz band functions as an historical remnant of jazz history, and the death of its drummer stands for the ascension of the saxophone and the white symphonic jazz composer—Lord Henry, John van Maray, and Paul Whiteman. Yet within Schickele's novel, this transformation from drum to saxophone, from jazz band to symphony, neither removes race from jazz's identity, nor guarantees its aesthetic success. Like the German music establishment and like Janowitz, Schickele will also render the age of symphonic jazz a failure or, rather, as insufficient from a purely aesthetic perspective. Within Schickele's novel, there is a distinction between the material success John van Maray's "symphony for jazz, strings, and organ" will no doubt have and the aesthetic potential of jazz to narrate the history of humanity. Regarding its economic prospects: long before it is completed, photographs of van Maray working on the symphony appear in the illustrated press, portending the success to come (SFJ 188). Yet throughout his separation from Johanna and work on the symphony, van Maray's life swings back and forth between his career as a popular jazz musician and the spiritual life as an artist-composer of a jazz symphony. To help balance these and to escape the negative influence of the jazz singer Ursel Bruhn, he works in concert with other artists, namely a sculptor, as well as in a church. Yet even after van Maray seemingly overcomes these difficulties and declares the symphony, this "great work," complete (SFJ 277), he finds himself continuing to compose in his dreams. In order to stop, he is compelled to return to the world, to a "jazz music that does not speak as I do" (SFJ 278). Van Maray, following the symphonic jazz model, sought to separate the jazz of entertainment, the jazz of the world, through the creation of his own artistic jazz of and within the symphony. Yet though he may be capable of achieving this in the abstract, the completion of the symphony, not to mention its commodification as "jazz symphony," ultimately will not spare him the deleterious effect of the materialism symbolized by this jazz music of the world.

Failing to reach personal equilibrium through completion of the symphony, he seeks refuge in the Black Forest and then in St. Moritz, where he meets Angelica, a young girl who turns out to be van Maray's daughter from an earlier affair. After she arrives, the two quickly become very close until Angelica leaves one day to go out into the wintry landscape. When she doesn't return, van Maray goes in search of her, only to find her severely injured and alone in the snow. It is only after she dies as a result of her injuries that van Maray realizes he was her father. After her death, he retreats to his home on Lake Constance, and enraged for having squandered his life and fearful that he will lose Johanna forever, he goes to the lake intent upon destroying the symbol of the materialist side of his life and of the jazz of the world: his saxophone. It has finally become clear to him that this metallic instrument, no matter its potential, is not capable of creating a form of art untainted by the materialism of modernity.

> "Down with dancing Nigger bottoms (*Niggersteiß*)!" he called out and lifted the instrument up so that he could smash it on the cliff.
> "Down with black money (*schwarze Kasse*)!"
> "Long live the forty-eighth parallel with all its fruits and vegetables and wine and the women—if things like that also flourish there! Down with I.G. Jazz-Industry!"
> As he held the saxophone in his raised hand, about to execute the destructive blow, John noticed to his surprise how the silent water was washing a star on the stone, a magical movement, always the same, tiny star.
> "I see," he said—"Of course."
> And instead of continuing his rant, he went quietly into the house and came right back out with a cord and an iron weight.
> He took the saxophone and sank it, like a cat's cadaver (*krepierte Katze*), into the lake. (SFJ 352)

Here van Maray does more than merely reject jazz and the racial difference and materialism for which it stands to him; he simultaneously recognizes that his pursuit of jazz was spurned on by a desire within himself to throw off the civilization that would support it. That he does not destroy, but rather sinks, the saxophone may result from the universal connection he sees between nature and music; in other words, the potential reconciliation symbolized by the idea of the jazz symphony may still be attainable, though not for him and not in this life.[78] As he looks into the lake, the water's motion across the star's reflection on the stone reminds him the same daring combination of high and low, of symphony and now sunken jazz that had once inspired him.

When *Symphony for Jazz* is viewed in comparison to Janowitz's *Jazz: A Novel*, a number of important parallels, as well as differences, emerge. In both novels, an attempt is made to formally recreate the aesthetic principles of jazz through language and innovative narrative form. While Janowitz carries this experiment to a much further extent, both texts eventually abandon the ephemeral modernity of jazz in favor of tradition—death in Janowitz and nature in Schickele. At the same time, in its deployment of race and Blackness as a means of figuring jazz's difference, Schickele's work anticipates the turn taken in the final example of symphonic jazz literature, Gustav Renker's *Symphony and Jazz* from 1931.

Requiem for the Jazz Symphony

If Schickele's *Symphony for Jazz* and Janowitz's *Jazz: A Novel* would seem to generally fit within a modernist debate surrounding jazz, symphonic and otherwise, and the possibility of a German jazz literature, the Swiss-Austrian author Gustav Renker's contribution occupies a more tenuous position. Perhaps best described as a melding of the jazz novel with the genre of the *Heimatroman*, this work fails to make any attempt at incorporating jazz, formally or structurally, and instead narrates a fairly typical tale of city versus country, young versus old, sick versus healthy. At the same time, Renker's work is significant not only for the ways it differs from Janowitz and Schickele, but for how, in its own way, it continues the project of jazzing up German literature. Selectively taking up the idea of the symphonic jazz novel as it had been developed in Janowitz and Schickele, in Renker's work, key elements, such as the saxophone, drums, the mountains, and, of course, the jazz symphony, receive new meaning.

Whereas the previous two examples displayed an at times positive, if ultimately negative, relationship to jazz, Renker's *Symphony and Jazz* for the most part dispenses with any such pretenses. Indeed, the binary relation between the terms implied in the title is furthered through the splitting of the composer character well-known from Janowitz and Schickele into two figures. First there is Othmar Wehrberg, an aging composer residing in Vienna whose brightest days seem to be behind him. As the novel opens, he is struggling to finish his latest symphony and the reasons for this soon become clear: in the urban, "Jewish" Vienna he has lost all relationship to his native Alpine village Maltatal. It will only be through his return to his *Heimat* towards the end of the novel that Othmar Wehrberg will regain his rootedness and once again be a creative composer. The work of art resulting from this turn homeward will by no means consist in his combining jazz and symphony, however. Instead, this task will fall to his son, Richard "Ricki" Wehrberg, who, like Lord Henry and John van Maray, will rise to international success through the composition of a jazz symphony. His youth and interest in jazz and "primitive," non-European music mark his relationship to his father and, as Tobias Nagl notes, shape the narrative as "an Oedipal conflict carried out through music."[79] Yet whereas the other two jazz-symphony composers maintain an indirect and tenuous relationship to Blackness, Ricki cultivates not merely a connection to African American culture but to the African continent itself. Unlike the implicit historical development of jazz within the previous two novels, in which the music progressed from Blackness to whiteness, Ricki's vision of symphonic jazz would seek to return jazz to an original, "Black" state. As he notes of his artistic goals: "I want to remain at the source, to go to it. With the first big royalty fee that I earn, I will travel to Africa" (SUJ 29).[80] He further states that supposedly great German composers like Pfitzner, Strauss, Wagner, and Mahler are degenerate, claiming that they are examples of "music that has lost its foundation. Music is authentic only insofar as it is primitive" (SUJ 31). What emerges over the course of the novel is that both father and son represent less opposites than two sides of the same issue—the loss of *Bodenständigkeit*, or "rootedness," in German art. This lack in each is further highlighted through their shared relationship to the "rootless" music critic Paul Hirsch, whose Jewishness and degeneracy are referenced throughout the novel.[81]

The ultimate terminus of the false path of the prodigal son Ricki is embodied in the figure of Hesekiel Makua-Taka. In this African American figure named after a Hebrew prophet, Renker remixes elements from Janowitz, Schickele, and the German reception of Whiteman to create a monstrous image of a Black mammonite, whose sole desire in the novel is to monetarily exploit Europe for the last of its cultural potential. More than this, the alignment of an African American jazz musician with Jewishness, in addition to the stereotyped presentation of the critic Hirsch, amount to something qualitatively new in the symphonic jazz novel. As I want to argue, Makua-Taka's inclusion is indicative of an important shift within the German theorization of jazz that takes place towards the end of the 1920s and one that intensifies with the rise of National Socialism. Specifically, the linkage effected here between urban, foreign Jewishness and the modernist, popular music jazz takes up the long-standing trope of "Jewish modernism" ("*die jüdische Moderne*") that, as historian Scott Spector has shown, was particularly pronounced in German-speaking Central Europe. [82] This idea acts within discussions of modernism and modernity as a trope for the fear over the dissolution of deep rooted traditions and their substitution with a superficial, ephemeral, nonunique urban popular culture. In other words, the discourse on "Jewish modernism" enables speakers within this space to mediate between "true," "authentic" art and "mass culture" like jazz. As Spector summarizes: "The complexity of the relations between the figures of modernism and of Jewishness stems in no small part from the famously ambiguous status of modernism itself, as well as its relationship to modernity on the one hand and popular culture on the other."[83] According to Spector, this notion of the "Jewishness" of the modernism and modernity, which reaches at least as far back as Richard Wagner, served this crucial role not only for conservatives like Renker but also shaped the self-understanding of modernism itself. It is thus important to see how Renker's figuration of Makua-Taka profits from both of these strains within German culture. As we will see in chapter 6, from the late 1920s onward, this connection between Jewishness, Blackness, jazz, and modernism will become increasingly prevalent, not only in the writings of jazz's detractors but, through the translation of Harlem Renaissance poetry, also in those of its modernist defenders.

At the same time, Renker's characterization of Makua-Taka not only draws on the idea of the "Jewish modernism" but on a Weimar jazz reception caught between Black and white, between, for example, Sam Wooding and Paul Whiteman. For Makua-Taka is not only Jewish and Black, he is also the novel's saxophone-playing "King of Jazz" (*Jazzkönig*) (SUJ 32).[84] There were, of course, Black jazz performers who were called or went by the name "jazz kings" and/or "kings of jazz" during the 1920s, beginning at least with Mitchell's Jazz Kings in 1920 but also including George Barthelme's 1919 reference to James Reese Europe as "jazz master" and the Black jazz musician Evandale Roberts in Berlin in the summer of 1921, not to mention the marketing of Wooding as the "King of the Jazz Band" as early as August 1925.[85] For Renker, by contrast, one fundamental aspect of Whiteman's symphonic project remains inaccessible for the Black Makua-Taka: the composition of the jazz symphony itself. The call for the creation of a corpus of jazz compositions, it will be recalled, was an essential complaint by Berlin music critics against Whiteman's concerts. In *Symphony and Jazz*, Makua-Taka's genius, however, is merely imitative and the promethean act of creation is left to the white European Ricki Wehrberg.

After enjoying initial success in America with a jazz piece, a "blues," Ricki next composes a jazz symphony, later premiered by Makua-Taka at an American concert hall. The description of the concert reveals not only the success but the construction of the difference between American culture's productive primitivity and the stilting weight of cultural tradition in Europe:

> If someone were to start dancing to Bruckner's Fifth in one of our philharmonics, he would be thrown out with grand effect. In America the noble benefactor of our Ricki [i.e., Makua-Taka] just played his jazz symphony in a concert hall where the middle was open. This removed the ceremonial constraints on our instinct to move. The band plays and people listen. But if one of the listeners feels the need, if the rhythm sparks in him the need to shake about (*durchrüttelt*), he is free to do so and to heed the call. (SUJ 161)

As with Makua-Taka's use of the saxophone, Ricki's jazz symphony mediates between the body and the mind, between high and low culture, rhythm and melody, and serves to reawaken the "natural" relationship between the *Volk* and culture. At the same time, it is important that the success of the jazz symphony takes place outside of Germany. While jazz and symphony may coexist in America in a productive relationship, in Europe, jazz is a symptom of the degeneracy of culture and its combination with the symphony but the worst imaginable scenario. So though the novel may contain surprisingly positive remarks about the jazz symphony, these primarily act as a reminder of what European music has lost: namely the connection to its folk culture.

This didactic element of *Symphony and Jazz* becomes especially apparent after father and son travel back to Maltatal and the Alpine community Wehrberg left when he departed for modern Vienna. Father and son are here aided by a female figure, Hilde, who, through her gender and Swiss roots, still seems to possess the healthy relationship to nature the two men lack. In Maltatal, all three share experiences of beautifully simple local folk culture and the invigorating natural surroundings. As we have already seen with Schickele and as is the case in Ernst Krenek's jazz opera *Jonny spielt auf* (*Jonny Strikes Up*), the Alps function within the German jazz imagination as an inexhaustible source of cultural invigoration.[86] The corrosive influence of Hirsch and Makua-Taka slowly recedes in this space, and once there, Wehrberg begins to understand all he has lost in his twenty years in the city, overcomes his compositional difficulties, and, finally, is able to produce a new work, albeit a requiem. This rural paradise, acting as nature's sanatorium, also comes with significant danger, and in the novel's climactic scene, a violent storm strikes the village. The sublime power of Alpine nature causes within Wehrberg an epiphany that the nearby Malta river will flood, destroy the house, and kill him and a little village girl playing there. With this insight Wehrberg rushes into action, taking the young girl into his arms and leaving the doomed house. Though he is successful in his rescue of the girl, his exposure to the storm makes him ill, and he soon lapses into a coma. Upon waking fourteen days later, he finds Hirsch at his bedside and learns that his son Ricki's latest work *Das Weinen des Urwalds* (*The Weeping of the Jungle*) is at that very moment having its European premiere in Munich. Though there is no radio, Wehrberg mystically hears the music. Surprisingly, in his dying words, Wehrberg mollifies his opinion regarding jazz, remarking of the saxophone, "I wouldn't have thought one could get so much from the instrument," and praising his son's work as "entirely new, sounding like a distant call" (SUJ 233). If death brings the elder Wehrberg to at least partially recognize all that he has lost and that which his son is attempting to regain, neither the experience of his father's *Heimat,* nor even his father's death alters Ricki's path. Instead of embracing his Alpine heritage and a heterosexual pairing with the Swiss Hilde, following his father's funeral, Ricki embarks with Hirsch on a trip to Africa. Unmoved, unchanged, at the novel's end, the symphony embodied by the father exists only as a requiem, while the false-folk culture of jazz continues to lure European youth ever further from its cultural heritage.

Between Symphonic Jazz and Jazz Symphony

In this final act of cultural resignation, Renker's novel joins those of Janowitz and Schickele. Each of their separate attempts to reconcile the conflict between ascendant jazz and declining symphony ends with resignation. For all three, symphony and jazz may coexist, but never harmoniously and hardly in a manner that can guide Europe towards a better future. Like the Berlin critics of Whiteman, each author also sees in symphonic jazz the music's apotheosis and ultimate failure. Even so, it is equally clear that symphonic jazz became a means for them to respond to the challenge of jazz in both modern and traditional aesthetic forms.

Behind this shift lies Whiteman's symphonic jazz. In many ways legitimizing the very idea of jazz as art, Whiteman's music laid the groundwork for a German jazz literature by showing that the music could also function as a formal, aesthetic principle. Here, it is important to note that though clearly influenced by Whiteman, in their German form, symphony and jazz stand in inverted relation to Whiteman's own experiment in modern music. Whereas Whiteman desired to create a symphonic jazz and to make jazz music respectable for a bourgeois public, the novelists created jazz symphonies. In other words, they sought to bring jazz to the symphony rather than the other way around. The hierarchy in this envisioning clearly favors the symphony, which remains the universal category of musical production, while jazz is tested as to whether it can fulfill this promise, in a strange way echoing Warschauer's concern over the European method for judging new cultural forms, that is: "to point a pistol at every new phenomenon with the demand that it reveal its ultimate aim and pass the test of whether it can be designated art."

If these experiments in symphonic jazz literature remain marked by ambiguity, both on their own terms and as attempts to incorporate jazz into German literature, the persistent and repeated attempts to do so hint at a more fundamental change to the function of jazz within German literature ushered by

Whiteman's idea of symphonic jazz. Before Whiteman, jazz in Weimar literature existed as a symbol—of chaos, revolution, disorder—and such one-
dimensional use of jazz is precisely the reason why so many other novelists
seemed to exhaust the subject with little discussion, through the addition of a
secondary character or a particularly salacious scene for example. Yet in the
wake of Whiteman's concerts, jazz also became more than a symbol; it became
a project, a shifting, moving, living thing. It is thus significant that each fictional composer of a jazz symphony, Lord Henry, John van Maray, and Ricki
Wehrberg is associated with water.[87] While this certainly positions jazz as a
floating music and culture, aligning it with the mobility of modernity against
the fixity of tradition, the very same idea of fluidity can be applied to the project of German jazz literature. Each author works with and through an almost
identical knot of questions in order to present a vision, not "just" of jazz but of
cultural production more generally. From Janowitz's almost abstract representation of narrative form; to Schickele's rumination on the relationship between
humanity, nature, and art in modern Europe; and finally to Renker's requiem
for the lost relationship between them, these are less reflections of an abstract
Zeitgeist than variations, or rather, improvisations on a common theme. That
each chose to do so via the jazz symphony was neither accidental, nor coincidental. For these three novelists, symphony and jazz were anything but an
empty field into which they inserted themselves, and Whiteman's symphonic
jazz can be said to have legitimized the high stakes of their own literary, rather
than musical, experiments. Through Janowitz, Schickele, and Renker, as well
as the many other discussions and applications of symphonic jazz, Whiteman
became a figure of even wider cultural significance. For better and for worse,
Whiteman's claim to have elevated jazz's cultural status made possible the
creation of the grand, if flawed, literary genre of the symphonic jazz novel.

It is also clear, however, that these jazz novels were exceptions to the
many other literary works that sought to incorporate jazz. Yet even these exceptions followed one rule of representing jazz in Germany: women and, in particular, the "new women" of Weimar Germany were essential players within
Weimar jazz culture. From white women like Madame Mae R. or Johanna
dancing to jazz music, to the inclusion of a series of Josephine Baker clones,
and even the Swiss Hilde's short cropped hair, these jazz novels draw upon the
debate over the shifting boundaries of gender identity and sexuality. Though
there were many cultural spaces where this debate was carried out, perhaps
none was as conspicuous as the popular revue stage.

CHAPTER 4

Syncopating the Mass Ornament:
Race and *Girlkultur*

> Supposing truth to be a woman—how? is the suspicion not well founded
> that all philosophers, as far as they have been dogmatists, have had a poor
> understanding of women?
> —Friedrich Nietzsche (1886)

Nietzsche's homology between truth and woman raises more than the question
of (male) desire and the production of knowledge. His provocative assertion
also turns on the incongruous grammatical gendering of "truth" (*Wahrheit*) and
a pejorative term for "woman" (*Weib*) in the German language. While *Wahrheit*
is figured through the feminine definite article *die*, Nietzsche's woman, *das
Weib*, at least grammatically speaking, is no woman at all. She is, rather, a sex-
less neutrum.[1] To Nietzsche, this contradiction between truth (*Wahrheit*) and
woman (*Weib*) is indicative of much more than "some play on words, a grammatical seduction."[2] To him, this faulty logic reveals the falsity of philosophical knowledge itself, asking us to move away from the idealist construction of
truth as embodied in some otherworldly ideal and instead to concentrate on a
multiplicity of truths. Nietzsche's configuration of women, truth, and philosophy, of course, also begins to unravel the complex interweaving of women and
modernity in German culture. For in spite of Nietzsche's warning, male Weimar theorists will see in woman, in particular the "New Woman" (*Neue Frau*)
the origin and essence of modern life.[3]

   As Rita Felski argues, the history and theorization of the modern is overdetermined through narrative oppositions of the feminine and masculine.[4] Felski's analysis of philosophical, sociological, and literary texts suggests not one
but multiple configurations of the modern and the feminine. In the Weimar
Republic, this relationship expressed itself to a large degree through a conflation of the feminine with the mass, be it through the feminization of the masses
as irrational or through the ideal of an undifferentiated, monolithic, feminine

mass culture. Succinctly summarizing the Weimar modality of mass/feminine, Andreas Huyssen writes: "The fear of the masses in this age of declining liberalism is always also a fear of woman, a fear of nature out of control, a fear of the unconscious, of sexuality, of the loss of identity and stable ego boundaries in the mass."[5] To this conflation of the feminine with the mass belonged the discussion of the cultural significance of the New Woman as a unique creation of modernity. In literature, theater, film, and music, the image of a liberated and independent New Woman littered the cultural landscape of the 1920s. Like her American counterpart, the "flapper," Germany's New Woman epitomized the liberation, economically, politically, and sexually, of women from nineteenth century society. Of course, as Atina Grossmann and others have pointed out, the reality for these "new" women was not so new at all and most languished under the double burden of housework and professional work.[6]

Within the culturally constructed image of the New Woman, as Lynne Frame has argued, the abstract idea could be further divided into three ideal types: Gretchen, Girl, and Garçonne.[7] Essential here is that all three simultaneously signify racial, gender, and national identities of Germany, the United States, and France, respectively. Of all three, the idea of the American Girl represented a most foreign and threatening variation on the theme of the New Woman.[8] This was because she was structured as a synthesis of the two other forms. She lacked the saturnine intellect of the French *Garçonne*, yet could still rival the latter in her androgynous play with the masculine and feminine. With the German Gretchen type, the Girl shared an innocence, in this case a residuum of America's supposedly pubescent culture from which she derived, but also distinguished herself through corporeal and sexual rationalization.

During the Weimar Republic, there was no more quintessential expression of the Girl than the Tiller Girl. Tiller Girls, the most recognized formation of female dance troupes at the time, performed widely on the popular revue stages of Berlin. Though originally founded by British businessman John Tiller, the Girls themselves were viewed as archetypally American. The cultural impact of the Tiller Girls derived from the precision and athleticism of their dancing. Unlike the highly sexualized female dance numbers of the prewar period, the athleticism of the Tiller Girls seemed to portend, or rather to index, the rationalization of entertainment and society.[9] Further, the Tiller Girls were imagined as an active and, for that very reason, threatening form of femininity. Ideologically positioned as modernized popular culture for a modern republic, the Tiller Girls and the revue stage they occupied became primary sites through which the gender of modernity was imagined in Weimar Germany.

It is here, however, that Nietzsche's suspicion regarding philosophers can

Figure 11: The Tiller Girls, the "Classical Form of American Group Dance," from Fritz Giese, *Girlkultur. Vergleiche zwischen amerikanischem und europäischen Rhythmus- und Lebensgefühl* (Munich: Delphin-Verlag, 1925).

be of aid. For all too often, a focus on rationality unwittingly leads to the essentialization of the Girl as a young, healthy, white woman (figure 11). The hypostatized legs of the Tiller Girls depicted in so many commentaries of the time and in contemporary scholarship have themselves come to act as a synecdoche of the Weimar vision of the Girl. In other words, they end up obstructing our ability to get at the multiple truths of this discourse.[10] In the following, I want to suggest that the Tiller Girls and Weimar *Girlkultur* more generally were not nearly as antiseptic as such images would lead one to believe and argue that Weimar *Girlkultur* should be seen as emerging out of the heterogeneous space of the theatrical revue that was populated with Black and white, male and female, German, American, and many other nationalized bodies.[11]

Girlkultur: Visions in Black and White

Figure 11 derives from industrial psychologist Fritz Giese's 1925 work *Girlkultur: Vergleiche zwischen amerikanischem und europäischem Rhythmus- und Lebensgefühl* (*Girlkultur: Comparisons of the American and European Sense of Rhythm and Life*).[12] A foundational text of Weimar's *Girlkultur* discourse, Giese's work contains over fifty such illustrations, taken from both popular and scholarly sources and for which he provided original captions. Introducing his object of study, the first illustration is of the Tiller Girls—legs extended in the air, frozen in uniform majesty, and described by Giese as the "classical form of the American group dance." As they will later be for Siegfried Kracauer, these icons of Weimar modernity are Giese's starting point, the surface phenomenon upon which he will build his argument. Turning the page, however, one discovers two images captioned as "Models of primitive ritual dance (*Kulttänze*) / The ancestors of Girl-culture." These two images depict dancing Black figures who are neither American nor European but nondistinct "primitives" (in fact, at least one image is of the Aranda people from Australia) intended to suggest a universalized age of primitive Blackness.[13] With the next two illustrations, Giese leaves this eternal-primitive for the world of the metropolis, not of Tiller Girls, but of African Americans, jazz bands, and Black revues, specifically the *Chocolate Kiddies*—one photograph shows performers from the *Chocolate Kiddies* revue, while another features a caricatured image of a Black jazz band with the words "USA Made in Germany" visible in the background.[14] The ultimate connection between these images and the Tiller Girls begins to emerge in the series' final image. Displayed on the next page is the end product of Giese's visual history of *Girlkultur*: two photographs of the young, white Girls, one simply identified as the "Ideal of Youth," while the other, an image of Alaska Liederman, is captioned as "An American Venus." What this visual narrative suggests and what this work as a whole argues is that, for Giese, *Girlkultur* is both mediated through and directly influenced by non-Europeans and Blackness.

Such mediation is reflected within the very notion of Giese's *Girlkultur*.[15] At least since the late eighteenth century, there existed in German cultural-political discourse an opposition between the supposedly profound, organic, often German *Kultur* and a superficial and materialist *Zivilisation,* usually French or American.[16] In this context, the combination of the American Girl with German *Kultur* (and not *Zivilisation*) is counterintuitive. It acts to unite the "superficial" and modern Girl with the very traditional, natural idea of *Kultur*. The "contradictory" nature of the concept was remarked upon by at least one commentator, Dadaist Richard Huelsenbeck. Neatly encapsulating the German distinction between *Kultur* and *Zivilisation*, Huelsenbeck wrote in his review: "Even the title of the book, *Girlkultur*, demonstrates . . . an extreme misunderstanding. The work can really only be about Girl-Civilizations in that the word culture implies a duration, consciousness (*Besinnung*), and valuation of natural ties which are entirely foreign to American progress."[17] To the contrary, I would suggest that Giese did not misunderstand the import of his title.

Instead, in this provocative title, he consciously plays off this central opposition of the German discourse on modernity. Instead of constructing America and Europe according to a binary logic of opposition, his concept of *Girlkultur* begins to point towards the ways in which America and Germany are growing closer rather than farther apart. Put differently, Giese's text can be seen as an attempt at mediation between what was for him the false opposition of Europe and America in the Weimar Republic. To return to the question of race within *Girlkultur*, one might argue that although Giese's placement of the African American at the center of his discussion must necessarily be interrogated, it is equally important that one not dismiss it outright. For in it is displayed the same type of cultural mediation that he endeavored to enunciate through his combination of Girl and *Kultur*.

Adhering to sociology of the surface, Giese constructs a "pathology" of the modern through analysis of its superficial manifestations—*Girlkultur* as embodied in the Tiller Girls. "Every case has its prehistory," he writes to open his analysis, adding: "The doctor must learn from its anamnesis, if he wishes to test the results or heal the sickness. Even our 'case' is in need of recollection of the conditions which led to its fashionable behavior (*Gebarung*)" (GK 9). Here, as elsewhere, Giese's text hovers between phenomenological and normative modes of argumentation, between merely wanting to diagnose and wanting to cure modern culture. In this, he parallels Georg Simmel, for whom modern culture, though assumed to be deleterious to individual subjectivity, was to be diagnosed, not morally judged. Giese's text oscillates between a fatalistic conceptualization of *Girlkultur*, i.e., as objective culture in control of and destined to determine the future of humanity, and as an ambiguous marker of transition between past and future. Thus at times, he argues, "The metropolis has us, technology has us, the economy has us: not we them!" (GK, 27), while at others he notes: "At the same time we want to be clear that Americanism as a fashionable interest should be overcome. America has its advantages and its serious dark side. What fascinates us here as a model are only the things we lack, not those that we also or even more fully possess (*noch besser besitzen*)" (GK, 141).

Giese's anamnesis of *Girlkultur* proceeds along ten different axes of interest. Each section presents an alternate version, or vision, of *Girlkultur*: aesthetically, philosophically, economically, politically, sexually, and racially. Following the visual narrative of the illustrations discussed above, Giese concentrates in the first section, labeled "Time Movement and Rhythm," on the position of African Americans in American society. As was argued in chapter 2, the performance of the *Chocolate Kiddies* marks both a quantitative and qualitative break within Weimar jazz culture. Written in the same year, 1925, Giese's text's references to this group and their inclusion in the text's initial visual narrative provide yet further substantiation of this argument. Unlike conservative rants against a soulless, calculating American modernity, Giese's America is a brutally and racially divided society that has been formatively influenced by slavery and its colonial past.[18] According to him, contemporary American culture, society, and identity result from the complex triadic relationship between European male settlers, African slaves, and European women.

America was long seen in Europe as a "feminine" state, perhaps beginning with the earliest representations of the Americas after Columbus' "discovery," but certainly continuing in the belief that women in America possessed inordinate power.[19] The variant of this argument found in Giese is based on the idea that colonial settlements would have been largely male, making the few European women especially prized. With the introduction of slaves from Africa, however, the issue shifts from a question of pure scarcity, to one of fear. He writes: "The Negro and the white woman, this becomes a matter of prestige!" (GK 64). Giese postulates that while the Euro-American male viewed relationships between himself and African women as unproblematic, contact between white women and Black men was construed from the beginning as taboo. For Giese, the relative scarcity of white women in colonial America, when combined with an emerging ideology of "racial purity," granted white woman a disproportionate amount of power in American society. Using Giese's terminology, this situation led to the dissolution of the masculine state (*Männerstaat*) of early colonialism and to the creation of a female state (*Frauenstaat*), in which women overpowered men because of their racial value. Of the early colonial era of the United States, Giese summarizes that "in this masculine state woman was scarce. She was so scarce as today the white woman in Africa or in the colonies, as today still often scarce in areas of new oil sources or gold mines. She was a jewel, an object worthy of fierce battle" (GK 105).

At this point, the colonial past of the United States becomes not just an explanation of American *Girlkultur* but a direct corollary to the German present. With the occupation of the Rhineland by French colonial troops from Africa, the specter of interracial relationships between Black men and white women was certainly on the minds of many Germans and, as we have seen in previous chapters, an important element of German jazz discussions. Giese, as well, draws upon the similarity between this homegrown example and America's racially divided history and present. "The Negro Question and the problem of the 'Black Horror,'" he writes, invoking both German and American vocabularies of race as a problem or question, "they are related" (GK 64–65). As modern nations existing in an era of colonialism, the United States and Germany share fundamental similarities concerning the relationship between Black and white. "We know from the south," he continues, "know from the colonies, that the relationship of the black man to the white woman is something entirely different than that of the white man to the black woman" (GK 65). Again, Giese's German audience would have been familiar with his discussion of race and the role of women in (colonial) European society. Specifically, Lora Wildenthal argues that the racialized colonialist space became a site for the articulation of German women's political aspirations at home, a space in which "self-defined colonialist women used ideas of race and gender in the context of formal empire both to gain new freedoms as women and to assert German superiority over 'backward' societies."[20] Around the issue of "race mixing" in the colonies, divisions within and outside of Germany grew between those asserting the "right" of German colonialists to sexual relations with colonial subjects and others who saw in any such relations a dissolution of national and racial boundaries.

Yet if it appears as if for Giese the descendants of slaves were but psychological projections through which an American national identity could be formulated, he complicates this situation by ascribing to African Americans various forms of cultural agency. In parallel to the mediation of "Girl" and "*Kultur*" in the title, Giese's reading vacillates in its description of African Americans between the concepts of *Kulturvölker* ("cultured peoples") and *Naturvölker* ("natural peoples"). Giese states: "The Negro discovered and was the first to artistically form the new rhythm of the metropolis" (GK 29). He adds: "Not the primitive Negroes of Africa. At least not directly these, the first generation. The natural people of the black portion of the world and other foreign primitive peoples stand too close to the primal rhythm of nature" (GK 29). Placing the African American into a line of development from nature to culture, Giese positions them as existing between these two poles. Within the metropolis of the new world, the "natural people" of Africa became the "grown cultural child (*erwachsenes Kulturkind*)" of America (GK 32). Indeed, as many others had since around 1900, Giese mentions both W. E. B. Du Bois and Booker T. Washington as examples of African American intellectual achievement (GK 31). Implicit within such proclamations of advancement was quite often a paternalistic attitude that such progress was predicated upon the help of Europeans. In this, his reading of African American culture shares a degree of similarity with other writers of the period, most notably with Arthur Rundt, whose translations of African American modernist poets like Langston Hughes are discussed in chapter 6.

Here, however, Giese unexpectedly argues that such progress carries with it the possibility of critique, even revolt. He sees in jazz a form of critique produced out of interaction with the dominant white society and also, and equally, a musical translation of modernity. Put differently, jazz functions as a musical translation of the cacophony of modernity and the modern metropolis. The African American, writes Giese, "was the first person to completely, intuitively sense this rhythm of the metropolis, technology, the economic, and circulation (*Verkehr*)" (GK 31–32). With this first moment, Giese falls neatly into European theories of the mimetic capacities of "primitive" peoples, with African Americans appearing as children in a world of adults, blank slates through which the modern environment could be seamlessly translated. Yet in jazz, there also exists a critical impulse against white America and the figuring of African Americans as "second-class civilized human beings" (GK 66). More than a reflection of American modernity, jazz for Giese originates not only in the mimetic recreation of modernity, but in its peculiarity and satire:

> Peculiarity (*Kuriosität*) of the music as it is delivered (*herausgeholt*) by high-spirited students on pianos, on whose resonance boards are laid newspapers and cigarette butts and a round of beer poured on top. Satire, revenge, and irony are practiced by the Negro on this world of the whites . . . , which ostracizes, separates, and doesn't consider him a full human being and yet needs him. He imitates the acoustics of the metropolis and mimics in this way the people and their rhythm. This is the first hidden, let us say provincial bar beginning (*Vorstadtkasinoanfang*) of the jazz band. (GK 33)

The jazz band for Giese is a satire of the metropolis, an ironic enactment of the sounds through which modernity excludes and persecutes African Americans and yet ideologically (and economically) needs them. It is an expression of the repressed, repressive, and, as he suggests, "hidden," elements of modernization.

The naïve mimesis with which he had described African American interaction with white culture is gone here, or at least supplemented by his ascription of a critical agency to African Americans. Jazz is not only to be conceived of as the mechanical reproduction of the sounds of city streets but as an ironic and satirical commentary on white metropolitan culture. In this reading of jazz as, amongst other things, an African American satire of white modernity, Giese combines the reading of jazz as satire with racial critique. Jazz transforms through innovative application and material mistreatment, in the case of the piano, the very normative framework of acceptable and unacceptable sound.

Instead, as in the passage from Giese cited in chapter 2, listening to jazz music recalls for him experiences of the disruptive, fragmentary, and terrorizing side of modernity. Disjointed and discomfiting, it is brought forth via the marginalized figure of the African American. In emphasizing the underside of modernity, while at the same time refusing to seek refuge in an imagined pastoral past, jazz articulates an alternate discourse of progress and modernization. It registers both the inescapability of modernity and the danger it represents to the individual.

Yet while Giese rhapsodized on the revolutionary parody of jazz music, he was only imperfectly able to integrate it with his wider discussion of *Girlkultur* and the Tiller Girls. The uncomfortable proximity of Black man and white woman implied by his argument was perhaps too much. Towards the end of his discussion, Giese suggests that jazz has meanwhile undergone a process of "acculturation" and appropriation by imitative white bandleaders, and he specifically names the London Sonora Band, which had visited Berlin in late 1924 (GK 33). In order to place jazz within the rationalized world of the Girl, to emphasize the discipline of her rhythm over the raucous parody of the jazz band, Giese must gradually strip jazz's rhythm of syncopation.

The relatively belated entrance of African American jazz and African American revues, however, complicates this move. In other words, he needs to reconcile the fact that African American revues like the *Chocolate Kiddies* arrive in Germany only after the Tiller Girls, while according to his developmental narrative, they should have appeared first.[21] Of the appearance of African Americans on the revue stage, he writes:

> There were operetta troupes of colored peoples and one of their best performances was the *Chocolate Kiddie*s, who toured Berlin, London, and the continent even after the first appearance of the American Girls. These musically, rhythmically, and theatrically talented, outstanding Negro troupes closed the ring of development and only served to make clear how America in itself came to this novel phenomenon of the Girl troupe— amongst other things. (GK 35)

In the end, though Giese is able to explore the relationship between white women and African American males at the conceptual level, the actual encounter with African Americans in the contemporary disrupts his analysis, forcing him to close "the ring of development." It is here that one comes up against the limitations of Giese's analysis, as well as a further example of how African, Afro-German, and African American performers in Weimar could resist European exoticism and primitivism and disrupt German representations of American modernity as ultramodern and ultraprimitive.

Girls and Saxophones, or Blackness
and the Weimar Revue Stage

As I want to suggest, the origins of Giese's resistance are to be located on the Weimar revue stage. Through the performances of African American stars like Josephine Baker,[22] Louis Douglas,[23] and many others, this space quickly became a racial "contact zone" in the middle of Weimar Berlin, to use this term from Mary Louise Pratt.[24] Epitomized by the productions of theater directors Hermann Haller at the *Theater im Admiralspalast*, Erik Charell at the *Grosses Schauspielhaus*, and James Klein at the *Apollo-Theater*, the revue was an especially important form of popular culture during the mid-1920s and acted, on- and off-stage, as a site of the enactment and theorization of modernity and modernism.[25] Reflecting the move towards visuality and surface culture, the revue distinguished itself from earlier theatrical modes through a fragmentary narrative and emphasis on *Schau*, or show, over content.[26] At the same time, it is important to remember that the revue was not merely a show to be seen but also a performance to be heard and jazz and syncopated popular music its perpetual accompaniment. Theodor Lücke commented at the time: "A revue without syncopation appears almost unthinkable today."[27] Or as Alfred Polgar wrote: "Syncopation is the salt and pepper of the up-to-date dance music. And not only dance music. Syncopation is a symbol of our unruly times, the symbol of a world that has come out of time."[28] Here, I am less interested in quantifying the actual extent of syncopation within German revues and their jazz symphony orchestras, than in the framing of the revue under this term. Simply stated, my argument here is that Lücke's and Polgar's use of the term "syncopation" reveals as much about *Girlkultur* as the more common tropes of machine-like precision and/or its relation to Fordist production in relation to Weimar women.[29] Instead, like Giese's racially hybrid genealogy of the Girl, the following will attempt to sketch a counter narrative of the revue around the question of race and gender, to listen for the syncopation of the jazz band, even while seeing synchronized Tiller Girls.

In order to do so, it is first necessary to consider African American, Afro-German, and other performers of African descent as essential, rather than as ancillary to Weimar revue culture. Black performers were present within the capital (and elsewhere) throughout the 1920s and early 1930s, both individually and as part of larger all-Black casts.[30] Most notable in this regard is the series of three "Negro revues" that appeared in the capital between 1925 and 1926: *Chocolate Kiddies* in May 1925; *La Revue nègre* in January 1926, famously starring Josephine Baker, Louis Douglas, and the jazz band of Claude Hopkins;[31] and finally, the production *Black People* in July 1926, choreographed and authored by the African American Louis Douglas.[32] Though these three shows are fairly well-known, they were by no means the last. In 1928, Sam Wooding returned to Berlin with his *Die schwarze Revue* (*The Black Revue*), which premiered in Berlin's *Ufa-Palast* in June. Unlike the *Chocolate Kiddies*, this show remained but a few days in Berlin. It featured Sam Wooding's jazz band performing symphonic pieces like Gershwin's *Rhapsody in Blue* alongside jazz standards such as "Tiger Rag." According to the program, it was choreographed in part by Louis Douglas, a figure who represents one of the most important lines of continuity within this period for African American performers on the Berlin revue stage.[33] Performers listed in the program and in advertisements include Johnny Hudgins, Greenlee and Drayton, U. S. Thompson, Edith Wilson, Hilda Rogers, and Benise Dant.[34] Finally, Louis Douglas and Marion Cook starred in their revue *Louisiana,* which played in Berlin July 1931.[35] Alongside jazz music by the "Louisiana-Jazz-Band," the show included the African American performer Rose Poindexter, who was also featured in the German film *Der brave Sünder* (*The Good Sinner*, dir. Fritz Kortner, 1931).

Even later still, a unique theatrical space for Black performers was created at the *Biguine*, an entertainment establishment named after the dance of the same name, which had been popularized in 1931 through the Paris colonial exhibition and the activities of musicians like the Martinican Alexandre Stellio.[36] The Berlin bar, which advertised for itself as "Germany's first Negro-Bar," opened in February 1932 under the direction of Viktor Skutezky, a film producer involved, for example, in E. A. Dupont's *Variete*.[37] If this late date meant that the *Biguine* would enjoy an existence of less than one year, it was frequented on two occasions by modernist Max Hermann-Neisse and was referenced in the *Zeitschrift für Musik* and the satirical Munich-based periodical *Fliegende Blätter*.[38] More specifically, *Biguine* featured jazz and other performances of African Americans, such as Elisabeth Welch[39] and Louis Douglas,[40] as well as other Black performers like Dinah from Montparnasse,[41] Berthe Vitalien,[42] and others. That in 1932 Skutezky opened a bar featuring Black performers, music, and staff serves as an important reminder that Black performers were present throughout the Weimar Republic.

Beyond such large-scale examples lay further, individual cases, in particular of former German colonials and African migrants, who, often because of scarce employment opportunities elsewhere, took positions within the popular variety theaters (*Scala* and *Wintergarten*), the film industry, and in the circus acts of Hagenbeck and Sarassani, as well as in jazz bands. For some members of the Afro-German and African migrant community, the entertainment industry offered a modicum of economic stability when other work was difficult to find.[43] Similar to the situation Tobias Nagl describes for Black actors in Weimar cinema and for jazz bands in early Weimar, the names of these performers rarely surface in contemporary reviews and, because of their great mobility within the European performance circuits, appear and disappear in official registers.[44] In addition, determination of their identity can be complicated by the fact that such performers regularly took on Anglicized names such as "Jonny," "Jimmy," "King Charles," "Louis," or "Tom."[45] Still, one might mention here the case of François Benga, better known in the period as Féral Benga, a Senegalese dancer who had worked in Paris with Josephine Baker at the *Folies Bergère* and whose signature act at the time was a parody of Baker. During late 1920s and early 1930s, Benga also worked in Berlin at *Wintergarten*, at the *Atrium-Beba-Palast*, and the *Alhambra*, the latter two being primarily movie houses.[46] While working at the revue, such performers of African descent could also encounter African American performers who found themselves in one of the many revue theaters. Rarely stars in the German press, African American performers like Ralph Grayson, Fernandes "Sonny" Jones, Marion Cook, Sadie Hopkins, Ruth Walker, Ruth Bayton, and Nina McKinney performed in a variety of shows and venues and, in the case of Bayton, were seemingly able to profit greatly.[47]

If this often meant the adoption of roles that fit with the mix of exoticism, eroticism, and internationalism so typical of the revue, these representations need to be interrogated as much for what they reveal about German images of Blackness as what they conceal about them. On the Weimar stage, racial stereotyping tended to work via the types of roles offered Black performers: they were often, though not always, employed as dancers or as background figures to indicate an exotic milieu. Yet as a result, the German revue became a space of interracial encounter in which Black and white regularly came into contact, often staging the very same racialized identity formation between Black man and white woman analyzed by Giese. In the following, special attention will be paid to instances of contact between Black performers and white Girls via jazz and the saxophone. Though as discussed in chapter 1, such examples hardly constitute the first or the only examples of Black and white performers on the Weimar stage, their unique status, situated between discourses of gender, race, sexuality, and music, position them as jazz effect.

Before proceeding, I want to take a moment to explain my focus on images containing the saxophone, an instrument that by 1926 had become an important icon of jazz.[48] In each of the jazz novels analyzed in the previous chapter, the figure most representative of jazz possesses a saxophone (Lord Henry, John van Maray, and Makua-Taka). As such, it functions as much more than synecdoche for jazz *writ large*; those who possess the saxophone also symbolically possess jazz. Given the racialized construction of jazz within Weimar, Black performers were regularly depicted holding saxophones, regardless of whether they played the instrument, to signify their authentic relationship to jazz and jazz's relationship to Blackness. The example of Ernst Krenek's Jonny from *Jonny spielt auf* (*Jonny Strikes Up*) is again a paradigmatic example of this use. Though Jonny is a jazz fiddler (the entire opera revolves around his theft of a violin) and also plays the banjo, he is introduced carrying a saxophone.[49] While he will blow a few notes on this instrument in this opening scene, the saxophone has no significance for the remainder of the plot. Of course, in promotional material, Jonny was regularly depicted blowing on this saxophone in order to index his jazz bona fides. A mobile icon of the jazz republic, the saxophone proved particularly useful as a signifier of jazz legitimacy.

Given this context, it is significant that the saxophone and its attendant associations also came to play a conspicuous role within the representation of the Girl and New Woman. On the one hand, saxophone-playing Black men were regularly depicted alongside white women in both avant-garde and more popular representations.[50] If in many cases the saxophone remained within the hands of a Black performer, there exist numerous examples that depict not African Americans, but New Women playing, i.e., possessing, the saxophone. As Michael Cowan has shown, the phenomenon of the *"Saxophonbläserin"* (female saxophone player) was widespread within Weimar culture, existing in film (*Saxophon Susi*, dir. Carl Lamač, 1928), popular song (*Die Susi bläst das Saxophon / Susi Blows on the Saxophone*) and the revue, marking the "female saxophonist as the pinnacle of a new autonomous and career-oriented womanhood."[51] Indeed, images of saxophone-playing women are extremely common, such as actress Brigitte Helm in publicity stills for *Metropolis*, cabaret performer Rosa Valetti posing in a shot for the magazine *Uhu*, actress Hertha Schroeter in a photograph by Yva, a shot of the dancer Trude Hesterberg from a revue, or even in the painting "The Female Saxophone Player" by the British artist Laura Knight that accompanied Vicki Baum's serialized novel *Feme* (*Secret Sentence*) in the *Berliner Illustrirte Zeitung*.[52] These saxophone-playing New Women can be said to appropriate jazz's status as a cultural marker of empowerment, as had the male jazz protagonists in Janowitz's and Schickele's jazz novels. More than this, I would also argue that these solo performances articulate the New Woman's possession of jazz at the same time as they displace the threat of Black masculinity. At once exorcizing and appropriating jazz's Blackness, such representations are powerful reminders of race's presence within Weimar jazz culture, even when seemingly absent.

While the latter two image types, Black saxophone player with white woman and solo white female saxophone player, are the predominant modes of representation, there is one further modality. This form, which includes all three elements, the Girl, the saxophone, and a Black man, also existed in representations of the Weimar revue stage. The first example (figure 12) comes from the Haller revue, *Wann und Wo* (*When and Where*), which premiered in Berlin's *Admiralspalast* on September 2, 1927. Haller's fourth great revue of the decade, the program was written by director Haller himself, along with Rideamus (pseudonym for Fritz Oliven) and Willi Wolf, featuring the music of composer Walter Kollo. Though none of the contemporary reviews mention this fact, *When and Where* was also a revue featuring Black male and white female performers sharing the same stage.

At the same time, there is also something unique and uniquely significant to this scene's placement of a Black performer alongside the omnipresent Girls. This becomes clear when compared to standard representations of the Tiller Girls. In images like those from Giese, the Girls are depicted in a linear fashion, often encompassing the entire breadth of the image, and are presented so that the individuality of the performers becomes overpowered by their sartorial and physical uniformity. Further, the Girls typically are presented with exposed legs, preferably performing some sort of recognizable motion which functions to reference the synchronized movements for which they were best known. Frozen and desiring of reanimation by the viewer's imagination, the Girls are abstracted from the original context of performance. By contrast, in the image from *When and Where,* the Girls appear almost miniaturized in comparison to the overpowering scenery. Indeed, the set design plays a role equal in symbolic power to the action on the stage. While images of naked women were by no means exceptional on the Weimar stage, the scenery's combination of the nude woman with a saxophone is important as a further iteration of the solo saxophone-playing Girl. In addition, her slick, short hair, large bracelets, round hips, and faux banana skirt should be seen as in conversation with images of Josephine Baker and other Black performers circulating during this time. Moving down from the scenery to the Girls themselves, one immediately notices their asymmetrical grouping on either side of the saxophone's bell. In

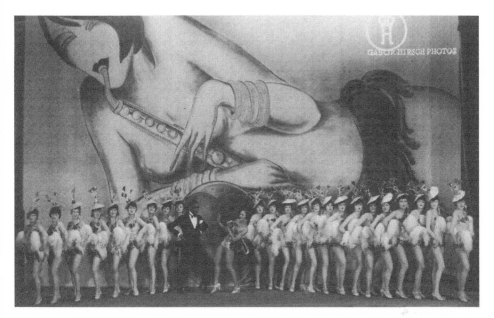

Figure 12: **Marcelle Rahna and Fernandes "Sonny" Jones in the revue Wann und Wo from 1927. Photo by Gabor Hirsch, courtesy of Dr. Hedwig Muller of the Theaterwissenschaftliche Sammlung University of Cologne.**

relation to the Black performer in the middle, the Girls are not only disrupted by his presence, they are also displaced. Temporarily removed from the logic of rationalization, the line formed by their bodies appears less refined than in other images, despite this image's obvious staging.

The fundamental importance of this image, however, is contained within the relationship between the two central figures standing in the midst of the girls. Positioned around the opening of the saxophone's bell, an instrumentless Black man stands facing a Girl holding a prop saxophone. The two performers here are likely to have been Marcelle Rahna, the revue's French star, and the African American dancer Fernandes "Sonny" Jones.[53] Jones was the long-time partner of Louis Douglas, and he had first come to Europe and Germany in the pre-war era as part of "Belle Davis and her Piccaninnies."[54] In 1917, he had also performed as a dancer in drummer Louis Mitchell's Seven Spades, an important example of early African American bands in Europe during World War I. Jones' presence in this jazz-age production is thus a further reminder of how Weimar jazz culture is marked as much by rupture as by continuity in terms of the Black presence.[55] Turning again to the image, while Jones' location vis-à-vis the oversized saxophone suggests his connection to the instrument, his physically present partner draws away from him, holding her palm up to him. What the image depicts, then, is a battle over representation, of jazz and the Girl. Though creating proximity and, indeed, contact between Black and white performers, the staging also suggests the attempt to control this.

As the foregoing has argued, the more the Girl and New Woman came to approximate her American counterpart, to not only dance to, but also perform jazz via the saxophone, the more her identity threatened to "darken."[56] Specifically, the revue performer Jenny Steiner developed an act that centered around a parody of Josephine Baker in performances between 1926 and 1929.[57] If, following Patrice Petro, one sees in the New Woman and Girl "as much a racialized as a gendered ideal," [58] encounters like that staged in *When and Where?* play off (and into) the German public's concern over the racial health and purity of white German women, the fear, for example, that these women were "becoming less motherly, both quantitatively and qualitatively."[59] Yet pushing Petro's argument a bit, one can suggest second that this racialization occurred not only along the axis of German racial purity in opposition to Blackness, but that the image of the New Woman itself bordered on a racially hybridized identity between Black and white.

Recuperating Jazz's Whiteness and the Rejection of the Black Revue

Towards the end of the 1920s, the revue underwent a period of crisis that ultimately resulted in the end of the era of the grand revues. The live, theatrical revue was gradually replaced, on the one hand, by the much more mobile and potentially more profitable sound film and, on the other, by the less modern but potentially less offensive operetta.[60] For example, Charell quit the revue business, eventually directing the grand film *Der Kongress tanzt* (*The Congress Dances*) in 1931. Haller himself put on his last revue in 1928, *Schön und schick* (*Pretty and Fashionable*) and the *Admiralspalast* would likewise turn to operetta in the early 1930s. In the midst of this period of transition, Josephine Baker returned to Berlin to star in the revue *Bitte einsteigen!* (*All Aboard!*) at the *Theater des Westens*. The music for this production was composed by Friedrich Hollaender, author of amongst many other things, the unforgettably jazzy music featured in von Sternberg's *Der Blaue Engel* (*The Blue Angel*) from 1931.

Despite the combination of these two figures, the revue was an unmitigated financial flop. As Alan Lareau argues, the show's failure was due both to the small size of the theater, the general crisis in the revue and its Blackness. He argues that the show's failure indicates that the interest in Baker had been primarily a fad and that by 1928, "the discourse of the 'primitive modernity' of blacks and jazz had already run dry."[61] Lareau is certainly correct to note that this period witnessed a significant number of attacks on jazz and Blackness, which can be seen across a wide range of issues—in the waning enthusiasm over Wooding, the negation of the jazz symphony in Weimar literature, and now in the apparent rejection of Baker. For me, however, the critiques of the late 1920s reveal less the superficial nature of the investment than their opposite, namely insecurity over the depth of connection between jazz and Weimar culture. In other words, in Baker's less than triumphal return to Berlin, one witnesses not the death knell of jazz's or Baker's relevance for Germany but a reinterpretation of the relationship.

At the same time, the turn "away" from jazz did impact the ways in which the connection between the New Woman, the Girl, Blackness, and jazz was framed. The period between 1929 and 1933 witnesses multiple voices within the German jazz discussion, who figure Black jazz and its popularity as an historical moment to be relegated to the background, an ephemeral fling with modernity, despite the ongoing presence in Berlin of African American and Black performers in revues such as Douglas' *Louisiana* or at the *Biguine*. Just as Giese tried to explain away the coexistence of Sam Wooding's Black jazz and the white Tiller Girls by suggesting the former closed the ring of development, such writers and artists push against the ongoing presence of Black performers. The 1931 film *Die große Attraktion* (*The Great Attraction*, dir. Max Reichmann) represents a case in point of this tonal shift. Ostensibly a vehicle for the tremendously popular singer Richard Tauber, the thin plot revolves around the love life of the fictional tremendously popular singer Ricardo, played by Tauber. It features numerous performances by variety show artists, acrobats, strongmen, and tango dancers (one of which is played by the famous Weimar-era actress Margo Lion). In fact, given that the film's second act takes place in Berlin's *Wintergarten,* it is likely that these represent actual performers of the period. *The Great Attraction* is thus as much filmic representation as rare document of Berlin popular culture in the early 1930s.

The manner by which Blackness and jazz are thematized within the film reveals how their relation to the Girl and New Woman were reframed for this period of crisis. Specifically, we see this in the narrative arc of the main female protagonist Kitty, played by the 21-year-old dancer Marianne Winkelstern, who had performed as a soloist for Charell at the *Grosses Schauspielhaus* during the latter half of the 1920s. During this period she performed alongside Black revue performers, for example, in Charell's 1927 production of *Madame Pompadour*, which starred Fritzi Massary and Walter Jankuhn, but also featured, in addition to Winkelstern, the African American Ruth Walker and "Snowball," whose real name was Charles Harris, an African American youth who had appeared with Paul Whiteman in New York.[62] Winkelstern's dance and revue background is put to use in the first scene of the film, which takes place at a Parisian music hall. After a series of establishing shots that overlay Parisian streets, the Eifel Tower, and blinking advertisements for Ricardo's performance at the *Casino de Paris*, the initial scene opens unexpectedly onto a shot of a blackfaced Winkelstern carrying a saxophone in her hand in a manner reminiscent of Krenek's Jonny. Wearing an Afro-wig that will soon carry symbolic importance for the film, she performs on the instrument while the background fills with a large troupe of dancing girls, later to be revealed as the Jackson Girls, one of many Tiller Girl clones of the period. The editing crosscuts images of Kitty's racialized, sexualized jazz performance with the chorus-line kicks of the Girls. In other words, this presentation telescopes the two aforementioned image modalities: the blackfaced Kitty is both the Black man playing a saxophone for white women and a New Woman playing a saxophone solo. Further, it is significant to note that her name "Kitty," both infantilizes her as well as resonates with the description of Blacks as "chocolate kiddies" following on the revue of 1925. Indeed, Rose Poindexter portrayed the Black dancer "Kiddy" in the previously mentioned film *The Good Sinner*, also from 1931.[63]

At the same time, in *The Great Attraction,* this intensification of Blackness vis-à-vis the white New Woman serves a primarily negative function in the plot. After finishing her performance, the blackfaced Kitty runs offstage, only to come to an abrupt halt as she sights members of Ricardo's entourage. Through shot-countershot editing, the viewer watches Kitty watch as she waits for Ricardo. After entering the scene, Ricardo pauses for a moment before looking directly in Kitty's smiling direction. Though the viewer registers through his pause that he has caught a glimpse of her, Ricardo does not stop and merely continues on his way. At this point, Kitty looks to her right and left and comes to see for herself what Ricardo (and the viewer) has already realized: two bare-chested Black Africans are standing next to her (figure 13). These two figures are in the far background when Kitty stops mid-run to look for Ricardo and then suddenly appear, like a trick-shot effect from cinematic history, the moment Ricardo's gaze meets hers. Turning towards first one and

Figure 13: Still from the film *Die große Attraktion* (*The Great Attraction*), 1931.

then the other Black male, she looks down at her own cosmetically darkened skin and breaks out in laughter. Now realizing that Ricardo had ignored her because he had taken her for Black, after a quick rub of her similarly black-faced cheek, she takes off her wig, revealing the white skin around her hairline.

In an inversion of the well-known scene at the end of American film *The Jazz Singer* (1927) in which Jack Robin (Al Jolson) applies blackface make-up in front of a dressing-room mirror, Kitty, now seated in front of a mirror, re-moves her blackface makeup for the audience. As Kitty continues to remove her Blackness and reveal her whiteness, we witness, through a series of cross-cuts, the first performance by Ricardo. Significantly, Ricardo is seen with a modern dance band, which includes, amongst other instruments, a saxophone. In this way, Ricardo himself can be considered part of Weimar jazz culture, a culture that, while still foreign, has become Europeanized or, rather, whitened. So if Kitty's initial performance represents the dangers of Blackness and Americanized femininity, Ricardo can be said to represent its overcoming through white male masculinity. In other words, through the opposition be-tween the "Black" jazz Kitty and the white jazz Ricardo, *The Great Attraction* stages the whitening of jazz via the prism of gender.

The interweaving of these elements continues as the plot progresses with Ricardo heading to Berlin and Kitty, leaving the Jackson Girls behind, follow-ing him. When she next approaches Ricardo on the train, she has transformed herself from the foreign, Black New Woman of Paris into a more suitable white German woman. Nonetheless, Ricardo still resists her, at this point profes-sional, advances. Her contractual obligations play a pivotal role here and even though she will impress him in Berlin through an impromptu saxophone per-formance (this time without blackface), he forbids her from officially joining his troupe until she is released from her contract by Jackson. Given that the film will end the heterosexual union of Kitty and Ricardo, the preexisting contract functions both as economic and marriage contract, with possession of Kitty transferring from one white male to the next.

It is important here to consider how jazz and its Blackness, or rather whiteness, inform Kitty's transformation. During the early 1930s in particular, numerous authors sought to account for what they viewed as a disconnect between what European jazz musicians performed and the images and sounds evoked by the word "jazz," namely Black dancing and music, especially within the right-wing and fascist politics. Here, it is useful to recall that in April 1930 in Thuringia, the Nazi culture minister Wilhelm Frick issued a "Decree Against Negro Culture."[64] This decree was largely viewed as directed against jazz and one of the ways jazz's defenders came to its aid was to distance the music from the "Negro culture" being attacked by the Nazis and others. Though as we will see in the next chapter, this type of argument does not arise in the 1930s, it does solidify during this period and, to no small degree, is due to the threat of state intervention against jazz. In one such article published in 1932, the mathematician A. Sacher-Woenckhaus sought to "defend" jazz and its associated dances by arguing "our modern dances *are not* nigger-dances anymore."[65] Indeed, this statement echoes that given by "Bruno Weil," potentially Kurt Weill, in response to the April 1930 ban on jazz referred to above: "The claim that jazz music, as it is exclusively practiced today, is Negro music, demonstrates a degree of ignorance that calls into question Mr. Frick's qualifications to carry the title 'minister of culture.'"[66] Sacher-Woenckhaus goes further, however, arguing for the progressive whitening of jazz, so that if it started out as Black, its true value lies today in the hands of white European composers. He suggests: "There are no Black Hindemiths, Honeggers, Weills, Stravinskys and others, who have shown how to master jazz, to make it into a source of unheard of tonal appeal . . ."[67] Sacher-Woenckhaus' broader point here is that the European dominance of jazz has reached the point at which the name jazz is no longer useful to describe such works; while they have been influenced by jazz and African Americans, their current form is due primarily to Europeans, and just as one today accepts previously foreign cultural artifacts like tobacco or potatoes as European, so too should Germans accept this new jazz.

Ricardo's character and his music fall broadly into line with the argument of Sacher-Woenckhaus and others: while Ricardo's music is influenced by African American culture, it is presented in a deracinated, universal, and nonthreatening form. Significantly, Ricardo's current status hides an earlier traumatic encounter with dangerous female sexuality. As the viewer learns, Ricardo's initial resistance to Kitty's advances was rooted within the trauma of his ex-wife's decision to leave him to pursue an illicit affair with another man and a career in America. It is only after Ricardo himself confronts this, his own jazz past, that his masculinity can be fully recuperated. In a scene occurring towards the end of the film, Ricardo's wife's ex-lover appears in a bar where Ricardo, Kitty, and other members of the troupe are dining. In Ricardo's rage at seeing him, he grabs the man by his coat and drags him outside of the restaurant. After the tussle, the two men leave and go to another establishment, with an appropriate text appearing on its window: "Restauration." In the following scene, the former lover hands Ricardo a picture of his ex-wife, revealed in a close-up to be a young cigarette smoking New Woman. After contemplating the image, Ricardo tosses the photograph back to him, signaling his complete break with her. Having finally overcome the trauma inflicted by the New Woman, Ricardo is now ready to return to normalcy and to do so with the equally transformed Kitty.[68] The film's final scene features a joint performance by Ricardo and Kitty of the song "Du warst mir ein Roman" ("You were a Novel to Me").[69] Yet when Kitty emerges from the back of the music hall to accompany his singing on her saxophone, the Blackness ascribed to her, to the saxophone, to the New Woman and jazz, has all but been erased.

In the early 1930s, the ideas surrounding the whiteness of jazz and female sexuality served to disperse the threat of Blackness and the New Woman that had been central to Giese's *Girlkultur* from 1925. Across a variety of cultural works, this shift can be seen as an important index of a conservative turn in German culture, something accelerated, though by no means initiated, by the Great Depression in 1929 or by governmental actions taken against jazz by the National Socialists beginning in 1930. Nonetheless, this shift had important ramifications for the German engagement with jazz in the late 1920s and early 1930s, which will be discussed in the following chapter in greater detail. Still, as should also be clear, the revue stage played a central role in the contestation and construction of both jazz and the New Woman. From Josephine Baker to Louis Douglas, Fernandes "Sonny" Jones and beyond, the African American and Black presence on the stage did not merely exist alongside, but lay at the very heart of the debate over *Girlkultur*, with the whiteness of the Girl, like that of Kitty, emerging at their points of intersection.

Rereading Kracauer and the Mass Ornament

One question arising out of the foregoing analysis is whether (and how) the connection between Blackness and the Girl entered the work of surely the most famous commentator on the subject, Siegfried Kracauer. Or, as James Donald suggestively asks: What if Kracauer met Josephine Baker?[70] Certainly, given the prevalent use of Black performers in Weimar revues, it is unlikely that Kracauer did not have opportunity to meet any number of Black performers, and so it is less a question of counter-factual history than whether he chose to document these encounters in his writings. As Hans Pehl notes, Kracauer did in fact review the performance of the African American dancers "Myron and Pearl" in late 1928, yet he did so without mentioning that they were Black.[71] Given this and other examples of Kracauer's response to Black performances discussed below, the more relevant question to ask is why Kracauer's work, in particular that on the revue, generally elided discussion of race.

Before proceeding to address this question directly, it is first necessary to look at Kracauer's perspective on the revue and the Tiller Girls. Kracauer's texts on revue culture and the Tiller Girls act, as in Giese, as an object of analysis through which to model his unique methodology for analyzing seemingly insignificant cultural ephemera like the Tiller Girls. In his 1927 "Mass Ornament," the Tiller Girls come to stand for an entire era, one struggling to comprehend the radical changes resulting from a totalizing and rationalizing capitalist system. Of course, as Miriam Hansen has recently argued, what makes Kracauer's essay so valuable is not the comparison between the legs of the Tiller Girls and hands of the workers on Ford's assembly lines, each standard tropes of Weimar-era discourse on *Girlkultur*.[72] Instead, she argues that "in contrast with either enthusiastic or lapsarian accounts, Kracauer's essay assumes a more dialectical stance towards the phenomenon, reading it as an index of an ambivalent historical development."[73] For Hansen, the Tiller Girls in Kracauer's theory are "heuristic and symptomatic": they both suggest the extent to which capitalist rationality has inserted itself into the natural world (here, the human body) as well as point towards what is missing, namely conscious understanding on the part of the audience, i.e., more enlightenment.[74] As Kracauer once wrote, capitalism's shortcoming is not that "it rationalizes too much but rather *too little*."[75] At the same time, it is precisely this functionalization of the Tiller Girls within his broader theory of modernity that lends itself to the antiseptic portrayal one often finds in Kracauer: they are synchronic, rather than syncopated, abstracted rather than contextualized on the Weimar stage, geometry machines rather than the imperfect human bodies we see in the image from *When and Where?* Closer inspection of Kracauer's texts from the period reveals a series of questions relating to racial contact that are nonetheless present within his work. While in his texts on the revue and Tiller

Girls these tend to exist as traces, other texts of his, in particular those on jazz performances and Blacks in Paris, push their presence to the foreground.[76]

Generally, and much in tune with his discussion of gender, racial difference functions primarily as an absence with Kracauer's thought. Just as the Tiller Girls cease to be feminine individuals within the mass ornament and instead serve primarily to "point [. . .] to the locus of the erotic," Africans and African Americans, as well as cultural expressions like jazz, cease to be "Black" in his work. [77] They point instead to the function of race as a sign of ideologically constructed difference. One intention behind this negation of difference is to show the global reach of capitalist rationality. With this argument, one imagines, he hopes to convince his European readers to forego the exoticist escapism of the revue or travel films and to instead focus on becoming conscious of the inner workings of their world's reality.

Kracauer's method here is to simultaneously point towards the banality of things treated as radically different by mainstream culture, while highlighting the exoticness and strangeness of mainstream, middle-class German culture. In this, he invokes the idea of a dialectics of identity in difference and difference in identity, a procedure that simultaneously serves to familiarize the foreign and defamiliarize the self in an act of enlightenment. A particularly striking example of this tactic occurs within the initial framing of his 1930 study of white-collar workers, *Die Angestellten* (*The Salaried Masses*). As Kracauer implies, the white-collar worker, at least according to a Marxist theory of development, should have been in steady decline. Yet during the Weimar Republic, their ranks swelled as much as their politics appeared to veer to the right. Yet another non-synchronous moment of capitalism, their existence is to him an example of the "exoticism of a commonplace existence."[78] Turning the tables on the white-collar workers, Kracauer writes that their daily life is "more unknown than that of the primitive tribes at whose habits those same employees marvel in films."[79] Indeed, Kracauer sees himself as a Kurtz of sorts, journeying into the heart of darkness that is the modern metropolis, suggesting that his exploration of the salaried masses' culture is "perhaps more of an adventure than any film trip into Africa."[80] This satirical and self-deprecatory gesture indicates the extent to which Kracauer's use of tropes relating to Blackness was a highly self-reflexive one, simultaneously eliding and invoking a crude dialectic of primitivism and modernity.

The most explicit example of Kracauer's ironic deployment of this vocabulary is the 1928 article "Negerball in Paris" ("Negro Ball in Paris").[81] The mise-en-scene of Kracauer's short vignette is a small, inconspicuous Parisian locale for Black Parisians in the *Quartier de Grenelle*. He uses this setting to hint at the distinction between the Black inhabitants of Paris and Black entertainers and performers, like Josephine Baker, to whom visitors flock in order to experience "exoticism." Yet, as he suggests, even these rather uninteresting Blacks of the suburbs are hunted by white tourists as entertainment game, having had to repeatedly change gathering locations in order to avoid what Kracauer calls "white curiosity."[82] For Kracauer, this is but a "futile game of hide-and-seek, as the foreigners always follow again on their heels."[83] This inversion of foreign and foreigners is central to his argument. Blacks are identified not through their difference but through their identity with their fellow Parisians. Meanwhile, the foreigners are the white (German?) visitors seeking to find their vision of Blackness reinforced through "real" experience. Throughout the text, Kracauer plays with the primitivist imagination of his readership. For example, he writes of the scene inside as being marked by the "impenetrable darkness of the haircuts, the red, green, and yellow vestments glisten like tropical flowers towards the heavens."[84] His language here mirrors the organic metaphors typically used to describe Black subjectivity. However, he inverts their normal meaning when he corrects himself, stating: "This is no Negro ball, this is a Parisian provincial ball, which just happens to be put on by blacks." In a word, these Blacks are "indigenous products," with little other than their skin color to differentiate them from other Parisians.[85] As the Tiller Girls point towards the erotic, these figures point towards the exotic, and in revealing their ideological function within the capitalist entertainment system, Kracauer seeks to disrupt the myth of Blackness within Europe and Germany.[86] Having deluded his reader into imagining the people of the hall forming an organic forest of "Black savages," he instead proceeds to unmask the European public's image of Blackness as an artificial, white projection.

Kracauer concludes his short discussion by considering the symptomatic meaning of the scene. For him, these Blacks' non-difference signals not merely the interrelation and ultimate similarity of different groups but is a "sign of the exoticism of the Parisian population, that true exoticism that cannot be derived from geography."[87] We have already encountered this double move of familiarizing the "exotic" and "exoticizing" the familiar before, namely in his better-known studies of the white-collar workers and the Tiller Girls. Yet here, Kracauer also, even surprisingly, suggests the existence of actual, rather than merely ideologically, produced difference. Kracauer's own "exotic" is neither defined by nor reducible to race; instead, his exotic is something metropolitan, modern: "Paris takes Africa into itself too. For this reason it can become a harbor for the Negroes."[88] As Theodore Rippey suggests, Kracauer potentially has in mind "Paris as exotic zone a vision of a necessarily urban, modern space, in which different groups experience continuous, multifocal [contact], and where equal cultural footing guarantees each group the freedom to appropriate any other's ways on its own terms."[89] To be sure, such a situation was hardly common, and one might counter that Kracauer's optimistic vision of the equality experienced by Africans in Paris is overstated. At the same time, both this text as well as the ethnographic framing in *The Salaried Masses* point to the important role Blackness and Black cultural expression could play in his work. Working with the same methodology employed to decipher the mass ornament, i.e., working "through the center of the mass ornament, not away from it," Kracauer deciphers the meaning of Black performance for white European audiences. While validating its desire for the exotic, for difference in the undifferentiated mass metropolis, he wants to redirect such energies by debunking the associated natural-organic vocabulary and by gesturing towards a conceptualization of modern identity that would welcome, rather than extinguish or ideologically exploit, such difference.

Still, as Kracauer would have been aware, this ideal was all but impossible given the economic, social, and cultural position of Africans, Afro-Europeans, and African Americans in Europe. Indeed, in a short review article written a few months before "Negro Ball in Paris," Kracauer himself struggles with his own fascination with Blackness, the revue, and jazz. Not coincidentally, it is a review of a 1928 performance of Sam Wooding, who was this time performing in Frankfurt's *Schumann Theater*. Though he devotes but a paragraph to their contribution to the show (which also featured Russian, French, and Chinese performers), the dancing girls, step dances, and singers do not fail to leave an impression on him. Of the music, he writes: "It rustles as if from jungles, derisive laughter brays into the sweet pianissimo and the desire wallowing in the darkness is disenchanted by loud tumult."[90] An aural analogue to match his own unique methodology, Sam Wooding's jazz sets out from the audience's primitivist inclinations only to break with them. And just as he was wont to place himself alongside the pleasure-seeking white-collar workers, here too he finds himself enthralled by the music. In a passage similar to Lion's later account of his first experience of Wooding or the discussion of the fictional jazz concert in America by Makua-Taka, Kracauer notes: "It's a hard lot to only be allowed to look; the music drives into your legs and they want do dance along at any price."[91] Of course, Kracauer doesn't dance, doesn't take part, both because of the setting and, one suspects, because he didn't allow himself to. To have danced, with the girls, to jazz, would have been to collapse what he viewed as a necessary critical distance, no matter how slight, so that he could point the way out from within.

Yet if Kracauer ultimately resists the temptation to create jazz, rather than merely enjoy it from a distance, a unique experiment in jazz was already underway in Frankfurt, little more than a mile away from where Kracauer was sitting in the *Schumann Theater*. In January 1928, the local music conservatory, Dr. Hoch's, began teaching American jazz to its German students, developing an entire program of study devoted to the music under the direction of a 22-year-old Hungarian composer Mátyás Seiber. Bringing the bar, revue, and street into its esteemed institution, the creation of the *Jazzklasse* unleashed a debate about jazz and its role in Weimar society that has few parallels.

CHAPTER 5

Bridging the Great Divides:
Jazz at the Conservatory

> Jazz could be a bridge between entertainment music and high art. For it
> makes not only in technical aspects the highest demands on the performer,
> it also demands improvisatory, in other words, real musical abilities—
> entertainment music should not be fought, it should be raised. Its eradica-
> tion would be utopia.
> —Alfred Baresel (1927)

In late 1927, the director of Hoch's Conservatory in Frankfurt am Main, Bernhard Sekles, issued a circular announcing that a program in jazz instruction, a
Jazzklasse, would begin next January at the conservatory. News of Sekles' plan
spread quickly as it moved through the daily press to the German music press,
the Prussian state parliament, and even across the Atlantic, where the *New York
Times* recapitulated the debate for its American readership under the somewhat
misleading headline, "Jazz Bitterly Opposed in Germany."[1] As the first example of post-secondary education in jazz, in Germany and in Europe, there was
something unique to this announcement from Frankfurt am Main. From the
point of view of jazz's opponents, talk of jazz colonizing German music and its
institutions no longer appeared mere idle chatter. This very real incursion of
jazz into a conservatory pointed to them to the dangers of the contemporary
moment. Both American and African, jazz symbolized the absolute worst the
contemporary musical world had to offer. Those voices supportive of jazz, on
the other hand, viewed in Sekles' plan a pragmatic approach towards adjusting
musical education to the realities of the modern music profession. Specifically,
they referred to the large number of musicians who depended on jazz and popular music for their livelihood, without, however, ever having undergone any
systematic training in such music. Interestingly, few questioned whether jazz's
translation into the academy would result in something essential about it being
lost. For most, it was of little concern whether jazz gained or lost through the

Jazzklasse. It seemed the more pressing question was rather: Did Germany and German music and musicians have anything to gain from it?

Bound up with these particular, musically oriented questions is a number of other, broader cultural thematics of the period. Sekles' announcement ignited, among others, smoldering debates about the relationship between music and race, the fate of German national identity in modernity, and the division between high and low culture. This chapter will look specifically at the latter question in order to highlight the ways in which the question of "jazz at the conservatory" became a moment of crystallization in this wider discussion. The *Jazzklasse* debate undoubtedly marks an intensification of the struggle to define the changed and ever-changing relationship between high and low culture. A central cause of much of the acrimony aroused by the *Jazzklasse* resulted from a generalized anxiety over the apparent disintegration of the boundary between these spheres of art. While such anxiety certainly does not stem exclusively from jazz, throughout the Weimar Republic, this music from across the Atlantic consistently acted to disrupt and problematize long-standing assumptions regarding the division.

As we have seen, during the early 1920s and then with greater intensity after the concerts of Sam Wooding and Paul Whiteman, jazz became a mainstay of German popular music and could be heard, often in its symphonic form, in bars, cabarets, and cafes from Berlin to Frankfurt and beyond. Equally important, however, were developments within so-called art music, symphonies, operas, and other works by contemporary composers that seemed to be drawing increasingly upon the low world of jazz for inspiration, rather than from the three Bs of Bach, Beethoven or Brahms. Paul Hindemith, Darius Milhaud, and George Antheil, not to mention Kurt Weill, all produced works inflected by what they took to be the jazz idiom. And their works were often massively successful. Perhaps no better example of this exists than Ernst Krenek's "jazz opera," *Jonny spielt auf* (*Jonny Strikes Up*).[2] Whether one would today term the music employed by Krenek "jazz," the piece was incessantly discussed under the rubric of the "jazz opera" and, for better and worse, few questioned whether this "jazz opera" was at all jazzy. Enjoying around 500 performances across cities stretching from the Baltic to New York, the seemingly unending run of Krenek's *Jonny* in 1927 appeared to have ushered in a new era in which jazz's popularity had reached critical mass. In a word, by November 1927 when Sekles made his announcement, jazz seemed to be conquering the world, both high and low, through its invasion of the concert and opera hall and now something perhaps even more sacrosanct: institutions of higher learning. The combination of jazz, a mass-produced, racially foreign cultural commodity, with a tradition-rich conservatory such as Dr. Hoch's left little doubt, for proponents and opponents, that the dividing line between the high culture of operas, symphonies, and conservatories and the low culture of jazz, jazz bands, revues, and cafés was vanishing before their very eyes.

Still, the *Jazzklasse* was never only a debate carried out in the press, a theoretical encounter over ideological abstractions. Instead, its very creation and five-year existence are testament to the concrete ways by which jazz changed the cultural landscape of Weimar Germany. In order to explain why it was in Frankfurt am Main, rather than elsewhere in Germany, France, or Great Britain that the first academic program in jazz was created, it is necessary to consider, after a short history of Dr. Hoch's Conservatory, the social impact of the hyperinflation that culminated in 1923. Next, through an examination of the writings of Bernhard Sekles, the program's initiator, both material and aesthetic reasons are presented as to why it was Hoch's and nowhere else that offered the first formal academic instruction in jazz in Germany. After which, I turn to the discussion sparked by Sekles' November announcement, with special emphasis on how the *Jazzklasse* occupied a privileged position in the crisis of the high/low ideology during Weimar. Yet, my consideration concludes not with this debate but with discussion of the activities and writings of the *Jazzklasse*'s director, Mátyás Seiber, who, through radio concerts, publications, and pedagogical innovations, practiced what so many others merely preached: the jazzing up of German culture.

A Conservatory in Crisis

In 1923, due to the disastrous effects of almost a decade of inflation, the once well-funded Hoch's Conservatory was in financial dire straits and saw itself confronted with the increasingly real threat of a state takeover of the institution. Though only four years would pass before Sekles would make his scandalous announcement, there was at the time little to indicate that this esteemed conservatory would begin teaching a low and popular music like jazz. Indeed, the conservatory movement in Germany, which began in the nineteenth century, had been pivotal to defining the boundary between high and low culture. For the creation of conservatories like Dr. Hoch's can be understood as one important element in the growth of bourgeois culture in Germany in that such institutions occupy a new space within social hierarchies. French economist and cultural theorist Jacques Attali sees the conservatory movement as belonging to a much larger process of what he calls the "normalization of the musician." By this, he means to indicate a process by which universal aesthetic forms and practices were imposed on music practices. Attali writes that conservatories "were charged with producing high-quality musicians through very selective training. Beginning in the eighteenth century, they replaced the free training of the jongleurs and minstrels with local apprenticeship."[3] Neither courtly nor sacred, conservatories grew out of the perception of a lack of professionalism and training in music with the intent to remove the stain of the dilettante from music and to transform it into a distinct and honored form of art. Conservatories thus mark a disciplining of musicians in both senses of the word. They appropriate the dispersed power of local musicians and create a system under which these institutions possess great power in the conferral of aesthetic legitimacy. Simply put, conservatories served to distinguish between those who belonged to the "higher" realm of the musical artist and those who remained at the "lower" level of untrained or amateur musicians.

As is so often the case, it was a dilettante, lacking cultural capital and thus legitimacy in the eyes of the guardians of culture, who provided the financial capital necessary for the founding of Frankfurt's first conservatory. Born in 1815, Dr. Joseph Hoch began his life in a relatively wealthy family and is said to have had pretensions to a career in the diplomatic service. He also seems to have fancied himself a musician, taking piano and violin lessons in his youth. Hoch eventually became a lawyer, accumulating a tremendous amount of wealth over his lifetime. When he died in 1874, his will decreed that were he to have no offspring (he did not), "it is my dearest wish that my entire estate serve the purpose of founding and maintaining an institute for music under the name Dr. Hoch's Conservatory in Frankfurt am Main, the city of my birth."[4] His original endowment was a tremendous sum of over 900,000 Goldmarks to be managed by a board of seven trustees. Dr. Hoch's Conservatory opened on September 19, 1878, four years after his death.

With teachers such as Clara Schumann and students like Hans Pfitzner, Percy Grainger, and Paul Hindemith, Hoch's Conservatory became a highly reputable and successful institution over the course of its first thirty years. Its enrollment increased from an original number of 139 in 1878 to over 400 in the academic year directly preceding the First World War.[5] The period between 1914 and 1923 was to be a very difficult one for Hoch's Conservatory, as it was for most such institutions in Germany. For one, it faced diminishing enrollment numbers due to the war, although it did not suffer as terribly as female students had from the beginning outnumbered male students. More importantly, the conservatory had to cope with a steadily rising rate of inflation, which began, at first only slowly, to diminish the size of its endowment.

Yet, it was not merely the economy that was impinging on the desires of the Frankfurters. With the November Revolution of 1918, the Social Democratic Party had come to power, bringing with it a general belief in greater educational opportunity for all citizens and the idea that the state was the best means to achieve this. Under Leo Kestenberg, Social Democrat and head of the music division of the Prussian Ministry of Science, Art, and Education (*Volksbildung*), a major reform of the music education system was undertaken. A musician by training, Kestenberg felt strongly that music was an essential component of a general humanist education. His overall goal, as he put it in his programmatic *Musikerziehung und Musikpflege* (*Music Education and the Cultivation of Music*) from 1921, was to help realize music's potential to create "a new humanity according to the law of community and music."[6]

During his tenure as head of the music division between 1918 and 1932, he attempted to bring about radical change in the area of music pedagogy. The so-called "Kestenberg Reforms" were in some ways an extension of the professionalization of musicians to which the founding of the conservatories also belonged. Yet this time, it worked against rather than for the conservatories. Kestenberg began by standardizing teacher training, which now required of all instructors an *Abitur*, as well as the successful completion of a state examination. To this end, Kestenberg envisioned the creation of state committees to design the test and state music colleges to prepare students for it. Of all Kestenberg's reforms, this last one was most disconcerting to private institutions like Hoch's Conservatory. In cities like Frankfurt, Kestenberg did not foresee the construction of a new school, opting instead to simply take over the existing institution. Of course, had the hyperinflation not decimated the conservatory's original endowment, there would have been much less to fear. Yet, because it was now forced to rely on the city of Frankfurt and the state of Prussia for its funding, Hoch's Conservatory had lost the autonomy from state and market that had defined its early history. Indeed, a state takeover of a previously private conservatory was not without precedence. One had to look no further than the city of Cologne. The Cologne Conservatory, which had stood since 1850, became a public institution in 1925, and Kestenberg was overtly working to achieve the same result in Frankfurt.[7]

It was under these circumstances that Bernhard Sekles became director of Hoch's Conservatory. In 1923, Sekles was appointed director of Hoch's Conservatory against the explicit wishes of Kestenberg, who had supported another candidate for the position, Hermann Scherchen.[8] Kestenberg's resistance to Sekles proved well founded. Under Sekles, Hoch's Conservatory was revitalized through a period of reform and rebirth that helped to stave off a takeover by the state until 1938, long after Sekles had been "relieved" of his position by the Nazis. One such reform was the *Jazzklasse*.

Bernhard Sekles, the *Jazzklasse*, and the Reform of Dr. Hoch's Conservatory

Before looking at the reforms put through during these years, it is necessary to understand Bernhard Sekles, who was to become a central figure in the debate about the *Jazzklasse*. Born in Frankfurt in 1872, the son of a Jewish business-man, Sekles studied under Iwan Knorr at the institution he was later to head. After successfully completing his studies, he acted for a short while as the *Kapellmeister* of the Heidelberg and Mainz Operas. Thereafter, he returned to Frankfurt, where he began teaching at Hoch's Conservatory in 1896. There, Sekles oversaw courses in music theory, instrumentation, and composition. It was in the latter function that he met an aspiring young Frankfurt musician, Theodor Adorno, who will later play a crucial role in German jazz reception and theory as is discussed further in chapter 7. Equally notable amongst Sekles' students was Paul Hindemith, who studied under Sekles between 1912 and 1913. Not merely an instructor, Sekles was also a composer in his own right, authoring works such as *Scheherazade* (1917), a three-stage opera after *1001 Nights*, the comedic opera *Die Hochzeit des Faun* (*The Marriage of Faun*) (1921), and *Die zehn Küsse* (*The Ten Kisses*), a light opera from 1926.[9] His earliest work revolved around the *Lied* and it was in this general arena that he produced what was to be his most famous work, *Aus dem Schi-King* (*From the Shijing*), op. 15 (1907), a cycle of eighteen songs for high voice and piano.[10] As can be gleaned from the titles of these works, Sekles drew consistently upon an imaginary East for inspiration, be it Eastern European, Middle Eastern, or Asian. Further, from the few theoretical writings left by Sekles, the image of music that emerges from them is one defined by his concept of nature, which Sekles declares to be the ultimate aim of all music. As he writes in his unpub-lished *Grundzüge der Formenlehre* (*Fundamentals of the Theory of Form*), "The organism is the highest miracle in nature as well as art."[11]

This proclivity for the natural qua exotic other will surface again in the announcement for the *Jazzklasse*. In it, Sekles will use the metaphor of blood transfusion to describe the transfer of jazz from the new to old world. Although it appears he never wrote explicitly about jazz outside of the announcement, Sekles did in fact compose at least one jazz-influenced piece. Contained in the

1927 *Das neue Klavierbuch* (*The New Piano Book*), this song, "Kleiner Shimmy" ("Little Shimmy") is demonstrative of the fact that Sekles was potentially more than casually interested in jazz and jazz music.[12] More important in this context are his comments on what will later become a central issue for defenders of the *Jazzklasse*: improvisation. In *Fundamentals of the Theory of Form*, Sekles points out that what differentiates an improvised piece from one composed in advance is precisely the formers' lack of form. "Improvisation," he writes, "is a skill of the *moment*. With it, therefore, the time to form the received is lacking."[13] In other words, the perfection of form achieved in the works of great composers cannot be achieved in the improvised work. At the same time, this does not mean that improvisation is without musical validity. Sekles argues: "That which it [the improvised piece] lacks and must necessarily lack in final formal boundaries (*Formgebundenheit*), it replaces in greater or lesser degree through the *musical mental readiness (Geistesgegenwart)* of the improviser."[14] The musical justification of improvisation comes from the act of the performance, from the performer's intellectual and/or spiritual presence, his/her bodily and mental quick wittedness.[15]

This appreciation for improvisation, coupled with Sekles' Orientalist inclinations, constitute essential components of the conditions of possibility for the *Jazzklasse*. While by themselves insufficient, they reveal a certain level of receptivity to the idea of teaching jazz at a conservatory. Equally necessary, however, was the fiscal crisis of the post-war years. For without the hyperinflation, it is highly unlikely that the reforms undertaken by Sekles would ever have come about. In response to the Kestenberg reforms and the conservatory's need to improve its financial situation, Sekles instituted an internal reform of the conservatory's structure. He resurrected the conservatory's orchestra, founded an opera school at the conservatory, and, as a countermeasure to the Kestenberg reforms, in 1926/27 offered courses designed to prepare students for the state examinations. As he wrote on the occasion of the fiftieth anniversary of the conservatory's existence: "An art institute that ignores the legitimate demands of the times ultimately loses its connection with reality and thereby simultaneously its right to exist."[16]

It is then as part of this broader set of institutional reforms that the decision to offer a program in jazz can best be understood. That such a program would be controversial was without question, though it is hard to believe that Sekles had even the faintest inkling of the scandal his decision would provoke. Be that as it may, Sekles personally authored the announcement, and in November 1927, he sent copies to an unknown number of publications, though the

Zeitschrift für Musik, Deutsche Tonkünstler-Zeitung, and *Der Auftakt* reprinted the advertisement in full. Addressing the question of jazz's place vis-à-vis the music establishment, he begins:

> Does a seriously conducted conservatory have the right to erect a program in jazz?
>
> Not only the right, but even the duty, assuming that the head of this program is not any slick jazz drummer (*geschickter Jazz-Schläger*), but has studied jazz on-site, i.e. in America. More than this, he must possess a most thorough general education and above all have at his disposal masterful compositional technique as well as possess the pedagogical ability to systematize the material in a progressive manner. Today, more than half of all musicians are forced to regularly or occasionally play in a jazz ensemble, without ever having learned it. Jazz accordingly appears in a distorted image that goes far towards explaining many people's aversion to it. Of course there are nasty excesses in jazz, and Siegmund von Hausegger is correct, when he publicly protests that included among these is the jazzing of the motifs of our great symphonic masters. He is incorrect, however, to judge an aesthetic branch against its degenerations. Not only for opportunistic reasons, but also for pedagogical ones can a *cultivated* (*gepflegter*) jazz be of use to the youth.[17]

Adorno once described the Sekles' compositional style as one of "mild exoticism,"[18] a description that goes to the heart of the conceptualization of jazz expressed here. Sekles' thought straddles the two worlds of the folkish and primitive and technical mastery. This ambivalence, this position between "high" and "low," structures the announcement as it slides in and out of these worlds. Sekles begins by contesting the belief that jazz and conservatories are inherently opposed and asserts not only that he is justified in his actions, but that he sees the teaching of jazz as an ethical duty. Part of Sekles' reasoning here remains pragmatic. If, as he says, more than half of all musicians are already playing in jazz ensembles, should they not also be educated in the correct way of playing it? By offering a program in jazz, one could ensure a higher quality of the music that will be played, regardless of whether there is a *Jazzklasse* or not.

To this practical and pragmatic argument, he couples the idea of taming jazz, of creating a cultivated form of jazz. While he does not clearly delineate this concept, such jazz would most likely have been a version of Whiteman's symphonic jazz. As Sekles' thought remained torn between his desire for the organic, natural, and unaffected and his adoration of form, the announcement for the *Jazzklasse* balances these two sides of his musical personality by incorporating the exotic in a highly technical manner. Further evidence of this ambivalence is demonstrated by his discussion of the ideal program head. Sekles derides the "slick jazz drummer" and says instead that the person must not only be a classically trained musician, but also have experienced jazz firsthand in America. As we will see, the man who eventually headed the *Jazzklasse*, Mátyás Seiber, could claim to fill both these requirements.[19] Acquiring such a person, Sekles hoped, would dispel the idea of jazz as a chaotic, revolutionary music that must necessarily signal the end of dominance for European and German music within the conservatory.

It is easy to see Sekles as a hero of jazz fighting against the reactionaries who rejected his plan. However, any such romanticization of the progressive and sympathetic Sekles falters under the weight of his own language. In the second half of the announcement, he writes:

In the creations of our day an increasingly abstract-speculative moment is coming to light. Here, only a transfusion of unspent nigger blood, if mediated by a tactful musician, can be of aid. For music without any impulsiveness (*Triebhaftigkeit*) does not deserve the name music any more. If jazz is a good pedagogical means for the producer, then it is to no less a degree for the reproducer. Though difficult to explain, it is a fact that the German, who after all has achieved the highest in music, demonstrates conspicuously little joy in the *rhythmic*, despite the fact that it is generally recognized that rhythm is to be seen as the pulse of all music. One can, however, view the sense of rhythm as a special discipline—in other words, removed from all the other musical elements—in that it can be taught only inadequately. No one knows this better than the head of a conservatory who can continually observe how students perform the most neck-breaking rhythmic arts in gymnastics without, however, it ever having the least use value for their musical practices. Jazz, on the other hand, is so totally constituted by the rhythmic that, under a superior and systematically led practice, it can develop the rhythmic feeling in an incomparably surer way. Dr. Hoch's Conservatory wants therefore to be *the first* to attempt, with sufficient enrollment, to form a program in jazz. The instruction will apply not only to the typical jazz instruments, as they are: drums, saxophone, banjo, trumpet, and trombone, but also to practicing ensemble

performance. Eventually there should also be a corresponding vocal program connected. Instruction begins in the middle of January 1928. Bro-
chures can be requested from the offices of Dr. Hoch's Conservatory.[20]

Like many before him, Sekles saw contemporary music as hyper-rationalized
and overly abstract, perhaps even overly civilized. Implied here is that the *Neue
Musik* (*New Music*) of Schoenberg, as well as the *Neue Sachlichkeit* of his
former student Hindemith, has led German music down the false path of abstraction. Against this, jazz could function as a transfusion of cultural vitality,
promising to bring with it a spontaneity, even carnality, absent to him in contemporary German art music. Not just the stylized version as he felt his own
compositions to be, in jazz he felt he had found an "unspent," untainted, pure
source of vitality. For Sekles, then, jazz was to become part of the academy, not
as an equal of European music but as raw material to be turned into a finished
product. Despite its revolutionary call for the inclusion of jazz at the conservatory, in many ways, Sekles' announcement remains true to the ideal of the
conservatory: to create a distinction between artist and amateur, between high
and low.

The *Jazzklasse* Debate

Nonetheless, jazz's opponents immediately saw in the announcement a direct
attack on German culture and music and seized upon Sekles' wording and
the transfusion metaphor in particular.[21] Already by late November, a chorus
of disapproval issued forth from the conservative press. Sekles' call for a
"transfusion of unspent nigger blood" was explicitly quoted and referred to
ad nauseam, supplemented by a hefty bantering about of racial epithets
against Africans, African Americans, white Americans, and Jews. Deriding
the *Jazzklasse* as another example of Germany suffering under a "Black Horror," cultural reactionaries rejected Sekles' claims about the faltering rhythm
of German music, and it was this debate that caught the attention of the
broader public, including the Prussian state parliament and the *New York
Times* referred to at the outset.[22]

Alongside such ad hominem and ill-informed rants, there proceeded another, equally revealing debate. This concerned the question of whether *Unterhaltungsmusik*, or music for entertainment, belonged at all in the halls of conservatories, private or otherwise. Sekles' announcement raised a number of

important questions relating to jazz and its status vis-à-vis European art music. For example: Is it necessary to teach jazz music to "serious" musicians? Further, is all entertainment music to be banned from the conservatories? Finally, what is, in fact, jazz? Is it African or American, a *Volksmusik*, art music, or merely a commodity?

One of the first to react to Sekles' circular was the conservative *Allgemeine Musikzeitung*, which published a piece by Paul Schwers entitled "Jazz als akademisches Lehrfach!" ("Jazz as Academic Subject!").[23] Schwers vehemently rejects Sekles' arguments and demands that the latter "justify" himself: "How will you justify yourself now? *You will have to do so*, if your name is not to suffer permanent damage."[24] The personalization achieved by Schwers was generative of a split within the debate. On the one hand, there existed personal, often anti-Semitic, attacks on Sekles, while on the other, a discussion of jazz's contribution and relation to European music took form.[25] In the attacks of Schwers and many others, one again sees the linkage of Blackness, jazz, and Jewishness encountered in Renker's novel *Symphonie und Jazz*. It is, moreover, an element of German jazz reception that will reach fever pitch in the reaction to the operetta *Schatten über Harlem* by Russian-Jewish dramatist Ossip Dymow to be analyzed in the following chapter. Following a strategy of bonding Jewishness to Blackness (and vice versa) as a means of rejecting popular culture, Schwers denies jazz any aesthetic value.[26] Employing the same organic language Sekles had used in the announcement, Schwers demonizes jazz as a plague and chides him for wanting to help bring the "filth of the every day" into the conservatory.[27] Referring to the many German musicians who play jazz, he writes:

> It is hunger which drives by far the most to choke down this repulsive nigger food [. . .] These young people will tell you that even a "cultivated jazz" cannot be the object of academic instruction. For every musician, as far as he is prepared for public ensemble performance can without difficulty master the essentially stereotypical rhythmic structure of jazz music, which incidentally is not and can never be music in the pure sense. In the best case it is a music substitute: rough and in the long run an abhorrent, superficial surrogate (*widerlich anmutendes Surrogat*).[28]

The racialized descriptions of the economic situation will repeatedly be called upon to reject the *Jazzklasse*. To Schwers, jazz is merely another example of how high culture is no longer able to remain "above" the everyday, profane, and racially other world of popular music. Schwers' description of jazz as an impure surrogate can be read as an attempt to redraw the boundary between high and low and, at least partially, to do so along racial lines.[29]

Schwers' attack on Sekles and jazz did not go unnoticed, and counterattacks came from both the practical and theoretical side. For the professional musicians who read *Der Artist*, jazz was much more than an ideological bogeyman; it was an artful means to earn a living. It is hardly surprising then that Schwers' words hardly struck a chord there and were severely criticized by Leon Lencov. Reprinting Schwers' comments for his readers, Lencov writes: "The presumption is hard to resist that while Paul Schwers is unquestionably well versed in many musical matters, he has occupied himself with jazz only in a most superficial manner."[30] Further, from the *Frankfurter Zeitung* came another positive response. In his discussion from November 25, 1927, music critic Karl Holl highlights three positive aspects to the idea of the *Jazzklasse*.[31] First, he maintains that the *Jazzklasse* could be valuable not only in "raising the general standard of the culturally much too little attended to entertainment music, but also in the strengthening of the German musician's relatively underdeveloped rhythmic sense."[32] Like Sekles, Holl sees jazz as a means to invigorate German music. Against nationalist conservatives like Schwers, he ironically adds that it is only through the adoption of an "unspent foreign substance" that degeneration through musical incest is to be averted.[33] Lastly, Holl valorizes the effort to bring folk and serious music together. He argues that anyone who fully grasps the contemporary situation in music,

> will still have correctly understood the great severity of the problem of folk art and high art, entertainment music and intellectual music, when, as in the present case, the attempt at a bridging of that opposition, lamented again and again as a "tear" in our cultural situation, is introduced with inadequate propagandistic means.[34]

Though without embracing what he sees as Sekles' unfortunate choice of vocabulary, Holl does view the *Jazzklasse* as an opportunity to revisit the oppositions within music between high and low culture. It is an attempt to repair the torn halves of art, to bridge, in other words, high with popular culture.

Yet this recognition is coupled with the disdain Holl exhibits for Sekles' conceptualization of jazz as art in the strong sense of the word. In this, the liberal Holl and the conservative Schwers are united. "Jazz," he writes, "is truly not to be placed on the same level as our received forms of art music. It is, if we wish to use the concept responsibly, as it has been handed down by our great cultural tradition, not musical art at all, but . . . *'musical arts and crafts.'*"[35] Holl reproaches Sekles for overestimating the aesthetic value of jazz, seeing "dangerous irony" (*gefährliche künstlerisch-ethische Spitze*) in Sekles' concept of cultivated jazz.[36] Unlike Holl, Sekles appeared to judge all works of art by the same fundamental premise; that they should strive to reproduce the ineffable formal beauty of the natural. Sekles cared little from where it originated, whereas Holl, although positively reacting to jazz's use as a bridge between entertainment and serious music, wished to retain a conceptual distinction between art and the economy.

Each author can be seen as representative of a different bridging strategy available to Weimar-era commentators. In the case of Sekles, one encounters a strategy of "Romantic reaction," while in Holl, one sees an attempt at what I wish to call "bourgeois reconciliation." Sekles represents a strategy of Romantic reaction in that his organic concept of art and culture signify a desire to overcome the division between high and low through recourse to an idyllic, even atavistic, precapitalist unity of art and nature. This form of bridging seeks to unite high and low through a circumvention of their division in capitalism. Romantic reaction calls for a return to a form of art that is capable of unifying the two realms. To be sure, Sekles had been forced to recognize their ultimate unity largely as a result of the incursion of the economy into the academy, something that explains much of the tension between his practical and aesthetic grounding in the *Jazzklasse* announcement. Ultimately, however, his conception of art elides these economic aspects in favor of the notion of art as natural organism.

Holl's mode of argumentation, conversely, is indicative of a strategy of bourgeois reconciliation in that while he desires a unification of the two realms, he envisions this process as taking place under the hegemony of high culture, much like the authors of the symphonic jazz novels previously encountered. While he appears to argue for an equalization of the relationship, for Holl, the *Jazzklasse* also signifies a moment for high culture to reassert its dominance over popular culture. Central here is his idea that low culture and non-European cultures in general have little to add to high culture. At best, they can allow Europeans to regain lost or forgotten aspects of their past. In the *Jazzklasse* debate, the primary example of such remembering was the lost ability to improvise that was now to be regained through jazz.

In response to the debate generated by his announcement, Sekles issued a second declaration to clarify his original position.[37] This second circular avoids any reference to the blood transfusion metaphor and instead concentrates on the gains to be made from the inclusion of jazz in formal music education.

First, Sekles repeats his argument that regardless of one's personal opinion, one cannot ignore the fact that a high percentage of contemporary musicians is forced to play in a jazz ensemble without being either stylistically or technically prepared.[38] Second, he raises for the first time the issue of improvisation, which will later become a centerpiece of the defense of the *Jazzklasse*. Expanding on his original statement that jazz could serve to bring rhythmic joy back into German music, he now states that instruction in jazz could be used as a means to relearn the lost art of improvisation. "For the reproducer it [jazz] represents the most vital means of rhythmic education known to me. Furthermore, it revives the capacity to improvise which has almost become lost to us."[39] The ability to improvise is recast in this second statement as a primary quality of jazz, which, to the European, is something not foreign, but forgotten. Mixing his own Romanticism with the bourgeois sensibility of Holl and others, Sekles' turn towards improvisation in this second statement marks an important shift within the debate.

While Sekles and the *Jazzklasse* continued to be critiqued from the conservative camp, his argument that jazz ought to be conceived of as a means to revitalize German and European music found support with the progressive music critic Heinrich Strobel.[40] In "Unzeitgemäße Proteste" ("Untimely Protests") from the modernist periodical *Musikblätter des Anbruch*, Strobel maintains that jazz is valuable insofar as it not only has engendered a return of rhythm to German music but also a return of improvisation. Citing Hindemith, Stravinsky, and Weill as examples of high art that would be unthinkable without jazz, Strobel praises the incorporation of jazz into art music. Of improvisation specifically, he notes:

> The art of improvisation which was jettisoned in the 19th century is reborn in jazz. We have known for a long time that it is not so much about the piece itself, but about what the jazz band makes of it. The jazz band demands creative activity from the individual. It awakens the joy in elemental music making. It is a sign of accountability vis-à-vis our time when a leading conservatory takes up these problems of today.[41]

Strobel's impassioned defense of jazz and the *Jazzklasse* does not necessarily view jazz as existing on a distinct plane from European art music. Nonetheless, Strobel as well falls at times into the strategy of bourgeois reconciliation in that, in the final analysis, his justification of jazz assumes European primacy in music. In other words, the joy in rhythm and the art of improvisation that are to be found in jazz are desirable primarily as remnants of the European past. In a sense, one might say that for Strobel, what the civilized European has forgotten, the barbarians of jazz will allow them to master once again.

In the attention paid to the European elements of jazz, one sees evidence of an attempt on the part of these liberal defenders to come to terms with the transformation of music and art under capitalism. By arguing that one could return via jazz to a musical quality believed to have been lost to progress, supporters were able to point towards an alternative vision of modernity, one not completely determined by the market or racial others. Developing this idea most fully was Leipzig music critic Alfred Baresel, a figure previously encountered in the discussion of Paul Whiteman. A prolific writer, Baresel wrote numerous articles on jazz and entertainment music and authored the first German-language study of jazz music in 1925, *Das Jazzbuch (The Jazz Book)*.[42] Through his *Jazz Book,* as well as numerous other essays, in many ways Baresel became Weimar Germany's authority on jazz music. Given his stature, it is not surprising that on two separate occasions he commented on the scandal in Frankfurt, first in the *Neue Musik-Zeitung* and then in *Melos*.

Predictably, Baresel entered the debate as a defender of the *Jazzklasse* and attempted to dispel certain myths about jazz propagated by the program's antagonists. He begins his article from the *Neue Musik-Zeitung* by suggesting that only through music education can the split between high and low be bridged. To him:

> The baleful division of our present music in edifying and entertaining can only be bridged through pedagogy . . . . This division is especially noticeable today in Germany, where the extremes are marked by the small intellectual circle around Schoenberg and the large art-averse masses, on whom musical influence is possible *only* at places of entertainment.[43]

For Baresel, contemporary music has split into, on the one hand, an intellectualized form characterized by Schoenberg, and, on the other, the *Schlager*-consuming masses. In this situation, he argues that it would be best to raise the level of music at such establishments to that of high art. At the same time, he makes clear that, for him, entertainment music has certain advantages over art music, especially in the area of rhythm. Equally important in this regard is the economic side of the argument, namely, because German musicians are not entirely competent in the field of entertainment music qua jazz, they have suffered financially. "For years," he writes, "German musicians have been waging a difficult battle against the preference for their foreign colleagues, who because of more thorough, specialized training (*Durchbil-*

dung) are mostly superior."[44] In other words, a program in jazz such as the one planned by Sekles could enable them to compete more ably against their non-German competition.

This defense of the *Jazzklasse*, oriented as it was towards the practical advantages to be gained through education in jazz, was supplemented by a second, more ideologically charged article in the journal *Melos*. In this second article, "Kunst-Jazz" ("Art Jazz"), Baresel focuses specifically on the relationship between jazz and art music, seeking to determine the extent to which jazz has already been absorbed by European art music. To a certain extent presaging Sacher-Woenckhaus' later argument, Baresel begins by commenting:

> I do not see anything more or less in the dust raising decrees of the Frankfurt jazz conservatory than the first, extremely necessary attempt to put control back into the hands of responsible music authorities over this, in the final instance inherently foreign, but no longer removable entertainment art.[45]

The watchword here is control. For him, pure American jazz is less an expression of musical development than a reflection of a society in transformation. It is mass music for the masses. Referring twice to jazz's "sporty" quality, Baresel maintains that it has been left up to Europeans to make jazz into "actual" music.[46] Already before the war, he argues, Debussy's ragtime pieces displayed the impact of African American music on Europe. Baresel thus repositions later pieces like Stravinsky's ragtime works, not as belonging to a post-war invasion from America but as an extension of an already existent trend in European, especially French, art music. Of this, he writes:

> Jazz, as it came to us from America, was . . . in many ways already permeated by elements of the new art music, namely of the French kind. Even its most characteristic instrument, the saxophone, is of French invention. [. . .] The motoric element attributed to jazz, the stomping rhythm amongst the syncopation is found just as well in Stravinsky and Bartok's gravitation towards indigenous folk music (*Hinstreben zur heimatlichen Folklore*).[47]

The emphasis here on the European elements of jazz can in part be read as overcompensating for the depiction of jazz as foreign and barbaric, as "international" and "anti-German." Yet, it is equally evident of an attempt by Baresel and others to reassert European mastery against jazz.

In raising jazz from mere entertainment to European art form, there is not only a desire to avoid the fate of atonality and its unpopularity with the populace at large but to circumvent the colonization of European music by racial others. As he wrote in the passage cited at the beginning of this chapter: "Entertainment music should not be fought, it should be raised. Its eradication would be utopia." The potential utopia Baresel glimpses in jazz's eradication is one in which the deleterious effects of capitalist production on European music are negated through a reinvigoration of the European high cultural tradition. Such a turn was only possible, however, through the strategic reconfiguration of improvisation as European. Through the idea of improvisation, jazz enabled liberal critics like Holl, Strobel, and Baresel to postulate the rebirth of a European past once thought destroyed but that could now be regained through the modern entertainment music known as jazz.

Interrupted Crossing: The *Jazzklasse* between Theory and Praxis

Despite the vehement protest, Sekles carried on with his plans and the *Jazzklasse* opened in early 1928. Enrollment in the program hovered around 15, and, through the activities of its director Mátyás Seiber, made substantial contributions to the local Frankfurt music scene. Still, after but a five-year existence, it was forcibly closed in April 1933, and its Jewish faculty members notified of their impending dismissal. As with other short-lived examples of Weimar jazz culture, it is crucial that we recognize the *Jazzklasse* as much for its five years of existence as for the debate recounted above and its inevitable closure. As such, I would like to conclude with a consideration of the jazz practices of the program and its director.

Mátyás Seiber's biography is fascinating, yet in many ways also typical of this period's jazz innovators.[48] Hungarian by birth, his particular path led first to Budapest and Zoltán Kodály, where he studied Hungarian folk songs. After completing his studies, but before landing at Hoch's Conservatory, Seiber took a temporary position as a musician on a transatlantic ship's orchestra and worked for a few months in late 1927 on a ship of the famous Hamburg-America line. [49] Though it is highly unlikely that Seiber procured an education in jazz on these short travels between Hamburg and New York, they are nonetheless important reminders of the flow of peoples, cultures, and ideas across the Atlantic in the period. More interesting in terms of Seiber's engagement with popular music were his associations with the *Südwestdeutscher Rundfunk (Southwest German Radio Station)*, or *SWR*, based in Frankfurt. Beginning in 1925, *SWR* had its own jazz band, which was led by Paul Hindemith's brother, Rudolf.[50] At its peak in 1927, *SWR*'s jazz band played weekly on German radio, though in years afterward the regularity of its performances dropped off noticeably.[51] The radio also supported professional, non-academic music from the *Amar Quartett*, which premiered a "Jazz Dance Concert" in September 1926.[52] Even before taking over the *Jazzklasse*, Seiber participated in two small ensemble formations, the *Caféhaus Trio* and the *Lenzewski-Quartett*, the former headed by Erich Itor Kahn and the latter by Gustav Lenzewski, many of whose members were also part of *SWR*'s house band. Thus, by the time Seiber took over the *Jazzklasse* at the beginning of 1928, he not only had a claim of having years of practical experience but could demonstrate thorough knowledge of European classical and folk music. Each of these traits came into play over the course of the next five years; these years witnessed the *Jazzklasse* presenting its and Seiber's work to the public through performances by his students, which in a few instances were broadcast on the radio.[53]

Yet even before then, Seiber entered the ongoing debate on the program in a 1928 article "Jazz als Erziehungsmittel" ("Jazz as Educational Method") published in *Melos*.[54] Deftly extricating himself from the dominant terms of the debate, Seiber is the first to ask whether instruction in jazz is at all possible. As other defenders, he points to the great number of musicians who are already playing and for whom jazz instruction certainly would do no harm. But this argument remains too abstract, especially for someone who must develop a program of academic training in what had up to this point been an informal, commercial practice in Europe. The difficulties of systematizing the study of jazz into different courses and instructional principles are potentially in his mind when he writes that, in addition to the provocative question of whether one should teach jazz, one must add: "whether one *can* instruct jazz (and *how* one can do this)."[55]

Seiber next discusses the rhythmic particularities of jazz and from there moves onto the art of improvisation. For both these aspects, Seiber argues on the basis of cultural, rather than racial, difference. He sees rhythmic syncopation in jazz as, for the most part, determined by the creation of *Scheintakte*, or "pseudo-measures," a concept later taken over by Adorno.[56] As Seiber wrote in his *Schule für Jazz-Schlagzeug* (*Manual for Jazz Percussion*):

One group among the shifts of accent is of particular importance, one which stands out for its regularity. For example, if in a row of 4/4 measures one continuously emphasizes every third quarter-note, in this way an impression of many 3/4 measures is produced. Thus are created a form of "pseudo-measures" against the original measures. These are of extraordinary importance for jazz.[57]

Seiber later served as jazz expert to Adorno for his essay "Über Jazz" ("On Jazz") from 1936, and Adorno will make much of the false, apparent, or pseudo-character of these measures. Yet for Seiber, the term "pseudo-measure" is less an ideological critique of jazz's originality than an attempt to frame jazz rhythm for a German audience unfamiliar with it. In other words, this concept makes jazz rhythm understandable through its translation into preexisting European musical vocabulary. In this regard, it is also important to note that Seiber places quotation marks around this term. It is as if he were aware of the terminology's insufficiency, yet unable to proceed without it. In "Jazz as Educational Method" and his jazz manual, Seiber consistently emphasizes the incompleteness of the study of notes and repetition of rhythms. For him, these are necessary, but not sufficient, to jazz performance.

Seiber further develops this position in his comments on improvisation. Though to a certain extent Seiber also relies on the idea of jazz as a reawakening of improvisation, his execution of the argument is unique. Seiber's essential point about improvisation, and one that reinforces his faith in the idea that jazz can be taught and is not an "inborn" ability, is that improvisation, too, can be instructed. The problems with improvisation that seem to plague Germans and not Americans (he does not specify white or Black) have to do with the context of musical instruction in Europe. As he writes:

Certainly the Americans do it [improvise] entirely "unconsciously," i.e. similar to the way the Gypsy in Hungary decorates the melody, plays around "by ear," adds "countermelodies," etc. But we must consider that the American grows up in the middle, so to speak, of this music. He hears it resounding from every street corner, before every store, every house, through speakers, gramophones or in the orchestra itself. This music plays in America the role of a sort of "folk music" and "popular music," it has its own tradition and through the repeated acts of hearing "sits" in the strictest sense of the word in every American's "blood."[58]

It is important to read Seiber's use of the "blood metaphor" in relation to its use in the *Jazzklasse* debate by Sekles, Schwers, Holl, and others. Though seeming to rely on an assumption of naiveté within non-European cultures, it is also evident that Seiber wishes to signal the fundamentally questionable nature of such concepts through his repeated use of scare quotes. As with the term "pseudo-measure," Seiber's text carefully navigates, albeit without transcending, the given framework of the debate.

Another powerful example of such ambiguity is contained in Seiber's references to the use of improvisation in the European past. This section of his argument comes after his cultural definition of improvisation. He begins by looking to European handbooks on improvisation from the sixteenth century. These he sees as analogous to the current use of such handbooks within jazz instruction in Germany, for example his own *Manual for Jazz Percussion* published a year later. Seiber is acutely aware that learning improvisation through a handbook would seem to be a contradiction in terms. Yet what critics of German jazz practices in the 1920s often miss, and conversely what Seiber recognizes here, is that, given the dependence on the written note in European musical life, it was perhaps unavoidable that the path to freeing oneself from notes had first to begin with them. As Seiber himself puts it, these handbooks and their formulas for improvisations and breaks are "naturally only a teaching aid for beginning . . . , both today and in the past; the ultimate goal towards which one strives was and is . . . to gain such practice in the matter that the book is no longer necessary and one is capable of playing in an impromptu manner."[59] This piece is perhaps the most optimistic of Seiber's. Written at the beginning of his career in jazz instruction, at a time before the economic slump and the rise of the Nazis, it displays a rare openness to jazz and the music's aesthetic potential.

Seiber, like so many others, shifted his position on jazz during the final few years of the republic, and scholarship on Seiber's jazz writings has sometimes focused its attention on later, more skeptical moments in his work.[60] Yet here, one must be attentive to the fact that the general tenor of writing on jazz during the late 1920s and early 1930s would take a critical turn, with many voices declaring the jazz revolution of the early and mid-1920s to be at an end. For example, composer Alban Berg, who would incorporate elements of ragtime into his work, most notably the later *Lulu* opera, responded to Sekles' plans that while he found the idea laudable, he feared jazz's time was already past.[61] Or as Seiber himself wrote in 1930, "Jazz has its stormy youth behind it. It stands now in the mature 'prime of its life.' We ought not expect many surprises from it."[62] Seiber's position here can not only be compared with that of Berg, but also with that of Kurt Weill, who in 1928 proclaimed that "today we are doubtlessly standing at the end of the epoch during which one could speak of the influence of jazz on art music."[63] Yet Weill closes his essay with a demand that jazz practices, in particular of collective music making, be used to break apart the "rigid system of musical practice in our concerts and theaters."[64] Like Weill, Seiber's "negative" comments regarding jazz belie his continuing faith in jazz's potential for development. Yet while Weill's thoughts remained at the level of abstraction, Seiber developed a theoretical and practical basis for achieving such a jazz breakthrough.

In his 1931 article, "Jazz und die musikstudierende Jugend" ("Jazz and Youth Music Learners"), Seiber follows up on his earlier claim of jazz having left its wild childhood behind, claiming that the music has entered a "quieter, more measured, and more orderly phase of life."[65] Indeed, he at first seems to abide by a developing undercurrent of German jazz criticism during the early 1930s that jazz's Blackness is a "fable" rather than fact, yet another element of Seiber's writings later propagated by Adorno.[66] If Seiber here diminishes the Black contribution to jazz, he is equally concerned with debunking the essentialized ideology of Black jazz that embraced groups like The Revelers and Singing Sophomores as "Negro Quartettes," only later to learn they were just "conventional (*bieder*) whites."[67] As in his other writings, Seiber is as much concerned here with the proper production of jazz as he is with its conditions of possibility. For him, America's vanguard position in jazz music has nothing to do with race but with the American "milieu," put another way, the social context. "Playing jazz well is not . . . a question of race, but one of familiarization. The German musical youth can—or rather could—play jazz just as well as the American, if the *conditions* were the same as in America."[68] While he understands that conditions in the two societies and cultures will never be identical (nor does he feel they should be), there are specific measures that can be taken to raise the level of German jazz. This begins for him with the creation of a jazz milieu, a "'jazz culture'" in Germany.[69] He suggests that this is already happening to an extent in bars and other entertainment establishments across Germany where jazz has become part of the lived environment. But, argues Seiber, it is also necessary to promote its creation through training like that offered by the *Jazzklasse*, because, as he rightly claims, the public will only take jazz seriously when German musicians take it seriously.

One of the primary means through which Seiber and the *Jazzklasse* aspired to take jazz seriously and thereby change the public perception of the music was through radio broadcasts. The *Jazzklasse* presented itself for the first time in a radio concert on March 3, 1929. The program featured various Tin Pan Alley tunes like "Igloo Stomp," "Miss Annabelle Lee," and "Virginia Stomp." It also featured Stravinsky's "*Suite Nr. 2*."[70] Amongst the performers for that first concert was the German-Jewish musician Eugen Henkel, playing banjo and guitar. Henkel later became a significant figure in popular music and jazz during the Third Reich.[71] After praising Henkel's performance in particular, the reviewer from Frankfurt's *General-Anzeiger* concluded: "It was a nice success . . . for the new jazz program and for all future Paul Whitemans, Jack Hyltons, and Bernhard Ettés. Maybe you'll even make it to 'Jazz Doctors.'"[72] A "symphonic jazz concert" then took place on February 20, 1930, featuring Gershwin's *Rhapsody in Blue*, selections from Weill's *Dreigroschenoper*, and *Jazzolette*, an original composition by Seiber. This same concert was then offered as a matinee performance on March 11, and nationally broadcast on the *Berliner Funkstunde*.[73] Yet another appearance of the Frankfurt *Jazzklasse* occurred in November 1931.[74] Additionally, Seiber and in all likelihood the students of the *Jazzklasse* were part of the performance of the German-version of Vivian Ellis and Richard Myer's operetta *Mr. Cinders* (German title: *Jim und Jill*) when it debuted in Frankfurt in December 1931, and also took part in numerous performances of Brecht and Weill's *Threepenny Opera* in Frankfurt's *Neues Theater* in October 1928.[75]

If these concerts and Seiber's own compositions from the period indicate that his approach to jazz was heavily indebted to Whiteman's symphonic jazz rather than African American jazz musicians, they equally reveal a high degree of public engagement on the part of Seiber.[76] Through these concerts, locally and nationally broadcast as some were, the *Jazzklasse* remained in the public eye long after the fury of the initial debate had subsided. In what was for him an extremely positive review, Adorno wrote of the first concert: "The *Jazzklasse* of Hoch's Conservatory, which brought its initiator, Sekles, so many stupid (*töricht*) attacks, introduced itself to the public under the extraordinary and knowledgeable leadership of Mátyás Seiber and legitimated itself splendidly."[77] The concert also provided the opportunity for Adorno to comment on the already cold *Jazzklasse* debate. Against the attackers of Sekles and Seiber, Adorno maintains that jazz is an unavoidable fact of contemporary music culture and that without question jazz will have a positive effect on the reproductive capacities of German musicians. At the same time, he relativizes jazz's importance and hints that with the *Jazzklasse*, i.e., with jazz as a pedagogical subject, the music no longer seems as modern as it once did.

Yet, the ultimate significance of the *Jazzklasse* may not lie with such radio concerts or reviews but with the program's students themselves. Along with their teachers, the students who came through the *Jazzklasse*'s doors were daily dedicating themselves to jazz.[78] As such, I would like to conclude with a moment of unique insight into Seiber's pedagogical method, which comes in the form of a November 1932 article on the *Jazzklasse* from the *Frankfurter Zeitung*.[79] Written on the eve of Germany's descent into National Socialism, the tone of this piece betrays little of the high stakes associated with the earlier debate. Quickly rehashing the now-forgotten scandal, the text reveals what a typical hour of instruction at the *Jazzklasse* looked like. It describes how Seiber stood before the class, directing its members with various commands: to repeat a particular passage, go over a section without the melodic line, repeat it again, but this time now only with the horn section, etc. Seiber emerges in the piece as a demanding and serious instructor, someone who expects as much of his jazz students as he would of classical musicians. Tellingly, it suggests how serious the issue of jazz remained for him.

Perhaps most interesting, though, is the reference to the "real" instructor of the class: the gramophone. Seiber's instructional method was to have his "syncopators," as the article calls the program's students, repeatedly and intensively practice with each other as described above. Yet, the moment of truth was not faithfulness to a text or to Seiber's ideas alone. For afterwards, the group sat in a circle around a record player, listening to a jazz record, comparing it with that which they were playing and answering technical questions from Seiber about the piece as performed on the recording. The article does not reveal which jazz album the students were practicing to, and it is unlikely to have been a name like Duke Ellington, Fletcher Henderson, or Louis Armstrong. But, to paraphrase Seiber's comments about the jazz culture he was aspiring to create with his class, it might have or, more precisely, could have been had the experiment of the *Jazzklasse* not been cut short, forcing this emerging jazz culture into hiding and exile.

Still, Sekles' and Seiber's *Jazzklasse*s had a long-lasting effect on Frankfurt, Germany, and, indeed, European jazz history. Part of this jazz culture in hiding was Frankfurt's *Hotclub Combo*, a formation that included two students from the now jazz-less Hoch's Conservatory,[80] Carlo Bohländer and Emil Mangelsdorff (brother of the world famous jazz trombonist Albert Mangelsdorff).[81] More to the point, one of the *Jazzklasse*'s actual students, Dietrich Schulz-Köhn, became a pivotal figure of the German jazz scene, both during and after the Third Reich. Though he never officially became a "jazz doctor" as the reviewer of the first concert by the *Jazzklasse* had suggested might occur, he did choose "Dr. Jazz" as his moniker and purchased letterhead to reflect this.[82] I reference him here because during the 1950s, Schulz-Köhn was also a player in yet another rediscovery of Weimar culture in the Federal Republic. While visiting the United States in late 1957, he acquired the address of the African American poet Langston Hughes. Though he wasn't able to personally visit Hughes at that time, he began corresponding with him after returning to Germany. It was as "Dr. Jazz" then that Schulz-Köhn sent Hughes clippings from German articles in which the poet's name had been mentioned. In one letter, Schulz-Köhn tells Hughes that he and his wife have been working to make Hughes' poetry known in Germany.[83] Though Hughes doesn't mention it in his response, he was certainly aware of the German interest in his work. Indeed, he had been corresponding with German-speaking fans like Schulz-Köhn since the 1920s when his jazz and blues poems, and with them the African American modernist movement known as the "Harlem Renaissance," first became known to a German-speaking audience.

CHAPTER 6

Singing the Harlem Renaissance: Langston Hughes, Translation, and Diasporic Blues

> The mood of the Blues is almost always despondency, but when they are sung, people laugh.
> —Langston Hughes (1927)

In June 1932, "loaded down with bags, baggage, books, a typewriter, a victrola, and a big box of Louis Armstrong, Bessie Smith, Duke Ellington and Ethel Waters records," the African American modernist poet, jazz and blues fan Langston Hughes embarked from New York on a trip that eventually took him across the Soviet Union, Central Asia, and, for one, maybe two nights, to Berlin, Germany.[1] Already widely recognized as one of the most important poets of the New Negro modernist movement also known as the Harlem Renaissance, Hughes set sail with a small group to film "Black and White," a Soviet-financed depiction of racism in the United States. On this journey, Berlin and with it Weimar Germany were but temporary stops and his first experience of the German capital was not a particularly positive one. About this "wretched city," he later commented: "The pathos and poverty of Berlin's low-priced market in bodies depressed me. As a seaman I had been in many ports and had spent a year in Paris working on Rue Pigalle, but I had not seen anywhere people so desperate as these walkers of the night streets in Berlin."[2] Yet it was also in Berlin that Hughes came to experience the African American presence in Germany. At the *Haus Vaterland*'s Turkish café, Hughes observed a Black waiter pouring coffee, whom he describes as a "Blackamoor in baggy velvet trousers, gold embroidered jacket and a red fez."[3] Assuming him to be African, none in his group attempted to speak to this foreigner in a foreign land, but when the waiter heard the group speaking English, he burst out: "'I'm sure

glad to see some of my folks!' [. . .] 'Say, what's doing on Lenox Avenue?'"[4]
If Hughes relates no further information regarding who the waiter was or why
he was in Germany, the presence of this Harlemite in Berlin can stand in for the
current state of knowledge regarding the Weimar encounter with the Harlem
Renaissance and its jazz poet laureate Langston Hughes: virtually unknown,
often misrecognized, and yet there, waiting to speak.[5]

Indeed, the German translation of Langston Hughes began in 1922, at a
time when Hughes was but 21 years old, long before he became a dominant
figure of African American poetry, and it continued almost unabated until
1933. Translators of the period were particularly attracted to his work—all
told, there were seventeen different translators of his poetry into German, who
produced more than sixty individual translations of his work. To be sure, these
are not evenly distributed, neither chronologically nor geographically—most
were published between 1929 and 1931 and had at least some connection to the
Austrian capital, Vienna. Still, the poems, their translators, and the various
modalities, personal, textual, and political, by which German-speaking authors
came to engage with his work have much to say to us. They speak not only
about the importance of Hughes and Harlem for Weimar culture but also about
the need to develop new methodologies to account for cultural transfer and
translation in the interwar period.

For one, the interpenetration of jazz, blues, and other forms of African
American music in Hughes' work shows how the impact of jazz, in America
and Germany, was by no means limited to music alone. So if discussion of an
African American poet would at first glance seem misplaced here, it is important to recall the broader categorization of jazz in the 1920s: as music, as dance,
as drum, but also as art and culture. In other words, we would do well to heed
Hughes' claim in "To a Negro Jazz Band in a Parisian Cabaret"—that jazz has
"seven languages to speak in / And then some."[6] More concretely, like no other
artist associated with the Harlem Renaissance, Hughes embraced jazz and the
blues in his work as a means of validating the originality and value of African
American vernacular culture. As Brent Hayes Edwards writes of this poem:
"The many languages in the poem are a means of apprehending a music so
intimately concerned with dialogue and exchange among a group of performers and the audience that it can be approached only through a kind of critical
multilingualism."[7] Indeed, German interest in jazz and interest in Hughes and
the Harlem Renaissance reciprocally reinforced one another, regularly bleed-
ing into each other through the translation of Hughes, "the original jazz poet."[8]
Tobias Nagl writes of the interest in jazz that it "was conceptualized in the best
of circumstances as a means of communicating to Europe the political and

cultural emancipatory movements of the Black diaspora, the Harlem Renaissance, Pan-Africanism, and Civil Rights Movement."[9] And yet a monolingualism nonetheless rules over current scholarly discussions of jazz in Germany, a mode of inquiry in which German jazz reception can only ever include reactions to jazz music, rather than the culture of jazz; its fans; and, as I argue here, its poetic language. Breaking out of this monolingualism, this chapter will attempt to learn how to speak one of jazz's languages, that of African American modernist poetry.

For one, Hughes' suggestion regarding the polyglot nature of jazz can be taken to also refer to the fact that jazz has always existed in multiple places and forms at the same time. Just as the famous jazz bands and African American revues of the period did not impact German cultural history alone, but rather the entire American and European continent, so too should it come as no surprise that the German translation of Langston Hughes weaves in and out of European national boundaries.[10] Indeed, Hughes' peripatetic life in many ways mirrors that of his translators, many of whom were of Jewish descent. Born to communities that after World War I had lost their prior national belonging or migrated to one of the major German-speaking metropolises like Berlin or Vienna, they often found themselves caught between national boundaries during the interwar period. More to the point, Hughes' poetry and its call for self-recognition and empowerment resonated particularly powerfully with many German-language translators, be they Zionist, socialist, or otherwise affiliated.

Specifically, I want to suggest that in the German translations of Langston Hughes and other poets of the Harlem Renaissance, German-language writers of Jewish descent took part in what Edwards calls an act of diasporic reciprocity. "Reciprocity," for Edwards,

> is less an originating appeal that is answered than a structure of mutual answerability: articulations of diaspora in tension and in dissonance, with necessary resolution or synthesis. [. . .] Diaspora can be conceived only as the uneasy and unfinished *practice* of such dialogue—where each text both fulfills the demand of the other's "call" and at the same time exposes its necessary "misrecognitions," its particular distortions of the way race travels beyond the borders of nation and language.[11]

At the most basic level, the diasporic reciprocity of the Jewish and African diasporas is evidenced in the personal contact between Hughes and three such translators (Hans Goslar, Arthur Rundt, and Anna Nussbaum), even while such individual contact never meant that the translators or their translations were without prejudices, of nation and language. That the diasporic reciprocity of the Jewish and African diasporas was both a point of contact as well as conflict is not particular to German-language translations of Hughes but is rather, as Edwards shows, the very definition of the practice of diaspora.

The most significant moment of diasporic reciprocity between Hughes and his Central European translators of Jewish descent occurred via the translators' focus on the multivalent idea of voice. In this focus on the voice, Hughes' translators repeatedly showed themselves to be exceptional. While much writing on jazz and African American culture shares a focus on the ineluctable rhythm of the jazz band, its saxophones and drums, Hughes' translators instead tended to focus on the human voice and its expression in song. Voice should be understood here musically, but it is important to recognize how voice could be understood politically—as an agent of self-assertion in the face of constant oppression, as protest against pressure to assimilate, and, finally, as a call to value one's origins. As one commentator, the Austrian writer Else Feldmann noted, these works of poetry showed how African Americans "are no longer dependent on someone white coming and 'representing' them. They, the 'savages,' sing their life themselves and they don't sing it any less beautifully than the best whites."[12]

Yet if Hughes' translators for the most part avoid direct reference to jazz, their work reveals a potentially even deeper engagement with jazz and the culture from which this music springs. So if it is often not jazz that dominates their work, then it is the culture and music standing behind jazz—what Hughes calls "that tune / That laughs and cries at the same time"—namely the blues.[13] The blues are a foundational aesthetic of Hughes' work, both in terms of form such as in his blues poems and also in terms of an overarching ethos of African American culture.[14] This blues disposition of Hughes' work is perhaps best expressed in the lyric: "When you see me laughing, I'm laughing just to keep from crying." This combination of laughter and tears, comedy and tragedy was essential to Hughes' deployment of the blues and jazz. Against a view of African American culture as one-dimensional, either comic or tragic, Hughes' poetry works dialectically, imbuing the frenetic rhythms of the jazz band with tragedy and the languid despondence of the blues with comedy. This message was undoubtedly heard by his translators and their focus on voice and song invoked this dialectical sense of the blues not only implicitly but, as we shall see, quite explicitly. As the translation of the African into the Jewish diaspora, as an example of the sounding of repressed voices in Weimar culture, the significance of the translation of Langston Hughes into German is hard to overestimate. On the one hand, it opens up study of the African American diasporic voice within Weimar culture by the revealing of the tragi-comic blues song behind the joyous dance of the jazz band. On the other hand, it offers a moment to theorize the relationship between African American and Jewish diasporic identities in the interwar period. In sum, the translation of Langston Hughes into German is a call to view in the exchange and contact between an African American modernist and his Central European Jewish interlocutors a complex and contradictory act of communication.

"Negro": From Harlem to Berlin and the Rhine[15]

In January 1922, *Crisis*, the main periodical of the NAACP published its third poem by Langston Hughes. Entitled "Negro," it was to become one of Hughes' most famous works and can today be found in almost all anthologies of his work. Hughes himself would shortly thereafter end his time as a student at Columbia University; meet Alain Locke and Countee Cullen; and eventually embark as a seaman for Europe, Paris, and the West African coast. In the meantime, he floundered financially, searching for a job in a city still very much closed to African American workers but embraced the culture of Harlem, its cabarets, and jazz. Then in April 1922, something curious happened. Hughes learned that one of his poems had appeared in a Berlin newspaper.[16] Ironically, or better yet tellingly, Hughes' poem had traversed the Atlantic before he had himself and long before he ever visited Berlin.

This first translator of Hughes' work was Hans Goslar, at the time a senior civil servant within the Prussian government and later press secretary of the Prussian ministry of state. Born to a German-Jewish family in Hannover, Goslar was known at the time equally as Zionist and journalist. Through important, if controversial, works like *Die Sexualethik der jüdischen Wiedergeburt* (*The Sexual Ethics of Jewish Rebirth*) and *Jüdische Weltherrschaft! Phantasiegebilde oder Wirklichkeit?* (*Jewish Dominance of the World! Figment of Imagination or Reality?*), Goslar was a recognizable public figure within Berlin and a strong supporter of Weimar democracy. Arriving in New York on December 28, 1921, during his travels in America Goslar sent home articles about American life and then collected these in his travelogue *Amerika 1922*.[17]

Goslar's activities in the early 1920s are themselves indicative of the widespread interest in the United States by Weimar Germans. Many journalists and authors went to the United States in this period and returned home with strong impressions of this land of "unlimited possibilities" and, in the process, produced a staggering number of publications.[18] Learning about and speaking to African Americans was an important part of the travel itineraries of many visiting German writers. As the impact of the Great Migration became unmistakable in northern urban centers like New York, acquainting oneself with African American culture meant trips not only to the American South but, above all to the wondrously unique "black city" Harlem, as it was described in many contemporaneous accounts. Such interest may have peaked in the late 1920s, but, as Goslar's early texts show, it was present from the very beginning and in dialogue with the early jazz enthusiasm of Siemsen and Tucholsky discussed in chapter 1. For example, the important journalist and theater critic Alfred Kerr undertook his own visit to New York in 1921. While there, he witnessed a major moment in the history of Black musical theater, Noble Sissle and Eubie Blake's *Shuffle Along* at Daly's *63rd Street* theater. *Shuffle Along* was an important step not only in Josephine Baker's career, who wowed German audiences in 1926, but also in Adelaide Hall's, who performed with the *Chocolate Kiddies* in 1925. As Kerr presciently wrote of *Shuffle Along*, it "is at once striking . . . and inward. At once entertaining . . . and deeply felt — A symbol of the future?"[19] Still, it was not only Goslar and Kerr who took note of Harlem, two further articles appeared in the *Vossische Zeitung* in 1922, discussing its Black millionaires and the new sense of racial empowerment expressed in movements like Garveyism.[20] So while Goslar's inclusion of Hughes may be the earliest known German translation of his work, its treatment of African American culture and the city of Harlem was by no means isolated or unique.[21]

Like many other translations of Hughes into German, Goslar's was not published as a stand-alone work of poetry. Instead, his setting of Hughes' poem was embedded within a broader, journalistic account of African American culture and society, first within the April article "Der amerikanische Neger" ("The American Negro") and then later within his travelogue.[22] In his chapter "Afrika in U.S.A.," an expanded version of the article from April, Goslar attempts to dispel any number of prejudices against African Americans, both those of Europeans and of white Americans. Though his tone tends towards paternalism, referring on more than one occasion to the childlike nature of African Americans, his argument is more historically than racially rooted. For him the fact that African American children tend to do well in early grades, only to falter in later ones, is "a given with a race that has not yet been intellectually trained, one unaccustomed to mental work."[23] Goslar further argues that differences between whites and Blacks in political, economic, and social matters are shrinking and that, for the most part, it is only a matter of time and opportunity before they disappear. He ends his section on the African American in the United States calling for "the complete emancipation of Negroes and the systematic education of this group of 11 million to morally full-fledged, socially and politically equal Americans."[24]

Goslar's interest in the struggles of African Americans did not emerge from mere curiosity alone. As a German-Jewish Zionist, it was also personal and political. He takes note of a tendency within the African American community towards a self-understanding as belonging to a wider community of Africans living in diaspora. "Even if the great majority of American Negroes feel themselves thoroughly rooted within their home country and there do not remain many traditions of the homeland," he suggests, "there nonetheless exists in many circles a general feeling that is not dissimilar to what is happening today under the name Zionism amongst the Jews of the world."[25] Both the growing Pan-African movement and the awakening of racial pride in the African American community following the war struck a chord with his own experiences as a German Jew.

In this, Goslar's writings fit the mold of "Jewish traveling cultures" outlined by historian Nils Roemer. Looking at works by Arthur Holitscher, Joseph Roth, Egon Erwin Kisch, and others, Roemer traces the development of travel writing by Central European Jews to Eastern Europe, Palestine, America, and the Soviet Union as a "cultural practice that involved transcending cultural, political, and national boundaries."[26] While traveling necessarily involved reflection about differences between the foreign and the home, for German-speaking Jewish writers like Goslar, "traveling became more often a search than an experience of homecoming that testified not only to a great deal of curiosity but betrayed a profound sense of not feeling at home at home."[27] In other words, Goslar's notes about African American cultural strivings can also be read as a reflection of the lack of acceptance he would have to face when he returned home. Given the June 1922 murder of Walther Rathenau, the German-Jewish industrialist and presiding foreign minister, it was a struggle that remained all too present for German-Jewish writers like Goslar.

Yet if the connection drawn by Goslar between Zionism and the Harlem Renaissance was one typical concern of the translators, so too was the framework by which he sought to understand Hughes' work: music and voice. Unlike so much of the early jazz discussion, which focused almost exclusively on rhythm, Goslar frames his account of African American musical achievement via the voice. It is thus not only as a poetic work of art but also as a "little song" that he offers his "loose translation" of Hughes' poem "Negro."[28] Tellingly, though many changes to sentence structure and wording are present throughout the translation, it is the fourth stanza on music that Goslar most radically alters. Compare Hughes' words on the left to Goslar's translation on the right.

I've been a singer:	Aber immer hab' ich gesungen,
All the way from Africa to	Auf dem Wege von Afrika nach
Georgia I carried my sorrow	Georgia ertönten meine
songs.	traurigen Lieder.
I made ragtime.[29]	Und dabei tanzte ich im
	Rhythmus.[30]

Curiously, the translation gives music an almost greater power than it holds in the source text. The addition of "aber immer" ("but always") to the opening line marks the musical voice as a continuing source of resistance to the oppression that surrounds it. Goslar's gloss on the musical genre of ragtime, *"Und dabei tanzte ich im Rhythmus"* ("and I danced around to the beat"), is equally telling because it is less a future point in the development of African American song than an act taking place in parallel.

For a variety of reasons, I want to argue that Goslar's setting of Hughes' "Negro" follows what translation theorist Lawrence Venuti has called a domesticating, rather than foreignizing, method of translation. Following Friedrich Schleiermacher, Venuti distinguishes between "a domesticating method, an ethnocentric reduction of the foreign text to target-language cultural values, bringing the author back home, and a foreignizing method, an ethnodeviant pressure on those values to register the linguistic and cultural difference of the foreign text, sending the reader abroad."[31] Most striking in this regard about Goslar's translation is that while each stanza of Hughes' poem begins with "I" or "I've," the German translation does not once begin a line with the equivalent, transforming, for example, the first line "I am a Negro" into "Ein Neger bin ich" ("A Negro am I").[32] Later translators like Anna Nussbaum will not follow him in rigid adherence to German stylistic rules; and with good reason. Though Hughes' original poem structures the identity of the lyric "I" through its copula with "Negro," this equation is part of a complicated enunciation of African American identity that takes place in and against a temporal element. In Goslar's rendition, however, the individuality of the poem's lyrical subject is diminished through this series of inversions that, when taken together, act to place an ahistorical racial identity over individual, historical subjectivity. While this is in tune with Goslar's use of the poem as a demonstration of the feeling of solidarity with Africa, of Pan-Africanism qua Zionism, this abstract framing of the Black subject will take on a different tone when the political stakes of the context shifted from the left to the right.

Attesting to the broadening interest in African American culture that already existed in the early 1920s, Goslar's Zionist reading of Hughes was to be ripped out of its context and inserted into a proto-fascist critique of the French occupation of the Rhineland in Georg Widenbauer's "Die schwarze Weltgefahr" ("The Black Threat to the World") from 1923. As discussed in chapter 1, the French occupation of the Rhine, which began in 1919 and continued until 1930, involved some 80,000 soldiers in total, of which between 30,000 and 40,000 were African. It will further be remembered that the debate was marked by a vitriolic comingling of racial, national, and sexual metaphors, leading to discussion of the occupation as a violation and defilement of the nation. In "The Black World Danger," Widenbauer sees in the occupation more than German suffering at the hand of Blacks. He argues instead that it marks but the first stage in a worldwide revolt of non-whites against whites. "By itself," he writes, "the Black Horror encompasses only a part of the horror facing the entirety of white humanity, should the black race awaken."[33] For Widenbauer, the African American is the pivotal figure in this awakening of the Black race as he is representative of not one but two victors of the war: American modernity and non-white races.

It is into this racial phantasmagoria of globalized Black rebellion that Widenbauer plunges Goslar's translation of Hughes, though, significantly, without attributing the translation to the Jewish Goslar. At the same time, Widenbauer's text, like Goslar's, contains surprising moments of identification with Hughes and African Americans. As he writes to introduce the poem: "We understand the deep melancholy that speaks from the sorrow song of the American Negro Langston Hughes."[34] Just as Goslar had set up a parallel between Jews and African Americans, Widenbauer implicitly places the white German and the African American on equal footing, as both are, at least to him, victims of the victors. Commenting on Hughes' poem, he writes: "This sorrow song of blacks breathes life not only from an insatiable longing for the motherland Africa. Alongside this homesickness there resounds in the soul of the black resentment (*Groll*) over his previous oppression as well. From this, he creates the indestructible hope of throwing off his yoke of oppression."[35] Were one to replace in this passage "Black" with "German" and "Africa" with "Germany," it could very well describe the revanchist sentiment of right-wing radicals regarding the occupation and loss of eastern territories after the Treaty of Versailles.

At the same time, Widenbauer's argument as a whole and the presence of Hughes in particular act to reestablish distance between white Europe, Black Africa, and a racially suspect America. Again revealing the crucial role played by music within Hughes' German-language reception, though Widenbauer makes but two changes to Goslar's translation, they both occur in the fourth stanza on music. First, he Germanizes the proper name "Georgia," which Goslar and later Nussbaum retained. By turning "Georgia" into "Georgien," he thereby furthers Goslar's domesticating strategy and replaces a clearly American location with one that also carries connotations on the European continent. More significantly, Widenbauer removes the point of origin, Africa, from line 11, which now begins *"Auf dem Wege nach Georgien"* ("On the way to Georgia") rather than "All the way from Africa to Georgia."[36] Through this deletion, Widenbauer's translation abstracts Black musical culture from any specific historical context. Hughes' poem had insisted that African musical traditions have not only been preserved in spite of the arduous journey wrought by the Atlantic slave trade but have developed (from sorrow song to ragtime) and become historical. In sum, Widenbauer's subtle alterations act to figure the African American as a dancing "Negro" from nowhere, always on a journey, always the same, and always marching in a foreign land *a la* Germany's Rhineland.

"I, Too": Of German Mimicry and African American Originality

In the mid-1920s, travel to New York, and by extension also to Harlem, continued. This led to a number of further cases of Hughes appearing in the German press in both translated and untranslated form.[37] The most significant examples of the translation and transmission of Hughes in the mid-1920s derive from Arthur Rundt, a German-Jewish journalist born in Katowice, today in Poland, but at the time part of the disputed territory of Upper Silesia. Rundt himself was an especially mobile figure, spending much of the early twentieth century in Vienna before finally emigrating to New York where he passed away in 1939. His life and works exist between and beyond Germany and Austria, an element characteristic of many of Hughes' translators. It was in 1924/25 that he undertook his first trips to New York, arriving on April 20, 1924, and then returning on January 17, 1925. During this period and afterward, Rundt wrote extensively for German-language newspapers and journals between Berlin and Vienna on issues related to America. More importantly, it was through his travels and writings that he came personally to know Alain Locke and Langston Hughes. Between 1927 and 1929, Rundt corresponded and met with Locke, in both New York and Washington, D.C., where Locke was a professor at Howard University.[38] Sending his greetings to Hughes in one of his letters to Locke, Rundt also seems to have met

Hughes personally on at least one occasion.[39] Yet while in New York, Rundt not only met with African Americans but gave a lecture at the New York Labor Temple based upon his recent trip to Palestine.[40] As such, one can count Rundt as well as belonging to Roemer's "Jewish traveling cultures," whose third main destination, the Soviet Union, Rundt also visited.[41] Finally, note should also be made here of Rundt's attempt to publish a German edition of Locke's seminal anthology *The New Negro: An Interpretation* with one of the most important German publishers of the period, the S. Fischer Verlag. Though this project did not come to fruition, Rundt's personal contact with Locke and his attempt to publish a translation of this central work of the Harlem Renaissance yet again show how German knowledge and engagement with African American culture were rarely produced within a vacuum.[42]

Unlike Goslar or Widenbauer, Rundt generally portrays African Americans not in terms of their difference from the American mainstream but in their similarity to it. Harlem may excite him as "a complete, enclosed social machinery . . . , a black city,"[43] yet it is not the city's Blackness, but its Americanness, ultimately meaning its whiteness, that fascinates him. Rundt's interpretation of African American culture is that it is fundamentally determined by a need to mimic and recreate white culture. As he writes: "Over and over again there sounds in the speaking and writing of the Negro this passionate cry of blood: for sameness (*Gleichsein*)."[44] "Sameness" for Rundt oscillates between demands for political and social equality and a racially rooted drive towards cultural assimilation. Yet while Rundt does retain the idea of "blood" race as an ultimate marker of difference, the assimilation of African Americans to (white) American culture is part of his general interpretation of American culture as the result of racial contact and hybridization. As Dorothea Löbbermann writes, "The culture of modernism (*Moderne*) in which creative people come into contact with each other and with their audience is for Rundt the result of a racial mixture to which African Americans have made decisive contributions."[45]

In total, Rundt translated five pieces of African American poetry and published them, along with numerous references to Hughes' work in periodicals and newspapers in Prague, Vienna, Berlin, and Frankfurt.[46] Yet, it is his translation of "I, Too" that is most deserving of mention.[47] Again highlighting the speed with which Hughes' poetry was translated into German—while "I, Too" debuted in America in March 1925, it was already being read in Rundt's German translation in May of that very same year. More importantly, Rundt uses his translation of "I, Too" as the lynchpin of his interpretation of African Americans as mimetic. Indeed, he employs the English title "I, Too" as a *leitmotif* throughout these writings. For example, in his article "Die schwarze Welle"

("The Black Wave"), Rundt constructs a parallel between the concept of mimicry and Hughes' title, writing: "*I, too! I, too!* Mimicry! Mimicry."[48] While in his travelogue *Amerika ist anders* (*America Is Different*), he glosses the title by writing: "'*I too! I too!*'—'I also want to be like that! I too.'"[49] In yet a third context, he notes: "The '*I too*' of the American Negro, the call for sameness (*Gleich-Sein*), the will to mimicry is most clearly present in the New York Negro quarter Harlem."[50] In point of fact, it is hard not to suspect that for Rundt, the "too" of Hughes' title was also to be understood as its English homophone "two," in which the African American "I" is but a doppelgänger of the white American.

Accordingly, Rundt's translation of the poem revolves around and resolves into mirrored pairs. Though slight variations exist between the published versions of his translation, in all, he adds the words "I, too" to the end of the first line of the poem and consistently punctuates this new sentence with an exclamation mark. Rundt also adds an exclamation point to Hughes' line 13. These additions may make the poem seem more overtly political, but in their repetitiveness, these screams also read as childishly impertinent. In a more substantive manner, he achieves this mirroring effect through alterations to the structure and language of the second stanza of "I, too." These become especially clear when Rundt's translation is compared with Hughes' source text.

Tomorrow,	Morgen
I'll be at the table	Will ich bei Tische sitzen,
When company comes.	Wenn Gäste kommen.
Nobody'll dare	Morgen
Say to me,	Wird niemand sich trau'n,
"Eat in the kitchen,"	Zu mir zu sagen:
Then.[51]	"Iß in der Küche!"[52]

It should further be noted that Hughes' original second stanza is bookended by the temporal modifiers "tomorrow" and "then." These are certainly parallel but not identical. The concluding "then" exists as a part of a series, an embedded moment that follows on the past but occurring at an uncertain, i.e., historically dependent, point in the future. Rundt's restructuring removes this carefully composed temporality by translating the indeterminate "then" with a repetition of "tomorrow" and moving it to the middle of the stanza. In this way, Rundt's translation undercuts the development implied within the poem, just as Widenbauer and to a lesser extent Goslar had done in the stanza on music from "Negro." Moreover, in the second line, Rundt has exchanged the future tense for the modal verb "*wollen*," meaning to want or intend.[53] In switching out future reality for desire, Rundt subtly shifts the message of the poem away from the importance of African American belief in oneself and towards the desire to repeat, to copy whiteness.

In the example of Rundt, German mimicry of Hughes' English reveals itself to be a distorted mirror, reflecting as much Hughes' own poetics and politics as that of his German mediators and translators. If much of the original was lost in translation as it made its way back and forth across the Atlantic, it is equally significant that Rundt knew both Hughes and Locke personally. That he should have not only have traveled to Harlem but brought back the very latest work by one of its greatest representatives speaks to the growing significance of Harlem, not only as an important site for African American but for German culture as well. If the case of Rundt presents a deeply ambiguous example of how Hughes' poetry was both recognized and misrecognized, such damage was not always irreparable, as we will see in the case of Anna Nussbaum.

"The Negro Speaks of Rivers": Cultural Flow between African Americans and German-Speaking Europe

By the time Langston Hughes first heard from Anna Nussbaum in late 1927, he was well aware of the interest in his work in the German-speaking world. At the same time, Nussbaum quickly eclipsed all others, both in the number, quality, and impact of her translations. Through the publication of *Afrika singt. Eine Auslese neuer afro-amerikanischer Lyrik* (*Africa Sings: A Selection of Recent Afro-American Poetry*), she was responsible for the publication of almost forty translations of his poetry and around one hundred translations of contemporary African American poets. Born in Eastern Galicia in 1877, the Austrian-Jewish Nussbaum moved sometime in her childhood to Vienna. First attending university in Switzerland, she eventually received her doctorate from the University of Vienna in 1907. Following the war, her activities focused on two areas, translation and journalism. To begin with, during the first half of the 1920s, she was active as a translator of French authors, translating the works of Rousseau and Rabelais, as well as Henri Barbusse.[54] She also took great interest in American authors and, in 1929, published a translation of Theodore Dreiser's novel *Sister Carrie*.[55] Nussbaum additionally worked as a journalist for a number of Viennese newspapers, first for *Die Neue Freie Presse* and then more consistently for *Der Tag*. She was further engaged in socialist and feminist organizations like the *Internationale Frauenliga für Frieden und Freiheit*. This combination of journalism and activism, according to historian Lisa Silverman, was typical of Vienna's Jewish community: "In an era when a filiative identification with Judaism declined, many Jews felt the pull of more affiliative cultural networks such as journalism and socialist organizations."[56] In the case of Nussbaum, one such affiliative network became the Harlem Renaissance.

Already in 1922, the same year as Goslar's visit to New York, she had taken note of African American culture, jazz music, and spirituals. In an article appearing in the *Sozialistische Monatshefte*, Nussbaum reviewed three works in French by or about members of the African diaspora. Discussing novels by Paul Reboux, Rene Maran, and Lucie Cousturier, she demands greater realism within fictional portrayals of Africans. In the present context, however, it is the short note at the end of her article that will prove most germane to her future activities as translator of Hughes. There, she writes with passion about a personal experience with African American music:

> Recently I had the opportunity to get to know the exceptional musical and rhythmic talents of Negroes, their fine feeling for humor and parody. For some time, they've been playing, dancing, and singing at the Prater. Of course, they've done so according to the demands of the public, above all the frenetic vitality of jazz band melodies, but at personal request they'll also sing their wondrous, old nigger songs, in which a centuries-old longing for freedom, a heartfelt, intimate (*rührend-innig*) love of home is expressed. May the best amongst the whites finally find the courage of conviction to raise their voice for justice and understanding for a race that like everyone has a right to pursue, according to its individuality (*Eigenheit*), a beneficent development in its own, free country.[57]

Here in its earliest form is Nussbaum's ambiguous understanding of African American culture, in which received tropes of African American culture are interwoven with unique insight. On the one hand, she repeats the idea of a rhythmically and musically superior Black subject, so often present in European appraisals of jazz music, not to mention her use of racially insensitive vocabulary. On the other hand, she senses that what African American performers offer to the public is not always a true reflection of their own culture but rather a show for the public. Furthermore, she recognizes the necessity of Africans and African Americans to develop their own culture without European and/or American domination, echoing, if only faintly, Goslar's reading of Pan-Africanism via Zionism.

The performers to which she was responding are as important as what Nussbaum has to say, however. Nussbaum's comments were written in response to the performances of the *Southern Syncopated Orchestra* (*SSO*) in Vienna, which took place at the Prater between May and September 1922 and featured many of the most famous African American artists of the period, jazz and otherwise. Aside from Sidney Bechet, Buddy Gilmore, and the composer Will Marion Cook, one must also make note of singer Abbie Mitchell, first mentioned here in the discussion of the *Chocolate Kiddies*. In a curious twist of fate, Mitchell will cross paths with Nussbaum via her translation work once more. In 1931, Mitchell will give concert performances in America of Nussbaum's German translations of Langston Hughes. Given Mitchell's performance of these songs and her involvement in the prehistory of the *Chocolate Kiddies*, it is thus fitting that the likely impetus for Nussbaum's process of discovery began with an encounter with the *SSO* and Abbie Mitchell.[58]

Between Nussbaum's experience of the *SSO* and the beginning of her writings on African American music and translation of Harlem Renaissance poetry, five years elapsed. There were numerous modalities through which Nussbaum might have come into contact with African American performers and artists, jazz and otherwise, in these intervening years.[59] Still, the exact details of how her interest spread from the experience in the Prater to the translation of African American modernist poetry remain unknown. What is known is that from late 1927 onward, she took a great interest in this subject, beginning with an article in September of that year. Entitled "Neger-Musik" ("Negro Music"), the immediate occasion for this was an upcoming performance of the Utica Jubilee Singers, one of the African American vocal groups that regularly toured European metropolises in the 1920s.[60] In this piece, she discusses the history of ragtime and jazz, as well as African American spirituals via collections by Stephen Foster, James Weldon Johnson, and J. Rosamond Johnson, and presents information about figures such as Ira Aldridge, George Bridgetower, Sissieretta Jones, Roland Hayes, and Paul Robeson. Just three months later, Nussbaum began writing about and to African American modernists like Hughes. In her first letter to Hughes from December 7, 1927, she introduces herself, asks permission to publish translations of his work, and, because a young composer is interested in setting his poems to music, for an example of the blues.[61] On December 25, she then publishes a short article on Hughes' life, his thought, and his poetry in the Vienna newspaper *Der Tag*, calling him "a poet of the colored proletariat, of the proletariat as such," closing the article with two translations of Hughes' work, "The Negro Speaks of Rivers" and "Porter."[62] As she had with her other correspondents, she sent a copy of this article to Hughes himself, something, which as we've seen, Frankfurt jazz fan Dietrich Schulz-Köhn would also do some thirty years later.

The intellectual and material exchange between Nussbaum and African American modernists that took place between 1927 and her untimely death in 1931 produced a flood of translations and publications out of the trickle that had come before. For Hughes was but the first of many African Americans that she reached out to: W. E. B. Du Bois, Countee Cullen, Claude McKay, George Schuyler, and Georgia Douglas Johnson can all be counted amongst her correspondents. Though unlike Goslar and Rundt, she never travelled to America or Harlem, Nussbaum's words and thoughts traversed the Atlantic many times through her prodigious letter writing. Her contact with Du Bois proved especially useful, as through him she was able to contact other figures and acquire a subscription to the *Crisis*, as well as access important works by African American authors. Indeed, she profited so much from this exchange that Hughes and her other African American correspondents can be said to have shaped her anthology *Africa Sings*. To begin with, her interlocutors supplied Nussbaum with works to which she would otherwise have had no access. Before she began corresponding with Hughes in late 1927, Nussbaum seems to have possessed Hughes' *Weary Blues* and his *Fine Clothes to the Jew*, as well as Locke's *The New Negro*.[63] Yet by the time the anthology was published, it contained works from ten separate poetry collections as well as poems from the journals the *Crisis*, *Opportunity*, and *Carolina Magazine*. In other words, it was only after Nussbaum began corresponding with Hughes that the breadth and variety of texts and authors began to take shape, and it is this element more than any other that makes *Africa Sings* so unique.[64]

As was the case with her initial correspondence with Hughes, Nussbaum not only received texts from African American authors, she returned her own works to them. With her letters to Hughes, Du Bois, or Cullen, she included press clippings from the German and Austrian press discussing or defending African American culture. Writing in the *Pittsburgh Courier*, George Schuyler relays that she contacted him in 1928 asking for facts and materials related to African American life.[65] He responded by giving her photographs of African Americans from a variety of professional backgrounds as well as further addresses. When a racially motivated campaign emerged in Vienna to protest a planned performance by Josephine Baker, Nussbaum had the materials and knowledge to intervene. She quickly published an article in *Der Tag*, "Die afro-amerikanische Frau" ("The Afro-American Woman"), presenting in both textual and pictorial form a diverse image of Black women in the arts, education, entertainment, and politics.[66] As Schuyler, who received a copy of the article, noted: "With the information obtained from this side of the water, Dr. Nussbaum has written several articles on the Negro which appeared in leading Austrian and German newspapers. She has made the public in those two countries familiar with artistic development among Negroes along all lines. Thousands of people over there are now aware of the poetry of Langston Hughes, Countee Cullen, and Arna Bontemps."[67]

Indeed, transfer between Nussbaum and the Harlem Renaissance was in at least one case reciprocal. Nussbaum's "The Afro-American Woman" was itself translated and appeared, likely via Du Bois' help, in the *Norfolk Journal and Guide*, an important African American periodical.[68] Comparison between the translation found in Du Bois' papers, likely Nussbaum's work, and the published version reveals key differences and points towards conflicts over the representation of African American culture between German-speakers like Nussbaum and African Americans themselves. For one, while Nussbaum translates her original reference to the "*einfache Verse*" of Phillis Wheatley as "simple verses," the published version takes instead "plain verse," a selection that shifts the meaning of "*einfach*" from uncomplicated to unadorned. Further, while Nussbaum writes in reference to African American perseverance in the face of racism and violence that "Der Geist läßt sich nicht morden" ("One cannot murder the spirit."), the published English version reads: "His [the African American] spirit won't allow him to perish."[69] Localizing Nussbaum's universal claim written from a socialist and Jewish diasporic perspective, the English translation refocuses the energies of the piece towards the more immediate political ends of African Americans. As this and the preceding examples demonstrate, Anna Nussbaum and *Africa Sings* reveal not a one-sided German-Austrian interest, but cooperation, collaboration, and an example of diasporic reciprocity with diverse African American artists and intellectuals like Schuyler, Du Bois, and Hughes.

The collaborative quality of Nussbaum's work on *Africa Sings* was furthered through the participation of three other translators. In addition to Nussbaum, Anna Siemsen (sister of early jazz commentator Hans Siemsen), Josef Luitpold Stern, and Hermann Kesser each contributed translations and each of them had their own views on African American culture and poetry. This resulted in many of the translations engaging in domesticating strategies reminiscent of those analyzed in Goslar and Rundt.[70] Yet Nussbaum's own translations, all poems by Hughes, are marked by Venuti's strategy of foreignization. Consider, for example, her translation of Hughes' fourth stanza on music from "Negro," in particular in relation to Goslar's (see above).

I've been a singer:	Sänger war ich:
All the way from Africa to	Weit her von Afrika nach Georgia
Georgia	Brachte ich meine Leidgesänge.
I carried my sorrow songs.	Ich habe Ragtime geschaffen.[72]
I made ragtime.[71]	

In wording, structure, even punctuation, Nussbaum models her translation on the source text, retaining, for example, the proper names "Georgia" and "Ragtime," rather than replacing them with German equivalents as had Goslar and Widenbauer and as would later translators Hannah Meuter and Paul Therstappen.[73] Further, her early use of the term "afro-amerikanisch" ("Afro-American") in the collection's subtitle is yet another indication of the foreignizing tendency of her translation strategy. Such remnants of the source text demand that the reader understand the poet Hughes as much on his own terms as on the terms of the language into which he has been translated. To speak with Venuti, Nussbaum's translation sends the reader abroad, rather than back home.

The reasoning behind such, albeit relative, fidelity is laid out in Nussbaum's preface to *Africa Sings*. She begins by justifying the peculiar title. Following Alain Locke, Nussbaum defines such poems not as "Negro poetry," but as "Afro-American poetry: songs of Negroes living in America that are first and foremost rooted in race feeling, in solidarity with Africa."[74] This "race feeling" is not the triumph of biology over individuality, but, as she explains, "a thoroughly noble feeling grounded in the human experience (*im menschlichen Gemüt*)."[75] It is a feeling that is both aesthetically productive and a means of aiding, rather than inhibiting, understanding between cultures and peoples. In addition, if the title's reference to Africa would seem to emphasize the past rather than present of African Americans, it is important to point out that Nussbaum's anthology contains only works produced in the contemporary, i.e., the 1920s, and the timeliness of the poems works dialectically with the title's African framing, allowing the works to be understood in a modern, political, and historical context.

This dialectical movement linking past and present is further expressed in the anthology's ten thematic divisions. These are "I am a Negro," "The White God," "The New Homeland," "Work," "You Whites," "The Black Woman," "Harlem," "Poet's Dream," "Love," "Liberation," and "In Folk Sound (Blues) (*Im Volkston [Blues]*)." These divisions can and should be read chronologically, but it is neither a timeless nor a reductive history. Instead, they document the re-articulation of African American history by the poets themselves, in which progress is marked both by a growing independence from white culture as well as by the development of racial pride. So while the beginning four sections focus on the legacy of slavery and dislocation, beginning with the seventh section on Harlem, there is a shift towards issues facing African Americans in their own community. For example, the poems collected under the heading "Liberation" are not about liberation from physical, but rather the mental and spiritual, bondage of pervasive racism and racial oppression. It is this logic that justifies the anthology's closing with Hughes' blues poems. For Nussbaum, these blues have been "invigorated" by Hughes "with a new spirit and timeliness" and reveal the soul of his people in a way that is free from the deformities of white representations of Blackness.[76] Despite these major differences from other translators, Nussbaum's conception of African American culture and many of the individual translations themselves remain to a large degree informed by European and German cultural notions of African vitality, musicality, and naïveté. Their difference lies in the fact that unlike other translations these were to no small degree counteracted through her direct contact and exchange with the African American artists themselves.

Further, if translations like those of Goslar and Rundt were scattered throughout the press, appearing at irregular intervals, *Africa Sings'* status as an anthology containing around one hundred translations quantitatively and qualitatively altered the German-language encounter with Hughes. What makes the anthology noteworthy, then, is not simply Nussbaum's personal contact with figures like Hughes and Du Bois, but the amount of publications it inspired about African American poetry and its translation into German, and their importance abroad and at home. Indeed, the work's cultural resonance upon publication was striking. For one, *Africa Sings* was widely and positively reviewed, receiving discussion in the German, Austrian, and even American press.[77] In *Crisis*, African American chemist Percy Julian, who had studied at the University of Vienna, wrote that *Africa Sings* "marked a new epoch in European effort at interpretation of American Negro Youth."[78] Of the impact of the work on the broader public sphere, he notes: "in 1930 one found a copy of 'Afrika Singt' on the bookshelf of nearly every cultured German home."[79] If this is surely an exaggeration, partial confirmation comes from the unlikely source of novelist Hermann Hesse, author of his own jazz-influenced novel, *Der Steppenwolf* from 1927. Indicative of the type of informal circulation amongst left-leaning artists and intellectuals likely to have been prevalent at the time, Hesse writes:

> Recently while travelling I found a book lying in the guest room of a friend in Munich. For three nights I read in it with excitement and great interest. It is called *Africa Sings* and contains a selection of Negro poetry,

not from Africa, but America, that were translated into German by various translators. I will buy this book, it captivated me. Ancient things sound there in a new key and move the heart.[80]

If someone like Hesse could come across the work in the guest room of Rein-hold Geheeb, editor of the journal *Simplicissimus*, others need not have known such literary luminaries or have left their exposure to mere serendipity. For there were three further means by which *Africa Sings* came to exert its influ-ence on the German and Austrian public sphere.

The first of these occurred through the republication of the poems in a variety of journals and newspapers. In the many reviews of the work, the min-iature form of the poem proved particularly advantageous to spreading Hughes' name, with examples of his poetry and the poetry of others easily reprinted. Between 1929 and 1933, *Africa Sings'* translations of Langston Hughes appear in at least nine further publications in Germany and Austria.[81] This also in-cluded the reproduction of Nussbaum's translation of "Negro" in Alfons Gold-schmidt's 1931 pamphlet in support of the Scottsboro Boys *8 Menschen in der Todeszelle (8 People on Death Row)*.[82] This global movement to free a group of African American youths who had been falsely imprisoned and convicted of rape in 1931 had a surprisingly broad impact in Germany, as we shall see in the next chapter. Beyond such republications, *Africa Sings* also spurred others on to translate Hughes, producing a total of seven further translations. In the so-cialist journal *Urania*, Anna Siemsen, co-translator with Nussbaum, intro-duced four new translations by "comrade Kurgass," likely Paula Kurgass, noted feminist and later German-Jewish exile.[83] Then there is the case of Thomas Otto Brandt. During the 1920s, Brandt was part of a group of young Austrian writers involved with a short-lived journal *Literarische Monatshefte*, in which two new translations of Hughes appeared.[84] Though the readership for this journal was extremely small, these poems later made their way across the Atlantic to the pages of *Crisis* where Percy Julian reproduced them for his African American readership. Finally, *Africa Sings* gave speakers of German outside of Germany, Austria, and Switzerland access to Hughes' poetry, and Slovene translations of Hughes, based not on the originals, but upon the trans-lations in *Africa Sings*, were published in the early 1930s.[85] Such reprintings and new translations, within and outside of Weimar Germany, not only magni-fied the effect of *Africa Sings*, they stand as an index of a broad European and German-speaking interest in African American culture and modernism. Like ripples in the water, the translations of *Africa Sings* spread out from Vienna and Germany throughout Central Europe and then back to the United States, completing the cycle begun by Goslar's first translation and the letter back to Hughes in 1922.

Still, perhaps the most lasting way Nussbaum's translation work moved beyond the containment of the poetry anthology was through music, in particular through song. Between 1929 and 1931, no less than eight composers set the poems of *Africa Sings* to music: Helmut Bornefeld, Wilhelm Grosz, Werner Richard Heymann, Fritz Kramer, Edmund Nick, Kurt Pahlen, Eric Zeisl, and Alexander Zemlinsky (figure 14).[86] Further, Ossip Dymow and Béla Reinitz produced an operetta, *Schatten über Harlem* (*Shadows over Harlem*) with songs based on poems from *Africa Sings*.[87] Named after McKay's 1922 poem and anthology of the same name, this important work will be discussed below. Still, working only from the uneven translations of *Africa Sings*, these young composers often found themselves in a difficult position.[88] Even if in such imperfect form, their musical interpretations of Hughes' work soon found their way onto German, Polish, and Czech airwaves.[89] Both Pahlen (1930) and Zemlinsky (1935) had their works debuted on *Radio Brünn* and, in an unlikely squaring of the circle, Grosz's *Afrika Songs* premiered in February 1930 on the *Schlesische Funkstunde* simultaneously broadcast to Berlin, Leipzig, and Cologne under the musical direction of Edmund Nick, himself author of a composition inspired by *Africa Sings*.[90] Importantly, the reach of Nussbaum's translations and their musical settings was not limited to Europe alone. As referenced above, between the spring and fall of 1931, the African American singer Abbie Mitchell, whom Nussbaum had first seen in Vienna in 1922, gave a series of concerts in Chicago and New York in which she performed songs from Pahlen's settings.[91] Like the translation of Nussbaum's "The Afro-American Woman" and Brandt's poetry, Hughes' poetry, transposed into music and translated into German, went back across the Atlantic where it was heard anew.[92]

Through these reprintings, new translations, musical productions, and national radio programs, the poems of *Africa Sings* reached a German- and non-German-speaking audience outside, but also inside, Weimar Germany. Through the constant endeavors of Nussbaum, but also the actions of others like Kurgass, Brandt, Bornefeld, Goldschmidt, and Mitchell, *Africa Sings* was elevated beyond the isolated endeavor of one exceptional woman in Vienna. In giving access to Hughes' poetry and providing a focus to such energies, *Africa Sings* and Anna Nussbaum were able to bring to surface a subterranean flow of interest. Of course, when such interest surfaced, it could also provoke, and the history of Ossip Dymow and Bela Reinitz's *Shadows over Harlem* is a prime example of the tragic (and comic) fate of Langston Hughes in German translation.

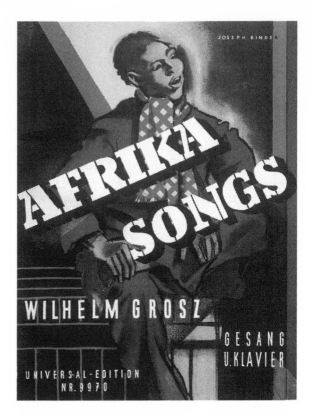

Figure 14: Sheet music for Wilhelm Grosz's *Afrika Songs*, 1931. Used with permission from Universal Edition.

Weimar Gets the Blues:
New Negro Culture Meets Nazi Politics

In the early evening of October 19, 1930, a group of brown shirts lingers in a park to the north of Stuttgart's city center on a plane tree path.[93] They gather in preparation of *Shadows over Harlem*, a musical comedy that at 7:30 that evening will have its premiere at the *Kleines Theater*. With a Jewish author and African American culture as its subject, to them, the piece is a prime example of the cultural bolshevism seemingly so prevalent in Weimar Germany and an affront to the German nation and race. They are, however, not the only group on alert that evening. Having become aware of the Nazis' intentions, the Stuttgart police has increased their forces in the area and taken measures to block the way leading from the theater to the nearby state parliament.[94] Should things get out of hand, they have two extra squadrons standing at the ready.[95] Both groups will play their role tonight.

Regrettably, for the Nazis at least, the play has first to be performed before it can be protested. To this end, a group of them enters the theater, where they intend to disrupt the performance. Yet because this is a premiere and no one is aware of the particularities of the piece, the group must lie in wait for an offending scene or utterance. In fact, the first act will proceed relatively quietly, with only a single whistle of disgust issuing from the audience. The second act will not proceed so smoothly. During a salacious song-and-dance scene, the youths finally take sufficient offense and seize the moment to halt the performance (figure 15). As Karl Konrad Düssel described the scene in the *Stuttgarter Neues Tagblatt*: "It is a scene played with virtuosity. Both characters, the acting, the songs, the dances, everything magnificent [. . .] But it is a rather direct scene. An extremely unseemly scene, the protesters must have said to themselves. And now there's no more restraint. Now it breaks loose. Whistling, noise, yelling. 'Filth' is the least one hears."[96] Some audience members decide to protest the protesters and cries to play on compete with the chants of the Nazis.[97] The house lights are turned on, restoring order and weakening the protest, but as soon as the room is once again darkened, the shouting match begins anew. This process repeats itself, until, after a delay lasting several minutes, the scene can finally be completed. Despite further incidences, though none as memorable, the play eventually reaches its finale, after which, with author and cast standing on stage, another battle of wills, hands, and voices takes place between the Nazi scandalizers and members of the audience supportive of the piece. Yet the scandal has by no means reached its climax. Departing audience members are met outside by the group of young men from the park. Here, the theatergoers will endure, amongst other insults, repeated chants of "*Deutschland erwache. Juda verrecke*" (Germany awake. Die Jew) lasting for around thirty minutes. Eventually, the police enter with their reserves and forcefully clear the area with nightsticks, arresting many of the protesters and finally restoring order.

Shadows over Harlem will have only two more performances, after which it will be permanently cancelled. The official reason given is the failing health of Emil Heß, Toomer from the offending scene, but neither its proponents nor opponents put much stock into that explanation. Instead, the cancellation of the play, alongside the scandal of its premiere, stood as a sign of the increasing power of the National Socialist movement, in particular as the scandal occurred directly on the heels of the Nazis' breakthrough performance in the September 1930 elections. Bolstered by the Nazis' success in disrupting and then removing the play from the theater, local right-wing politician Franz Mergenthaler gave a speech in the state parliament calling for a review of the the-

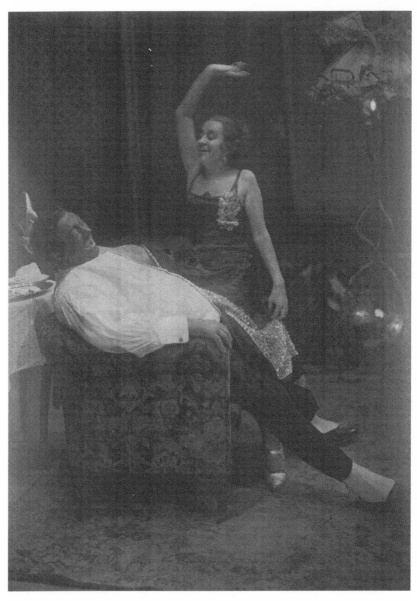

Figure 15: Scene from Ossip Dymow's *Schatten über Harlem* in Stuttgart, 1930. Staatsarchiv Ludwigsburg of the Landesarchiv Baden-Wurttemberg.

ater's funding and leadership. In a related incident, Stuttgart's Nazi leadership threatened to send all 21,000 of their supporters to the theater should the play ever be performed again.[98] Like the counter-protesters in the theater, the liberal press, local and national, defended, if not the piece itself, then the theater's and Dymow's right to free expression.[99] The socialist press as well criticized the Nazis' actions and was generally more sympathetic to intentions of the piece, if it also found fault with the execution.[100]

As can be gleaned from these notes based upon the vast press coverage, the actual content of *Shadows over Harlem* quickly receded behind its scandal, and, other than those present at the premiere, it was not only forgotten but never known.[101] To this day, it has enjoyed but those three performances in Stuttgart in 1930. Current scholarship on interwar German culture contains but the barest of details concerning the piece, and, when mentioned at all, *Shadows over Harlem* exists primarily through the Nazi scandal recounted above. As Hans-Martin Ulmer notes in his study of antisemitism in Stuttgart, the focus on the idea of the scandal then (and I would add now) amounted to the "adoption of the National Socialist *topos* of the 'theater scandal.'"[102] In order to extricate discourse from this Nazi bind, we need first to rethink this work's history and performance, not with an eye towards its disappearance but towards the conditions of its very appearance in an attempt to give voice back to an author, cast, and cultural movement silenced that evening.

The first note to make about *Shadows over Harlem* is that it was a collaborative effort uniting cultures and artists across Europe and the Atlantic. In addition to musical settings by the Hungarian composer Béla Reinitz and additional song texts supplied by the German communist poet Erich Weinert, its Russian-Jewish American author, Ossip Dymow, was heavily inspired by the New Negro movement, with which Dymow was potentially familiar from the time he spent in America and New York between 1913 and 1925.[103] The title references the poem "Harlem Shadows" by Afro-Caribbean poet Claude McKay, first published in 1922. Furthermore, the cast reads as if it came from a *roman à clef* of the New Negro movement. The lead character is named Langston Johnson, a combination of Langston Hughes and James Weldon Johnson, author and first African American secretary of the NAACP. Dymow's Langston also has a love interest, Gwendolyn, referencing the poet Gwendolyn Bennett whose poetry also appears in *Africa Sings*. Then there is Toomer, the Black millionaire, clearly inspired by the author Jean Toomer, whose novel *Cane* serves as the basis for two songs set by Reinitz. Though such references would have likely remained opaque to the audience, potentially explaining much of critics' and audience members' difficulties with the work, these references to the Harlem Renaissance are crucial to understanding the cultural stakes of Dymow's project.

The plot, which covers a single day, takes place in a Harlem cabaret named *"Afrika."* The cabaret contains three levels: a kitchen where African Americans work almost without any contact with whites, a second level for the offices of the white owner Joe Hopkins, and a restaurant above where Blacks serve white guests. In this regard, the cabaret *"Afrika"* may have been modeled on the famous Cotton Club in Harlem, which showcased some of the greatest African American jazz bands and performers of the period, in particular Duke Ellington, but which was owned by the white bootlegger Owney Madden, hired light-skinned female dancers, and remained off-limits for most African Americans in Harlem. At any rate, the racial dynamics at the fictional cabaret reflect to a large degree the realities of Black-white relations in American society during the 1920s. For example, while the external conditions of segregation continue, they are beginning to fray as a result of ever-greater numbers of African Americans in northern cities and their demands for equality. Concretizing the link between his play and the New Negro movement, Dymow sets the club *"Afrika"* not just anywhere in Harlem but at 135th street, a location that has been called "the heart and soul of Black Harlem."[104] This street was the location of the Harlem YMCA, where Langston Hughes and other famous figures from the Harlem Renaissance lived, as well as the site of the 135th Street Library, now the Schomburg Center for Research in Black Culture.

The plot revolves around the two figures Langston and Gwendolyn, both recent transplants from the South, or *"Dixieland"* as it's referred to in the play. Early on, Gwendolyn is given a mysterious telegram by the owner Hopkins and commanded to deliver it to Mr. Williams, a white guest, whose sexual advances she has already rebuffed in an earlier scene. Knowing that bringing anything to his room will result in Gwendolyn's rape, Langston volunteers to deliver it for her. Yet, Langston's motives are not entirely altruistic. As he says to Gwendolyn: "I want to tell you something. I've been thinking about this for a long time: We work—but the whites make the money. And how do they do that? Not with work [. . .] With telegrams. Whites make love with the telephone and make money through telegrams. I need money at the moment."[105] Opening the telegram, he discovers that it is an offer to purchase a huge tract of land in the American South, but payment in full must be made within the next twenty-four hours. This telegram sparks in Langston the idea of Harlem pooling its money to buy a kingdom for African Americans.

The cabaret workers choose their leadership and Langston serves the dual role of treasurer and messiah. For the constitution of their new country, Dymow ironically models it on the democracy of the United States. As the stoker Esra, newly elected president of the republic, says: "We will lynch the whites! We will hang them. We will have a democracy. We will douse them with gasoline and burn them alive!"[106] Parts of the German audience would surely have recoiled in shock at such images and some conservative commentators referenced the "Black Horror" in their critiques of the play. Yet, the horrible acts recounted here are based not on German but American conditions, and in all likelihood, it is the savagery of whites recounted here, such as the brutal lynching and burning of the African American George Hughes in Sherman, Texas, in May 1930 that was reported on in Germany as well.[107] In referencing the brutality of what was known as "lynch justice," Dymow may have been attempting to bypass the racial prejudice of the audience by, however clumsily, having the white German audience imagine itself as victim of this order. In the right-wing press, this strategy played into the hands of those who viewed in Blacks an animal and savage race. Thus, in the report issued by conservative media-mogul Alfred Hugenberg's *Telegraphen-Union*, which appeared in numerous newspapers across Weimar Germany, the play's plot was summarized as depicting Black longing for "bloody revenge against their white oppressors."[108]

Naming their new country *"Aetiopia,"* the leadership further declares its intention to create a union of peoples of color, which will include their nation, as well as China and the Soviet Union. As was to be expected, the positive references to communism, along with a Jewish author, became the main points of reactionary attacks on *Shadows over Harlem*, which tended to interpret the piece as an allegory of communistic Zionism. The Nazi newspaper *Der Angriff* commented: "Threatening, muffled, future-oriented [*zukunftsschwangere*] revolt against centuries of injustice? Fine. One might forget that the author says 'the Negroes' and means 'the Jews.'"[109] Meanwhile, the *Süddeutsche Zeitung* will summarize the plot as a *"grotesque*, failed experiment in a Zionism for *colored people*."[110] While such attacks can be rejected for the ideological fantasies they are, it is also noteworthy that like Goslar, Rundt, and Nussbaum before him, Dymow's *Shadows over Harlem* also plays off resonances between Zionism and Pan-Africanism.[111] As we have seen throughout, German-speakers of Jewish descent not only were some of the most important translators of Hughes, they also framed their work in ways that invited parallels between their experience of diaspora and that of African Americans.

In this way, the German translation of Hughes' modernist work, including its rejection as "cultural bolshevism" by the right, shares an investment in the trope of "Jewish modernism" (*"die jüdische Moderne"*) previously discussed in chapter 3. Here again, I will follow Scott Spector's consideration of the contradictions and tensions that surround the overdetermined relationship between "Jewishness" and modernism in Central European discourse, as it is something clearly at work within the translation and reception of Hughes in German, though in ways that differ from its treatment in Gustav Renker's *Symphony and Jazz*. Spector describes this idea as an "elusive object that is not a body of work nor a register of authors, but a way of thinking about oneself and one's place in relation to the past, the future, and creativity."[112] In other words, modernism and Jewishness are, for better and worse, intimately related within the Central European cultural imaginary; it is a way of thinking that produces such strange bedfellows as Goslar and Widenbauer, Dymow and his Nazi critics. More importantly, attempts to revalue the connection through inversion of the Nazis' racist reading or even through disavowal of the connection are equally problematic. In Spector's view, both the valorization of modernist works like *Shadows over Harlem,* as having been decidedly shaped by Central European Jews, as well as its opposite, namely the insistence upon the "Gentile" origins of modernism, share particularly discomfiting Nazi analogues: in the rhetoric of "cultural bolshevism" on the one hand and in the Nazi requirement of baptismal certificates to prove "Aryan" heritage on the other.[113]

In the case of works like *Shadows over Harlem*, Spector's argument suggests, scholars must both avoid reading it solely as a "Jewish" text, while at the same time striving to uncover the specific ways Dymow's experience of diaspora informs the piece's modernism. In the examples of Dymow, Goslar, and Nussbaum, this could begin with an acknowledgement of the multiple ways in which their displaced, peripatetic lives created a situation that fostered diasporic reciprocity between their own experience and that of the African American authors they were translating. At the same time, to view their works primarily through their "Jewishness," in other words, to replace Dymow's African American characters with Central European Jews, would, in many ways, reproduce the same ideological matrix that led to the right-wing rejection of the piece. A reading of *Shadows over Harlem* as an allegory of European Zionism would depend not only upon erasing the history of contact and exchange between African American and German-language Jewish authors, it would also ignore the ways in which Dymow ironizes, indeed undercuts, the plan of the cabaret workers through comedy and exaggeration. Rather than allegorizing Zionism through the New Negro movement, Hughes' Central European Jewish translators and adaptors Dymow, Goslar, Rundt, and Nussbaum are all after something rather more complicated.

In *Shadows over Harlem*, Dymow intends not only to depict the exploitation and persecution of African Americans but also their strategies for countering it. Though by no means wholly successful in this endeavor, the finale of *Shadows over Harlem* points towards such a deeper engagement with the aesthetics of the New Negro movement. Towards the end of the work, Langston is duped into handing over the telegram to the callous Black millionaire Toomer, who promises to pay for the land himself and then share it with the others. When Langston realizes that Toomer's real intent is to exclude him and the rest of Harlem, he protests, only to have Toomer call the police and claim that Langston has stolen money from him. The police discover $250 on Langston, the money collected from the cabaret workers, and arrest him. Though he adamantly denies having stolen the money, he also refuses to say where it is from. As the police investigate further, they eventually speak with Gwendolyn. She deceives them, saying that the money is hers, earned as a prostitute for Langston. This explanation suits the white policemen and Langston is promptly released. Now freed and back amongst the cabaret workers, he admits to having lost the telegram to Toomer. Upon learning this, the cabaret workers turn on Langston and threaten to lynch him. Fleeing the mob, Langston escapes and finds refuge in one of the cabaret's private rooms. There he finds Gwendolyn and the telegram's original owner Mr. Williams. It is at this point that Williams reveals to both of them that the telegram was a fake all along, an invention meant to lure Gwendolyn to his room. In other words, Gwendolyn and Langston learn that there never was any land to be bought, never any republic to be founded, and that the entire dream of independence had been built upon white deception.

Without any time to let this fact set in, the Black lynch mob breaks into the room and is told of Williams' machinations. Yet, the assembled cast neither cries nor rises up in anger but laughs heartily and goes immediately, quietly back to work. As Dymow writes in the final stage directions: "One after the other, the Negroes begin to laugh, ever wilder and louder. A sympathy of laughter comes into being."[114] For critics, on the left and right, it was at this point that the integrity of the piece eroded entirely.[115] They simply could not grasp why the situation should provoke laughter; it was clearly a tragic, rather than comedic, ending. As Düssel wrote: "A tragic, frantically wailing conclusion to a comedy simply makes no sense."[116] This seemingly inexplicable laughter is followed by the assembled cast's recitation of Hughes' 1922 poem "Laughers," in its English original no less. The poem includes the lines: "Dream-singers, / Story-tellers, [. . .] / Loud laughers in the hands of Fate."[117]

As mentioned earlier, for Hughes, laughter is not only a product of happiness but is part of a blues aesthetic in which the absurdity of American racial realities intertwines comedy and tragedy so fully that they become indistinguishable. As he writes in his gloss on the genre cited at this chapter's outset: "The mood of the Blues is almost always despondency, but when they are sung, people laugh."[118] Or as he states elsewhere, the blues is a form defined by "hopeless weariness mixed with an absurdly incongruous laughter."[119] Blues qua laughter acts as a survival strategy of African Americans in the face of oppression. For such laughter is, amongst other things, also a mask, a projection of happiness and docility that can function as subterfuge amongst those aware of its ironic intent. This type of laughter, like that occurring at the end of *Shadows over Harlem*, provokes laughter of laughter, ironizing and indeed inverting the agreement normally associated with the act. The African American characters at the end of the piece laugh neither at their dream nor its failure but in the face of oppression. Their laughter suggests they will carry on and live to dream again. As Dymow wrote less than six months after the play's cancellation in a piece about Harlem and its poets Hughes, McKay, and Toomer in the Vienna newspaper *Das kleine Blatt*: "Their poems reveal what is hidden behind the ever-friendly, naively-sincere (*kindlich-aufrichtig*) smile of the American Negro."[120] One might suggest, therefore, that under the cover of comedy, Dymow has smuggled in an African American aesthetic form and that *Shadows over Harlem* can stand as a, albeit awkward, translation of the blues for German theater.

Such an endeavor in Germany in 1930 was ultimately destined to failure in a very important sense: its call to understanding and sympathy could not depend on a knowing response from the Stuttgart audience, and Dymow's rich web of allusions fell mostly on deaf ears, its irony taken by many critics for literalness. Yet, the play's transatlantic call did elicit a response in the African American press. In the *Baltimore Afro-American*, there appeared a short note on the scandal.[121] After referring to the plot of the play as a depiction of the "oppression of the Negro in America" and recounting what it terms the "riot" of October 19th, the short review concludes: "The play was objected to because a group known as the 'Nazis' believe that the new Negro culture is ruining the German culture."[122] Unlike other articles in the American press, this piece adds an important, if seemingly trivial, detail. In this report, the Nazis don't merely object to African American culture, "Negro culture," as the *New York Times* put it,[123] they object to the "new Negro culture." To its African American readership, this would have meant, amongst other things, the modernism of the Harlem Renaissance. No author is given for the report, and it is unclear whether this addition was based on knowledge or merely surmised. Of course, such a quiet moment of dialogue between Weimar culture and African American modernism is all but inaudible against the loud chants of the brown shirts outside the theater. Still, the message it carries, of a neglected history of communication and miscommunication between African and Jewish diasporic communities between Russia, Vienna, Berlin, Stuttgart, and Harlem, is certainly one worth hearing.

"As I Grew Older:" Weimar Culture
and African American Modernism

Back in Vienna, Anna Nussbaum followed the events surrounding *Shadows over Harlem* and reported on the situation to W. E. B. Du Bois, on November 7 and December 29, 1930.[124] She continued to correspond with him through the spring of 1931, sending him a final note on May 31, after which she unexpectedly passed away on June 28.[125] In her death, the focus and drive behind the dissemination and translation of African American poetry in Germany and Austria had suffered a loss from which it did not recover until the after the Second World War.[126] With Nussbaum's death, the economic downturn, and the rise of the Nazis, the Weimar encounter with Hughes is one that seemed to go missing after 1933. After 1945, new translators worked to make Hughes, once again, known to the German public in the East and West. While such postwar efforts perhaps bore greater fruit in terms of the overall public recognition of Hughes,[127] Dymow's *Shadows over Harlem* and Nussbaum's *Africa Sings*, as well as the other examples analyzed here, cannot simply be written off as islands of insight in a sea of "jazz age" ignorance. Instead, they need to be seen as having been on the forefront of something much larger and deeper: a new sense of the aesthetic and cultural achievements of African Americans and peoples of African descent. And if the Stuttgart audience had not been able to answer the transatlantic call of Dymow's text, the translation of Langston Hughes more generally can be viewed as an example of Edward's idea of "diasporic reciprocity" as a "call to translate."[128] This unique state of affairs was indebted as much to the status of German-speaking Jews in Central Europe as to the transnational reach of Black modern expression. It is only as a result of the modernist movement of the Harlem Renaissance and the concomitant interest in jazz across the United States, Europe, and Germany that writers like Goslar, Rundt, Dymow, and Nussbaum, along with many others, were no longer merely speaking about African Americans but, rather, also having African Americans like Langston Hughes speak through them.

To be sure, the translation of Langston Hughes' poetry was not the only example of American and African American culture speaking in Weimar Germany. As we have seen throughout, exposure to American culture produced complex responses on the part of Weimar Germans as they struggled to reconcile the seemingly irreconcilable elements of music, race, and American culture. If many of these instances like those of Dymow and to a lesser extent Nussbaum were largely forgotten, the struggles of one young philosopher *cum* musician to make sense of this new culture have remained especially audible within the history of jazz in Germany. This is Theodor W. Adorno, whose works such as *The Dialectic of Enlightenment* (cowritten with Max Horkheimer) have influenced generations of scholars. From the 1930s to 1960s, Adorno and other philosophers associated with the Frankfurt School, such as Walter Benjamin and Herbert Marcuse, supplied scholars and radical thinkers with a new vocabulary to analyze and critique capitalist culture. In the most positive sense, Adorno and the Frankfurt School were amongst the first to discuss popular culture with the same theoretical rigor that had previously retained for high culture alone. In a more negative way, they used the standards of high cultural analysis to do so. Of course for many, no better example of the limitations of Frankfurt School critical theory can be found than in Adorno's thoroughgoing and long-standing rejection of jazz. From the 1930s to the 1950s, Adorno repeatedly sought to debunk jazz as reactionary, rather than progressive, as repressive, rather than liberatory; a position that could lead to inflammatory statements such as that "jazz and the pogrom belong together."[129] Still, as I want to explore in my final chapter, even as staunch a critic as Adorno was not free from the influence of Weimar's jazz republic.

CHAPTER 7

Jazz's Silence: Adorno, Opera, and the Decomposition of Weimar Jazz Culture

> It is hardly an exaggeration to claim that every consciousness today that has not appropriated the American experience, even if with resistance, has something reactionary to it.
> —Theodor W. Adorno (1968)

Like so much else that had defined the first decade of Germany's democracy, jazz was very much under attack during the final years of the Weimar Republic. A critical turn set in around 1930 that had as much to do with transatlantic trends in popular music as with the crises in politics and the economy that dominated the republic during the last years of its existence.[1] If jazz, and with it jazz effects, nonetheless continued to be produced—through musical works like *Shadows over Harlem*, films such as *The Great Attraction*, and concerts by the *Jazzklasse*—as we've seen throughout the past chapters, jazz's position within Weimar culture was also clearly threatened, evidenced not in the least through the ban on "Negro culture" and its expression through "jazz bands, drum music, Negro dances, Negro music, negro songs (*Negerstücke*)" by the National Socialist Wilhelm Frick in Thuringia in April 1930.[2] It was during this period of Weimar jazz culture's decomposition that Theodor W. Adorno first achieved and then lost his academic position at the Goethe University in Frankfurt, produced an opera on America, rejected jazz, and, like many others, left Germany for England and then the United States.

It is, of course, the Adorno of a few later years who will come to loom over so much of the historical discussion of jazz in Germany, casting a shadow over German jazz criticism that stretches back into Weimar and forward into the present. Between his "Über Jazz" ("On Jazz") in 1936 and "Zeitlose Mode: Zum Jazz" ("Perennial Fashion–Jazz") from 1953, Adorno repeatedly rejected jazz as a progressive, revolutionary, or otherwise critical music. [3] Indeed, Adorno's earliest extended treatment of jazz, "Abschied vom Jazz" ("Farewell to Jazz") published in April 1933, would seem to put Adorno's loathing of this music on early display. Just two months after Hitler became chancellor and in the midst of severe economic depression and continuing political violence, Adorno responded with apparent sanguinity to the prohibition of jazz by the *Berliner Funkstunde*, a national radio station based in Berlin. Whether as foil or as model, his scathing critique has informed most scholarly thought on the subject of jazz in Germany and no account of jazz's presence in early twentieth-century Germany can get around Adorno.[4]

For the present purposes, the most important aspect of Adorno's anti-jazz legacy is that his appraisals have, for various reasons and to various degrees of success, consistently been applied to the study of jazz in the Weimar Republic. Specifically, scholars of the past twenty years have tended to read Adorno's post-1933 writings as a continuation of Weimar-era jazz discourse, bolstered in this contention by the fact that Adorno's terminology and overall stance on the music would appear to remain unchanged over the course of his lifetime. As J. Bradford Robinson argues: "Adorno's jazz writings, although post-dating the Weimar Republic, must be read within the context of Weimar Germany's commercial music scene as a whole."[5] In one way, such an interpretation acts as a defense of Adorno's critique of jazz—not as a valid interpretation of jazz but as an incisive critique of German and European ideologies of jazz in the 1920s and early 1930s. Robinson's work is but the most compelling and nuanced of many attempts to remove the stain of Eurocentrism, cultural snobbism, and even racism from Adorno's jazz texts by anchoring them in Weimar.[6] At the same time, this defense of Adorno rests on one very important assumption, namely that the jazz of Weimar Germany was out of touch with the developments in America and the rest of the European continent, with Weimar's supposed ignorance ultimately functioning as scapegoat for Adorno's. While there are many problematic elements to this idea, most relevant in this context is the idea that Weimar Germany was somehow backwards in its understanding of and engagement with jazz and that writers such as Adorno were free to make their jazz theory as they pleased. Adorno and jazz, Adorno and America, are thus ideal candidates to evaluate the present work's primary argument, namely that Weimar culture was produced through fractious contact with American culture and the Gordian knot of music and race via jazz.

At the same time, any attempt to uncover Adorno's experience of jazz and his engagement with the music, its performers, and its cultural significance must confront the fact that Adorno wrote relatively little about the music between 1918 and 1933. Still, Adorno's works from the 1920s and early 1930s do contain telling, if scattered, references to notable figures from Weimar's jazz culture such as Paul Whiteman, The Revelers, Josephine Baker, Frankfurt's *Jazzklasse*, and the Louis Douglas revue *Black People*, under the musical directorship of jazz icon Sidney Bechet no less.[7] So if there can be little doubt that Adorno was exposed to a wide array of jazz styles and potentially as early as 1925, when he may have heard Arthur Briggs, another veteran of the *SSO*, such references and biographical details can only hint at what ultimately remains an absence in his early work.[8] Expressed more positively, Adorno's relative silence on jazz during the period does not mean he wasn't listening, that he wasn't paying close attention to questions of music, race, and American culture as part of his philosophical and musical education in the 1920s.

On the other hand, Adorno may not be as silent on these matters as it would at first appear. For the relative scarcity of his comments on American and African American culture disappears as soon as one considers his incomplete musical work *Der Schatz des Indianer Joe. Singspiel nach Mark Twain* (*The Treasure of Indian Joe*. Singspiel *after Mark Twain*). (Hereafter referred to as *Treasure*.)[9] Initially produced between November 1932 and August 1933, I want to suggest this unique work was the result of Adorno's cultural apprenticeship during the 1920s. Indeed, though *Treasure* is a piece very much of its time, it is in certain ways out of step with Adorno's later works, on jazz and otherwise, that have defined his legacy as one of the most important thinkers in twentieth-century European thought. Tellingly, and unlike his jazz writings, this work has largely been ignored, both by critics and defenders. Excluded from the twenty volumes of his collected works, the libretto was published as a limited edition in 1979, and the two compositions he completed for the work were published a year later in a separate volume.[10] After offering an insightful reading of the libretto in the context of Adorno's work, Adorno scholar Rolf Tiedemann closes his afterword to the publication by noting:

> If one were to offer *Schatz des Indianer Joe* as pre-Christmas entertainment . . . the piece would hardly fail to impress. But one must not, as this would almost certainly be the exact opposite of what Adorno himself had intended to bring to the stage. Only the composition is capable of fully bringing out what the author has let seep into the text. Unfortunately, too little of the composition is extant for the work to be completed. Adorno did not plan to publish the libretto independently of the music; he knew too much about literature (*Literatur*) to consider the libretto by itself to be poetry (*Dichtung*).[11]

Following these notes from Tiedemann, few authors have tackled the libretto or its place within Adorno's thought. Indeed, as much as, if not more so than, his jazz writings, Adorno's American opera has become an open secret of Adorno scholarship, though recently it has begun to garner more interest.[12]

When read as belonging to the complex of the jazz republic, however, *Treasure* can be viewed as a singular achievement of Adorno's early thought and marks an important moment in his development as a thinker. For in this fragment of an opera, Adorno not only entered into dialogue with the great American author Mark Twain but with the thorny issue of race and Blackness in US culture via music. As I want to show, his attempt to imagine American society as operatic text pushed him to confront questions of racial difference in ways that his later analyses of jazz did not.

Adorno's American Opera as Anti-*Zeitoper*

The first step in locating Adorno's work within the jazz republic is to put aside Adorno's authorship of the work for a moment. When one considers *Treasure* purely from the perspective of a Weimar-era musical work set in America, it immediately enters into conversation with a host of further works from the period. In particular, Adorno's American setting invites comparisons to the group of *Zeitopern* ("operas of the times") produced roughly between 1927 and 1930 that broadly share an American theme: Krenek's *Jonny spielt auf (Jonny Strikes Up)* (1927), Max Brand's *Maschinist Hopkins* (1928), Eugen d'Albert's *Die schwarze Orchidee (The Black Orchid)* (1928), Karol Rathaus' *Fremde Erde (Foreign Soil)* (1930), Kurt Weill's *Aufstieg und Fall der Stadt Mahagonny (Rise and Fall of the City of Mahagonny)* (1930), and George Antheil's *Transatlantic* (1930). Such *Zeitopern*, as Susan C. Cook shows, were above all a response to the perception of a crisis in opera. Confronted with diminishing demand for this baroque product, composers of *Zeitopern* sought to incorporate modern culture into their works as a means of speaking to the audience's contemporary life. *Zeitopern* prominently feature technology like automobiles and trains; new media like film, radio, and phonographs; and urban locales such as bars and hotels. These are introduced not only to reflect current society but also to critique and parody it. As Cook explains:

> The *Zeitoper* was firstly a comic genre and typically relied on parody, social satire, and burlesque as dramatic tools. [. . .] *Zeitopern* were obvi-

ous expressions, even celebrations, of modern life. Composers tried to incorporate as many attributes of contemporary life into all facets of the operatic production as possible. The libretti were set in the present; characters were typically everyday people or were presented as recognizable modern stereotypes.[13]

A crucial component of *Zeitopern* was their use of jazz and other forms of syncopated popular music, be it through instruments like saxophones and banjos and/or through music written in the style of blues, foxtrot, and tango. While one may certainly question the authenticity of the terminology, the intention of the composers was to signify popular music and jazz to their audience. Moreover, the music of these *Zeitopern* is without question some of Weimar culture's most memorable. The collaborations of Bertolt Brecht and Kurt Weill have longest remained in the minds of German and not only opera but also jazz and rock enthusiasts. From Louis Armstrong's or Ella Fitzgerald's performances of "Mack the Knife" to The Doors' rendition of the "Alabama Song," Weimar's "operatic" jazz has enjoyed a spectacular afterlife.

In choosing to set his first opera in America, Adorno was consciously engaging with this tradition. Yet, he was also faced with a difficult proposition. How does one, for example, satirize satire and how can one avoid the danger of this critique of modernity being read in a prelapsarian, reactionary manner? Adorno's solution, I argue, was to create an anti-*Zeitoper*, a work that critiques both the form and musical content of a *Zeitoper* without suggesting a return to the past as a means of escaping the present. The first point to make here is that he sets his opera not in contemporary, urban America but in the rural, pastoral American past of the mid-nineteenth century. Yet this space, as I discuss below, represents neither escape from nor an antithesis to the present. Instead, the libretto highlights both consonances and dissonances between present and past that work together to track the origins of the contemporary crisis in the 1930s. Second, Adorno's incomplete opera is the only one of these operas to have been based on an American literary source, let alone of the caliber of Twain. That this was a risky endeavor on Adorno's part cannot be ignored. The end result is no doubt messy, and the difficulty he faced in adapting Twain goes a long way to explain the uneven reception of the work. Third, Adorno is the only composer not to use jazz and jazz-like elements. Setting the opera in the past freed him in many ways from the necessity of incorporating jazz but not entirely, as in his score, he also does not attempt to reproduce nineteenth-century music, American or otherwise. Instead, in the two completed compositions, Adorno has produced twelve-tone serial compositions.[14] While it would surprise few that Adorno does not include jazz and instead composes a la Schoenberg and Berg, jazz's absence is nonetheless significant.

As this point, it is important to consider in some detail the music he did produce. The two completed songs are "Hucks Auftrittlied" ("Huck's Entrance Song") and "Totenlied auf den Kater" ("Death Song to the Tomcat"). In each, Adorno overlays his dystopian vision of American society with an atonal score, producing a disorienting and chilling effect, particularly for anyone approaching Twain or *Tom Sawyer* with naïve notions. At the same time, music and text exist in dialogue with each other, at least according to musicologist Martin Hufner. Of "Huck's Entrance Song," Hufner writes: "the musical structure (*Gestaltung*) is in essence based upon the text. One can almost hear the dog's 'barking at the moon,' the 'catching of flies with the mouth' . . . . These textually based impressions have their musical analogies. They are almost executed as program music (*musikbildlich umgesetzt*)."[15] Although it is impossible to know how other songs would have dealt with the relationship between music and text, Hufner suggests that the music would have underscored, rather than introduced or contradicted, key elements of the text.

By breaking with the established rules of the *Zeitoper* such as the jazz milieu of the modern metropolis, yet still remaining in dialogue with the genre through its setting in America, Adorno's opera may have been able to reconfigure the question of American culture and, by extension, the cultural meaning of America and American jazz for Weimar Germany. In particular, in refusing to relegate jazz music either to an impossible and implausible utopian promise or even to satirize and ironize it, jazz's silence in the opera could have acted as a negative space that, in concert with the libretto, might have created a new model of critical engagement with both the American present and past. Still, all these thoughts must ultimately be attenuated through the use of the subjunctive. The fact that Adorno never completed the opera is as telling as the fragment that exists. The missing music points not only towards a lack within his opera, it also hints at the fragility of the jazz republic and much else at Weimar Germany's end.

Between 1932 when Adorno began work on the project and his departure for England in 1934, Adorno's personal situation grew untenable. Already, the first nine months of the Nazi dictatorship had brought terrible, if uncertain, change: from the suspension of civic liberties, to the dismissal of politically and racially undesirables from state-funded positions, to even more ominous events like the construction of a concentration camp for political opponents in Dachau. Adorno's own experience of the events of 1933 was unexceptional, if no less tragic.[16] While visiting in Berlin with his future wife, Gretel Karplus, the Institute for Social Research was forcibly closed and Adorno's work at the University of Frankfurt ended that year as well.[17] On a more personal note, his house in Frankfurt was searched, and he feared that his mail was being opened. Then, when he attempted to switch career paths to music instruction, he was informed that because of the "Law for the Restoration of the Professional Civil Service," he would only be allowed to instruct "non-Aryans."[18] In sum, every month the Nazis held power, Adorno's prospects seemed to grow bleaker. As he wrote to his mentor, composer Alban Berg, on November 13, 1933:

> At the moment things are not going very well with my own work. My *venia legendi* has now indeed been revoked as a result of the Aryan paragraph and I'm spending a great amount of time and energy looking for a new teaching position. This by itself would not be so terrible, but for weeks I was so generally depressed that I lacked the freedom to compose. I have to work at gradually (*mühsam*) reacquiring it. [. . .] Nevertheless, I believe that my libretto [i.e. to *Treasure*] and the pair of pieces I composed (which already exist as scores) are meaningful (*etwas taugen*). But such an ambitious (*weitschichtige*) work truly demands a more open horizon of fantasy than I have today.[19]

In this note to his friend and teacher, one senses the thirty-year-old's frustration and desperation. By the end of 1933, Adorno no longer felt he possessed the "freedom to compose," the intellectual space to create a work of art that could speak, if only from a place of privilege, to the injustice surrounding and impacting him.

In his inability to progress in his own work and through the institutional, legal, and social repression mounting around him, Adorno's place in Weimar culture, along with his opera, was decomposing before his very eyes. This state of affairs no longer supported the idealized stakes of Weimar's engagement with music, race, and American culture that it had even as late as 1932. In other words, it no longer provided for a "horizon of fantasy" in which a meeting of the American author Mark Twain and a German philosopher-composer could mean something significant. It did not matter that text and music were effective in themselves—they were losing their addressee.

In the Ruins of the Jazz Republic

After more than a decade of critics, authors, musicologists, and artists rhapsodizing on the dangers and dreams of contemporary America across Weimar culture, for Adorno, there seemed to be no place better suited to tracing the origins of the current crisis than in the American past. At the same time, Adorno's choice of source material is both curious and significant: Mark Twain's *The Adventures of Tom Sawyer* (1876). Perhaps the best-known American novelist at the time, Twain was widely read in Germany, and his works were regularly translated into German. *The Adventures of Tom Sawyer*, moreover, is a founding myth of childhood and children's literature in America. Though written in the 1870s, Twain sets his novel in the antebellum South in the fictitious town of St. Petersburg on the Mississippi river. In episodic manner, it tells the story of the rapscallions Tom Sawyer and Huckleberry Finn, Tom's companion and titular hero of Twain's later novel *The Adventures of Huckleberry Finn* (1885). The narrative is propelled by the boys' witnessing of a murder by "Injun' Joe," a half-Native American, half-white criminal. The boys swear an oath to never speak a word about the murder, for fear that Joe will seek retribution if he ever found out that they had witnessed the act. After the murder is blamed on Joe's innocent associate, Muff Potter, Tom breaks his oath of silence by testifying in court against Joe. Yet Tom's testimony only serves to put him in immediate danger, as his appearance in court is promptly followed by Joe's escape. Living for the remainder of the novel in fear, Tom eventually meets up with Joe in a labyrinthine cave located on the outskirts of town. There, the criminal will fall to his death in an act that ends both Tom and Huck's fear as well as makes them rich. It turns out that the cave was the hiding place of Joe's treasure, the inspiration for Adorno's title. Twain's novel thus ends on a relatively happy note with both boys ostensibly reborn as wealthy, respectable figures of the town.

Taking place across seven scenes, Adorno's libretto retains the central episodes and overall arc of the novel, yet also makes key alterations and additions.[20] Most glaringly, Adorno shifts the setting of the story from the fictitious St. Petersburg to the real birthplace of Twain, Hannibal, Missouri. Though based in reality, the name Hannibal is significant because of the associations the city's namesake would have had for the classically educated Adorno. The historical figure Hannibal possessed, for at least one important figure of the period, special significance for the situation of Jews in Europe: Sigmund Freud. Having engaged with Freud's writings at least since 1927, Adorno was thus likely familiar with the following passage from Freud's *Interpretation of Dreams*: "To my youthful mind Hannibal and Rome symbolized the conflict between the tenacity of Jewry and the organization of the Catholic church. And the increasing importance of the effects of the anti-Semitic movement upon our emotional life helped to fix the thoughts and feelings of those early days."[21]

Indeed, Adorno was potentially motivated in his choice of Twain for reasons of solidarity. Twain was rumored by those on the right to have been a Jewish writer (he was not), and in the 1933 edition of *Handbuch der Judenfrage* (*Handbook of the Jewish Question*), Twain is described as having a "Jewish" writing style.[22] Hannibal, however, was not just a "Semitic general," he was an African general, and it is in this doubling of Africanness and Jewishness that the shift from "St. Petersburg" to Hannibal takes on further significance. In thereby invoking the interweaving of Blackness, Jewishness, and American-ness that was so common during the final years of the Weimar Republic, Adorno positions his text in response to the poisoned atmosphere of early 1930s Germany and the function of jazz therein. Further indicating that ques-tions of race and Blackness in American culture were on his mind is Adorno's important alteration to the *mise-en-scéne*. Whereas Twain clearly sets his novel in the antebellum period of Southern slave society, Adorno indicates that his story takes place in the 1860s.[23] Because he does not specify an exact date, but only a decade, emphasis is placed on this period's transitional nature, one in which the slave-holding South lost the Civil War, African Americans were freed from slavery, and the entire region underwent rapid transition to free-market capitalism. Though the analogy remains intentionally imprecise, the implied connection between the revanchist American South and the radical right wing in Germany, between anti-Black racism in America and anti-Semitism in Germany, powerfully informs the libretto.

At the same time, though *Treasure* sets up parallels between 1860s Amer-ica and 1930s Germany, between African Americans and German Jews, it would be a mistake to view this work as but an allegory of the present. Ador-no's choice of a relatively outdated author like Twain shows that he is equally interested in highlighting dissonances between the eras. By 1932, Twain's popularity in Germany had diminished, with fewer editions of his works and fewer discussions of his work appearing in the press.[24] In a word, Twain's work had become *passé* for an audience beginning to discover modern American authors like Fitzgerald, Dreiser, Hemingway, not to mention African American authors like James Weldon Johnson and Langston Hughes. Second, Adorno's choice of translation intensifies the distance between Twain and the German present. Adorno bases his text not on the most recent translations of the 1920s, but on Margarete Jacobi's 1892 translation, *Tom Sawyers Abenteuer und St-reiche*.[25] Adorno not only adapted Jacobi's translation, he leaves significant portions of the translation untouched.[26] This means that Adorno's libretto at times hardly reads like Adorno, whose own writing style was notoriously dif-ficult and dense. It should then come as no surprise that, like Tiedemann, Walter Benjamin took offence at the libretto's language, calling out *Treasure* for the "straightforward, rustic tone of the dialogue."[27] Yet this, I would argue, was Adorno's intention. The datedness of the language and of Twain himself are crucial coordinates within the force field linking, but never telescoping, Twain's America of the mid-nineteenth and Adorno's Germany of the early twentieth centuries. Together, the elements of Twain's Americanness and "Jewishness," the overdetermined place of Hannibal in the 1860s, and its rural setting, in addition to the archaic language, act to simultaneously historicize the present and actualize the past.

One reason for this complicated procedure is that Adorno viewed *Treasure* as an opportunity to provide an aesthetic response to his and Walter Benjamin's theorization of the ruin in capitalism. Indeed, he understood *Treasure* to be of a piece with Benjamin's *Arcades Project* and the ideas of allegory and ruin undergirding it. Viewing in Benjamin *Treasure*'s "ideal reader," after completing the libretto, Adorno sent him a copy for his reaction.[28] When Benjamin finally responded after several months of delay, he critiqued the work not only for its language but more fundamentally suggested that, in its present form, *Treasure* amounted to a "reduction to the idyllic."[29] Adorno in turn delayed for over a month before reacting. In his response, he insists regarding the tone specifically:

> The hearty language is not the heartiness of real children, so much as that encountered in the literature written for children; [. . .]; if it doesn't sound too arrogant, I would perhaps suggest that I have smuggled a great deal into the piece, that nothing is quite intended in the sense in which it immediately appears, and that I am using the childlike imagery to present some extremely serious things.[30]

These "serious things" may refer to the theoretical import of *Treasure* as a reflection on the aesthetic of the ruin, an important synthesis of his philosophical and musical investigations up to this point in his career.

This idea of *Treasure* as an enactment of the Benjaminian ruin comes into particular focus when the work is read in relation to Adorno's lecture on *Naturgeschichte*, or "natural history." Delivered to the Frankfurt *Kantgesellschaft* in July 1932, that is just three months before he began work on *Treasure*, Adorno elaborates in this lecture on his ideas about nature and history in ways that not only pay homage to Benjamin but also prefigure the central arguments of his and Horkheimer's later *Dialectic of Enlightenment*. Adorno begins with a discussion of the traditional understanding of nature and history. Following a strategy of immanent critique, he accepts these terms for the moment in order to push "these concepts to a point where they are mediated in their apparent difference."[31] As Adorno well knew, while the enmeshing of nature and history represented an important step away from the idealist tradition, it was not enough. Instead, the purpose of natural history had to be a reorientation of the very practice of philosophy, a "change of perspective" as he put it.[32] This was to be achieved through an allegorical deciphering of the ruin.

For Benjamin, as for Adorno, the ruin stands as the physical embodiment of the idea of natural history. "In the ruin," Benjamin writes in his *Origin of the German Tragic Drama*, "history has physically merged into the setting. And in this guise history does not assume the form of the process of an eternal life so much as that of irresistible decay."[33] Ruins signify not only the meeting of nature and history, they also reveal the lie of historical progress and lay waste to the idea of capitalist society as a harmonious self-identical totality. As Susan Buck-Morss notes about the ruin in capitalism: "The debris of industrial culture teaches us not the necessity of submitting to historical catastrophe, but the fragility of the social order that tells us this catastrophe is necessary."[34] Due to the split vision of natural history, the world as experienced by the subject loses its appearance of wholeness, transforming itself into shards and rubble in need of signification and (allegorical) interpretation.

It is this idea of natural history as ruin that lies at the center of *Treasure* and one Adorno makes quite explicit within the text itself. While Tom and Huck dig for buried treasure in a haunted house, Tom stops to pick up a brick. Holding it in his hand, he comments to Huck: "with a brick like this we could have a nice game of treasure" (*S* 62). Here, Tom resignifies the search for gold into a game in which the ruins of commodity culture become the object of desire. Tom elaborates that these "stones were made by people long ago in the brickworks on the river. You still feel that they were baked in the mold. Now they are a ruin. They lie there broken like real stones, as if they had been lying there forever. Just like the treasure" (*S* 62). Tom's immediate insight here is to recognize the social construction of wealth, with the bricks' ruinous state breaking down the perception of capitalist value as impervious and solid. Yet, this passage also acts as a map to Adorno's text. In connecting the ideas of the ruin and treasure, it suggests that the treasure(s) of Adorno's opera will be found precisely in such collisions of nature and history, of myth and reason.

To achieve his natural historical reading of nineteenth-century American society, Adorno strategically intertwines three groups that represent an enmeshing of nature and history: animals, children, and marginalized racial groups. What potentially drew Adorno to *Tom Sawyer* was that Twain himself uses the negativity of these groups in relation to the bourgeois' self-definition in order to achieve his own critique of American society. In Adorno's *Treasure*, however, the exclusion of these groups attains theoretical weight. Their mistreatment and exclusion, individually and in concert, mark the space of the freedom that remains unfulfilled, yet that is promised by Enlightenment reason.

Of Dogs, Cats, and Nature's Repression

Adorno maintained a life-long fascination with animals, something he shared with Twain.[35] Adorno had pet names for his family members and friends, including "giraffe" for his wife and "mammoth" for his long-time collaborator Max Horkheimer. More to the point, Adorno consistently used animals throughout his philosophical work, and according to Christina Gerhardt, in his works this fascination became a subject "inscribed in a whole network of theoretical concerns."[36] In the early 1930s, these ideas were still in embryonic form. Writing to the composer Ernst Krenek in 1934, who shortly thereafter received a copy of the libretto, Adorno asked that Krenek pay particular attention to "the consistent animal symbolism of dog and cat, for which I have no theory, yet is perhaps the most important thing."[37] Gerhardt's arguments about animals in Adorno's *oeuvre* generally line up with this missing theory. Gerhardt suggests that in Adorno's work animals and "animality function [. . .] as an index of what reason has repressed."[38] Specifically, they act as a rejoinder to Kantian ethics, which in part sought to define humanity through its opposition to animals. Animals, their treatment by and interaction with humans, act dialectically to denote humanity's in/humanity. In the opera's libretto, cats, dogs, bats, and flies, as well as unidentifiable animals, are present or referred to throughout the text and signify a liminal sphere of intersection between reason and the repression of nature under capitalist culture.[39]

As Adorno makes clear in his letter to Krenek, it is domestic animals, cats and dogs, that stood for him at the center of this problematic in *Treasure*. Such animals are enchanted, mythical figures for Tom and Huck, imbued with the power to invoke an otherworldly, uncanny sphere of haunted houses and cemeteries. Cats, dead ones in particular, carry significant symbolic weight in both Twain and Adorno. In Twain, Tom gives his cat Peter a painkiller originally intended for him, resulting in the animal jumping through a window, never to return. In Adorno's version, Tom also gives Peter the painkiller, but instead of an ambiguous fate, Adorno specifies that the cat eventually dies from the medicine, an addition meant to link violence against animals with violence against humans. Despite a proclamation of guilt over Peter's death in the opera's first song, "Death Song to a Tomcat," Tom will merely discard the cat's dead body and move on. It is at this point that his comrade Huck enters and claims Peter's corpse for use in a ritual ceremony to cure him of his warts. Both in Twain's original and Adorno's setting, a dead cat thus serves as the intermediary for Tom and Huck between the living and dead worlds, a ruin of life imbued with the power not only to invoke but to control the spirit world. Both Tom and Huck's proximity to the cat serves to animalize the boys. Indeed, it can hardly have escaped Adorno's attention that Tom Sawyer's first name is also that of a male cat in English, and, as in the case of the painkiller, what happens to Tom and what happens to the cat reciprocally inform each other. Furthermore, Huck communicates with Tom as a cat, signaling his presence to him through a meow in the night.

While cats are primarily linked to the children, who suffer at the hands of others, dogs are more closely aligned with the perpetrators of such violence. This association of dogs with perpetrators potentially led Adorno to choose the pseudonym "Hektor Rottweiler" when publishing his highly controversial "On Jazz" in 1936. As he later explained to Peter von Haselberg, the name "appeared so German and dangerous that no one would suspect a Jew behind such a name."[40] Meanwhile in *Treasure*, the criminal of the story, Indian Joe, is consistently related to dogs. Tom calls him a "dog catcher" (*S* 26) and Huck will later term him an "Indian dog" (*S* 34), while Joe himself says at one point that he is "dog tired" (*S* 66). Still, though Joe may be the tormentor to the boys, as a person of Native American descent in a world defined by whiteness, he also belongs to a group in danger of eradication. The exclusion and repression suffered by Indian Joe due to his race simultaneously animalizes and humanizes him. In a word, he is the beaten dog who has bitten back at society through his criminality. I will return to the function of racial others later in my analysis, but it is important to see how the character Indian Joe functions both as perpetrator and victim.

Models of Childhood in Modernity

The connection in *Treasure* between reason's repression of nature and the violence of and against humans is echoed in its portrayal of children and childhood. For indeed, children stand in Twain and Adorno on the precipice between animality and humanity, nature and history. To an even greater degree than domestic animals, children and childhood represent a troubled area for defining humanity against nature within Enlightenment thought. Though children were said to lack the reason through which humanity's difference from animals was defined, children also obviously possessed human form and would eventually acquire reason. As Anthony Krupp notes in his study of childhood in early modern philosophy, within encyclopedias and dictionaries of the eighteenth century: "The higher cognitive faculties (namely, reason and intellect) define . . . what it means to be fully human; since children lack these faculties and adults possess them, childhood per se is defined negatively, as a period of 'lack,' an age under the sign of 'not yet.'"[41] Given this model of childhood, it is unsurprising that, in *Treasure,* children are so intimately linked to animals. Yet rather than imbuing childhood with any utopian ideal, Adorno seeks to uncover the bourgeois model of childhood as a period of "lack" for what it is: a projection exposing the return of bourgeois humanity's repressed nature through its representation of children.

Treasure's representation of children and childhood is, as is the case of domestic animals, represented through a dialectical pair. The two main figures, Tom and Huck, embody competing ideals of childhood that stand in tension with each other. On the one hand, Adorno's Tom begins as a capitalist entrepreneur, who, instead of money, trades in remnants of the adult world that have fallen into children's hands—apple cores, a kite, marbles, a piece of blue glass, a glass stopper, a piece of rope, etc. (*S* 12). Famously, Tom acquires these goods by having the neighborhood children pay him to paint a fence, a task which had been intended as punishment for his bad behavior. Though the other children at first resist his offer, Tom convinces them, telling those who would mock him: "Can you paint a fence everyday? There's something to this punishment (*Strafarbeit*). For Tom Sawyer it's a lot of fun" (*S* 13). Transforming work into fun is Tom's capitalist trick, and like their elders, the neighborhood boys fall for his deception. Indeed, Tom earns a bounty so plentiful that he delights in wasting one of his valuable matches by stomping on it, commenting: "never before have I had so much. There's no telling what one can do with it" (*S* 12).

While Tom busies himself with the acquisition of objects for their exchange value, the *lumpen* Huck needs them for their use value alone. When Huck first emerges from the barrel he lives in, Adorno describes his clothing as the "utterly ragged clothing of an adult, folded-up pants with only one suspender, a much too long jacket, and a hole-filled hat" (*S* 14). Like Tom's profit, Huck's clothing consists of the ruins of adult society; ill-fitting and ill-preserved, they are composed of capitalism's waste. In his embodiment of that which this society no longer values, Huck is marked as the "pariah of Hannibal" (*S* 21) and, like Joe, remains as an outsider and, as such, a potential threat to the community.[42] Huck is not only a threat to capitalism as a class system, he also threatens its ideologies of masculinity. To wit, Adorno's Huck is both hypermasculine and effeminate. While he may physically best Tom in their initial encounter, any such masculine prowess would have been upset by Adorno's choice to have the character sung by a soprano.[43] In the end, then, the two boys signify competing models of childhood development. Tom, the bourgeois man-child, is well prepared to become fully human for this system, to forever leave behind this period of "not yet," while Huck's position as ambiguously gendered vagrant guarantees that his humanity will likely remain partial.

Though counterpoised to each other, the two figures nonetheless remain in a state of dialectical enmeshment: Tom's maturation into the fullness of white male humanity is constantly threatened by his youth and association with Huck, while Huck, through the treasure he and Tom acquire at the story's close, will become wealthy enough to be accepted into Hannibal's high society. Yet if both carry the potential of turning one way or the other, each makes a decision within the opera that ensures he will stay on the path laid out for him in their initial introductions. In Tom's case, his downward trajectory is halted by breaking the oath he swears with Huck, i.e., to never speak of Indian Joe's murder of Dr. Robinson. As Adorno explained in his letter to Krenek: "Tom becomes 'free' through the violation of the oath and the exploding of the mythic-ethical sphere of the oath, just as in a certain sense the entire thing is the fulfillment of a dialectical de-mythologization (*Ent-Mythologisierung*)."[44] Read in the context of nature-history, the initial oath in the cemetery, signed on a piece of bark in the boys' own blood, signals the boys' acquiescence to the mythic, natural world. In breaking with this oath, Tom is able to escape from it. However, as Tiedemann astutely notes, Tom's emancipatory act would have been followed by another oath, this time before the court of Hannibal.[45] So though Tom may have escaped the mythical-natural world, he now enters the historical-rational world symbolized by the bourgeois legal system. One might therefore suggest that Tom commits an Odyssean act of Enlightenment in the sense developed in *The Dialectic of Enlightenment*: in breaking the initial oath, Tom overcomes his fear and thereby breaks with the mythical past, yet in this very act, he is simultaneously sworn into the new mythic structure of capitalist logic and instrumental reason. With his entry into this realm, that which is dangerous and threatening to Tom changes. No longer a societal outsider, he is free to enjoy the privilege of white, male power. As Christopher D. Morris writes, "Adorno depicts [Tom] as the Enlightenment spirit that remains unconscious of its preconceptions, its hermeneutic circle, its imperialism."[46] While Tom ultimately is able to find safety in this space, it is one that remains inaccessible to the marginalized members of this society, most notably Joe, Huck, and, as we will see, African Americans.

Given how true to Twain and the translator Jacobi Adorno's libretto remains, it is all the more telling that Adorno makes an important addition concerning race and the possibility of justice. After Tom and Huck have taken their oath of silence, they reflect on its implications for others. In Twain's original text, Huck makes reference to the fact that their silence will likely result in a hanging. While nineteenth-century readers of Twain may also have understood him to mean the hanging, or lynching, of an African American, Adorno not only makes explicit this subtext of Twain's text, he uses this moment as an opportunity to further differentiate the social position and consciousness of Tom and Huck.

> TOM: If the doctor dies, someone will be hanged.
> HUCK: It'll be a nigger that gets hanged.
> TOM: But he didn't even do it.
> HUCK: No one was there. A nigger will get hanged. (*S* 31)

Other than the initial line, which had been originally spoken by Huck, these words are wholly of Adorno's invention and have no correlate in Twain's text. Significantly, they reveal Tom's naïve assumptions about the bourgeois legal system as well as Huck's more pragmatic and realist position that has been informed by his position as town pariah. While Tom's words reflect his unflinching faith in the legal system as rational arbiter of guilt and innocence, Huck understands that, whether real or imagined, a violation of one of this society's members (here, the murder of Dr. Robinson) must be recompensed. Though Adorno's libretto follows Twain and it is ultimately not an African American who is to be hanged but the white Muff Potter, such additions suggest that race, Blackness, and "half-breeds" like Indian Joe were not only on Adorno's mind in 1932/33, but they potentially serve an important function within *Treasure*.

At the same time, the full extent of the importance of racial others within this constellation of oaths, testimony, witnessing, and justice remains opaque, limited in part by Twain's blunted vision of race in *Tom Sawyer*. Yet Adorno's adaptation of Twain's text was never meant to stand for the 1860s alone, but it was intended to speak with and to the early 1930s; in the minds of many Germans, Europeans, and Americans, reference to the execution of an African

American for a crime he did not commit had a very contemporary resonance: the tragedy of the Scottsboro Boys.

Adorno and the Scottsboro Boys

On March 25, 1931, nine African American youths were travelling on the Southern Railroad's Chattanooga to Memphis freight train.[47] Their names were Charles Weems, Clarence Norris, Ozie Powell, Olen Montgomery, Eugene Williams, Willie Roberson, Roy Wright, Andy Wright, and Haywood Patterson. Aging in range from 13 to 19, they, along with some sixteen other, mostly white male youths, were riding the train illegally. After a white rider stepped on the hand of an African American rider, a fight broke out between the two groups, with most of the white riders soon jumping off board. After the defeated whites informed the stationmaster in Stevenson, Georgia, that a gang of African Americans had attacked them, the train was stopped in the town of Paint Rock, where local sheriffs and a hastily organized group of men met the train. Authorities then discovered nine African American youths, a white male, and two young white women, Ruby Bates and Victoria Price. The two women would soon report that they had been raped. The implication of this charge was clear for the African American riders. As Clarence Norris later stated: "I was scared before, but it wasn't nothing to how I felt now. I knew if a white woman accused a black man of rape, he was as good as dead."[48] A mere twelve days later the first of the so-called "Scottsboro Boys Trials" was held. Splitting up the defendants, Weems and Norris were the first to be prosecuted, and the all-white jury quickly delivered a guilty verdict with a sentence of death by electrocution. In all, four separate trials of the defendants were held in 1931, each with the same result. The only aberration to this rule was the trial of thirteen-year-old Roy Wright, whose case ended in mistrial because the jury refused to acquiesce to the prosecution's request for life imprisonment, with jury members insisting on the death penalty.

While the injustice perpetrated against these young men remains shocking, the case might have been forgotten were it not for the national and international campaign against the injustice at Scottsboro. The movement to free these innocent young men resulted in protests across the globe and a series of retrials and appeals, eventually reaching the Alabama and United States Supreme Courts. In particular, the communist International Defense League (IDL) elevated the status of this small-town Southern matter to a level of notoriety equal to that of Sacco and Vanzetti. As historians Miller, Pennybacker, and Rosenhaft write:

The Scottsboro case has been called one of the great defining moments of the twentieth century, providing a vocabulary and constellation of images not only for its own time but for subsequent generations as well. . . . The mythic power of the case did not derive from the fact of injustice alone. It depended on the way the case was publicized—and its outcomes shaped—by the campaign on behalf of the defendants organized by the international Communist movement.[49]

News of Scottsboro quickly reached Germany, and a campaign in support of the defendants was organized through the Berlin offices of the *Internationale Rote Hilfe* (*International Red Aid*) and Willi Münzenberg's *Liga gegen Imperialismus* (*League Against Imperialism*).[50] Exposure to the case was heightened through the speaking tour of the mother of Roy and Andy, Ada Wright, who arrived in Hamburg on May 7, 1932, and appeared in Berlin on May 12. Though Wright was officially prohibited from publically speaking in many cities, as was the case in Berlin, her tour publicized the plight of the African American youths for the German public. As Louis Engdahl, who accompanied Wright on her travels, reported: "The total result . . . has been to set all Germany thinking about the Scottsboro case to the extent that on trains, in streetcars, and even on the public highways, the Negro mother, her likeness being made familiar by pictures and publicized everywhere, was continuously asked by those interested, 'What can we do to help?'"[51] If the extent of discussion referred to by Engdahl can be questioned, his remarks nonetheless contain a great deal of truth about the breadth of the impact of Scottsboro on the German public. For example, Das Komitee zur Rettung der Opfer von Scottsboro (The Committee for the Rescue of the Victims of Scottsboro) founded in 1932 under the leadership of Alfons Goldschmidt, worked to increase awareness of the case and to stop the planned executions. This group issued a political pamphlet *8 Menschen in der Todeszelle* (*8 People on Death Row*) that explained the history of the case and of lynching in America. It ended with poems by Langston Hughes and Claude McKay from Nussbaum's *Africa Sings*. Indeed, a protest letter against the injustice of Scottsboro reprinted in *8 People on Death Row* included signatures of two of the most important public figures of the time, Thomas Mann and Alfred Einstein. Far from a trivial event, through the visit of Ada Wright, communist demonstrations, the organizational efforts of Goldschmidt and others, Scottsboro was on the minds of many leftists in the spring and summer of 1932.

If Adorno never made any public remarks on the Scottsboro case, this is not definitive proof of his ignorance either. Scottsboro was widely and publicly discussed, especially in the left-leaning intellectual circles in which Adorno traveled. More concretely, Adorno may have learned about the case through Godo Remszhardt, a Frankfurt associate at the Institute for Social Research. In the early 1930s, Remszhardt wrote the African American activist William Pickens, discussing with him his plans for a ten-volume series on African American culture.[52] Remszhardt also wrote to Langston Hughes, requesting his permission to reprint his work and asking him to pass along his address to Alain Locke, whom Remszhardt had apparently met on one of the latter's visits to the city of Nauheim located near Frankfurt.[53] Adorno could thus have known of the Scottsboro case either through the general public discussion or through personal contact with someone like Remszhardt.

By the same token, despite the reference to injustice against African Americans in his 1932 libretto, Adorno never made any knowledge of the case explicit. Here, one would do well to recall another philosopher's silence regarding race in an important early work, namely Hegel's. Susan Buck-Morss has recently offered a provocative reading of Haiti and the enslavement of Africans throughout the Western Hemisphere as an inspiration for Hegel's famous master/slave dialectic in *The Phenomenology of the Spirit*. Though the precise reasons for Adorno's silence on Scottsboro may differ from those of Hegel, Buck-Morss' description of Hegel's precarious professional and financial position at the time of his writing of *The Phenomenology of the Spirit* shares some similarity to Adorno's position in 1932/33. As she argues, the negative repercussions Hegel would have incurred for overt criticism of the state or for explicit references to Haitian revolution likely made him wary of making the connection overt.[54] Indeed, given Adorno's equivocal response to his status as racial outsider within Nazi Germany, he had many reasons to remain silent on Scottsboro.

I bring up Hegel and Haiti because, as Buck-Morss suggests, Hegel's silence is not only personal but carries methodological implications. As she writes in *Hegel and Haiti*: "What happens when, in the spirit of dialectics, we turn the tables, and consider Haiti not as the victim of Europe, but as an agent in Europe's construction?"[55] With this question, Buck-Morss challenges us to read European history from the "margins," to investigate how, in the age of colonialism, European history, including that of its philosophers, was in very important ways written from the outside in, shaped in turn by historical actors and events long considered unimportant. In order for this method to work to its fullest extent, one must begin not from an assumption of the insignificance of "minor" events but of their potential significance. In other words, Buck-Morss calls upon scholars to shift issues from the margins to the center of European history through exploration of provocative juxtapositions like Adorno and Scottsboro.

Indeed, when one compares the major fault lines of the Scottsboro trials and Adorno's *Treasure*, the points of contact between the two take on focus, namely witnessing, oath taking, and the possibility of justice for socially stigmatized groups. Throughout the Scottsboro trials, witnesses contradicted each other, equivocated, recanted, and adapted their testimony. To begin with, the testimony of Victoria Price and Ruby Bates, the two young women who levied the charge of rape, could not have been more disparate. While Price was gregarious and quick-witted, offering a compelling description of what had happened to her, Bates' testimony was halting and even contradicted Price's in certain points. In addition, while two local doctors provided evidence that immotile semen had been found in both girls, each also stated that they found little evidence to corroborate the violent acts described by Price. The defendants themselves contributed to the confusion. All initially denied that a rape had taken place, but, after Price and Bates' testimony, together with the hostile atmosphere outside the courtroom and mounting guilty verdicts, three of them testified that they had seen the others rape the girls but had themselves not taken part.[56] Further trials (and convictions) would ensue throughout the 1930s, each offering a new iteration of the same fundamental question: What claim on truth does witness testimony have in relation to guilt or innocence in an atmosphere poisoned by racial animus and oppression?

Further points of confluence exist between the case and Adorno's opera. Like Tom and even more so the proto-hobo Huck, Victoria Price and Ruby Bates existed on the margins of Southern society and lived lives that, in the words of Goodman, "mocked the white South's most sacred ideal," namely that of Black and white separation.[57] Bates and Price were raised and lived in interracial settings, and they, like the African Americans on the train, were subjugated to the system of agricultural and industrial exploitation that existed in the American South, though not to the same extent. Yet once they were discovered on the train, their accusation of rape against the African American youths invoked an as yet unclaimed privilege of whiteness. Again in the words of Goodman, Price and Bates:

> knew that the Black youths had not raped them or bothered them in any way. But they also knew that if they had said nothing or no—'No, those Negroes didn't even speak to us'—the people who asked [the deputies] would have thought of them the way respectable white men and women had always thought of them: as the lowest of the low, vagabonds, adulter-

ers, bootleggers, tramps. If, on the other hand, they complained or said yes, the same people would suddenly have thought of them as rape victims and treated them as white southern women, poor but virtuous, for the first time in their lives.[58]

As with the case of Tom, Bates and Price's testimony served as their entrance into the community from which they had previously been excluded. The courtroom acted as the symbolic site of their initiation.

"If No One's Looking": Race, Vision, and the Impossibility of Escape

As would be expected from an author interested in the role of race and the possibility of justice, as I believe Adorno to have been in 1932/33, *Treasure* accords to African Americans and their social exclusion and stigmatization a central place. At four moments in the libretto, African Americans figure prominently and, in at least two of these instances, in ways at odds with Twain's original novel. The importance accorded Blackness and African Americans in the libretto is particularly noteworthy because, other than in his jazz writings, where its significance is downplayed, Blackness as a meaningful category of social difference does not have a place within Adorno's thought, neither prior to nor after *Treasure*. Yet because of his source material, Twain, an author famous not only for his humor but for his controversial deployment of racial attitudes in America, as well as the debate about race, capitalism, and justice stirred by the Scottsboro case, African Americans become a fulcrum point of Adorno's text from the early 1930s. Like animals and children, they demarcate a space of violently repressed non-humanity, a space from which Tom will flee and into which Huck will attempt to escape.

The first appearance of an African American character occurs in the opera's opening scene: the previously discussed exchange of labor (fence painting) for childhood treasure. This episode has already been analyzed in relation to Tom's proto-bourgeois status. While Twain also uses an African American character, a young boy named Jim, there are vast differences between Twain's and Adorno's staging of the episode. Twain narrates the painting of the fence chronologically, proceeding from Aunt Polly's assignment of the task as punishment through its completion via Tom's cunning deception of his playmates. In Twain, the sequence begins with Tom's initial attempt to trick Jim into doing his work for him. But before Jim can accede, he is struck from behind by Aunt

Polly's shoe and immediately runs down the street and away from Tom. When Adorno's opera begins, by contrast, Tom has already succeeded in tricking the other neighborhood boys and, rather than desiring that Jim work for him, Adorno's Tom merely requests that Jim look at the painted fence. The opera opens with the following dialogue.

> TOM: Have a look, Jim.
> JIM: Can't look. The old aunt says I shouldn't do anything but fetch water, my head'll be ripped off if I look.
> TOM: Don't be fooled, she always talks like that, she can't even really hit, no one feels it (*das spürt kein Mensch*).
> JIM: I'm afraid (*Ich Angst habe*) (*S* 9)[59]

If in Adorno's version Tom's status as proto-bourgeois has already been established through his trickery and the accumulation of childhood treasure, the obvious question arises as to why he is so insistent that Jim gaze upon the fence? Unlike in Twain, where the focus is on the exploitation of labor, Adorno is interested in the culture that results from such exploitation. In a word: Tom's prompt is intended to initiate Jim into the realm of commodity culture. This is a culture where to look is to desire (and vice versa), and Tom's demand that Jim look is also an imperative to enter the realm of bourgeois capitalism. Further, Jim's fear of violence regarding Aunt Polly (read: the white adult order) is well-founded; as in Twain, Adorno's Jim is also struck by Aunt Polly, not by a slipper, but by the corpse of Tom's dead cat Peter. That Jim is struck in the opening scene by this symbol of reason's violent repression of nature and metaphor for children means that racial others, children, and animals are linked from the very moment of the opera's beginning. Threatened by the same system that will seek to exterminate and oppress these other groups, the African American Jim immediately comprehends the stakes of acceding to Tom's request, saying: "my head'll be ripped off if I look." Attempting to allay Jim's fear, Tom responds that Aunt Polly cannot really hit, that "no one [*kein Mensch*] feels it." As an almost fully white male bourgeois, Tom need not take the threat seriously. The problem for Jim is that for this system he is not a human, can never become one, and most certainly does feel it when Aunt Polly does strike him with the weight of Peter's limp body.

Significantly, Jim's exclusion at the libretto's outset removes African Americans from all subsequent direct action in the plot, and there are no further Black characters present within the text—other than those referred to by Huck. For it is through Huck that race will be repeatedly brought into the libretto. Huck's relationship to African Americans is most clearly suggested at the end of the libretto. In the opera's penultimate scene, Tom and Huck overcome their fear of the cave, Indian Joe perishes, and they discover his treasure, an act which transforms them into the richest people in Hannibal. Yet, that this victory is more pyrrhic than real is quickly revealed through Adorno's description of their entrance into the celebration being held in their honor: "Suddenly Tom and Huck appear in an unspeakable condition, in utter contrast to the gathering. They wear the oldest suits; Huck is totally ragged and scared. Both are smeared all over with soot and stearin" (*S* 94). Adorno thematizes here the fact that though Tom has inwardly appropriated the values of this society, he still appears to them as an outsider, symbolized in the tattered clothes he wears and in the boys' faces that at once display both whiteness (stearin) and Blackness (soot). Yet once the boys reveal the riches they have brought with them to the gathered party, each is given a new suit to put on. While Tom immediately begins to change, i.e., adapt himself externally to his new status, Huck remains unmoved and instead leans up against a window through which he will shortly escape. As Tom continues to change his clothes, he attempts to convince his skittish friend to stay. When Huck remains steadfast in his refusal, Tom makes a final request of him:

> TOM: Huck, one more thing: Are you going to be back in your barrel tomorrow? We have to bury Peter.
> HUCK: Who?
> TOM: The cat.
> HUCK: You think. If it rains or is too hot, I'll be in the Rogers' barn. Ben doesn't mind. There's an old nigger there who's often given me something to eat. I much prefer to eat lunch with him, if no one's looking, at the same table, than here. *Bon appétit*, Tom. (*S* 101–102)

In Huck's departing statement are united all the major components of the opera: death, animals, race, and the powerful violence of looking and witnessing. Huck's ensuing flight through the window, like that of the cat Peter or Jim's down the street, is anything but an escape into freedom. If Huck can now refuse this bargain, his incorporation into white bourgeois society, like that of Ruby Bates and Victoria Price, is but a moment away. Like the vagabond youths on a train from Chattanooga to Memphis, Huck lives on the edge of this world, but it is certain that he will again be confronted with the opportunity to join and with ever-increasing pressure as he ages.

While *Treasure* remains silent about jazz, Adorno himself did not, and as he worked on the libretto to an opera that was to forever remain a fragment, he published his first major treatment of the music in *Europäische Revue*.[60] Entitled "Farewell to Jazz," it has long served as testimony to Adorno's stubborn resistance to jazz and his flawed understanding of it. Lacking in specific examples, the article appears to conflate the Central European experience of the music for jazz itself, to measure it not against Ellington and Armstrong but against the jazz-like music of The Revelers and Zez Confrey. Yet if Adorno would seem to judge the art form by outdated examples that highlight not jazz itself but its white appropriation, this is not necessarily attributable to a lack of knowledge regarding issues faced by African Americans, musicians or otherwise. As my analysis of *Treasure* has shown, Adorno was hardly unaware of (or unaccustomed to) the ideological use of racial difference towards exclusionary ends. Instead, "Farewell to Jazz," its apparent agreement with the Nazi ban of the music, as well as its lack of reference to major figures from the jazz tradition, are part of an interpretive strategy dependent upon the power of silence, in particular of jazz's silence. While the ultimate end of this strategy remains opaque within the dense theoretical network of *Treasure*, "Farewell to Jazz" will make explicit that Adorno's intention is not to celebrate jazz's silence but to make it heard.

Adorno's Farewell to Jazz

"End of April 1933"—These words appear above Adorno's controversial article and confront the reader today as a paratext to the piece's original presentation. Punctuated with a colon, they almost seem to linger over the text: a question to which it responds, or, perhaps, an explanation of what follows. For despite his precarious personal and professional situation in early 1933, Adorno nonetheless took time to write a farewell to jazz. From one perspective, it is not so much Adorno's argument as the historical context of its publication that should give one pause. Had Adorno issued this farewell before April 1933, his argument would have fit relatively neatly into a main strain of critical writing on jazz in Germany in the early 1930s. In fact, 1932 saw Adorno himself declare in a short concert note that jazz had reached its end.[61] Further, even Adorno's title was not new. As will be remembered, Hans David had issued an identical "Farewell to Jazz" in 1930 on the occasion of one of Sam Wooding's final performances in Berlin.[62] What such appraisals do not share with Adorno's is their relative innocence vis-à-vis National Socialism. Earlier declarations of jazz's end had not been written directly in response to the music's prohibition but to what was seen as the music's decline as an avant-garde musical genre. Thus for Adorno to say what had been already said, what he himself had already said, and at the most inopportune of moments, seems to be without logic, unless Adorno genuinely disliked jazz and agreed with the ban; sought to curry favor with the new government; attempted to smuggle in dissent through apparent approval; or, finally, wanted to use the opportunity provided by the ban to critique Weimar culture. There may be some truth to all of these ideas.

In order to fully understand his position in "Farewell to Jazz," there is first need for clarity regarding its exact target. The prohibition referred to by Adorno did not create a new legal situation as he implies but was independently issued by the new political leadership of Berlin's oldest public radio station, the *Berliner Funkstunde*.[63] The recently appointed and soon to be replaced National Socialist director Richard Kolb, issued a decree on March 8, 1933, announcing the elimination of jazz from the station's programming.[64] Despite the provocative title, Kolb's ban was anything but clear. It begins: "In the first years after the war Germany came to know in 'jazz music' a form of dance music that was ruled by an unbridled, excessively sharp and accentuated rhythm, characterized by the piercing tone of horns and a diverse complex of percussion and noise instruments."[65] This opening frames its target as the jazz of the immediate postwar period, interpreting such early jazz as the musical analogue to the political anarchism of the November Revolution. In point of fact, the *Funkstunde* ban directs its ire almost exclusively towards such early jazz. Contemporary jazz, it insists, is a stabilized, non-revolutionary music in which the music's African American roots no longer play a significant role. "In the most recent developments," it continues, "much of the unaesthetic, the grotesque and provocative elements of jazz music have been taken out."[66]

In essence, the ban attempts to delineate a politically innocuous form of jazz from the dangerous and subversive jazz of the past. Thus, the actual wording of the prohibition runs:

> The *Funkstunde* bans all dubious dance music, that designated as 'Negro music' by the common sense of the people (*vom gesunden Volksempfinden*), in which a salacious rhythm dominates and the melody is violated (*vergewaltigt*). But the *Funkstunde* will continue to support modern dance music, insofar as it is not inartistic in its musical elements or offensive to German sensibility. The mere use of instruments favored by jazz, such as, for example, the saxophone and banjo, do not suffice to define a music as jazz.[67]

The *Funkstunde* prohibition walks an ideological tightrope between the opposed needs of popular music and politics. While it is clear that something called "Negro music" will disappear from the Berlin station, it is entirely unclear what, musically or aesthetically, differentiates such music from other types of jazz and dance music, other than what the leadership of the *Funkstunde* designates as Black dance music, or jazz.

Adorno's response in "Farewell to Jazz" acutely diagnoses the illogic of the ban. In anticipation of a centerpiece of the culture industry thesis, Adorno refuses to recognize the, for him, purely ideological distinction between Black and white jazz postulated by Kolb. Rather than accurately reflecting actual, musical differences, for him, such distinctions ultimately serve to conceal the essential uniformity of all mass culture. Adorno begins:

> The regulation that forbids the radio from broadcasting "Negro jazz" may have created a new legal situation; but artistically it has only confirmed by its drastic verdict what was long ago decided in fact: the end of jazz music itself. For no matter what one wishes to understand by white or by Negro jazz, here there is nothing to salvage. Jazz itself has long been in the process of dissolution, in retreat into military marches and all sorts of folk music."[68]

In asserting the end of jazz as a revolutionary music of modernity and hence the meaninglessness of the ban, Adorno draws not only on the widespread belief of jazz's pastness but also adds to this thesis in interesting ways. What concerns him in this opening remark is not whether jazz was destined to disappear overnight; he clearly felt that, despite the superficial actions of the government and individual institutions, jazz would for the most part continue uninterrupted under National Socialist rule. Instead, ironically employing the terminology of the new regime, he specifies that the target of his ire is not: "big city degeneration or deracinated exoticism. . . . Jazz no more has anything to do with authentic Negro music, which has long since been industrially falsified and smoothed out here, than it is possessed of any destructive or threatening qualities."[69] Indeed, the strength and weakness of his argument lie in this rebuttal of the dominant terms of Weimar and now Nazi jazz discourse. For what Adorno suggests is that critics of jazz unwittingly miss their target (race) when they aim at jazz (commodity).

One way to look at "Farewell to Jazz," then, is to frame the text as an attempt to turn the reactionary tendencies of National Socialism towards progressive purposes. What Adorno seems to have desired was recognition of the implications of the very real break between Weimar culture and National So-cialism within the consciousness of the public. That is to say, for Adorno, only through intensive critique of the present, through direct commentary on the events of the day, rather than merely proceeding as if nothing had changed, would contemporary consciousness be in a position to confront the new politi-cal and cultural landscape. What Adorno hoped, to be sure naïvely, was that the ban could be seized as an opportunity to extricate music culture from the false utopia of unmediated freedom represented by jazz.

Towards this end, Adorno moves explicitly to historically locate jazz's use by the bourgeoisie. Shifting to the past tense in the third paragraph, he states in a declaratory manner: "Jazz was the *Gebrauchsmusik* of the *haute bourgeoisie* of the post-war period"[70] *Gebrauchsmusik* is to be understood here in the two-fold sense of a music for everyday use, and as one to be used for ideological ends; it is a music that, for Adorno, is determined to be exploited. One mode of the bourgeoisie's exploitation of jazz was its elevation to a music freed from the contradictions of modern capitalism. Summarizing the dream given form in their jazz ideology, Adorno writes:

> The virtuoso saxophonist or even percussionist, who made audacious leaps in between the marked beats of the measure, who displaced the ac-cents and dragged out the sounds in bold glissandi—he, at least, should have been exempted from industrialization. His realm was considered to be the realm of freedom; here the solid wall between production and re-production was evidently demolished, the longed-for immediacy restored, the alienation of man and music mastered out of vital force.[71]

It is the, for Adorno, necessary inability of jazz to occupy this realm of freedom that makes it "false." Its failure, in other words, resides in the discrepancy be-tween jazz as promised by cultural critics and as delivered by musicians.

Seeking to demonstrate his thesis in the musical material through a struc-tural examination of jazz, Adorno shifts the level of his critique from one of the specifically German conception of jazz to an ontological reading of jazz in it-self. Ultimately, his interpretation here reduces jazz either to a simple recapitu-lation of Western art music since the mid-nineteenth century (chromaticism and rhythmic complexity) or to its failure to develop these tendencies to the same extent. Structurally, then, jazz can do no right for Adorno: it either fails to measure up to atonal music or, if it does so, will exist only as a second-hand copy.[72] Yet as Adorno would have been aware, this argument, though partially unique in its Marxian inflection, is nonetheless an equally standard variant of

Weimar jazz discourse. As such, why make it at all? Adhering to an argumentative structure common to Adorno's writings, the darkest and bleakest moments of his analysis immediately precede the slightest of hopes. He writes:

> Jazz has left behind a vacuum. There is no new *Gebrauchsmusik* to take its place, and it will not be easy to launch one. But this vacuum is not the worst thing. In it is expressed, wordlessly, like the alienation of art and society, a kind of overall state of reality that words are lacking to express. This vacuum may be wordless, but it is no false consciousness. Perhaps in the silence it will grow loud.[73]

Specifying the space vacated by jazz as the space of freedom is essential here. During the Weimar Republic, jazz had occupied this space as part of Weimar culture's desire for renewal and redemption after the war. When critics began to take leave of jazz, to declare jazz's present past, this did not erase the possibilities signified by the music—these remain intact but now empty. For this reason, the vacuum left behind by jazz becomes the most objective representation of the present for Adorno. And it is precisely in its negativity that this fragile space takes on extreme importance. Only by remaining unoccupied, only by remaining silent, is it capable of acting as the necessary and constant reminder of both freedom's possibility and impossibility under the current state. To occupy it with the "false freedom" of jazz, or anything else, could only degrade it. Not because jazz is low or racially other, but because like all products of capitalism, including so-called "high" or "serious" art, jazz cannot alone deliver on the promises made on its behalf.

Though in vastly different ways, Adorno's jazz theory of 1933 and his incomplete opera each mark an important moment within the decomposition of Weimar's jazz culture. If Adorno had still believed at the time of writing "Farewell to Jazz" that something like his *Treasure* could serve as an intellectual bridge between the positive liberation of Weimar jazz criticism and the negativity of jazz's absence, even this hope would eventually be extinguished. As his previously cited letter to Berg reveals, by late 1933, Adorno felt himself to have lost "the freedom to compose," to have lost "the horizon of fantasy" necessary to such a grand project as *Treasure*.[74] As Lydia Goehr suggests, *Treasure* was never completed not because Adorno's compositional talents failed him or simply because his personal situation grew untenable, but because he was confronted with something even more devastating, with "increasing awareness of the extreme difficulty, if not the impossibility, of composing an opera for the sake of a possibility he believed had a minimal chance of being realized in contemporary times: the possibility of social justice."[75] Neither Adorno's decision to abandon *Treasure* nor to leave Germany were taken lightly. He vacillated between remaining in Germany and emigrating either to Vienna, England, or Constantinople. Oxford and a position as an "advanced student" eventually won out in April 1934.

A little over a year later, Adorno returned to jazz, this time to collaborate with Mátyás Seiber, former head of the *Jazzklasse* and now fellow exile in England.[76] The result of their work together was Adorno's first substantial piece of jazz criticism, which, as noted earlier, he published under the pseudonym "Hektor Rottweiler." By the time "On Jazz" was published in the *Zeitschrift für Sozialforschung* in 1936, *Treasure* lay fallow and Adorno's life in Britain was hardly marked by the jazz's silence.[77] In February 1938, Adorno landed in New York and soon thereafter began work with Paul Lazarsfeld on the Princeton Radio Project. His first days in America not only saw him tackling new issues, they also saw him returning to old ones. In early 1938, he went back to work on *Treasure* and began composing three new songs, "Kinder im Labyrinth" ("Children in the Labyrinth"), "Huckleberry Finn," and "Säufer im Wasserturm" ("Drinker in the Water Tower").[78] Yet, America in 1938 was not Weimar Germany in 1932 and much had happened in between—to Adorno, America, and, of course, Germany. After working on these new compositions, the opera was abandoned once more, this time permanently.

Still, if his primary concerns in both *Treasure* and "Farewell to Jazz" were showing themselves to no longer carry the personal or political importance they had but a few years earlier, Adorno's late Weimar texts do something much greater than merely diagnose the lacunae of a culture in decomposition. More than transcending what Adorno viewed as the limitations of the German use of jazz and Blackness in 1920s musical culture, Adorno's American opera project provides an aesthetic and literary counterweight to the negativity of jazz within his "Farewell to Jazz." Emerging at the nexus of German and American history and society and mediated in a literary meeting with Mark Twain, Adorno's *Treasure* does indeed approach its subject with resistance, but so too does it put on display a consciousness that has appropriated the American experience like few others had during the Weimar Republic.

Conclusion

Good bye, Jonny
You were my best friend.
One day, one day, [. . .]
We'll be together again.
—Kreuder and Beckmann (1939)

The end of the Weimar Republic in 1933 meant, amongst many other things, that the stakes of jazz for German culture changed fundamentally, and Adorno's incomplete opera is but one example of this. Around the same time as members of Germany's internationalist avant-garde took leave of jazz as a progressive art form, the Nazi attack on "cultural bolshevism" further wed the rejection of "Jewish modernism" with Blackness and jazz.[1] What this ultimately meant for jazz was that, by 1933, there were but few voices remaining to defend the music and many more, including Adorno, invested in its critique. Having been so thoroughly identified with a now defunct and discredited republic, under National Socialism, the music was subjected to repeated attacks. Yet, jazz's fate under the Nazis was not to be systematically eliminated but to suffer sporadically according to the caprices of the new dictatorial regime. At times, the Nazis proceeded vigorously and publically against jazz and the "foreign" musicians associated with it—through radio bans in 1933 and 1935, through the prohibition of listening to foreign radio stations in 1939, or Goebbels' 1941 prohibition not of jazz but of music featuring muted horns, atonal melodies, or with a "deformed rhythm (*verzerrte Rhythmen*)."[2] Perhaps the most infamous example of jazz's pariah status during the Third Reich was the *Entartete Musik* (*Degenerate Music*) exhibition of 1938, which prominently displayed jazz, Jewish, and Black musicians as racial antipodes to National Socialist culture. To these instances of the Nazis' public war on jazz, however, must be added curious moments of toleration. For example, musical practices associated with jazz, like syncopation, even saxophone solos, by no means disappear in 1933.

Instead, they can be found in German popular music throughout the 1930s. Paralleling the *Funkstunde*'s ambiguous ban on jazz, during the first half of the Nazi regime at the very least, German musicians remained to a large extent free to connote jazz.

Obviously, the short space afforded by a conclusion can by no means serve as a thoroughgoing discussion of jazz under the Third Reich. As the work of scholars like Michael Kater, Bernd Polster and others has shown, jazz's fate under National Socialism was both complicated and convoluted.[3] What I offer instead is an attempt to trace the afterlife, or aftereffects, of the jazz republic during this period. Though jazz did not act in this period as an object through which Nazi culture defined itself, neither did Weimar jazz culture disappear overnight. Instead, certain elements, personalities, and figures from it lived on in the early Nazi era.

Following on Erica Carter's analysis of the role played by Weimar's cinematic ghosts of Marlene Dietrich in Nazi cinema, I would like to suggest that Weimar jazz culture lived on during National Socialism as specter of this time past. As Carter's study shows, Nazi cinema is filled with doubles of Weimar cinema, most notably the actress Zarah Leander, who filled in for absent stars like Marlene Dietrich. One strategy deployed within Nazi cinema in terms of compensating for the loss of émigré stars was to recall performances and roles from the Weimar period, such as the femme fatale, only to, in Carter's words, "obliterate that image in the actual or symbolic death of the characters."[4] At the same time, for Carter, such doubles not only registered a loss but could also serve the production of a new, National Socialist public sphere.[5] Weimar jazz, as well, existed as an uncanny double of a culture lost to emigration, incarceration, and death. Nazi-era evocations of Weimar jazz can be said, in Carter's terms, to compensate "by disavowal of that loss . . . with a fantasied double, copy or facsimile."[6] Though one could explore Weimar jazz culture's continued existence into the 1930s through a variety of examples, Willy Fritsch, Theo Mackeben, or via instrumentation, perhaps the most publically visible of these is the Jonny figure. This figure has shadowed the present work from almost the very beginning. First seen as Friedrich Hollaender's 1920 "Jonny (fox erotic)," it burst onto the national stage in Krenek's 1927 *Jonny spielt auf* (*Jonny Strikes Up*), the *succés de scandale* of the decade. From there, it fractures into almost innumerable forms: cigarettes, photographs, operettas, recordings, etc. In other words, by 1933, Jonny had achieved a form of iconic status and could thus stand to a large degree for the entirety of Weimar jazz culture.

Before exploring how the Jonny figure lived on during the 1930s, it is important to consider it in relation to the broader situation of jazz and African

American popular music during the Third Reich. Only in comparison with the wider question of jazz under the Third Reich does the Jonny figure's unique status come into view. For one, jazz and later Swing presented a number of practical difficulties in terms of governmental attempts to control them. Not only were they almost impossible to define in any objective, verifiable manner, as Guido Fackler suggests, the development towards Swing in the early to mid-1930s actually made the music less susceptible to Nazi control, at least for a time. With a new name, a more orchestral, more melodic sound, Swing enjoyed a degree of tolerance in the mid-1930s, in part due to Nazi censors' unfamiliarity with the genre.[7] By contrast, Jonny was most certainly a known quantity, closely associated with the "decadence" of the Weimar Republic and thus a likely target of Nazi censors.

And yet, the Jonny figure remains in the public eye during the period between 1933 and 1939. The examples of its use range from oblique to explicit and can be found within the political as well as cultural spheres. Already in 1934, Weimar's Jonny reappears in the 1934 popular song "Ich wünsche dir Glück, Jonny" ("I Wish You Luck, Jonny") with music by Ludwig Schmidseder and lyrics by Rudolf Grau.[8] Telling the story of a woman and her lover Jonny, this song's lyrics clearly took their impetus from Hollaender's original song and were read as such by at least one writer within the musical press.[9] Though recorded by three different female vocalists, in the following, special attention will be paid to the performance of Marita Gründgens. This is not only because she, sister of the famous actor Gustaf Gründgens, is the best known of the three, but, more importantly, because her fame in part derived from her ability to impersonate voices and take on various alter egos.[10] In fact, she is today best known for songs like "Ich wünsch' mir eine kleine Ursula" ("I'm wishing for a little Ursula of my own") in which she imitates the voice of a little girl asking her mother for blond-haired, blue-eyed little sister.[11] Less well-known is the fact that she apparently made a name for herself during the late 1920s through impersonation of, amongst other figures, the American blackface performer Al Jolson.[12] Equally germane to the present argument is that Gründgens was an exquisite mimic of Marlene Dietrich, who had previously released what was to become the most famous recording of Hollaender's "Jonny" in 1931. Gründgens' uncanny ability to mimic Dietrich is demonstrated on the September 1933 recording "Filmsucht" ("Film Addiction").[13] Featuring lyrics written by Gründgens and set to the well-known Hollaender tune of "Ich bin von Kopf bis Fuß auf Liebe eingestellt" ("Falling in Love Again"), she mimics the voices of three Weimar film divas: Marlene Dietrich, Greta Garbo, and Lilian Harvey. The apolitical song is an amazing display of her abilities and, though relatively obscure, deserving of rediscovery. At the same time, it is significant that all three performers invoked here were absent from Germany at the time (though Harvey would return in 1935). Within this context, Gründgens' mimicry of Dietrich, Garbo, and Harvey lends itself to a reading of the song as Nazi-era doppelgänger for an absent Weimar culture.

In "I Wish You Luck, Jonny," Gründgens impersonates not a specific person but the genre of the Weimar Jonny song more generally. Described as a chanson and blues,[14] the recording begins with three deep tones from a bassoon over which the piano adds a series of light arpeggios. As the listener soon learns, these initial tones indicate the sounding of a ship's horns at a nearby dock, from where Jonny will tomorrow leave. The year 1934 was a time of departure for many figures of Weimar jazz culture, and quite a few jazz musicians of the 1920s were already absent: Dajos Béla, Marek Weber, and Weintraubs Syncopators. Further, by November 1933, the *Reichsmusikkammer* (RMK, Reich Music Chamber), a subdivision of Goebbels' ministry of culture, had decreed that foreign musicians needed to register with the RMK and carry an identity card issued by this agency. This meant that they also would have to declare their race and religion, a potentially dangerous prospect for Jewish and Black artists.[15] As Jonny's lover, the female singer seems to sense that the sound of the ship's horn might have distracted him, and so her first words command him to "drink, drink, drink my blond Jonny / don't talk to me about tomorrow." While most immediately these lines refer to her concern over separation and the ensuing heartache both will suffer, here she is singing not to any lover, but to Jonny, whose name marks him as foreign. Continuing over a plaintive piano accompaniment, she consoles him, saying that nothing matters other than that: "I wish you luck, Jonny." Significantly, each time she sings this line, the song's tempo speeds up and a drum brush technique adds a syncopated, percussive element that enlivens both the piano and Gründgens' delivery. Viewed in parallel to Gründgens' mimicry of Dietrich, this flirt with jazz instrumentation intensifies the song's self-conscious play with Jonny as an icon of Weimar jazz culture. Exasperated at the recording, critic Kurt Herbst writes of Gründgens' song in *Die Musik*: "This sort of subject is too unimportant to discuss from the perspectives of morals, music, rhythm or anything else. It is simply boring, because this Jonny—pars pro toto—is simply overdone and with it the outmoded worldview (*abgeklapperte Gesamtschematismus*) from which we have to liberate ourselves."[16]

At the same time, I would suggest that "I Wish You Luck, Jonny" not only invokes Weimar jazz culture but it also situates itself outside of this culture, that is to say within a post-jazz, post-Weimar era. For one, the lyrics stabilize

Jonny's potentially ambiguous racial identity, referring to him as "blond Jonny" in the first line. Further, the overall tone to the song borders on mockery of Jonny—his anxiety and impending exile. Concurrent to a timbral change in her voice that suggests a smile, she tells him: "one day you'll come back to me anyway. So I wish you luck, Jonny, really, good luck." Whereas Weimar-era songs tend to position Jonny as a figure who will soon leave to return to his home, in Nazi-era versions, the figure's impending absence is often coupled with the promise of his, albeit indeterminate, return. While this surely compensates for Jonny's absence, marking it as but a temporary interruption within a long-standing relationship, Gründgens' delivery of this line is punctuated by an awkward, almost ominous laugh. As such, the song leaves the nature of his return open—will the two be united in a future in which they can once again be together, i.e., in a post-Nazi, post-Weimar state, or, given her mocking tone, will Jonny come to see his departure as an overreaction and return willingly? The second verse continues on in this vein, with Jonny being told to laugh and forget the sadness of tomorrow. At the song's close, the ship's horn returns and adds a tonal layer of dissonance to the piano accompaniment, reminding listeners of Jonny's and jazz's departure from their lives. Neither pro- nor anti-jazz, "I Wish You Luck, Jonny" addresses and compensates for jazz's absence in a manner that reflects, rather than rejects, the Third Reich's ambiguous relationship to the music.

In 1935, Jonny again reappears, in both popular song and a controversial radio program. The first of these occurs in the song "Jonny hat Sehnsucht nach Hawaii" ("Jonny's Yearning for Hawaii") with music by Hans Reinfeld and lyrics by Bruno Balz. It is described as a "Hawaiian Waltz" available in an arrangement for "jazz voice" and vocal trio.[17] While the word "jazz" appears regularly within the music publishing industry in this year and beyond (though rarely in titles), it is in fact the title "Jonny" that is unique. In the year of its release, the song was recorded by at least three separate groups, Hans Bund, Fritz Domina, and an anonymous male quartet for the discount label *Woolco*.[18] Before addressing the song itself, we should note the significance of the lyricist Balz, a homosexual songwriter from the Weimar cabaret scene who first became well-known for his work on the film *Viktor und Viktoria* (*Victor and Victoria*) (dir. Reinhold Schünzel 1933). During the 1930s, he survived, though not without being at one point imprisoned in a concentration camp, by exploiting his usefulness as a songwriter, in particular for the aforementioned Zarah Leander.[19] Like other Jonny songs from the 1930s discussed here, Balz's "Jonny's Yearning for Hawaii" would become an evergreen of the German popular music industry.[20] The song itself, though unique in its use of the topos of Hawaii, once again positions Jonny in an unnamed harbor. Rather than a young man, however, in Balz's version, he is a sailor past his prime, longing to escape the dreariness of his present life. As with "I Wish You Luck, Jonny," the male singer seeks to console Jonny. Though longing to go to Hawaii, the singer tells him: "Poor Jonny, forget your pain / Everything is past and everything is over." More sedate than anything, Balz and Reinfeld's version transforms Jonny into a non-threatening old man, longing to return home but unable to do so.

In the same year, Jonny's continued relevance and relationship to jazz returned in an even more direct manner. This occurred in the form of satirist Hugo Hartung's radio play *Jonny spült ab* (*Jonny Does the Dishes*),[21] which featured music by the composer Bernhard Eichhorn.[22] Its immediate purpose was to parody Weimar jazz culture and Ernst Krenek's *Jonny spielt auf* (*Jonny Strikes Up*) specifically. Perhaps best known today for authoring the novel *Wir Wunderkinder* (*Aren't We Wonderful*), at the time, Hartung was working as a dramaturge for the Bavarian radio station.[23] Broadcast in the evening of February 25, 1935, *Jonny Does the Dishes* is described as "a cheery play with deep meaning and a grand piece of opera parody."[24] Though other plot members are listed with the name of the actor who will portray them, the listing for "the Negro Jonny" remains blank, substituted by the presence of two question marks. In fact, the title and its obvious reference to Krenek's jazz opera created a difficult situation for Hartung. Though this would obviously be a satire, so directly invoking Blackness, jazz, and Jonny also carried the danger of attraction. Patrick Merziger summarizes the dilemma in the following manner: Hartung "wanted to eradicate Jonny by writing a satire on him, but the satire only kept his memory alive."[25] For Merziger, examples like Hartung's *Jonny Does the Dishes* are indicative of the broader failure of politically motivated satire during the Nazi era, which, according to him, became increasingly unpopular with critics and audience members alike.[26]

The tension within National Socialist satire of Jonny and other specters of the Weimar past is put on display in the published plot summary: "The piece takes place in a German cosmopolitan hotel in the age of inflation and the glorification of niggers. Interested in profit, the hotel's director Knölle pays homage to the fashionable interest in this rootless taste by hiring the world-famous Negro violinist Jonny for a guest appearance. We won't yet say how this affair (*der ganze Spuk*) ends."[27] Though the description invokes the vocabulary of "cultural bolshevism" and insists on the pastness of Jonny and his jazz, its suggestive use of the word "*Spuk*" (affair, ghost) also invites questions about Jonny's potential relevance to the Nazi present. Even more clearly demonstrating the idea that *Jonny Does the Dishes* is as much about the present as it is a parody of the past is the mock interview between the "Negro jazz king" Jonny and Hartung that appeared in *Der Deutsche Rundfunk*.[28] In this "Conversation with Jonny," Jonny and jazz's irrelevance are repeatedly called upon to satirize their popularity in the "golden twenties" and, one suspects, their continued presence in the new Germany. Of the 1920s, Hartung's Jonny says: "Those were the days! When I think back to the finale of this opera [*Jonny spielt auf*]—I struck up the band—and old Europe lay at my feet . . . A lot has changed since then—everything!!"[29] Hartung responds by saying: "Yes, actually you've been completely forgotten. More forgotten than forgotten. I don't think that even one young person today knows your name."[30] As Merziger argues, a problem in this interview is that it fails to justify the need to parody a so unimportant and irrelevant matter like Jonny.[31] The only justification for the parody comes from Jonny himself, who, after again hinting at a secret plot element, insists: "maybe it's not so bad to bring this forgotten so-called 'art' back into the light of day again and present it as reflected in parody."[32] Here, as in the plot description, the language struggles to contain the implicit power of Jonny and his jazz.

Unsurprisingly, the official reaction to *Jonny Does the Dishes* was severe. Writing in *Der Deutsche Rundfunk*, one critic bemoaned the fact that while satire of this depraved era and its music is a laudable endeavor, here it is superfluous and without impact.[33] While the plot begins as a satire of Weimar culture, according to the reviewer, by the end, it had turned into "a typical theater intrigue with masquerading," with the result that the piece's main targets, according to this critic racial and cultural miscegenation, were missed entirely.[34] Even more directly, another critic felt the only good thing about the work was its title, otherwise it, like its purported object of parody, lacked "sharp wit and trenchant satire. A copy, instead of parody."[35] Similarly, the same Kurt Herbst who had chided Gründgens for her Jonny recording, complains that Hartung's *Jonny Does the Dishes* is less parody than an example of base cultural production "for the purpose of 'popular' entertainment," i.e., kitsch.[36] Herbst additionally implies that this same tendency towards kitsch is present in further productions by Hartung and Eichhorn. Indeed, in an internal report on Hartung from 1937 by Willy Reichartz for the *Reichssendeleitung*, their use of satire as such is found to be "highly questionable."[37] Reichartz feared, for example, that the general public could not distinguish between the parody of Weimar jazz culture in Hartung's Jonny and the real thing.[38]

Though the relationship is in all probability coincidental, it is also noteworthy that 1935 is the last appearance of Jonny in popular song until 1939.[39] In the meantime, though, the Jonny figure will make one important detour in 1938. In this year, Jonny will again be mobilized towards propagandistic ends as part of the "Degenerate Music" exhibition. Held in the city of Düsseldorf and organized by Hans Severus Ziegler, this exhibition had been inspired by the more infamous visual exhibition "Degenerate Art" of a year earlier.[40] It was the occasion for the Nazis to present their ideological vision of jazz–the horrific caricature of a Black saxophone player, portrayed as more simian than human, that has in many ways come to stand in for the fate of jazz under the Nazis (figure 16). Here, one not only confronts National Socialism's racialized theory of culture but also an intensification and condensation of cultural motifs from the Weimar encounter with jazz. Though the figure bears the name "Lucky," as others have pointed out, in both form and content, the image clearly belongs within the genealogy of the Jonny figure.[41] For one, this image, created by the graphic artist Ludwig Tersch, draws on colonialist images of Africans, as seen, for example, in the figure's oversized hoop earrings. Further, we recognize in the Black saxophone player not only Jonny from Krenek's *Jonny spielt auf* but the broader visual trope of the Black saxophone player and his threat to the "racial health" of German women. Finally, the Star of David placed on the figure's lapel telescopes Nazi rejections of Blackness and Jewishness, a foundational element of the Nazi discourse of "cultural bolshevism." If hardly ambiguous in its depiction, the image nonetheless depends on and indeed invites comparison to jazz imagery and jazz musicians once present in Weimar and now missing. Still, the figure carries not the name "Jonny," but "Lucky." Thus, while the image depends on a visual vocabulary clearly legible as Weimar's Jonny, the title conspicuously avoids directly referencing it, contenting itself with connoting, rather than denoting this figure, who for many stood not only for jazz but for Weimar culture more generally.

Yet if Jonny was publicly, if obliquely derided as "cultural bolshevism," the figure still had not yet disappeared from popular music in the Third Reich. Jonny will make one final curtain call in the 1939 hit "Good bye, Jonny!" featuring music by Peter Kreuder and lyrics by Hans-Fritz Beckmann. Though this song will enjoy an important afterlife during the 1950s and beyond as an evergreen of German light entertainment, the song originates in the 1939 *Wasser für Canitoga* (*Water for Canitoga*, dir. Herbert Selpin), a frontier film taking place in 1905 in Canada and featuring the Third Reich's most important male star, Hans Albers. Lutz Koepnick has analyzed Albers' two versions of the song that appear in the film as examples of the reassertion of masculinity within Nazi culture. With this film and song, Koepnick argues, "Albers establishes himself as a roughneck whose aim is to evacuate women and uncontrolled passion from the Far West. [. . .] Albers's song intends to make language rough and dangerous again, to transform orality into a conduit for manly

Figure 16: *"Entartete Musik"* (*Degenerate Music*), 1938. Brochure published by the Weimar National Theatre. Courtesy bpk, Berlin/Art Resource, NY.

action."[42] Yet the versions presented in the film are not the only ones and, given the number of recordings of the song that exist by Albers and others, hardly the most familiar ones.

As released in a separate recording for the Odeon label, both the orchestration and lyrics to the film version of the song are substantially changed. Here, the misogyny referenced by Koepnick is excised in favor of the homosocial bond between the German Albers and his departed, foreign friend Jonny. "My friend Jonny was a fine boy (*Knabe*)," laments Albers at the opening of the song. Continuing on in this vein, he sings: "He was a tramp and had no home."[43] As in Krenek, Hollaender, Grau, and Balz, Jonny's status as wandering vagabond remains pivotal to his characterization. To these lyrics, Peter Kreuder, veteran composer of German film and revue music, added a very specific musical texture with important connotations in German popular song. In a word, Kreuder's composition (on the Albers' recording performed under the direction of Werner Eisbrenner) is jazz-inflected. In terms of instrumentation, it uses muted trumpets, clarinets, and saxophones, while rhythmically, it displays a slight syncopation throughout and features an instrumental break filled with a rich big band sound.[44] The success of the song's combination of Hans Albers, one of the remaining major film stars from the Weimar era, and American Swing reveals much about the vicissitudes of jazz in National Socialism.

Such partial tolerance of jazz on the part of National Socialist functionaries, however, did require implicit (and often explicit) acceptance on the part of artists of the entirety of the Nazi ideological system. Put differently, the music's continued existence depended upon musicians voicing jazz from within the hegemonic order, rather than outside of it, let alone against it. If they failed to toe this broader line, Nazi authorities could and did intervene.[45] It is thus no accident that the song as performed by the public star Albers begins with the death of Jonny, acting in parallel to the treatment of Weimar film stars and types in Nazi film.[46] In other words, any emotional cathexis Albers and his audience are allowed to exhibit vis-à-vis Jonny presupposes this figure's absence from the material world. So whereas in "I Wish You Luck, Jonny" and "Jonny's Yearning for Hawaii," Jonny still exists, however temporarily, within physical proximity to the singer, Albers' "Good bye, Jonny!" will only venture hope for reunion in the afterlife. "One day, one day," screams an emotional Albers in the song's concluding line, "whether in heaven or hell. / We'll be together again." What Koepnick suggests about the film as a whole thus applies to this recording as well: it seeks to control the passion for the foreign and racially suspect Jonny by channeling such desire through rather than against the Nazi vision of contemporary Germany.

Still, while Albers' is the most famous, it is hardly the only version of "Good bye, Jonny!" Indicative of the song's broad popularity, there were at least six further recordings of the song issued that year, one instrumental version and five with vocals.[47] Each in its own way engaged with the legacy of Jonny, jazz, and Weimar, often in ways at odds with the more controlled recording by Albers. For example, not only are the recordings by Otto Stenzel and Egon Wolff stylistically closer to Swing, but they feature substantially different lyrics. Most importantly, in their versions, Jonny is no longer a dead figure from the past. While in Albers' version, an exploding bomb kills Jonny at the song's openings, these recordings reinterpret the sound of the explosion, its "boom," as the pop of a bottle for the two to drink together. Accordingly, German listeners to these versions can imagine themselves meeting Jonny "on earth or in heaven." The closer proximity of Jonny to the Nazi present meant, in turn, that there was greater latitude in these recordings to connote jazz culture. Consider the presence of a slide whistle within Stenzel's recording. This instrument, today used primarily for sound effects in animation, was known in the 1920s as the "Swanee whistle" and had been a common instrument with 1920s jazz instrumentation, notably in Krenek's *Jonny spielt auf*.[48] Of course, Stenzel's use of a slide whistle functions at most as an inside joke to those already in the know. Instead, this hardly rebellious detail, to draw again upon Erica Carter's work, reminds and compensates German listeners for Jonny's and Weimar jazz's absence with a Nazi Swing fantasy.

This is not the only version of "Good bye, Jonny!" to directly reference Weimar jazz culture. As it were, Krenek and Jonny meet once again in Iska Geri und die Neun Casaleon's recording of the song.[49] Though two years later Geri will record "Känguruh" ("Kangaroo"), a parody of Swing music and dancing, her recording of "Good-bye, Jonny!" is one of the least identifiably jazzy of the group, for example, in its prominent use of the accordion.[50] Still Geri's recording is significant for two reasons. First, she is the only female singer to record this song in its entirety, whereas the Jonny songs during the 1920s and early 1930s had been primarily sung by female singers or from a female perspective. Second, though altered to fit her status as woman, her version uses the original lyrics as sung by Albers rather than the alternate version of Wolff and Stenzel. For these reasons, Geri's recording acts more directly than even Albers' as a Nazi double of the Weimar Jonny tradition. Most striking in this context is that after Geri concludes the second to last chorus, the instrumental break that follows begins by quoting the first two measures of

Stephen Foster's "Old Folks at Home" (better known as "Swanee River").[51] In referencing this foundational nineteenth-century American song, Geri's recording inserts itself into the long chain of German encounters with African American music and its appropriation by white Americans. These flow through blackface minstrelsy to ragtime, most notably Irving Berlin's *Alexander's Ragtime Band*'s citation of Foster's song and George Grosz's reference to Berlin's song in his "Song to the World," to Sam Wooding and the *Chocolate Kiddies* who performed "Swanee River" in 1925,[52] and finally to Ernst Krenek, who recycles the same two measures in *Jonny spielt auf*.[53] More than any other recording, Geri's version unearths Jonny's Black, American, and, of course, Weimar German heritage. Yet, this unearthing is framed within the restrained lyrics used by Albers. To a certain extent, Geri's "Good-bye, Jonny!" rewrites the history of German engagement with African American music and culture as simultaneously pre- and post-jazz. In a word, the non-jazz of Geri's recording erases Weimar jazz, even as it depends upon it for its legibility. In this, but a four-second instrumental flourish invoking the twisted history of African American music and culture, Geri's recording, like that of Gründgens, acknowledges and simultaneously negates Germany's own jazz history.

Reflected in the three competing versions of Albers, Stenzel/Wolff, and Geri, "Good bye, Jonny!" in many ways stands for the complex, if ultimately negative, deployment of Weimar Germany's jazz legacy in the Third Reich. This is even more so the case as 1939 was to be the last year in which a song featuring the Jonny figure was released during the Nazi era.[54] Soon new regulations forbidding the use of English and other foreign words in German popular song severely impacted the use of the figure, transforming, for example, "Good bye, Jonny!" into "Leb' wohl, Peter!" ("Long live Peter!").[55] Though Kreuder's song was hardly the sole target of such regulation, it is nonetheless tempting to see in the quantitative number of Jonny recordings and their connotations of Weimar jazz culture something troubling for Nazi functionaries in this first year of the Second World War.

Be that as it may, it is clear that by 1939 and the outbreak of war, the curious combination of music and race, American and German culture, that had produced Weimar Germany as jazz republic had reached the outer limits of its immediate cultural and historical impact. Six years of Nazi rule had driven into exile, hiding, or death almost all the major figures encountered in preceding chapters. While some found temporary refuge in France, at least until 1940; England; or the United States, it is telling that by 1940, few of the major figures discussed throughout *The Jazz Republic* could be found inside of the borders of what was once Weimar Germany. From the perspective of

1939, let alone 1945, Weimar jazz culture appears remarkable as much for its brilliance as its seeming impermanence. Perhaps this is a reason why the metaphor of Weimar Germany as a "dance on a volcano" has had such lasting explanatory strength. The idea of people enjoying themselves before their imminent demise seems uniquely suited to capturing the precariousness of this experiment in German democracy.

Yet as the current work has argued, such jazz dancing on a volcano should stand less as evidence of a different, repressed Germany than as a pivotal link of the cultural history of the Weimar Republic. Attempting to move beyond the appearance of jazz as an ephemeral flare that simply burst onto the scene only to later disappear, *The Jazz Republic* began by looking at the ways in which jazz's entry, as music and dance, was embedded within preexisting ideas about music, race, and American culture. It is a history defined by a series of musical encounters between Germans and jazz, mediated by very different experiences and traditions. Yet as I've also insisted throughout, Weimar Germany's jazz effects are in no way simple projections of the German cultural imaginary, let alone reducible, to indulgences in primitivist and/or modernist fantasy. Jazz's non-German origins did not merely function as a passive surface through which Germans could engage in discursive shadowboxing and simply create a new identity for themselves after World War I. Instead, jazz consistently acted to bring to the surface elements of discomfort and disjuncture, particularly as a result of its confounding racial origins. A presence at once at home within and alien to Weimar culture, German representations of jazz bring into focus both the overlap and friction between German and American society in the early twentieth century. As the cases of the syncopated Girl and symphonic jazz demonstrate, German understandings of white America were very much bound up with representations of Blackness, American and otherwise. To be sure, German discussions of African Americans and white Americans differ in significant ways. Yet, their respective treatments remained powerfully framed by each other. That Sam Wooding and Paul Whiteman could at times function as antipodal, ideal types of German jazz theory was due not only to an understanding of jazz in terms of race but because from the very first, white and Black America existed in close, if troubled, proximity to each other.

The new framework for understanding the German encounter with American culture developed in the introduction made it possible to attend to manifold configurations of jazz and jazz culture in the Weimar Republic. Most importantly, I've shown how early attempts at theorizing and practicing jazz in Germany did not emerge in isolation and according to a logic of their own. Instead, the Weimar-era understanding of jazz and jazz practices emerged at points of contact and conflict with American and wider European culture. Transcending the long-standing emphasis on the Germanness of Weimar jazz, in turn, yielded any number of fascinating and, at first glance, "exceptional" cases, yet which lay at the very heart of Weimar Germany as jazz republic. These stretch from the jazz band's entry into Berlin in 1921, to Frankfurt conservatory students being taught by jazz records, to the curious history of Langston Hughes' translation into German, and finally to Adorno's operatic adaptation of Twain via the Scottsboro Boys.

Weimar's experience of jazz left few of this period's ideas, artworks, and people unchanged and moving jazz to the center of Weimar culture has involved much more than the addition of detail to well-known facts and figures. Instead, *The Jazz Republic* shows how a cultural shift towards jazz and other forms of American culture in the 1920s shaped this period's modernism and modernity. Whether in the Dadaism of Grosz and Mehring, Herwarth Walden's Expressionism, the New Objectivity of Dix and Janowitz, or Kracauer and Adorno's initial elaborations of what became Frankfurt School critical theory, the German encounter, engagement, and theorization of jazz was in many ways elemental, rather than accidental to Weimar culture. From the high-cultural halls of conservatories and operas to the lowly spaces of bars and revue and variety theaters, not to mention those private moments enjoyed around a phonograph player, jazz produced an aural world of its own, both impressive and expansive. It is a world without which the culture of the Weimar Republic simply cannot be understood.

Notes

INTRODUCTION

The quotation cited in the front matter is from Hans Janowitz, *Jazz. Roman* [1927] (Berlin: Weidle, 1999), 8. Unless otherwise noted, all translations from the German are my own. This novel is further discussed in chapter 3.

1. The following details regarding the *Admiralspalast* are based upon Jost Lehne, *Der Admiralspalast. Die Geschichte eines Berliner "Gebrauchs" Theaters* (Berlin: Be.bra-Wissenschaft Verlag, 2006), 53–79.

2. Alfred Lion, interview in documentary film *Blue Note: A Story of Modern Jazz* (dir. Julian Benedikt 1997).

3. Significantly, Lion and his later label partner Francis Wolff (see below) were to no small degree responsible for making Wooding's Berlin recordings known to an American audience. Based upon their personal collections, there appeared in 1941 a short discussion of Wooding in the periodical *Jazz Information* ("Sam Wooding and His Orchestra," *Jazz Information* 2:16 [November 1941]: 89).

4. Lion arrived in New York on the *SS München* from Hamburg on September 16, 1926, and indicated that he had an aunt in Brooklyn. At the time, he was 18 years old and gave his profession as merchant (Ancestry.com. *New York, Passenger Lists, 1820–1957* [database online]. Provo, UT, USA: Ancestry.com Operations, Inc., 2010).

5. John S. Wilson, "Twenty Years in a Jumping Groove: The Blue Note Story," *High Fidelity Magazine* 8:12 (December 1958), 41.

6. On *Blue Note Records* and Alfred Lion, see Richard Cook, *Blue Note Records: The Biography* (Boston: Justin, Charles & Co., 2004), esp. 6–9; Carla Garner, "Alfred Lion," *Immigrant Entrepreneurship: German-American Business Biographies, 1720 to the Present*, vol. 5, ed. R. Daniel Wadhwani (German Historical Institute). Last modified June 26, 2013. www.immigrantentrepreneurship.org/entry.php?rec=112

7. Francis Wolff saw Wooding and the *Chocolate Kiddies* in 1925, though it is unclear whether Lion and Wolff saw the show together or separately. On Wolff's activities in the 1930s, see Michael Kater, *Different Drummers: Jazz in the Culture of Nazi Germany* (New York: Oxford University Press, 1992), 75–77.

8. Cornelius Partsch, *Schräge Töne. Jazz und Unterhaltungsmusik in der Kultur der Weimarer Republik* (Stuttgart: Metzler, 2000); Pascale Cohen-Avenal, *Si on a du jazz, pas besoin de schnaps: Jazz, négritude et démocratie sous la République de Weimar* (New York: Peter Lang, 2011).

9. Nora M. Alter and Lutz Koepnick, eds., *Sound Matters: Essays on the Acoustics of Modern German Culture* (New York: Berghahn Books, 2004).

10. There is a growing number of works in the field of sound studies, some of the most significant include: Friedrich Kittler, *Gramophone, Film, Typewriter* (Stanford: Stanford University Press, 1999); Jonathan Sterne, *The Audible Past: Cultural Origins of Sound Reproduction* (Durham: Duke University Press, 2003); Timothy Taylor, *Strange Sounds: Music, Technology, and Culture* (New York: Routledge, 2001). See also the more recent collections: Daniel Morat, ed., *Sounds of Modern History: Auditory Cultures in 19th and 20th-Century Europe* (New York: Berghahn Books, 2014); Florence Feiereisen and Alexandra Merley Hill, eds., *Germany in the Loud Twentieth Century: An Introduction* (New York: Oxford University Press, 2012). Further, Alexander G. Weheliye's *Phonographies: Grooves in Afro-Modernity* (Durham: Duke University Press, 2005) is a theoretical intervention into the field of sound studies as well as a probing account of the role of sound and technology within African diasporic thought and culture in the US and globally.

11. Celia Applegate and Pamela Potter, eds., *Music and German National Identity* (Chicago: University of Chicago Press, 2002); Celia Applegate, "How German Is It? Nationalism and the Origins of Serious Music in Early Nineteenth-Century Germany," *19th Century Music 21* (Spring 1998): 274–96; Celia Applegate, "What Is German Music? Reflections on the Role of Art in the Creation of a Nation," *German Studies Review* 15 (Winter 1992): 21–32; Pamela Potter, *The Most German of Arts: Musicology and Society from the Weimar Republic to the End of Hitler's Reich* (New Haven: Yale University Press, 1998).

12. Applegate and Potter, "Germans as the 'People of Music,'" *Music and German National Identity*, 21.

13. For representative texts of the *Amerikanismus* debate in Germany, see Anton Kaes, Martin Jay, and Edward Dimendberg, eds., *The Weimar Republic Sourcebook* (Berkeley and Los Angeles: University of California Press, 1995), 393–411.

14. Adolf Halfeld, *Amerika und der Amerikanismus: Kritische Betrachtungen eines Deutschen und Europäers* (Jena: Eugen Diedrichs, 1927); Bertolt Brecht, "700 Intellektuelle beten einen Öltank an," *Werke*, eds. Werner Hecht et al., vol. 11 (Berlin: Aufbau-Verlag, 1988): 174–76.

15. Wolfgang Schivelbusch, *Die Kultur der Niederlage: Der amerikanische Süden 1865, Frankreich 1871, Deutschland 1918* (Berlin: Alexander Fest Verlag, 2001), esp. 294–303. On the prehistory of Germany's image of America in relation to jazz, see Cohen-Avenal, *Si on a du jazz, pas besoin de schnaps*, 28–30.

16. Rudolf Kayser, "Americanism [1925]," *The Weimar Republic Sourcebook*, 395.

17. Tobias Nagl, *Die unheimliche Maschine: Rasse und Repräsentation im Weimarer Kino* (Munich: Edition text+kritik, 2009), 762.

18. Ralph Ellison, *Shadow and the Act* (New York: Vintage Books, 1995), 49–50.

19. Ronald Radano, *Lying Up a Nation: Race and Black Music* (Chicago: University of Chicago Press, 2003), 12–13.

20. W. E. B. Du Bois, *The Souls of Black Folk* [1903] (New York: The Modern Library, 1996), 6.

21. Andrew Zimmerman, *Alabama in Africa: Booker T. Washington, The German*

Empire, and the Globalization of the New South (Princeton: Princeton University Press, 2010).

22. Sara Lennox, "From Postcolonial to Transnational Approaches in German Studies," *Hybrid Cultures—Nervous States: Britain and Germany in a (Post) Colonial World*, eds. Ulrike Lindner et al. (Amsterdam: Rodopi, 2010), lxii. Sebastian Conrad and Jürgen Osterhammel, eds., *Das Kaiserreich transnational: Deutschland in der Welt 1871–1914* (Göttingen: Vandenhoeck & Ruprecht, 2004).

23. Lennox, "From Postcolonial to Transnational Approaches in German Studies," lxxi.

24. Fatima El-Tayeb, *Schwarze Deutsche: Der Diskurs um Rasse und nationale Identität 1890–1933* (Frankfurt am Main: Campus, 2001), 18–38.

25. Lora Wildenthal, *German Women for Empire, 1884–1945* (Durham: Duke University Press, 2001).

26. Robbie Aitken and Eve Rosenhaft, *Black Germany: The Making and Unmaking of a Diaspora Community, 1884–1960* (Cambridge and New York: Cambridge University Press, 2013).

27. On African migrant workers in Weimar, see also Robbie Aitken, "Surviving in the Metropole: The Struggle for Work and Belonging amongst African Colonial Migrants in Weimar Germany," *Immigrants & Minorities* 28:2–3 (2010): 203–23.

28. Jan Nederveen Pieterse, *White on Black: Images of Africa and Blacks in Western Popular Culture* (New Haven: Yale University Press, 1992).

29. David Ciarlo, *Advertising Empire: Race and Visual Culture in Imperial Germany* (Cambridge, MA: Harvard University Press), 2011.

30. Eric Ames, *Carl Hagenbeck's Empire of Entertainments* (Seattle: University of Washington Press, 2008); Rainer Lotz, *Black People: Entertainers of African Descent in Europe, and Germany* (Bonn: Birgit Lotz Verlag, 1997).

31. Fred Ritzel, "Synkopen-Tänze: Über Importe populärer Musik aus Amerika in der Zeit vor dem Ersten Weltkrieg," *Schund und Schönheit: Populäre Kultur um 1900*, ed. Kaspar Maase and Wolfgang Kaschuba (Cologne: Böhlau, 2001), 161–83. On availability of American popular music and ragtime in particular, see further the discography by Rainer Lotz, *German Ragtime and Prehistory of Jazz* (Chigwell, England: Storyville Publications, 1981).

32. Astrid Kusser, *Körper in Schieflage: Tanzen im Strudel des Black Atlantic um 1900* (Bielefeld: transcript, 2013). See also her English-language article "Cakewalking the Anarchy of Empire around 1900," *German Colonialism, Visual Culture, and Modern Memory*, ed. Volker Max Langbehn (New York: Routledge, 2010), 87–104.

33. To be sure, numerous researchers have long shown the significance of African American performers and other peoples of African descent in Europe in the pre-1914 era. On this, see Jeffrey Green, Rainer E. Lotz, and Howard Rye, *Black Europe: Sounds and Images of Black People in Europe Pre-1927*, 2 vols. (Hambergen: Bear Family Records, 2013).

34. Horst Lange, *Jazz in Deutschland. Die deutsche Jazzchronik bis 1960*, 2nd edition (Hildesheim: Olms Presse, 1996). Errors in Lange's work, originally published in 1966, have been corrected and amended in numerous works, e.g., those of Rainer Lotz and Konrad Nowakowski, but have long remained the foundation for "facts" regarding

which jazz bands played where and when. To take but one example, Lange claims that in 1924, the "Ohio Lido Venice Band" was the very first American jazz band to play in Berlin. As is discussed in chapters 1 and 2, this can no longer be considered the case.

35. Scott DeVeaux, "Constructing the Jazz Tradition: Jazz Historiography," *Black American Literature Forum* 25:3 (Autumn 1991): 525–60.

36. Ibid., 531.

37. On Duke Ellington's role in Weimar jazz culture, see the discussion in chapter 2.

38. J. Bradford Robinson, "Jazz Reception in Weimar Germany: In Search of a Shimmy Figure," *Music and Performance during the Weimar Republic*, ed. Bryan Gilliam (New York: Cambridge University Press, 1994), 107–34.

39. Ibid., 131.

40. One further issue with Robinson's work is that he does not differentiate between Germany and Austria, which share some similarities but are hardly identical histories in terms of their exposure to jazz. For criticism of Robinson's application of his analytic model to Alban Berg and Austria, see Konrad Nowakowski, "Jazz in Wien: Die Anfänge," *Anklaenge 2011/2012*, Special Issue: *Jazz unlimited. Beiträge zur Jazz-Rezeption in Österreich* (Wien: Mille Tre Verlag, 2012), 127–31.

41. Ibid. Ellington and Armstrong were hardly known in the US mainstream press during the early 1920s, especially compared to Paul Whiteman (Damon J. Philips, *Shaping Jazz: Cities, Labels, and the Global Emergence of an Art Form* [Princeton: Princeton University Press, 2013], 59). Indeed, even in the African American press, references to Armstrong remain irregular through 1926 and only in the final years of the decade will he and Duke Ellington become more common subjects of reporting (see Charlene B. Regester, *Black Entertainers in African American Newspaper Articles*, 2 vols. [Jefferson, North Carolina: McFarland & Company, 2002/2010]).

42. Scott DeVeaux, "Core and Boundaries," *The Source* 2 (2005), 24.

43. Paul Gilroy, *The Black Atlantic: Modernity and Double Consciousness* (Cambridge, MA: Harvard University Press, 1994), 80. Jürgen Heinrich's develops the connection between Gilroy's Black Atlantic and the visual iconography of jazz during the Weimar Republic in his *"Blackness in Weimar:" 1920s German Art Practic and American Jazz and Dance* (Yale University, PhD diss, 1999).

44. For example: Heribert Schröder, *Tanz- und Unterhaltungsmusik in Deutschland 1918–1933* (Bonn: Verlag für Systematische Musikwissenschaft, 1990); Michael Stapper, *Unterhaltungsmusik im Rundfunk der Weimarer Republik* (Tutzing: Hans Schneider, 2001); Christian Schär, *Der Schlager und seine Tänze im Deutschland der 20er Jahre: Sozialgeschichtliche Aspekte zum Wandel in der Musik und Tanzkultur während der Weimarer Republik* (Zurich: Chronos, 1991).

45. Thomas Saunders, "How American Was It? Popular Culture from Weimar to Hitler," *German Pop Culture: How "American" Is It?*, eds. Agnes C. Mueller (Ann Arbor: University of Michigan Press, 2004), 56.

46. As Philips shows, Berlin had more record labels involved in the production of jazz than either Paris or London and issued more jazz records than Paris in the same period. For Philips, the reason jazz produced in Germany is relatively unknown today is

not its difference or aberration from the norm of jazz in the 1920s, but its very same-ness. As he notes, "Germany was unique within Europe as it had the most advanced and intensive record production, but the bulk of the jazz produced from this system stylisti-cally replicated the symphonic jazz from places like New York and London" (Philips, *Shaping Jazz*, 75, see further 53–62).

CHAPTER 1

The quotation cited in the epigraph is from Hans Siemsen, "Jazz-Band," *Die Weltbühne* 10 (March 1921), 288.

1. Ignoring its presence within contemporary writings, Siemsen's article was one of a few German ruminations on jazz to garner mention in the US press. See "Jazz Would Have Saved World from War, He Says," *Baltimore Sun,* April 10, 1921, 5; George Seldes, "German Writer Asserts America Now 'Drinks' Jazz," *Washington Herald,* April 11, 1921, 10.

2. For biographical information on Siemsen, see Wolfgang Delseit, "Siemsen, Johannes Hermann Ernst," *Neue Deutsche Biographie* 24 (2010), 383–84. Online: http://www.deutsche-biographie.de/pnd11884699X.html

3. Damon J. Phillips, *Shaping Jazz: Cities, Labels, and the Global Emergence of an Art Form* (Princeton: Princeton University Press, 2013), 53–76.

4. Henry Ernst, "Meine Jagd nach der 'Tschetzpend,'" *Der Artist* 2134 (November 11, 1926). *Der Artist* contains no page numbers. This text is also reprinted, with some minor passages omitted, in Heribert Schröder, *Tanz- und Unterhaltungsmusik in Deutschland 1918–1933* (Bonn: Verlag für systematische Musikwissenschaft, 1990), 274–77.

5. Other than in Schröder, one finds discussion of Ernst's article in J. Bradford Robinson, "Jazz Reception in Weimar Germany: In Search of a Shimmy Figure," *Music and Performance during the Weimar Republic*, ed. Bryan Gilliam (New York: Cambridge University Press, 1994), 117–19; Cornelius Partsch, *Schräge Töne: Jazz und Unterhaltungsmusik in der Kultur der Weimarer Republik* (Stuttgart: J. B. Metzler, 2000), 61. Most recently, Michel J. Schmidt uses Ernst's story to argue for jazz reception in Weimar as predominantly marked by visual, rather than sound, culture (Schmidt, "Visual Music: Jazz, Synaesthesia and the History of the Senses in the Weimar Republic," *German History* 32:2 [June 2014], 201–2).

6. Theo Freitag, "Henry Ernst †," *Der Artist* 2154 (April 1, 1927).

7. "Henry Ernst †," *Der Artist* 2153 (March 25, 1927). On Ernst in Dortmund, see further "Kapellen und Ensembles," *Der Artist* 1323 (June 19, 1910). See as well his advertisement for "Henry Ernsts Wiener Salonorchester," then performing in Hamburg, where it is claimed he has been performing since 1904 (*Der Artist* 1349 [December 18, 1910]).

8. In October 1919, Wieninger published one of the first German compositions with the word jazz in it, "Ducky. Jazzband Rag" (Leipzig: Schuberth, 1919), as adver-tised in *Hofmeisters Musikalisch-literarischer Monatsbericht* 91 (October 1919): 122.

On similar compositions from the period, see the appendices in Rainer Lotz, "That Foolishness Rag: Ragtime in Europa—Neue Gedanken zu alten Tonträgern," *Jazzforschung = Jazz Research* 21 (1989), 110–35.

9. Ernst, "Meine Jagd nach der 'Tschetzpend.'"

10. Ibid.

11. Ibid.

12. Jazz's entry into Berlin via the zones of occupation was first discussed in Konrad Nowakowski, "Jazz in Wien: Die Anfänge," *Anklaenge 2011/2012*, Special Issue: *Jazz unlimited. Beiträge zur Jazz-Rezeption in Österreich* (Wien: Mille Tre Verlag, 2012), 43–44. Along with Nowakowski, Hans Pehl, an independent researcher in Frankfurt am Main has contributed to this project through several crucial discoveries about the presence of early jazz bands in Wiesbaden, most notably the Original Piccadilly Four (see below).

13. Harry A. Franck, "Through Germany on Foot, Part II: Coblenz under the Stars and Stripes," *Harper's Magazine* (June 1, 1919), 322. See further: Raymond S. Tompkins, "Living among Germans Has Become 'War Horror,'" *Baltimore Sun,* March 9, 1919, 1, 3.

14. Keith L. Nelson, *Victors Divided: America and the Allies in Germany, 1918–1923* (Berkeley & Los Angeles: University of California Press, 1975), 126.

15. Schröder, *Tanz- und Unterhaltungsmusik*, 272.

16. George Bartheleme, "Jazz," *Kölnische Zeitung,* June 5, 1919. Unfortunately, the occasion for Barthelme's article is the tragic death of Europe, who was murdered in May 1919.

17. "A German Interpreter of Jazz," *Literary Digest* (August 23, 1919), 31. The translation was heavily edited, making the ironic tone of the source text all but invisible. Reference to Barthelme within the American literature on jazz can be found, for example, in Lawrence W. Levine, "Jazz and American Culture," *The Jazz Cadence of American Culture*, ed. Robert G. O'Meally (New York: Columbia University Press, 1996), 441.

18. Barthelme, "Jazz."

19. Ibid.

20. Advertisement for the Apollo Restaurant, "Tanz mit Jazz-Band. Zum erstenmal in Deutschland!" *Wiesbadener Bade-Blatt*, December 13, 1919. The name of the group is specified in the same paper on December 18 as "Marcel's American Jazz Band and the Comic Trap-Drummer Harry," with the further detail that they are the jazz band from the *Folies Bergére* coming on February 1–2, 1920, in the *Wiesbadener Bade-Blatt*. This French jazz band, better known as "Marcel's Jazz Band des Folies Bergére," recorded in Paris in Spring 1919 before disappearing from the discographical record (http://www.redhotjazz.com/marcelsjazzband.html).

21. Advertisement in *Der Artist* 1862 (October 21, 1920). See Nowakowski, "Jazz in Wien," 44.

22. Advertisement in *Der Artist* 1872 (February 3, 1921).

23. Advertisement in *Der Artist* 1881 (April 7, 1921).

24. Advertisement in *Der Artist* 1880 (March 31, 1921).

25. Advertisement in *Der Artist* 1878 (March 17, 1921).

26. Advertisement in *Der Artist* 1903 (August 8, 1921).

27. Ibid.

28. Advertisement in *Der Artist* 1880 (March 31, 1921). See further Aitken and Rosenhaft, *Black Germany*, 150.

29. Advertisement for "Neger-Orchester" in *Wiesbadener Bade-Blatt* (October 1, 1921). My thanks to Hans Pehl for alerting me to the presence of this advertisement. Despite joint efforts, it has not been possible to further document this group.

30. On the *Southern Syncopated Orchestra*, its history, and its evolving roster, see Howard Rye, "The Southern Syncopated Orchestra," *Black Music Research Journal* 29:2 (Fall 2009): 153–228; Howard Rye, "Southern Syncopated Orchestra: The Roster," *Black Music Research Journal* 30:1 (Spring 2010): 19–70. See also Catherine Parsonage, *The Evolution of Jazz in Britain, 1880–1935* (Aldershot, England: Ashgate, 2005), 143–62.

31. Ernst-Alexandre Ansermet, "Sur un orchestre nègre," *La Revue romande* 3 (October 15, 1919), 10–13; translated as "Bechet and Jazz Visit Europe, 1919," *Reading Jazz: A Gathering of Autobiography, Reportage, and Criticism from 1919 to Now*, ed. Robert Gottlieb (New York: Vintage, 1999), 741–46. As noted in chapter 2, individual members of the *SSO*, such as Arthur Briggs, George Clapham, and Buddy Gilmore, did play in Berlin and as early as 1924.

32. "Carlisle and Wellmon," *Black Europe*, eds. Jeffrey Green, Rainer Lotz, Howard Rye, vol. 2 (Hambergen: Bear Family Records, 2013), 26–30.

33. On the performances of the *SSO* in Vienna, see Konrad Nowakowski, "'30 Negroes (Ladies and Gentlemen)': The Syncopated Orchestra in Vienna," *Black Music Research Journal* 29 (Fall 2009): 229–82. Further details, as well as new information regarding the development of the *SSO* in Vienna and beyond, can be found in Nowakowski, "Jazz in Wien," 58–77.

34. Bernhard Etté, "Zurück zur Geige!" *Berliner Montagspost,* September 6, 1926.

35. Ernst, "Meine Jagd nach der 'Tschetzpend.'"

36. Byjacco, "Dolores Jazz. Three Step. Creiert von Chitta und Prof. Arthur Dolores," (Songa Verlag: Berlin, 1919).

37. For example, Siegwart Ehrlich's "Erry-Merry. Jazztanz" was similarly named for the dance pair Erry & Merry, as was Bernhard Minte's "Damarow-Jazz. Threestep" for the duo Damarow. All three songs, as well as Garter and Spink's "Jazz. American Dance," the song whose advertisement marks the first incidence of the word "jazz" in *Der Artist*, are listed in the June issue of *Hofmeisters Musikalisch-literarischer Monatsheft* 91 (June 1919): 64–65. A reproduction of the advertisement in *Der Artist* 1790 (June 1, 1919) can be found in Schröder, *Tanz- und Unterhaltungsmusik*, 267.

38. Advertisement for *Simplicissimus* in *8 Uhr Abendblatt*, April 16, 17, and 22, 1919. The advertisement is also present on April 20, 1919, in the *Vossische Zeitung*.

39. Jeffrey H. Jackson, *Making Jazz French: Music and Modern Life in Interwar Paris* (Durham: Duke University Press, 2003), 21–22; Parsonage, *The Evolution of Jazz in Britain*, 16–18.

40. Jed Rasula, "Jazzbandism," *The Georgia Review* 60:1 (2006), 65.

41. There are two Berlin recordings of "Dolores Jazz" along with a few others that carry the word "jazz" in their title from fall 1919. The dance orchestra of a *Kapellmeis-*

248 Notes to Pages 29–32

ter Tauber recorded Byjacco's "Dolores Jazz" (Polyphon 15598) as did Marek Weber (Parlophon 1058–1). "Cuyaba Jazz" was recorded on Homokord (15852) in 1919 by an unnamed orchestra. For recordings and further examples, see: http://grammophon-platten.de/e107_plugins/forum/forum_viewtopic.php?8393

42. Ernst, "Meine Jagd nach der 'Tschetzpend.'"

43. Ibid.

44. Advertisement in *Der Artist* 1873 (February 10, 1921).

45. Ernst, "Meine Jagd nach der 'Tschetzpend.'"

46. On dancing and its politics within the immediate postwar period, see Wolfgang Schivelbusch, *Die Kultur der Niederlage: Der amerikanische Süden 1865, Frankreich 1871, Deutschland 1918* (Berlin: Alexander Fest, 2001), 319–26.

47. Schröder, *Tanz- und Unterhaltungsmusik*, 345.

48. Fth., "Silvester in Berlin," *Berliner Tageblatt*, January 1, 1919.

49. Karlernst Knaatz, "Der Tanz," *Vossische Zeitung*, January 1, 1919. Ellipses in original.

50. Ibid.

51. As Catherine Parsonage writes: "The fact that American syncopated styles had been the basis for most popular dance music in Britain from the late nineteenth century meant that jazz was perceived, initially at least, as merely another dance craze" (Parsonage, *The Evolution of Jazz in Britain,* 16). On the situation in France, see Mathew Jordan, *Le Jazz: Jazz and French Cultural Identity* (Urbana: University of Illinois Press, 2010), 45–47.

52. Poldi Schmidl, "Berlin," *Der Artist* 1772 (January 26, 1919).

53. A high-resolution digital copy of this image can be found at: http://www.loc.gov/pictures/item/2004665821/

54. The poster itself seems to have been constructed by the artist van Santen, who had ties to both the Anti-Bolshevist League and the German Publicity Office. See Sherwin Simmons, "Grimaces on the Walls: Anti-Bolshevist Posters and the Debate about Kitsch," *Design Issues* 14:2 (Summer 1998), 27. See further Kate Elswit, "'Berlin . . . Your Dance Partner Is Death,'" *The Drama Review* 53:1 (Spring 2009): 73–92.

55. Walter Mehring, "Dada-Prolog 1919," *Das politische Cabaret* (Dresden: Rudolf Kaemmerer, 1920), 9. Though another song in this collection bears the title "Berlin, dein Tänzer ist der Tod," it does not reference foxtrot or jazz dancing specifically (Ibid. 21–22).

56. Further information on this recording, long assumed to have been the product of a misguided German *Kapellmeister*, can be found at http://grammophon-platten.de/page.php?477

57. On jazz's use within American and European modernism in the period, see Rasula, "Jazzbandism," 61–124.

58. George Grosz, *Briefe 1913–1959*, ed. Herbert Knust (Reinbek bei Hamburg: Rowohlt, 1979), 65–74. On Grosz's use of American popular music, see Jeanpaul Goergen, "Apachentänze in Futuristenkellern: Dada—Grosz—Musik," *George Grosz: Berlin—New York*, ed. Peter-Klaus Schuster (Berlin: Ars Nicolai, 1994), 219–23.

59. Advertisement in *Jedermann sein eigner Fussball* 1:1 (February 15, 1919), n.p. The advertisement is reprinted in Goergen, "Apachentänze in Futuristenkellern," 221.

60. Jeanpaul Goergen, ed. *Urlaute dadaistischer Poesie: Der Berliner Dada-Abend am 12. April 1918* (Hannover: Postskriptum, 1994), 9.

61. Ben Hecht, "Dadafest," *Dada Performance*, ed. Mel Gordon (New York: PAJ Publications, 1997), 80–81. See also Beth Irwin Lewis, *George Grosz: Art and Politics in the Weimar Republic* (Madison: University of Wisconsin Press, 1971), 38–39.

62. On these examples as well as others, see Rainer Lotz, *Black People: Entertainers of African Descent in Europe, and Germany* (Bonn: Birgit Lotz Verlag, 1999), as well as the more recent two-volume *Black Europe* (2013). On minstrel imagery in German advertising, see David Ciarlo, *Advertising Empire: Race and Advertising* (Cambridge, MA: Harvard University Press, 2010).

63. Fred Ritzel, "Synkopen-Tänze: Über Importe populärer Musik aus Amerika in der Zeit vor dem Ersten Weltkrieg," *Schund und Schönheit: Populäre Kultur um 1900*, eds. Kaspar Maase and Wolfgang Kaschuba (Cologne: Böhlau, 2001), 167.

64. The first example is "Stepptänzer" from 1915 (reprinted as plate 12 in Serge Sabarsky, *George Grosz: Die Berliner Jahre* [Passau: Das Museum, 1993]). The second is "The Christmas Brothers" (reproduced in Sell Tower, *Envisioning America: Prints, Drawings, and Photographs by George Grosz and His Contemporaries 1915–1933*, 91). The third carries the title "Niggertanz," but Grosz himself had labeled it "Negertanz" (*Schall und Rauch* [February 1920], 3).

65. On the history of the discourse surrounding the French occupation in Germany, see Christian Koller, *'Von Wilden aller Rassen niedergemetzelt': die Diskussion um die Verwendung von Kolonialtruppen in Europa zwischen Rassismus, Kolonial- und Militärpolitik (1914–1930)* (Stuttgart: Steiner, 2001), 201–314.

66. Koller, *"Von Wilden aller Rassen niedergemetzelt,"* 202.

67. The term *"Schmach,"* meaning "shame," "dishonor," is regularly translated as "horror" within English discussions due to the popularization of the terms "Horror on the Rhine" and "Black Scourge on the Rhine" by E. D. Morel. The term *"Schmach,"* however, also carries connotations with the Treaty of Versailles, which Hindenburg and others termed a *"Schmachfrieden"* ("shameful peace"). On Morel's role within the debate, see, for example, Jared Poley, *Decolonization in Germany: Weimar Narratives of Colonial Loss and Foreign Occupation* (Bern: Peter Lang, 2007), 157; Robert C. Reinders, "Racialism on the Left: E. D. Morel and the 'Black Horror on the Rhine,'" *International Review of Social History* 13 (1968): 3–28.

68. Koller, *"Von Wilden aller Rassen niedergemetzelt,"* 220.

69. In addition to Koller, Poley, and Reinders, on the "Black Horror," see, amongst others, Sally Marks, "Black Watch on the Rhine: A Study in Propaganda, Prejudice and Prurience," *European Studies Review* 13 (1983): 297–334; Tina Campt, Pascal Grosse, and Yara-Colette Lemke-Muniz de Faria, "Blacks, Germans, and the Politics of Imperial Imagination, 1920–1960," *The Imperialist Imagination: German Colonialism and Its Legacy*, eds. Sara Lennox, Sara Friedrichsmeyer, and Susanne Zantop (Ann Arbor: University of Michigan Press, 1998), 208; Iris Wigger, *Die "Schwarze Schmach am Rhein": Rassistische Diskriminierung zwischen Geschlecht, Klasse, Nation und Rasse* (Münster: Westfälisches Dampfboot, 2007).

70. Partsch, *Schräge Töne*, 80–86; Schröder, *Tanz- und Unterhaltungsmusik*, 350–51.

71. Tom Black is described as a "Negro" (*Neger*), whose dances enthralled the audience at the relatively up-scale establishment in Berlin West (Poldi Schmidl, "Berlin," *Der Artist* 1839 [May 13, 1920]). See also advertisements for *Adi-Haus* in *Berliner Tageblatt,* May 8, 15, 22, and 29, 1920.

72. Popular theater and revue culture in Berlin is discussed further in chapter 4.

73. Advertisement for *Haremsnächte* in *Berliner Tageblatt,* October 1, 1920.

74. M. H. [Marie Happrich], "Berlin," *Der Artist* 1807 (September 28, 1919).

75. On Brody, see Tobias Nagl, *Die unheimliche Maschine: Rasse und Repräsentation im Weimarer Kino* (Munich: edition text+kritik, 2007), 559–90.

76. Quoted in Poley, *Decolonization in Germany*, 172. See further: "Varieté und Kino. Apollo Theater," *Welt am Montag,* November 18, 1920; "Das Apollo-Theater," *Vossische Zeitung,* October 6, 1920.

77. Poley, *Decolonization in Germany*, 172–74.

78. J. H. Morgan, *Assize of Arms: The Disarmament of Germany and her Rearmament (1919–1939)* (New York: Oxford University Press, 1946), 246.

79. The two affected groups were the Lola-Bach Ballet and its own *Haremsnächte* as well as the scene "Erotik" by the Erna Offeney Ballet. These prohibitions were issued not because of lewdness but out of concern for "public order" (Peter Jelavich, *Berlin Cabaret* [Cambridge, MA: Harvard University Press, 1993], 174–75).

80. Poley, *Decolonization in Germany*, 172–75.

81. Reinhard Mumm, "201. Sitzung, Montag den 3. April 1922," *Verhandlungen des Reichstags,* vol. 354 (Berlin: Norddeutsche Buchdruckerei und Verlags-Anstalt, 1922), 6826.

82. Nagl, *Die unheimliche Maschine,* 155n5.

83. Alan Lareau, *The Wild Stage: Literary Cabarets of the Weimar Republic* (Columbia, SC: Camden House, 1995), 23–69.

84. George Grosz, "Niggertanz," *Schall und Rauch* (February 1920), 3.

85. Advertisement for *Schall und Rauch,* featuring "Kirchner's Original-Jazz-Band" *Berliner Tageblatt,* April 15, 1921, while a later advertisement references "The High Life Jazz-Band" (*Berliner Tageblatt,* May 1, 1921).

86. Tucholsky's activities within *Sound and Smoke* are documented, for example, in Lareau, *The Wild Stage,* 28–32, 39–49. Jaap Kool, discussed below, appears in the program for *Sound and Smoke* as providing music for one of Anita Berber's dances (Program for "Schall und Rauch," April 1920, *Schall und Rauch* [April 1920], 4).

87. Klabund, "Rag 1920," *Hoppla, wir beben! Kabarett einer gewissen Republik,* ed. Völker Kühn, vol. 2 (Weinheim and Berlin: Quadriga, 1988), 61. Originally published in *Schall und Rauch* (September 1920), 11. Set to music by Friedrich Hollaender, it was sung by Mady Christians, who also performed Klabund and Hollaender's "Mady Foxtrott."

88. "Dada-Trott," *Schall und Rauch. Dada-Heft* (May 1920), 1mm [sic].

89. Friedrich Hollaender (words and music), "Fox macabre. (Totentanz.)," (Berlin: Heiki, 1920). Translation from Lareau, *The Wild Stage,* 45.

90. Like his "Jonny (fox erotic)," which is discussed below, the music for this song was announced in December 1920 (*Hofmeister Musikalisch-literarischer Monatsbericht* 92:12 [December 1920], 203).

91. Friedrich Hollaender, "Jonny (fox erotic)" (Berlin: Heiki Verlag, 1920).

92. In a 1922 discussion, Herwarth Walden references recordings by early jazz artists Eric Borchard and the Original Piccadilly Four in addition to Hollaender's "Jonny" ("Von den schönen Künsten," *Der Sturm* 13 [May 5, 1922], 71).

93. On these two versions as well as "Jonny" and Blackness within Weimar popular song, see Alan Lareau "Jonny's Jazz: From Kabarett to Krenek," *Jazz and the Germans: Essays on the Influence of "Hot" American Idioms on 20th-Century German Music*, ed. Michael J. Budds (Hillsdale, NY: Pendragon Press, 2002), 19–60.

94. In late 1919, the Austrian composer Robert Stolz, composer of "Bobby Jazz," released "Am Kongo und am Nil (Jonny um Mitternacht)" (On the Congo and on the Nile [Jonny at Midnight]), Op. 345 (Vienna: Bohéme-Verlag, 1919). Also predating Hollaender's piece are Franz Fischbach, "Jonny, mein Nigger" (Vienna: Rosé, 1920); Karl Weinstabl, "Jonny. Jazz f. Pfte" (Vienna: Pölzl, 1920); Siegwart Ehrlich, "Jonny vom Trokadero," (Berlin-Wilmersdorf: Hansa-Verlag, 1920); Ralph Benatzky, "Jonny-Foxtrott aus der Operette Yuschi tanzt" (Leipzig: Weinberger, 1920). Further discussion of Hollaender's work in relation to Fischbach's song can be found in Lareau, "Jonny's Jazz," 28.

95. Mehring's version was performed by cabaret artist Gussy Holl and set to music by Werner Richard Heymann (Walter Mehring, "If the man in the moon were a coon," *Chronik der Lustbarkeiten: Die Gedichte, Lieder und Chansons, 1918–1933* [Düsseldorf: Claasen Verlag, 1981], 95–98). Originally published in *Das politische Cabaret: Chansons, Songs, Couplets* (Dresden: Rudolf Kaemmerer, 1920): 71–74.

96. On Mehring's cabaret work, see Jelavich, *Berlin Cabaret*, 146–53; Lareau, *The Wild Stage*, 33–38.

97. Mehring, "If the man in the moon were a coon," *Chronik der Lustbarkeiten*, 96. English in original italicized.

98. As noted above, the first documented appearance of the word "jazz" this author has found for Berlin is the April 16, 1919 advertisement for Bella Chitta and Arthur Dolores' jazz dance in the *8 Uhr Abendblatt*. It is, of course, possible that earlier examples will be found. These would likely resemble one of three examples of the article "Die 'Jazz band' in Paris," which were published in Vienna (*Neues 8 Uhr-Blatt*, October 16, 1918), Bern (*Intelligenzblatt*, October 18, 1918), and Constance (*Konstanzer Zeitung*, October 30, 1918). As Konrad Nowakowski has shown, the Vienna article derives from critic Clement Vautel's column "Mon Film" in *Le Journal*, here from September 27, 1918 (Nowakowski, "Jazz in Wien," 34–35). There are thus potentially other versions of this article that appeared around mid-October 1918, but the *Konstanzer Zeitung*'s publication is currently the first published reference to jazz music within Germany's political boundaries. This article is discussed, albeit in a different context, in Wilfried Witte, *Erklärungsnotstand: die Grippeepidemie 1918–1920 in Deutschland unter besonderer Berücksichtigung Badens* (Herbolzheim: Centaurus-Verlag, 2006), 102.

99. There is some indication that "jazz bands" may have been present in the capital before January 1921 (Franz Wolfgang Koebner, *Jazz und Shimmy: Brevier der neuesten Tänze* [Berlin: Eysler, 1921], 3). However, thus far no evidence has surfaced regarding their presence, either in the form of advertisements or critical writing.

100. Rasula, "Jazzbandism," 70–71. As Arthur Briggs, who performed in Austria, Germany, France, and elsewhere, later stated: "For the French people the jazz band *was* the drums. They called [the drums] the jazz band" (Arthur Briggs, quoted in Mark Miller, *Some Hustling This: Taking Jazz to the World* [Toronto: Mercury Press, 2005], 72). On the terminology of jazz bands and jazz in Australia, see John Whiteoak, "'Jazzing' and Australia's First Jazz Band," *Popular Music* 13:3 (October 1994), 279–95.

101. Beginning in January, one finds advertisements for jazz bands in the *B.Z. am Mittag* and *8 Uhr Abendblatt*, while they begin in other newspapers (*Berliner Tageblatt, Berliner Lokal-Anzeiger, Vossische Zeitung, Berliner Montagspost*) in March and April. Though not included in this list, a second wave of jazz bands comes to Berlin in September 1921.

102. Advertisement for the "Cosmo Jazz Band" at *Wien-Berlin* in *Berliner Lokal-Anzeiger* March 6, 1921. Most advertisements repeat over a few days, in some cases longer, and appear simultaneously in multiple newspapers, e.g., the advertisements for "Cosmo Jazz Band" in *B.Z. am Mittag,* March 5, 1921, or the *Berliner Tageblatt,* March 6, 1921.

103. Advertisement for "Jimmi-Jazz-Band" at the *Rokoko* in *Berliner Lokal-Anzeiger* April 21, 1921. This formation may be identical to earlier advertisements for "Jimy Tanz mit Jazz Band" at the *Palais des Westens*, which began appearing in early March (*Berliner Tageblatt* and *B.Z. am Mittag,* March 5, 1921).

104. Advertisement for "Ballorchester Boesing mit Original Jazz Band" at the *Palais der Friedrichstadt* in *Berliner Lokal-Anzeiger*, April 3, 1921.

105. Advertisement for the "High Life Jazz-Band" at the *Schall und Rauch* in *Berliner Tageblatt,* May 1, 1921.

106. Advertisement for "Jazz-Band Max de Groot" at the *Luna-Palais* in *Berliner Tageblatt,* May 8, 1921.

107. At the *Apollo* in Wiesbaden, they are first advertised as "Neuer JAZZ-BAND. Die Original Piccadilli [sic] direkt von London" in *Wiesbadener Bade-Blatt,* October 14, 1920. They perform in Wiesbaden at the *Apollo* at least until January 1 (*Wiesbadener Bade-Blatt,* January 1–3, 1921). The group's presence in Wiesbaden was first discovered by Hans Pehl.

108. See *Journal de Geneve,* January 14, 1922; *Neue Zürcher Zeitung,* April 5, 1922; *Feuille d'avis de Lausanne,* June 16, 1923. This last advertisement refers to performances by the "Merry Harmony Makers and the Piccadilly Jazz Band." Whether this band is identical to the Original Piccadilly Four or merely an imitator is, at this point, unclear.

109. An overview of the group's discography and discussion of previous speculations regarding the group's personnel, in addition to recordings and reproductions of records and advertisements are available at: http://grammophon-platten.de/page.php?397

110. Advertisement for the *Scala-Casino* in *B.Z. am Mittag,* February 19, 1921. This band, too, may have come from Wiesbaden. In the *Wiesbadener Bade-Blatt*, one finds the last advertisement for an Original American Jazz Band on February 10, 1921, which fits well with the information regarding Eric Borchard contained in footnote 112. My thanks to Konrad Nowakowski for pointing this out to me.

111. Horst J. P. Bergmeier and Rainer Lotz, *Eric Borchard Story* (Menden: Jazz-freund, 1988), 1.

112. At the outbreak of the war, Borchard was working as a variety theater actor in England and traveled from there to New York in 1914. He arrived on the *SS St. Paul* from Liverpool on September 21, 1914, with his wife Marie Borchardt, originally from Hamburg (Ancestry.com. *New York, Passenger Lists, 1820–1957* [database online]. Provo, UT, USA: Ancestry.com Operations, Inc., 2010). He registers for the draft on September 12, 1918, giving his date of birth as February 7, 1886 and again listing his wife as Marie Borchard (Ancestry.com. *U.S., World War I Draft Registration Cards, 1917–1918* [database online]. Provo, UT, USA: Ancestry.com Operations Inc., 2005). Borchard's name and profession as "actor" also appear in conjunction with other entertainers in "Thousands Register in Draft," *New York Clipper,* September 18, 1918, 29. Though specifics regarding his activities during the war remain unknown, this information fits with American Banjoist Mike Danzi's recollection that "Borchard arrived in the U.S. a full-fledged Vaudeville artist, doing a Ted Lewis style of clarinet playing—had a partner for short period" (Quoted in Bergmeier and Lotz, *Eric Borchard Story,* 1). Some further details regarding Borchard's life and career have been documented by Ulrich Biller, who independently made the same discovery regarding Borchard's presence in New York City (http://grammophon-platten.de/page.php?447).

113. Borchard is cited on at least three occasions in the US press, and in all three, he references having played jazz in the US army in the German occupation zones. At the same time, this claim remains unsubstantiated. See: H. J. Mann, "Berlin Night Life Gayest in Europe," *Chicago Daily Tribune,* March 26, 1922, G12; "Germans Taught Jazz by Music Machines," *Washington Post,* January 20, 1924, EA17; "Germans Coming to Seek Jazz Singers Here to Satisfy Craze Started by Phonograph," *New York Times,* April 8, 1927, 4.

114. Though Borchard's earliest recordings had originally been dated to October 1920, this has been corrected to May 1921 (Rainer Lotz and Horst Bergmeier, *Der Jazz in Deutschland,* vol. 1 [Hambergen: Bear Family Records, 2008], 80). Though not included in the above discussion, note should be made of one further German jazz pioneer, Fred Ross, who recorded six sides for Beka in July 1921. Pianist Fred Ross, likely born as Erwin Rosenthal in Berlin, may also have spent time in the United States as indicated in advertisements for his group as "Ross Brothers from New York with Jazz Band" (*B.Z. am Mittag,* April 8, 1921). Unlike the case of Borchard, documentation of residency in the United States for Ross has yet to be found.

115. Roberts had originally come to Germany in the prewar era to study music from either Trinidad or Barbados, but, as a British subject, he was interned during the war. When the hostilities ended, he continued to perform music, only this time it was as a jazz drummer, in Wiesbaden, Berlin and beyond. My thanks to Konrad Nowakowski for sharing with me information on Roberts' background gleaned from his son, Ronald Roberts' memoirs (Ronald Roberts, "Autobiographical Account," *Personal Papers and Correspondence 1913–1994,* The Wiener Library, London).

116. "Köln," *Der Artist* 1904 (September 15, 1921).

117. Advertisement for Philipps-Neger-Jazz-Band at the *Scala-Casino* in *B.Z. am Mittag,* November 26, 1921.

118. Hans Erich Winckler, "Der rote Jazz," *Das schiefe Podium: Ein buntes Brett'l Buch,* ed. Walter Wenng (Berlin: Eysler, 1921), 104–6; Walter Mehring, "Groteksksong," *Die Weltbühne* 17:13 (March 31, 1921), 364; reprinted as Walter Mehring, "Jazz-band," *Das Ketzerbrevier* (Munich: Kurt Wolff, 1921), 36–38. Winckler's piece was set to music by Hermann Krome, reproduced in part in *Das Schiefe Podium,* while in 1923, Mehring's "Jazz-band" was set to music by Mischa Spoliansky (Lareau, "Jonny's Jazz," 38–40).

119. Franz Wolfgang Koebner, *Jazz und Shimmy: Brevier der neuesten Tänze* (Berlin: Eysler, 1921).

120. Of all the writers involved in this project, Kool had the most lasting impact on German jazz discussions, authoring important pieces on the history of jazz music for the German and US press as well as a book on the saxophone. See Jaap Kool, "Vom Negerdorf zur Philharmonie," *Uhu* 1 (November 1924): 31–41, 121–22; translated as Jaap Kool, "The Triumph of the Jungle," *Living Age* 324 (February 7, 1925): 338–44; Jaap Kool, *Das Saxophon* (Leipzig: J. J. Weber, 1931). Kool further authored works on non-Western dance culture, *Tänze der Naturvölker: Ein Deutungsversuch primitiver Tanzkulte und Kultgebräuche* (Berlin: Adoph Fürstner, 1921). On Kool in relation to dance and jazz, see Toepfer, *Empire and Ecstasy,* 167–70, as well as Michael Cowan, *Technology's Pulse: Essays on Rhythm in German Modernism* (London: Institute of Germanic and Romance Studies, 2011), 202–3.

121. Like "jazz" and "jazz band," the word "shimmy" was given a variety of spellings, most notably "Jimmy."

122. "Jazz-Band. Der neueste Berliner Rummel," *Berliner Tageblatt,* March 11, 1921.

123. "Jazz-Band. Die Modetänze in Berlin," *Berliner Tageblatt,* March 13, 1921. *Jazz und Shimmy,* 11–14; C. M. Roehr, "Von neuen Tänzen," *Der Artist* 1878 (March 17, 1921). On Roehr, see Schröder, *Tanz- und Unterhaltungsmusik in Deutschland, 1918–1933,* 268–72.

124. "Der Jimmy und der Shimney [sic]," *Berliner Illustrirte Zeitung* 30 (April 17, 1921), 232.

125. Herwarth Walden, "Von den schönen Künsten," *Der Sturm* 13 (May 5, 1922), 71.

126. Siemsen, "Jazz-Band," 288.

127. Kurt Tucholsky also refers to the girth of the jazz band players, though he specifies them as fat banjo players and fat clarinetists ("Die neuen Troubadoure," *Die Weltbühne* 17 [March 24, 1921], 343).

128. Koebner, *Jazz und Shimmy,* 109.

129. R. L. Leonard, "Jazz, Shimmy, Steinach & Co.," *Jazz und Shimmy,* 120. Ellipsis in original.

130. Wedderkop, "Shimmi greift ein," 88.

131. Pol., "Yazz-Band und Jimmy," *Berliner Illustrirte Zeitung* 30 (February 17, 1921), 116. This author here is likely Heinz Pollack, who wrote an early treatment of

popular dance *Die Revolution des Gesellschaftstanzes* (Dresden: Sibyllen-Verlag, 1922).

132. Siemsen, "Jazz-Band," 287.

133. Alice Gerstel, "Jazz-Band," *Die Aktion* 12 (February 4, 1922), 90. Translated as "Jazz Band," *The Weimar Republic Sourcebook*, eds. Anton Kaes, Martin Jay, and Edward Dimendberg (Berkeley and Los Angeles: University of California Press, 1994), 554.

134. Richard Effner, "Etwas über den Jazz," *Der Artist* 1890 (June 6, 1921).

135. Poldi Schmidl, "Berlin," *Der Artist* 1872 (February 3, 1921).

136. Kool, "Tanzmusik," *Jazz und Shimmy*, 103.

137. George Antheil, "Jazz," *Der Querschnitt* 2 (Weihnachtsheft 1922), 172.

138. On Dada and Expressionism in relation to jazz, see Partsch, *Schräge Töne*, 17–44; 75–92.

139. Futurism is referenced in Koebner, *Jazz und Shimmy*, 4, as well as in the three texts by Curt Max Roehr from *Berliner Tageblatt*, *Der Artist*, and *Jazz und Shimmy*, 11.

140. Cubism is referenced in Koebner, *Jazz und Shimmy*, 106; Siemsen, "Jazz-Band," 288; Gerstel, "Jazz-Band," 554 [90]; Bie, *Das Rätsel der Musik*, 98.

141. Herwarth Walden writes: "The musical arts are being Einsteined (*vereinsteint*). All knowledge is relative" ("Von den schönen Künsten," 70–71).

142. Herwarth Walden, "Shimmy," *Der Sturm* 13 (April 5, 1922) and Wedderkop, "Shimmi greift ein." These two authors will continue the debate over jazz in 1925 on the occasion of the Berlin performances of the African American revue *Chocolate Kiddies*. See chapter 2.

143. Gerstel, "Jazz Band," 554.

144. Tucholsky, "Die neuen Troubadoure," 46.

145. Ibid., 46, 47.

146. Pol., "Yazz-Band und Jimmy," 116.

147. Wedderkop, "Shimmi greift ein," 89.

148. Gerstel, "Jazz Band," 554.

149. Leonard, "Jazz, Shimmy, Steinach & Co.," 122.

150. Koebner, *Jazz und Shimmy*, 106.

151. Siemsen, "Jazz-Band," 287.

152. Gerstel, "Jazz Band," 554.

153. Wedderkop, "Shimmi greift ein," 88–89.

154. Bie, *Das Rätsel der Musik*, 100.

155. Schmalhausen's image is found on page 41 of Jaap Kool, "Vom Negerdorf zur Philharmonie" and is available online at: http://magazine.illustrierte-presse.de/die-zeitschriften/werkansicht/dlf/73406/53/0/

156. For example, both Kool's "Tanzmusik" and Siemsen's "Jazz-Band" frame their judgments of jazz with prewar experiences of Black musicians (Kool, "Tanzmusik," *Jazz und Shimmy*, 100; Siemsen, "Jazz-Band," 167).

157. Jeremy F. Lane, *Jazz and Machine-Age Imperialism: Music, "Race," and Intellectuals in France, 1918–1945* (Ann Arbor: University of Michigan Press, 2013), 1–18.

158. Walter Kingsley, "Whence Comes Jass?" *New York Sun* (August 5, 1917), 3. See

further Rasula, "Jazzbandism," 66–67. Indeed, Kingsley's work is equally notable for its speculation regarding the origin of the word "jazz." He suggests it derives from the vaudevillian term "jasbo." This is noteworthy as already by 1920 this idea had been taken up by Koebner via Paul Whiteman (*Das neue Tanz-Brevier* [Berlin: Eysler, 1920], 55). More generally, Kingsley's term "jasbo" can be further related to the apocryphal Black jazz musician from Chicago, "Jasbo Brown," who is often referenced in German discussions of the word's origin. This figure first appears in the United States and is picked up by the broader press in the United States and Europe (Alan P. Merriam and Fradley H. Garner, "Jazz-The Word," *Ethnomusicology* 12:3 [September 1968], 373–96, for "Jasbo Brown," 373–76). Examples of German use of "Jasbo Brown" include: Paul Bernhard, *Jazz: Eine musikalische Zeitfrage* (Munich: Delphin, 1927), 65–66; "Wie die Jazzband entstand," *Berliner Morgenpost,* January 1, 1926; Heinrich Wiegland, "Jazz," *Kulturwille,* Special Issue: "Yankeeland" 2 (1929), 33; E. F. Burian, "Revue!" *Der Auftakt* 8 (1928), 182; A. Sacher-Woenckhaus, "Unsere modernen Tänze sind keine Niggertänze mehr," *Uhu* 8 (April 1932), 85; Eduard Duisberg, "Jazz Band," *Das Magazin* 4 (May 1928), 2266–67. Via a variation on another origin story from American jazz musician Vincent Lopez, Kool propagated a similar story, but surrounding the figure of "Jack Washington" (Kool, "Vom Negerdorf zur Philharmonie," 32–33; Merriam and Fradley, "Jazz-The Word," 378). This version was later taken up by Bernhard Egg in his *Das Jazz-Fremdwörterbuch* (Leipzig: W. Ehler & Co., 1927), 4.

159. Harry Kessler, *Berlin in Lights: The Diaries of Count Harry Kessler (1918–1937),* trans. Charles Kessler (New York: Grove Press, 1999), 282.

160. Joseph Roth, "Jazzband," *Werke I: Das journalistische Werk, 1915–1923,* ed. Klaus Westermann (Cologne: Kiepenheuer & Witsch, 1989), 545. First published May 1, 1921, in the *Berliner Börsen-Courier.*

161. Tucholsky, "Die neuen Troubadoure," 342.

162. As Schmidl writes: "A true jazz band despises everything that is even somewhat musical and instead prefers Negro melodies. Now we understand why the drum plays such a tremendously important role" (Poldi Schmidl *Der Artist* 1872 [March 2, 1921]).

163. Theodor Leisser, "Der 'Jimmy,'" *Berliner Volkszeitung,* April 2, 1921.

164. Albert Held from the *Neues Wiener Journal,* September 15, 1921. Cited in Nowakowski, "Jazz in Wien," 134n389.

165. Poldi Schmidl *Der Artist* 1922 (January 19, 1922).

166. Ibid.

167. That Schmidl also has the occupation in mind is evidenced when he writes towards the end: "Let's assume that the French and with them their brothers, the honorable Senegal Negroes, marched out from the occupied territories and some of the Senegal Negroes stayed in Germany. This will one day likely be the case. With the blacks, the French will leave us a legacy undesirable to the civilian population, but that will be embraced as a sensation by the German audience of the entertainment establishments" (Schmidl, "Berlin," *Der Artist* 1922 [January 19, 1922]).

168. Susan Laitkin Funkenstein, "Man's Place in a Woman's World: Otto Dix, Social Dancing, and Constructions of Masculinity in Weimar Germany," *Women in German Yearbook,* 21 (2005), 163–64.

169. Though he is listed as a dancer for the first two appearances at Chemnitz in

1924, Tom Boston is elsewhere billed "the American Original-Jazz-Band-Canon," likely meaning that he was the drummer, in *Das Programm* (Hans Pehl, personal correspondence with the author, March 1 and 3, 2013; Rainer Lotz, personal correspondence with the author, January 22, 2013).

170. Both Dix and Gotsch were active in Dresden during the same period and in the same year, 1922, when Gotsch produced the woodcut "Jimmy [Tanzbar]" ("Jimmy [Dance Bar]"). On Gotsch, Dix and "Tom Boston," see Sell-Tower, *Envisioning America: Prints, Drawings, and Photographs by George Grosz and his Contemporaries 1915–1933* (Cambridge, MA: Busch-Reisinger Museuam, Harvard University, 1990), 92; Reinhold Heller et al., eds., *Stark Impressions: Graphic Production in Germany, 1918–1933* (Evanston, IL: Northwestern University Press, 1993), 152–53.

171. On jazz in Dresden, see the discussion below regarding Otto Dix's work, *An die Schönheit*. In Danzig, "Marcel's Jazz Band" appeared in November 1920 at the *Wintergarten* (*Gazete Gdanska,* November 24, 1920), though it is unclear whether this group is identical to the one that had appeared earlier in Wiesbaden. The group depicted here likely performed in the period between 1920 and 1923. In Prague, the early jazz formation, the "Ross Brothers," performed there with a Black dancer named "Mr. Bob" (*Prager Tagblatt,* October 8, 1921). For the developments in Vienna, as well as the connection with Berlin, see Nowakowski "Jazz in Wien."

172. Otto Dix, *Otto Dix: das Werkverzeichnis der Zeichnungen und Pastelle*, ed. Ulrike Lorenz, vol. II (Weimar: VDG, 2003), 590–92.

173. It is important that my argument here not be taken to indicate directionality in German jazz reception, e.g., from a consideration of jazz as white to one of jazz as Black music. Instead, throughout the period, both points of view are present and can, only with difficulty, be mapped chronologically and/or politically. The African American jazz musician Sam Wooding and the white jazz musician Paul Whiteman, examined in chapters 2 and 3, are examples of this difficulty.

174. On Berlin jazz bands in Vienna, see Nowakowski, "Jazz in Wien," 84–97.

CHAPTER 2

The quotation cited in the epigraph is from Hans Heinz Stuckenschmidt, "Lob der Revue," *Musikblätter des Anbruch* 8 (March/April 1926), 55.

1. Oscar Bie, "Chocolate Kiddies," *Berliner Börsen-Courier,* May 26, 1925.

2. As O. M. Seibt wrote from Berlin in the *Billboard*: "Ever since the French occupied large slices of German territory with thousands of black soldiers, who at the moment of writing are still stationed there, the majority of the German people do not exactly crave to see colored performers, and repeated experiences with such acts turned out indifferent successes, no matter how clever the individual artiste may have been" (Seibt, quoted in Mark Miller, *Some Hustling This: Taking Jazz to the World 1914–1929* [Toronto: Mercury Press, 2005], 123). In addition, Garvin Bushell, a member of Wooding's band, later reported the following story: "After opening night at the Admiral's Palace there were people out front crowding around the performers and musicians. Everybody was commenting on how well we'd performed, how much they loved our work,

and what a great show it was. But one German evidently had had too many drinks. He came right up into the crowd and tore open his shirt, saying in German (which I spoke), 'I'm a German to my heart. I don't understand why the government allows these black people to come to our country. During the war they cut off our noses and our ears.' He was speaking about the Senegalese, you know. The Senegalese didn't take prisoners: when a German went down they just cut off the end of his nose or an ear and put it on a string. That way when they went back home they could show how many men they'd killed. So this guy went on, saying, 'I have not forgotten what they did to us, and I won't stand for it. They should run them out of Germany'" (Garvin Bushell, as told to Mark Tucker, *Jazz From the Beginning* [Ann Arbor: University of Michigan Press, 1988, 57]).

3. One indication of the increasing importance of Wooding's jazz band to the show's success is that while original advertisements mentioned neither jazz nor Wooding, by the end of the show's run in July, the *Berliner Tageblatt* ran ads that referenced both jazz and Sam Wooding's name specifically (*Berliner Tageblatt,* July 2–5, 1925).

4. On Garland, see "William 'Will' Garland," *Black Europe*, eds. Jeffrey Green, Rainer Lotz, Howard Rye, vol. 1 (Hambergen: Bear Family Records, 2013), 227–32. See further: "Scala," *Berliner Börsen-Zeitung,* November 27, 1924; Ejk., "Scala Wihnachtsprogramm," *8 Uhr Abendblatt,* December 6, 1924; "Aus den Varietéprogrammen," *Berliner Tageblatt,* December 14, 1924; "Die Scala," *Berliner Volkszeitung,* December 14, 1924.

5. On the Fisk Jubilee Singers generally, see Andrew Ward, *Dark Midnight When I Rise: The Story of the Fisk Jubilee Singers* (New York: Farrar, Straus, and Giroux, 2000). On the group in Europe, see "Spirituals," *Black Europe*, eds. Jeffrey Green, Rainer Lotz, Howard Rye, vol. 1 (Hambergen: Bear Family Records, 2013), 32–37. Responses to their May 1925 Berlin performance include: Dr. Un., "Neger-Musik," *Berliner Morgenpost,* May 15, 1925; Li Zielesch, "Bei den schwarzen Sängern," *Berliner Tageblatt,* May 15, 1925; Z. "Plantage-Melodien," *Neue Berliner Zeitung. Das 12 Uhr Blatt* May 16, 1925; Klaus Pringsheim, "Die singenden Neger," *MM der Montag Morgen,* May 18, 1925.

6. The following examples were to my knowledge first traced in the *BZ am Mittag* by Konrad Nowakowski. See his "Jazz in Wien: Die Anfänge" *Anklaenge 2011/2012*, Special Issue: Jazz Unlimited: *Beiträge zur Jazz-Rezeption in Österreich* (Vienna: Mille Tre Verlag, 2012), 134–36.

7. "Pete Zabriskie," *Black Europe*, eds. Jeffrey Green, Rainer Lotz, Howard Rye, vol. 1 (Hambergen: Bear Family Records, 2013), 292–94. Advertisements for Zabriskie's jazz band appear in the *BZ am Mittag* from September 29, 1922, onward. They can also be found in the *8 Uhr Abendblatt* from at least October 3, 1922, onward. Advertisements for Hines and the "Bobo Jazzband" appear in the same newspapers from January 2 through January 13.

8. On Hayes in Europe, see "Roland Hayes," Green, Lotz, and Rye, *Black Europe*, vol. 1, 138–43. Hayes' appearance was widely advertised in Berlin newspapers and received a substantial amount of discussion as, for example, in: a. "Der schwarze Tenor," *Vossische Zeitung,* May 12, 1924; G. St., "Konzertwege," *Welt am Montag,* May 12, 1924; schr., "Der schwarze Tenor," *Deutsche Allgemeine Zeitung,* May 13, 1924.

9. Advertisements for Clapham's band appear, for example, in the *Berliner Morgenpost, Berliner Lokal-Anzeiger,* and *BZ am Mittag* between May 6 and May 12, 1924.

10. On Clapham and these recordings, of which no known copy exists, see "George Clapham," *Black Europe*, vol. 2, 232–34.

11. On the biographies of these jazz musicians in relation to the *Southern Syncopated Orchestra*, see Howard Rye, "Southern Syncopated Orchestra: The Roster," *Black Music Research Journal* 30:1 (Spring 2010), 22 (Boucher), 26 (Clapham), 34–35 (Buddy Gilmore), 36 (Mattie Gilmore). Rye indicates that Hines may also have been a member of the *SSO* at one point, but this remains unconfirmed (39).

12. Julian Fuhs (also Fuss) was born in Berlin but emigrated to the United States in 1910. In 1924, he returned to Germany and made a name for himself as a popular bandleader, in particular by performing jazz-like music in revues such as *An Alle* at the *Grosses Schauspielhaus* or *Wild West Mädel* at the *Neues Theater am Zoo* in late 1924 and early 1925. See Ulrich Biller's collection of facts and articles related to Fuhs' career at http://grammophon-platten.de/page.php?478.0. Significant here is that James Horton Boucher, a Black British violinist, also performed with the Julian Fuhs band in Berlin *Wild West Mädel*. Boucher had been a member of the *SSO* as well (Rye, "Southern Syncopated Orchestra: The Roster," 22).

13. Alex Hyde was born in Hamburg in 1898 but emigrated in the same year with his parents to the United States. In 1924, he returned to Germany via London, performing in Hannover, Berlin, and Munich in 1924 and 1925 as well as recording for German labels like *Vox*. See Horst Bergmeier and Rainer Lotz, *Alex Hyde. Bio-Discography* (Menden: Jazzfreund, 1985) as well as additions by Ulrich Biller at http://grammophon-platten.de/page.php?334

14. The London Sonora Band was a formation under drummer and saxophonist Bobby Hind. Like previous groups, it premiered at the *Scala* in September 1924 and then, in December, moved to the *Barberina*, where it would remain until May 1925, when Alex Hyde's formation replaced it. See "Aus den Varieteprogrammen," *Berliner Tageblatt*, September 12, 1924; advertisement for *Barberina*, "London Sonora Band. Das beste Jazz-Orchester der Welt," *Berliner Tageblatt*, December 14, 1924. On this band, see the collection of materials by Ulrich Biller at http://grammophon-platten.de/page.php?503

15. On this American group's very early appearance in Munich, see Nowakowski, "Jazz in Wien," 95n241. The group appeared in the *Lessing Theater*'s production in Berlin (Programm for "Wien gib acht!," ca. 1924, Theater, Berlin Collection; AR 3048/ MF 450; box 1; folder 3; Leo Baeck Institute).

16. Other than the evidence the group left in the discographical record, little is known about this group's impact in Berlin or its exact arrival. Period references to the band's presence in Berlin include: "Berlin Now Dancing Nightly; Ban Lifted," *Variety* (May 1925): 50; Rez., "Amateurjazzkapellen," *Deutsche Allgemeine Zeitung*, March 4, 1926.

17. Fritz Zielesch did, however, connect the Fisk Jubilee Singers with the *Chocolate Kiddies* revue in a discussion of race relations in America that appeared before the premiere of the revue ("Der Lebenskampf der schwarzen Rasse," *Berliner Tageblatt*, May

23, 1925). In addition, critic Leopold Schmidt, in a later piece from July 1925, contrasted the authenticity of the Fisk Jubilee Singers with the "ghastly [*gräßliche*] jazz band" in the *Admiralspalast* ("Rückblick," *Berliner Tageblatt,* July 22, 1925.).

18. For example, while the 1928 article "Jazz-Band" contains photographs of other African American jazz bands, Wooding's individual portrait and name are featured alongside white American, German, and European jazz musicians like Vincent Lopez, Paul Whiteman, Jack Hylton, Eric Borchard, and Fred Ross (Eduard Duisberg, "Jazz-Band," *Das Magazin* 4 [May 1928], 2265).

19. Mark Miller, *Some Hustling This: Taking Jazz to the World, 1914–1929* (Toronto: Mercury Press, 2005), 53–54.

20. Sam Wooding, "An American Dream for Harlem, New York (n.d. ca. 1980s)," *Sam and Rae (Harrison) Wooding Papers,* box 1, folders 1–2, Schomburg Center for Research in Black Culture, New York Public Library, NY.

21. Chip Deffaa, *Voices from the Jazz Age: Profiles of Eight Vintage Jazzmen* (Urbana and Chicago: University of Illinois Press, 1990), 19.

22. Though the complete history of the group remains to be written, Wooding and the *Chocolate Kiddies* toured Europe from May 1925 through June 1926. The show then fell apart, and Wooding continued on individually with some of the show's performers, e.g., Greenlee and Drayton. Wooding toured like this for the remainder of 1926 and into 1927 when he next departed for South America, touring there until around July when Dave Peyton wrote of Wooding's performance in Argentina (Dave Peyton, "The Musical Bunch," *Chicago Defender,* July 2, 1927; Miller, *Some Hustling This,* 155–59). After returning to the United States, Wooding performed in New York and then left again for Europe and Berlin in June 1928 to premiere *Die schwarze Revue* (*The Black Revue*), discussed in chapter 4. After Berlin, he played in Brussels, Paris, Copenhagen, and elsewhere. He left Europe in December 1931 and was back performing at Harlem's *Lafayette Theatre* (Advertisement for Sam Wooding and His International Chocolate Kiddies' Orchestra, *New York Amsterdam News,* January 27, 1932, 10). Though it differs in some details than what is presented here, see "Sam Wooding," Green, Lotz, and Rye, *Black Europe,* vol. 2, 280–90. Further details on the path of the *Chocolate Kiddies* revue across Germany and Europe between 1925 and 1926 are presented in Bo Lindström and Dan Vernhettes, *Travelling Blues: The Life and Music of Tommy Ladnier* (Paris: Jazz'Edit, 2009), 87–110.

23. The December 1925 return of the *Chocolate Kiddies* did not garner much notice in the Berlin press. Though advertisements can be found in major newspapers such as *Die Berliner Tageblatt, Vossische Zeitung, Neue Berliner Zeitung. Das 12 Uhr Blatt* beginning on December 20, 1925.

24. Sam Wooding, "Die Verklärung des Jazz," *Berliner Tageblatt,* July 31, 1926. Advertisement for the *Faun des Westens* for "Sam Wooding's Famous Symphonie-Orchestra of the Chocolat [sic] Kiddies," *8 Uhr Abendblatt,* June 22, 1926; Advertisement for the *Faun des Westens* for the "Greenlee-Drayton-Plantation-Revue. Musik des berühmten Sam Woodings Symphonie-Jazz-Orchesters," *8 Uhr Abendblatt,* July 21, 1926. See also Frank Warschauer, "Tanz bei Sam Wooding," *BZ am Mittag,* July 9, 1926.

25. Advertisement for "Sam Wooding's World Famous Jazz Orchestra," *Berliner Tageblatt,* October 10, 1926.

26. This second revue, which starred Johnny Hudgins, Edith Wilson, Greenlee and Drayton, Hilda Rogers, U. S. Thompson, Louise Warner, and Benise Dant, was widely reviewed, though less positively than the *Chocolate Kiddies.* See: G. "Schwarze Revue. Im Ufa-Palast am Zoo," *Neue Berliner Zeitung. Das 12 Uhr Blatt,* June 16, 1928; gol., "Die schwarze Revue," *Vossische Zeitung,* June 16, 1926; Georg Herzberg, "Die schwarze Revue," *Film-Kurier,* June 16, 1928; m., "Die 'Schwarze Revue.' Ufa-Palast am Zoo," *8 Uhr Abendblatt,* June 16, 1928; Oly, "Die schwarze Revue," *Berliner Börsen-Zeitung,* June 16, 1928; FB, "Die schwarze Revue," *Deutsche Allgemeine Zeitung,* June 17, 1928; lo., "Schwarze Revue," *Berliner Tageblatt,* June 17, 1928; s., "Die schwarze Revue," *Berliner Volkszeitung,* June 17, 1928; Hans W. Fischer, "Die schwarze Revue," *Welt am Montag,* June 18, 1928; "Sam Woodings Schokoladejungens und andere Berliner Ufa-Programme," *Der Artist* 2222 (July 20, 1928).

27. Discussions of this last documented appearance by Wooding in Berlin include: MK, "Sam Wooding spielt auf," *Tempo,* April 7, 1930; ü., "Sam Wooding und die Chocolate Kiddies," *8 Uhr Abendblatt,* April 9, 1930; ML, "Sam Wooding auf dem Dachgarten," *Neue Berliner Zeitung. Das 12 Uhr Blatt,* April 10, 1930.

28. Bernhard H. Behncke, "Sam Wooding and the Chocolate Kiddies at the Thalia-Theater in Hamburg, 28 July 1925 to 24 August 1925," *Storyville* 60 (1975), 217. On Wooding's opinion of Whiteman, see additionally Deffaa, *Voices of the Jazz Age,* 10–13.

29. "Sam Wooding and Orchestra Lead European Musicians: Makes Hit," *Chicago Defender,* July 12, 1930, 5.

30. Wooding, "Die Verklärung des Jazz."

31. Ibid.

32. John Howland, "Ellingtonian Extended Composition and the Symphonic Jazz Model," *Annual Review of Jazz Studies* 14, eds. Edward Berger, Henry Martin, Dan Morgenstern (Lanham, MD: Scarecrow Press, 2009) 4.

33. James A. "Billboard" Jackson, "Billboard Likes Johnny Hudgins," *Baltimore Afro-American,* January 10, 1925.

34. The information in this initial release was available by April 24 in Germany. *Der Artist* has a short note about a performance by forty African American artists that will premiere on May 25. Under the rubric "Was uns gerade noch fehlt" (The Last Thing We Need), an anonymous author bemoans the plan as yet another example of the "invasion" of Black artists in Berlin's entertainment district (*Der Artist* 2053 [April 24, 1925]). On the wider response to the *Chocolate Kiddies,* see below.

35. "To Offer Colored Revue in Europe," the *Billboard,* April 18, 1925, 5, 112.

36. The transliteration of Leonidoff's name varies. It is given both as "Leonidow" and as "Leonidov." The following discussion of Leonidoff's role is based on the author's joint research with Konrad Nowakowski.

37. On Leonidoff's activities with the MAT, see the retrospective account offered in his memoirs, published as Leonid Leonidov, *Rampa i zhizn* (Paris: Russkoe teatral'noe izdatel'stvo za-Granitsei, 1955). This account focuses almost exclusively on the person-

alities he encountered in the Russian theater, with no mention of his involvement with the *Chocolate Kiddies*. My thanks to Vlad Bilenkin for help in assessing this work.

38. Karl Schlögel, "Berlin: 'Stiefmutter unter den russischen Städten," *Der große Exodus. Die russische Emigration und ihre Zentren 1917–1941*, ed. Karl Schlögel (Munich: C. H. Beck, 1994), 237.

39. On Gest's biography, style, and position in the historiography of the MAT, see Valleri J. Hohman, *Russian Culture and the Theatrical Performance in America, 1891–1933* (New York: Palgrave Macmillan, 2011), 75–100.

40. "Negerexotik im Raimund-Theater," *Wiener Allgemeine Zeitung,* November 17, 1925. Leonidoff relates, however, that this initial project stalled when the salary demands became too high.

41. Advertisement for "Alabam Fantasies" at the Lafayette Theatre, *New York Times,* January 21, 1925, 5. For details on the contract as well as its London partners, see J. A. Jackson, "Around Harlem with Jackson," *Baltimore Afro-American,* February 7, 1925.

42. Abbie Mitchell, "Autobiographical Notes: Club Alabam," *Will Mercer Cook Papers,* Series G, 157–7, folder 20, Moorland-Spingarn Research Center, Howard University.

43. "'Alabam Fantasies' a Hit at the Lafayette Theatre," *New York Amsterdam News,* January 21, 1925, 6.

44. Howard Rye, "Three Eddies," *The New Grove Dictionary of Jazz, 2nd edition,* Grove Music Online (Oxford University Press). http://oxfordindex.oup.com/view/10.1093/gmo/9781561592630.article.J708100

45. On issues facing Black performers in the period immediately preceding the 1920s, see, for example, Karen Sotiropoulos, *Staging Race: Black Performers in Turn of the Century America* (Cambridge, MA: Harvard University Press, 2009).

46. "Lyons Suing Club Alabam," *Variety,* February 18, 1925, 37; "Lyons vs Alabam on Thursday," the *Billboard,* March 21, 1925, 22.

47. Sam Wooding, interviewed by Chris Albertson, New York, April 26, 1975. Originally conducted for the Smithsonian, these interviews with Wooding have been posted by Albertson on his website. The relevant section is at minute 44.00 and can be found at: http://stomp-off.blogspot.com/2012/03/sam-wooding-iii.html

48. It seems to have reached the Black community in Harlem as well. Abbie Mitchell remarks that when she returned from Europe in 1923, acting in New York had changed dramatically and everyone was speaking of Stanislavski (Abbie Mitchell, "Autobiographical Notes re: 1920s," *Will Mercer Cook Papers,* Series G, 157–7, folder 19, Moorland-Spingarn Research Center, Howard University).

49. My discussion of Greenlee and Drayton and the associated idea of the "class act" is based on Jean and Marshall Stearns, *Jazz Dance: The Story of American Vernacular Dance* (New York: Da Capo, 1968), 291–97.

50. On this period of Ellington's career, see Mark Tucker, *Ellington: The Early Years* (Urbana: University of Illinois Press, 1991).

51. Duke Ellington, *Music is My Mistress* (New York: Da Capo, 1973), 71.

52. Tucker, *Ellington: The Early Years,* 126.

53. "Jig Walk" alone was recorded on twelve separate occasions after its Berlin premiere (Tucker, *Ellington: The Early Years*, 135). See also the discography of European recordings of Ellington's tunes in the 1920s in Björn Englund, "Chocolate Kiddies: The Show That Brought Jazz to Europe," *Storyville* 62 (December 1975–January 1976), 50.

54. "Artists to Make Tour of Many European Capitals," *Baltimore Afro-American*, April 25, 1925, 14.

55. "Bamville Club Hosts Entertain Artists on Eve of European Trip," *New York Age*, May 9, 1925, 6.

56. Floyd G. Snelson, "'Chocolate Kiddies' Company Sails for Germany," the *Pittsburgh Courier*, May 16, 1925, 10. Though it is beyond the scope of this chapter, it is important to note that the revue received treatment in the African American press as well as in *Variety* throughout the summer, especially due to contract disputes that arose while the group played in Berlin. For example: "Two Artists Abroad May Quit Show," *Baltimore Afro-American*, July 4, 1925, A4.

57. O. M. Seibt, "Berlin News Letter," *The Billboard* (March 28, 1925), 86.

58. Peter Jelavich, *Berlin Cabaret* (Cambridge, MA: Harvard University Press, 1993), 165, 176.

59. Jacobsohn's role is acknowledged and praised in E. B–r, "Neger-Revue in Berlin. Gastspiel der 'Chocolate Kiddies im Admiralspalast,'" *Neue Berliner Zeitung. Das 12 Uhr Blatt*, May 26, 1925.

60. Advertisement for *Chocolate Kiddies*, *Berliner Tageblatt*, May 27, 1925.

61. Advertisement for *Chocolate Kiddies*, *Berliner Tageblatt*, June 6, 1925.

62. "Die Neger proben. Das schwarze Gastspiel im Theater im Admiralspalast," *Neue Berliner Zeitung. Das 12 Uhr Blatt*, May 22, 1925; M. P–t., "Chocolate Kiddies im Admiralspalast," *Berliner Morgenpost*, May 24, 1925; Li Zielesch, "Die 'Schokoladenkinder' in Zivil. Bei der ersten Probe der Negerkünstler," *Berliner Volkszeitung*, May 24, 1925; ls., "Die Neger proben," *Berliner Montagspost*, May 25, 1925.

63. A number of scenes of the group's appearance in Moscow can be seen in Dziga Vertov's film *A Sixth Part of the World* (1926).

64. "Program of Chocolate Kiddies Revue," Institut für Theaterwissenschaft der Freien Universität Berlin.Theaterhistorische Sammlung Walter Unruh, ca. May 1925.

65. On the role of Ellington and his music in the revue, see below.

66. According to the program, the performers were Thadeaus Greenlee and Rufus Drayton, the Three Eddies (Shakey Beasley, Tiny Ray, and Chick Horsey), Lottie Gee, Margaret Sims, Arthur Bryson, Bobby and Babe Goins, Arthur Strut Payne, Adelaide Hall, Charles Davis, George Statson, and Sam Wooding's Orchestra. The chorus was made up of Jessie Crawford, Viola Branch, Rita Walker, Thelma Green, Bobby Vincent, Thelma Watkins, Marie Bushell, Bernice Miles, Mamie Savoy, Allegritta Anderson, Lydia Jones, Helen Miles, and Ruth Williams.

67. This is a reference to the popular series of language instruction books promising to teach Germans 1000 words of a foreign language, e.g., *1000 Worte English* (Berlin: Ullstein Verlag 1925).

68. "Program of Chocolate Kiddies Revue."

69. Bushell, *Jazz From the Beginning*, 55.

70. Further details on song names and writers for all of the acts can be found in Englund, "Chocolate Kiddies: The Show that Brought Jazz to Europe," 45–46.

71. Ian Cameron Williams, *Underneath a Harlem Moon: The Harlem to Paris Years of Adelaide Hall* (New York: Continuum, 2002), 75.

72. Bushell, *Jazz From the Beginning*, 55.

73. Behncke, "Sam Wooding and the Chocolate Kiddies at the Thalia-Theater," 217.

74. Sam Wooding quoted in Egino Biagioni, *Herb Flemming: A Jazz Pioneer Around the World* (Alphen aan de Rijn: Micrography, 1977), 19. The band recorded at the *Vox* studio in July 1925 in Berlin and released the following sides: "Alabamy Bound," "By the Waters of Minnetonka," "O Katharina," and "Shanghai Shuffle." Each song was recorded and issued in 10- and 12-inch versions ("Sam Wooding," Green, Lotz, and Rye, *Black Europe*, vol. 2, 283–84).

75. On Whiteman's "Experiment in Modern Music," see chapter 3. Paul Whiteman and His Orchestra, "By the Waters of Minnetonka" (Victor 19391). On this song in the context of symphonic jazz, see John Howland, *Between the Muses and the Masses: Symphonic Jazz, "Glorified" Entertainment, and the Rise of the American Musical Middlebrow, 1920–1944* (PhD diss., Stanford 2001), 142–54.

76. Nora M. Alter and Lutz Koepnick, *Sound Matters: Essays on the Acoustics of Modern German Culture* (New York: Berghahn Books, 2004), 7.

77. Fritz Giese, *Girlkultur: Vergleiche zwischen europäischem und amerikanischem Lebens- und Rhythmusgefühl* (Munich: Delphin Verlag, 1925), 33. See chapter 4 for further discussion of Giese's work.

78. Miriam Hansen, "Benjamin, Cinema and Experience: 'The Blue Flower in the Land of Technology,'" *New German Critique*, 40 (Winter 1987): 179–224; Margaret Cohen, *Profane Illumination: Walter Benjamin and the Paris of Surrealist Revolution* (Los Angeles and Berkeley: University of California Press, 1995).

79. Walter Benjamin, *Illuminations*, trans. Harry Zohn (London: Fontana, 1992), 158.

80. Ibid., 159, trans. altered.

81. Here I am not as concerned about rehashing the Adorno-Benjamin debate of the 1930s in relation to experience as to read out of Adorno's own texts on music a set of questions and problematics. For a comparative view of their respective employments of the concept of experience, however, see Martin Jay, *Songs of Experience: Modern American and European Variations on a Universal Theme* (Los Angeles and Berkeley: University of California Press, 2005), 312–60.

82. Theodor W. Adorno, "Music in the Background," *Essays on Music*, ed. Richard Leppert, trans. Susan Gillespie (Los Angeles: University of California Press, 2002): 506–9. Originally published as "Musik im Hintergrund," *Vossische Zeitung*, January 31, 1934.

83. Adorno, "Music in the Background," 507.

84. Ibid., 508.

85. Ibid.

86. Ibid., 509.

87. Richard Leppert, "Music 'Pushed to the Edge of Existence' (Adorno, Listening, and the Question of Hope)," *Cultural Critique* 60 (Spring 2005), 95.

88. Adorno, "Music in the Background," 509.

89. Ibid.

90. Albrecht Riethmüller, "Hermetik, Schock, Faßlichkeit. Zum Verhältnis von Musikwerk und Publikum in der ersten Hälfte des 20. Jahrhunderts," *Archiv für Musikwissenschaft* 37 (1980), 48.

91. Adorno, "Music in the Background," 509.

92. Ibid.

93. Theodor Adorno, "On the Social Situation of Music," *Essays on Music*, 409, trans. altered.

94. Ibid.

95. Ibid.

96. Theodor Adorno, *Minima Moralia: Reflexionen aus dem beschädigten Leben*, *Gesammelte Schriften*, ed. Rolf Tiedemann, vol. 4 (Frankfurt am Main: Suhrkamp, 1997), 270.

97. Theodor Adorno, "On the Social Situation of Music," 409.

98. Riethmüller, "Hermetik, Schock, Faßlichkeit," 47.

99. The author consulted the following reviews in Berlin newspapers: Oscar Bie, "Negertheater," *Berliner Börsen-Courier* May 26, 1925; E. B–r, "Neger-Revue in Berlin. Gastspiel der 'Chocolate Kiddies im Admiralspalast," *Neue Berliner Zeitung. Das 12 Uhr Blatt,* May 26, 1925; Michael Charol, "Negritisierung. Die Chocolate Kiddies im Admiralspalast," *Berliner Börsen-Zeitung,* May 26, 1925; Fred Hildebrandt, "Negertheater," *Berliner Tageblatt,* May 26, 1925; P., "'Chocolate Kiddies.' Die Negertruppe," *Berliner Lokal-Anzeiger,* May 26, 1925; Kurt Pinthus, "Die schwarze Schau im Admiralspalast," *8 Uhr Abendblatt,* May 26, 1925; St., "Theater im Admiralspalast," *Neue Preußische Zeitung (Kreuz-Zeitung),* May 26, 1925; Erich Urban, "Die schwarze Revue. 'Chocolate Kiddies' im Admiralspalast," *BZ am Mittag,* May 26, 1925; Fritz Zielesch, "Chocolate Kiddies," *Berliner Volkszeitung,* May 26, 1925; a., "Neger-Operette. Die 'Chocolate Kiddies,'" *Vossische Zeitung,* May 27, 1925; gre, "Chocolate Kiddies," *Deutsche Allgemeine Zeitung,* May 27, 1925; RK, "Neger-Theater. 'Chocolate Kiddies' im Admiralspalast," *Berliner Allgemeine Zeitung,* May 27, 1925; "Schwarz-Weißes," *Vorwärts,* May 27, 1925; Yuri Ofrosimov, "негритянская оперетта (Admirals-Palast)," *Rul,* May 28, 1925; Klaus Pringsheim, "Neger Revue. Chocolate Kiddies im Admiralspalast," *MM Der Montag Morgen,* June 2, 1925; "Negertheater. Chocolate Kiddies," *Welt am Montag,* June 2, 1925; Jef., "Amerikanisierung mit Musik," *Berliner Montagspost,* June 8, 1925; Artur Michel, "Chocolate Kiddies. Ein Abschiedsgruß," *Vossische Zeitung,* June 13, 1925. Note should also be made of other reviews that appeared in newspapers and journals outside of Berlin, e.g.: "Berlin hat seine Negeroperette," *Der Artist* 2058 (May 29, 1925); George Stein, "Chocolate Kiddies," *Hamburger Anzeiger,* May 29, 1925; Arthur Berkun-Wulffen, "Neger-Revue im Berliner Admiralspalst," *Das Organ* 862 (May 30, 1925): 11; Herwarth Walden, "Schwarzkünstler," *Die Weltbühne* 21 (June 2, 1925): 818–19; Walther Hansemann, "Chocolate Kiddies," *Altonaer Neueste Nachrichten*; Hermann Wedderkop, "Chocolate Kiddies im Admiralspalast," *Der Querschnitt* 5 (1925): 653.

100. One article recounts a confrontation in a Berlin bar between two African American performers from the group and German nationalists. In this account, the nationalists are thrown out of the bar after the patrons stand up against this injustice (A. A., "Weiße Kulturträger," *Welt am Montag,* June 2, 1925). Regardless of whether the event took place in this manner, as noted earlier in footnote 2, troupe members later recalled similar incidents with German nationalists.

101. Sam Wooding quoted in Biagioni, *Herb Flemming,* 19–20. Various versions of this story have been given by Wooding and others from the band (Bushell, *Jazz from the Beginning,* 55; Deffaa, *Voices of the Jazz Age,* 17). "Bis" here refers not to the German preposition meaning "until," but to the French-language term for "encore."

102. Paul Bekker, *Die Sinfonie von Beethoven bis Mahler* (Berlin: Schuster, 1918), 17.

103. Bie, "Chocolate Kiddies."

104. Fritz Zielesch, "Chocolate Kiddies."

105. Michel, "Chocolate Kiddies."

106. Pinthus, "Die schwarze Schau im Admiralspalast."

107. Alfred Lion, interview in documentary film *Blue Note: A Story of Modern Jazz* (dir. Julian Benedikt, 1997).

108. Klaus Pringsheim, "Chocolate Kiddies," *Das Tage-Buch* 6 (May 1925), 805. See further his review from June 2 "Neger-Revue. Chocolate Kiddies im Admiralspalast."

109. E. B-r, "Neger-Revue in Berlin."

110. Nonetheless and demonstrating the wide range of views present at the time, the reviewer for the *Berliner Lokal-Anzeiger* suggested in a generally negative article that the "squawking and squeaking (*Gequäke und Gequieke*) was not as annoying" as usual, and that German jazz bands would do well to learn from them (P., "Chocolate Kiddies," *Berliner Lokal-Anzeiger*).

111. Rumpelstilzchen [Adolf Stein], *Haste Worte?* (Berlin: Winkler, 1925), 321.

112. Fred Hildebrandt, "Negertheater."

113. Urban, "Die schwarze Revue."

114. Walden, "Schwarzkünstler," 818.

115. Ibid.

116. Ibid., 818–19.

117. Bie, "Chocolate Kiddies."

118. St., "Theater im Admiralspalast."

119. Jacques Attali, *Noise: The Political Economy of Music,* trans. Brian Massumi (Minneapolis: University of Minnesota Press, 1985), 26.

120. Ibid., 26–27.

121. RK, "Negertheater."

122. Fritz Zielesch, "Chocolate Kiddies."

123. Li., "Black people. Neger-Revue im Metropoltheater," *Neue Berliner Zeitung,* July 14, 1926.

124. Born in Hungary, Ernö Rapée was an American composer of popular, jazz-inflected music of the 1920s, but who remained active in Europe and Berlin through his activities with music for silent film.

125. The *Funkstunde* was the first radio station in Berlin and all of Germany, opening in 1923.

126. Kurt Weill, "Tanzmusik [1926]," *Musik und musikalisches Theater: Gesammelte Schriften*, eds. Stephen Hinton and Jürgen Schebera. Mainz: Schott, 2000), 298.

127. On Rathaus' as well as other composers' use of jazz and America, see the discussion in chapter 7.

128. Karol Rathaus, "Jazzdämmerung?" *Die Musik* 19 (February 1927): 333–36.

129. Ibid., 333, 335.

130. Ibid. Italics in original.

131. Ibid., 336.

132. Ibid.

133. Ibid. Italics in original.

134. Ibid.

135. Hans David, "Abschied vom Jazz," *Melos* 9 (1930): 413–17. See chapter 7 for further examples.

136. See note 27 for further reviews of Wooding's last performances in Berlin.

137. David, "Abschied vom Jazz," 413.

138. Ibid., 415.

139. Excluding reviews of return appearances in Berlin, some of the most important post-1925 references to Wooding include: Alfred Baresel, *Das neue Jazzbuch* (Leipzig: Zimmermann, 1929), 13; Max Butting, "Jazz," *Sozialistische Monatshefte* (December 13, 1926): 879–80; Albert K. Henschel, "Paul Whiteman," *Die Weltbühne* 22 (July 13, 1926): 74–75; Karol Rathaus, "Jazzdämmerung?" *Die Musik* 19 (February 1927): 333–36; Heinrich Strobel and Frank Warschauer, "Interessante Jazzplatten," *Melos* 9 (1930): 482; Frank Warschauer, "Negerrevuen und Neger-Jazz," *Das blaue Heft* 8 (February 15, 1926): 108–12.

CHAPTER 3

The quotation cited in the epigraph is from Jaap Kool, "Vom Negerdorf zur Philharmonie," *Uhu* 1:2 (November 1924), 31.

1. On the debates over the jazzing of the classics, as well as other existing musical composition more generally, which was known as *Verjazzung* (jazzification/jazzing), see: Bernd Hoffmann, *Aspekte zur Jazz-Rezeption in Deutschland: Afro-amerikanische Musik im Spiegel der Musikpresse 1900–1945* (Graz: Akademische Druck- und Verlagsanstalt, 2003), 75–76; Eckhard John, *Musikbolschewismus: Die Politisierung der Musik in Deutschland 1918–1938* (Stuttgart: Metzler, 1994), 293; Cornelius Partsch, "That Weimar Jazz," *New England Review* 22 (Fall 2002), 186–90; Heribert Schröder, *Tanz- und Unterhaltungsmusik in Deutschland 1918–1933* (Bonn: Verlag für systematische Musikwissenschaft, 1990), 366–71; Jed Rasula, "Jazzbandism," *The Georgia Review* 60:1 (2006), 104–5.

2. It should be noted that while all three were born outside of Germany's borders at the time, each of their works were published by a German press, Berlin in the cases of Janowitz and Schickele and Leipzig in the case of Renker.

3. The recent collection edited by Kristen Krick-Aigner and Marc-Oliver Schuster, *Jazz in German-Language Literature* (Würzbug: Königshausen & Neumann, 2013), does address Schickele and Janowitz in articles by Eileen Simonow, Jürgen Grandt, and Pascale Cohen-Avenel, along with other examples of jazz in German-language literature. There is no mention of either Renker or the symphony in these works, however.

4. On Whiteman, see Don Rayno, *Paul Whiteman: Pioneer in American Music*, vol. 1 (Lanham, MD: Scarecrow Press, 2003); Thomas DeLong, *Pops: Paul Whiteman, King of Jazz* (Piscataway, NJ: New Century Publishers, 1983).

5. Paul Whiteman and Margaret McBride, *Jazz* [1926] (New York: Arno Press, 1974), 33.

6. Ibid., 27–28.

7. Max Brod, "Shimmy und Foxtrott" *Der Auftakt* 2 (1922), 256–59. This piece was also published under the same title in *Prager Tagblatt,* October 8, 1922.

8. Whiteman and McBride, *Jazz*, 26.

9. See, for example, Sieglinde Lemke, *Primitivist Modernism: Black Culture and the Origins of Transatlantic Modernism* (New York: Oxford University Press, 1998), 59–94.

10. Paul Allen Anderson, *Deep River: Music and Memory in Harlem Renaissance Thought* (Durham: Duke University Press, 2001), 235.

11. Paul Whiteman, quoted in Arthur von Gizycki-Arkadjew, "Zwei Stimmen zum Jazz," *Der Artist* 2239 (1928). Quoted in Schröder, *Tanz- und Unterhaltungsmusik*, 298.

12. On this space, see, for example, Janet Ward, *Weimar Surfaces: Urban Visual Culture in 1920s Germany* (Berkeley & Los Angeles: University of California Press, 2001), 176–77.

13. DeLong, *Pops*, 95.

14. *Lustige Blätter*, Paul Whiteman Collection, Berlin Folder, Williams College, ca. June 1926. My thanks to librarian Linda Hall, Whiteman author Don Rayno, and Meredith Soeder for helping make these materials available to me. Any document contained within the Whiteman Collection will be designated in the footnotes.

15. "Ein Paulus als Saulus," *Neue Berliner Zeitung. Das 12 Uhr Blatt,* June 15, 1926. Paul Whiteman Collection, Berlin Folder, Williams College.

16. Fred Hildebrandt, "Audienz beim Jazzbandkönig," *Der Tag* (Berlin) June 13, 1926. Paul Whiteman Collection, Berlin Folder, Williams College; Richard Dyck, "Der Mann, der den Jazz durchsetzte. Gespräch mit Paul Whiteman," *8 Uhr Abendblatt,* June 8, 1926. Paul Whiteman Collection, Berlin Folder, Williams College. Paul Whiteman, "Paul Whiteman," *Berliner Tageblatt,* June 22, 1926.

17. Albert K. Henschel, "Paul Whiteman," *Die Weltbühne* 22 (July 13, 1926), 74.

18. Paul Goldmann, "Paul Whiteman und sein Jazzorchester," *Neue Freie Presse,* July 5, 1926.

19. On this and band members' reactions to Berlin, see Rayno, *Paul Whiteman*, 135.

20. "Whiteman sucht den besten Foxtrott," *Vossische Zeitung,* June 12, 1926; an identical article is published in the *Deutsche Allgemeine Zeitung* on June 14, 1926, as well.

21. M. M., "Whiteman auf der Probe: Jazzband im Großen Schauspielhaus," *Vossische Zeitung,* June 15, 1926.

22. DeLong, *Pops*, 95.

23. Karen Painter, *Symphonic Aspirations: German Music and Politics* (Cambridge, MA: Harvard University Press, 2007), 185.

24. Schröder, *Tanz- und Unterhaltungsmusik*, 304.

25. Cover of *Simplicissimus* 31:14 (July 2, 1926): 185. Paul Whiteman Collection, Berlin Folder, Williams College.

26. Hans Siemsen, "Der Jazz-König kommt nach Berlin! Paul Whiteman," *8 Uhr Abendblatt*, May 28, 1926.

27. Ibid.

28. Ibid.

29. Whiteman, "Paul Whiteman."

30. Ibid.

31. Hans Heinz Stuckenschmidt, "Lob der Revue," *Musikblätter des Anbruch* 8 (March 1926): 153–55; "Mechanische Musik," *Auftakt* 6 (1926): 170–73; "Lob des Grammophons," *Das Kunstblatt* 10 (1926): 39–41.

32. Hans Heinz Stuckenschmidt, "Paul Whiteman," *Berliner Tageblatt*, May 29, 1926. See also the similar article Hans Heinz Stuckenschmidt, "Paul Whiteman, der Jazz-König," *Das Stachelschwein* 3:2 (1926): 9–10.

33. Stuckenschmidt, "Paul Whiteman."

34. Aside from Stuckenschmidt's and Siemsen's early pre-readings of the concert, Hungarian pianist and critic Arpad Sándor published "Jazz" in the *Berliner Tageblatt* on June 9, 1926, in which he, too, discusses Whiteman, though more generally. In addition, an excerpt from Henry Osgood's *So This Is Jazz* was reprinted as "Jazz-Anatomie. Zu dem Berliner Gastspiel des Whiteman Jazz-Symphonie-Orchesters," *Deutsche Allgemeine Zeitung*, June 24, 1926. Finally, Arthur Rundt, discussed in chapter 6, published an article about jazz, largely based upon his travelogue, *Amerika ist anders* (Arthur Rundt, "Jazz," *Berliner Börsen-Courier*, June 25, 1926. Paul Whiteman Collection, Berlin Folder, Williams College).

35. Hugo Leichtentritt, "Zur Einführung," program for Paul Whiteman's concerts at the *Grosses Schauspielhaus*, ca. June 1926. Author's personal copy.

36. On the second program, see Oscar Bie, "Das zweite Programm der Whitemankapelle," *Berliner Börsen-Courier*, June 29, 1926. Paul Whiteman Collection, Berlin Folder, Williams College; "Whitemans Sonntag," *Berliner Montagspost*, June 28, 1926.

37. Further details regarding Whiteman's itinerary and reception abroad are given in Rayno, *Paul Whiteman*, 127–38.

38. Rayno, *Paul Whiteman*, 135.

39. Goldmann wrote back home to Vienna: "Just like everywhere else, Paul Whiteman was an enormous success with the audience in Berlin. During the concerts there was tremendous applause after each number. The Berlin critics, however, rejected the 'symphonic jazz orchestra' for the most part, despite all recognition of the technical achievement" ("Paul Whiteman und sein Jazzorchester").

40. "Der Jazzkönig: Paul Whiteman im Großen Schauspielhaus," *Vossische Zeitung*, June 27, 1926.

41. Haf. [Hans Feld], "Paul Whiteman der Jazzkönig," *Film Kurier*, June 29, 1926. Paul Whiteman Collection, Berlin Folder, Williams College.

42. Leopold Schmidt, "Jazz-Konzerte im Großen Schauspielhaus," *Berliner Tageblatt*, June 26, 1926.

43. "Der Jazzkönig: Paul Whiteman im Großen Schauspielhaus."

44. "Whitemans Sonntag," *Berliner Montagspost,* June 26, 1926.

45. Wilhelm Klatte, "Whitemans Jazzmusik," *Berliner Lokal-Anzeiger,* June 26, 1926.

46. Klaus Pringsheim, "Jazz-Dämmerung," *Die Schallkiste* 1 (August 1926), 8. Italics in original.

47. Ibid.

48. Schmidt, "Jazz-Konzerte im Großen Schauspielhaus."

49. Oscar Bie, "Whiteman. Großes Schauspielhaus," *Berliner Börsen-Courier,* June 26, 1926. Paul Whiteman Collection, Berlin Folder, Williams College.

50. Walter Schrenk, "Whitemans erstes Konzert," *Deutsche Allgemeine Zeitung,* June 26, 1926. Paul Whiteman Collection, Berlin Folder, Williams College.

51. Frank Warschauer, "Jazz: On Whiteman's Berlin Concerts," *Weimar Republic Sourcebook*, eds. Anton Kaes, Martin Jay, and Edward Dimendberg (Berkeley and Los Angeles: University of California Press, 1994), 571. Translation modified. Originally published as "Jazz. Zu Whitemans Berliner Konzerten," *Vossische Zeitung,* June 19, 1926. Paul Whiteman Collection, Berlin Folder, Williams College.

52. XYZ, "Der Jazzkönig Paul Whiteman. Eine Auseinandersetzung aneinander vorbei," *Der Deutsche* (Berlin) June 27, 1926. Paul Whiteman Collection, Berlin Folder, Williams College.

53. Marc Weiner *"Urwaldmusik* and the Borders of German Identity: Jazz in Literature of the Weimar Republic," *The German Quarterly* 64:4 (1991): 475–87; Cornelius Partsch, *Schräge Töne. Jazz und Unterhaltungsmusik in der Kultur der Weimarer Republik* (Stuttgart: J. B. Metzler, 2000), 151–73. See further the recent collection by Krick-Aigner and Schuster, *Jazz in German-Language Literature.*

54. Felix Dörmann, *Jazz. Wiener Roman* (Vienna: Strache Verlag, 1925); on Dörmann, see Siegfried Mattl, "Dunkles Wien. Felix Dörmanns Jazz und die Wiener Unterhaltungskultur nach dem 'Grossen Krieg," *Pop in Prosa. Erzählte Populärkultur in der deutsch- und ungarischsprachigen Moderne*, eds. Amália Kerekes, Magdolna Orosz, Gabriella Rácz, and Katalin Teller (Frankfurt am Main: Peter Lang, 2007), 99–114.

55. Other than those discussed below, another possible exception to this rule is Erwin Sedding's *Jazzyn* (Berlin: Weltbücher Verlag, 1927). Sedding was a critic for *Der Artist* and wrote at least three articles on jazz: "Jazz," *Der Artist* 2072 (September 4, 1925); "Klavier und Jazzband," *Der Artist* 2076 (October 2, 1925); "Ia. Jazzschläger," *Der Artist 2086* (December 11, 1925). On Sedding's novel, see Pascale Cohen-Avenel, "An Epidemic of Jazz in German-Language Literature: 1920–1931," *Jazz in German Language Literature*, 137–46.

56. Weiner, *"Urwaldmusik* and the Borders of German Identity: Jazz in Literature of the Weimar Republic," 475.

57. Friedrich Hirth, "Der literarisierte Jazz," *Die Literatur* 29 (1927): 507–8.

58. Ibid.

59. Ibid.

60. Ibid.

61. Ibid.

62. Hans Janowitz, *Jazz. Roman* [1927] (Bonn: Weidle, 1999). Hereafter, references to the novel will be made in the body text with the abbreviation "JR." A portion of this novel has appeared previously in translation: Hans Janowitz, *Jazz*, trans. Cornelius Partsch and Damon O. Rarick, *New England Review* 25:1–2 (2004): 92–111. The implicit connection between Hirth's text and Janowitz's novel was first suggested in Philip Brady, "'Saxophon—guter Ton!' On Hans Janowitz's Jazz-Novel of 1927," *Expedition nach der Wahrheit: Poems, Essays, and Papers in Honour of Thea Stemmler*, eds. Stefan Horlacher and Marion Islinger (Heidelberg: C. Winter, 1996), 465.

63. See Anton Kaes, *Shell Shock Cinema: Weimar Culture and the Wounds of War* (Princeton: Princeton University Press, 2009), 46–86.

64. On the phenomenon of the *Eintänzer*, see Mihaela Petrescu, "Social Dancing and Rugged Masculinity—The Figure of the *Eintänzer* in Hans Janowitz's novel *Jazz* (1927)," *Monatshefte* 105:4 (Winter 2013): 593–608.

65. Jürgen Grandt, "The Colors of Jazz in the Weimar Republic: Hans Janowitz's *Jazz* Takes the Coltrane," *Jazz in German-Language Literature*, 78

66. Janowitz, *Jazz*, 24.

67. Oskar Maurus Fontana, "Jazz. Roman," *Das Tage-Buch* 8 (1927), 402. Further reviews of the novel include: Paul Leppin, "Jazz. Roman" [Review], *Die Literatur* 29 (1926/27): 483; Theodor Lücke, "Jazz. Roman" [Review], *Die literarische Welt* 3:9 (1927): 6–7.

68. These include modernist parody, as seen in the opening's homage to Dickens' *A Tale of Two Cities* and the modernist melding of music and text in Tolstoy's *Kreutzer Sonata*, as well as more vernacular variants like the detective novel implicated through the introduction of a serial killer and painter, Mr. Astragalus, to the novel. See further Cornelius Partsch, "That Weimar Jazz," *New England Review* 23:4 (Fall 2002), 189–91.

69. Eric Robertson, *Writing between the Lines: René Schickele, 'Citoyen Français, Deutscher' (1883–1940)* (Amsterdam: Rodopi, 1995), 126. On the specific meaning of the word "jazz" in the title, see below.

70. On the biographical elements within Schickele's novel, see Jean-Jacques Schumacher "'. . . mein persönlichstes Buch:' A propos du roman Symphonie für Jazz de Rene Schickele," *Recherches germaniques* 23 (1993): 155–64.

71. On this aspect in Janowitz, see Brady, 467–68.

72. Josephine Baker and figures resembling her were relatively common during the period. On these, see Tobias Nagl, *Die unheimliche Maschine: Rasse und Repräsentation im Weimarer Kino* (Munich: edition text + kritik, 2009), 660–69; Cornelius Partsch, *Schräge Töne: Jazz und Unterhaltungsmusik in der Kultur der Weimarer Republik* (Stuttart: J. B. Metzler, 2000), 141–60.

73. Rene Schickele, *Symphonie für Jazz* (Berlin: Fischer, 1929), 9. Hereafter abbreviated as SFJ and cited parenthetically in the main body text.

74. Kurt Martens, "Symphonie für Jazz" [Review]. *Die schöne Literatur* 30:9 (September 1929), 418.

75. Schröder, *Tanz- und Unterhaltungsmusik*, 157–59.

76. On production statistics for the saxophone, see ibid., 132. On the saxophone's cultural uses in the context of jazz and otherwise, see Daniel M. Bell, "The Saxophone

in Germany 1924–1935, A Cultural History," *The Saxophone Symposium* 29 (2004), esp. 14–25.

77. Schröder, *Tanz- und Unterhaltungsmusik*, 132. Though Schröder refers here to Baresel's 1929 *Das neue Jazzbuch*, the practice of doubling obviously starts much earlier, in Germany as well as in the United States.

78. For van Maray, the perfect jazz is that performed by the seagulls over the lake by the hotel, where he and Johanna first hear the jazz drummer and he decides to write his jazz symphony. They excite him because of their ability to travel between airy heights and watery depths: "They dove so deep that the tips of their wings became wet. Then they darted back above and the next cycle was a bit higher than the one from which they'd fallen. They gave me courage, the seagulls! They fit my music" (SFJ 56).

79. Nagl, *Die unheimliche Maschine*, 664.

80. Gustav Renker, *Symphonie und Jazz* (Leizpig: L. Stackermann, 1931). Hereafter cited as "SUJ" through parenthetical citations in the text.

81. Hirsch's Jewishness is referenced, for example, in his "sickly yellow (*fahlgelbes*) face marked by metropolis and civilization" (SUJ 89).

82. Scott Spector, "Modernism without Jews: A Counter-Historical Argument," *Modernism/Modernity* 13:4 (November 2006): 615–33.

83. Ibid., 623.

84. For Renker, the saxophone enables Makua-Taka to accommodate his African sound to the European ear, thus the statement: "The mediator to the world of culture was the saxophone that floated above it [the music], that gave the ears of whites the lyrical melody they demanded" (SUJ 35).

85. Advertisement for *Chocolate Kiddies Hamburger Anzeiger,* August 7, 1925, as well as *Altonaer Neueste Nachrichten,* August 12, 1925. This was also used in advertisements of the return of the *Chocolate Kiddies* to Berlin (advertisement in *Berliner Tageblatt,* December 20, 1925).

86. On the role of the Alps and mountains within German culture, see the recent collection *Heights of Reflection: Mountains in the German Imagination from the Middle Ages to the Present*, eds. Sean Moore Ireton and Caroline Schumann (Rochester, Camden House, 2012).

87. Janowitz writes that jazz band boys are all "sailors who always get seasick" (JR 18), it is a lake that marks the beginning of John van Maray's symphony and the end of his saxophone, while in Renker, Ricki Wehrberg is initially introduced as having a "passion for sailing" (SUJ 26).

CHAPTER 4

The quotation cited in the epigraph is from Friedrich Nietzsche, *Beyond Good and Evil,* trans. Michael Tannen (New York: Penguin, 1990), 31. Translation slightly modified.

1. While obviously the gender of a noun in German must not necessarily correspond to biological sex, there remains something uncanny to the neuter gendering of *Weib*. The entry for *Weib* in Grimm's *Wörterbuch* from the late nineteenth century, for example, states that any description of *Weib* must begin with a satisfactory explanation

of "the so conspicuous neuter gender of the word" (Jacob and Wilhelm Grimm, *Deutsches Wörterbuch* [Leipzig: S. Hirzel, 1878], s.v. Weib).

2. Nietzsche, *Beyond Good and Evil*, 31.

3. The literature on Germany's "New Woman" is vast, other than those works listed below, see for example: Atina Grossmann, "The New Woman and the Rationalization of Sexuality in Weimar Germany," *Powers of Desire: The Politics of Sexuality*, eds. Christine Stansell, Ann Snitow, and Sharon Thompson (New York: Monthly Review, 1983), 153–71; Atina Grossmann, *Reforming Sex: The German Movement for Birth Control and Abortion Reform, 1920–1950* (New York: Oxford University Press, 1995); Richard McCormick, *Gender and Sexuality in Weimar Modernity: Film, Literature, and 'New Objectivity'* (New York: Palgrave, 2001); Patrice Petro, *Joyless Streets: Women and Melodramatic Representation in Weimar Germany* (Princeton: Princeton University Press, 1989).

4. Rita Felski, *The Gender of Modernity* (Cambridge, MA: Harvard University Press, 1995).

5. Andreas Huyssen, "Mass Culture as Woman: Modernism's Other," *After the Great Divide: Modernism, Mass Culture, and Postmodernism* (Bloomington: Indiana University Press, 1986), 52.

6. Grossmann, "Girlkultur or Thoroughly Rationalized Female: A New Woman in Weimar Germany?" J. Friedlander et al., eds., *Women in Culture and Politics* (Bloomington: University of Indiana Press, 1986), 62–80.

7. Lynne Frame, "Gretchen, Girl, Garçonne? Weimar Science and Popular Culture in Search of the Ideal New Woman," *Women in the Metropolis: Gender and Modernity in Weimar Culture*, ed. Katharina von Ankum (Los Angeles and Berkeley: University of California Press, 1997), 12–40.

8. German discourse often employed the English term *Girl* instead of the German word for girl, *Mädchen*. I have therefore capitalized the word *Girl* throughout this chapter as a means of signifying the term's use as a conceptual device.

9. Peter Jelavich, *Berlin Cabaret* (Cambridge, MA: Harvard University Press, 1993), 177.

10. Other examples of writings on the Girl include: Erich Kästner, "Chor der Girls," *Lärm im Spiegel* (Leipzig: C. Weller & Co., 1930), 84–86; Siegfried Kracauer, "Girls und Krise [1931]," *Schriften*, ed. Inka Mülder-Bach, vol. 5.2 (Frankfurt am Main: Suhrkamp, 1990), 320–22; Paul Landau, "Girlkultur. Von der Amerikanisierung Europas," *Westermanns Monatshefte* 71 (January 1927), 565–68; Richard Huelsenbeck, "Girlkultur," *Die literarische Welt* 2:16 (April 16, 1926), 3; Alfred Polgar, "Girls [1926]," *Kleine Schriften*, ed. Marcel Reich-Ranicki, vol. 2 (Reinbek bei Hamburg: Rowohlt, 1983), 247–50; Joseph Roth, "Die Girls [1925]," *Das journalistische Werk, 1924–1928*, ed. Klaus Westermann, vol. 2 (Frankfurt am Main: Fischer, 1982), 393–94.

11. See Kerstin Barndt, *Sentiment und Sachlichkeit: Der Roman der Neuen Frau in der Weimarer Republik* (Cologne: Böhlau, 2003), 99–106 as well as Patrice Petro, "The Hottentot and the Blonde Venus," *Aftershocks of the New: Feminism and Film History* (New Brunswick, NJ: Rutgers University Press, 2002), 136–56.

12. Fritz Giese, *Girlkultur: Vergleiche zwischen amerikanischem und europäischem Rhythmus- und Lebensgefühl* (Munich: Delphin Verlag, 1925). All further references will be made parenthetically and indicated by "GK."

13. The images derive from Gustav Kafka, ed., *Handbuch der vergleichenden Psychologie*, vol. 1 (Munich: E. Reinhardt, 1922), plate III, fig. b and plate X, fig. b following 304. Giese himself contributed a lengthy section to this volume on child psychology (Kafka, *Handbuch der vergleichenden Psychologie*, 323–518).

14. This image from 1924 is from a scene at cabaret *Die Gondel (The Gondola)*. It originally appeared as "Karikatur einer Neger-Jazzband-Kapelle aus dem Kabarett 'Die Gondel,' *Uhu* 1:2 (November 1924), 31 as an illustration to Jaap Kool's article "Vom Negerdorf zur Philharmonie," which is also referenced in chapter 3.

15. Giese's title also plays off the more standard terminology of *Frauenkultur*, present at least since Georg Simmel's writings on the subject. See, for example, Georg Simmel, "Female Culture," *Simmel on Culture*, ed. David Frisby (Thousand Oaks, CA: Sage Publications, 1997), 46–54. On the development of the term in the Weimar Republic, see Kerstin Barndt, "'Engel oder Megäre.' Figurationen einer 'Neuen Frau' bei Marieluise Fleißer und Irmgard Keun," *Reflexive Naivität. Zum Werk Marieluise Fleißers*, eds. Maria E. Müller and Ulrike Vedder (Berlin: Erich Schmidt Verlag, 2000), 16–34.

16. Norbert Elias, *The Civilizing Process: Sociogenetic and Psychogenetic Investigations*, trans. Edmund Jephcott, eds. Stephen Mennell, Eric Dunning, and Johan Goudsblom (Malden, MA.: Blackwell Publishers, 1994), 5–30.

17. Huelsenbeck, "Girlkultur," 3.

18. Adolf Halfeld, *Amerika und der Amerikanismus. Kritische Betrachtungen eines Deutschen und Europäers* (Jena: Eugen Diedrichs, 1927).

19. Michael Taussig, *Mimesis and Alterity: A Particular History of the Senses* (New York: Routledge, 1993) 176–92.

20. Lora Wildenthal, *German Women for Empire, 1884–1945* (Durham: Duke University Press, 2001), 9.

21. There may also be a further reason for this connection, namely that Charles Davis, choreographer of the *Chocolate Kiddies*, had previously incorporated a variation of the Tiller Girls' routine for the show *Chocolate Dandies*, replacing the Tiller's kicks with taps. See Marshall Stearns and Jean Stearns, *Jazz Dance: The Story of American Vernacular Dance* (New York: Da Capo, 1968), 147. See further Nowakowski, "Jazz in Wien," *Anklaenge 2011/2012*, Special Issue: *Jazz unlimited. Beiträge zur Jazz-Rezeption in Österreich* (Wien: Mille Tre Verlag, 2012), 138n406.

22. Attesting to her fame, Baker's memoirs, as dictated to the journalist Marcel Sauvage, were immediately published in German translation as: Josephine Baker, *Memoiren*, ed. Marcel Sauvage, trans. Lilly Ackermann (Munich: Meyer & Jessen, 1928). On Baker in Germany, see Nancy Nenno, "Femininity, The Primitive, and Modern Urban Space: Josephine Baker in Berlin," *Women in the Metropolis*, ed. Katharina von Ankum (Berkeley and Los Angeles: University of California Press, 1997), 145–61; Tobias Nagl, *Die unheimliche Maschine. Rasse und Repräsentation im Weimarer Kino* (Munich: Edition text + kritik, 2009), 656–60.

23. The best source for details on Douglas' life remains Rainer Lotz, *Black People: Entertainers of African Descent in Europe, and Germany* (Bonn: Birgit Lotz, 1997), 297–389. Further discussion can be found in Leroy Hopkins, "Louis Douglas and the Weimar Reception of Harlemania," *Germans and African Americans*, eds. Larry A.

Greene and Anke Ortlepp (Jackson: University Press of Mississippi, 2011): 50–69; Andy Fry, *Paris Blues: African American Music and French Popular Culture, 1920–1960* (Chicago: University of Chicago Press, 2014), 70–78.

24. Mary Louise Pratt, *Imperial Eyes: Travel Writing and Transculturation* (New York: Routledge, 1992), 4.

25. In addition to Jelavich *Berlin Cabaret*, see Wolfgang Jansen, *Glanzrevuen der zwanziger Jahre* (Berlin: Edition Hentrich, 1987) and Franz-Peter Kothes, *Die theatralische Revue in Berlin und Wien, 1900–1938. Typen, Inhalte, Funktionen* (Wilhelmshaven: Heinrichshofen, 1977).

26. On the concept of surface culture in Weimar, see Janet Ward, *Weimar Surfaces: Urban Visual Culture in 1920s Germany* (Los Angeles and Berkeley: University of California Press, 2001), 9–10.

27. Theodor Lücke, "Gedanken der Revue," *Scene* 16 (1926), 114. See also Jelavich's discussion in *Berlin Cabaret*, 169.

28. Alfred Polgar, "Synkope [1924]," Alfred Polgar, *Kleine Schriften*, ed. Marcel Reich-Ranicki, vol. 2 (Reinbek bei Hamburg: Rowohlt, 1983), 173.

29. On rationalization discourse and the experience of it by women during the Weimar Republic, see Grossmann, "Girlkultur or Thoroughly Rationalized Female: A New Woman in Weimar Germany?"

30. Here it should be pointed out that in addition to Berlin, individual performers as well as entire shows travelled across Germany to large- and medium-sized towns, as well as touring internationally. Though my focus in this chapter remains on Berlin, individual histories of Black performers in other large cities are necessary as well. One important example of such work for Frankfurt am Main is Hans Pehl, *Afroamerikanische Unterhaltungskünstler in Frankfurt am Main. Eine Chronik von 1844 bis 1945* (Frankfurt am Main: n.p., 2010).

31. Contemporary reviews of *La Revue nègre* include: Alfred Polgar, "Abende in Berlin: Neger-Revue," *Die literarische Welt* 2:7 (1926): 3; m.l., "Negerrevue im Nelson Theater," *Vossische Zeitung*, January 4, 1926; Kurt Pinthus, "Neger-Revue. Nelson Theater," *8 Uhr Abendblatt*, January 4, 1926; Erich Urban, "Neger-Revue bei Nelson," *BZ am Mittag*, January 4, 1926; "Neger-Revue im Nelson-Theater," *Neue Berliner Zeitung. Das 12 Uhr Blatt.*, January 4, 1926; N., "Neger-Revue," *Berliner Börsen-Zeitung*, January 7, 1926.

32. Contemporary reviews of *Black People* include: AM, "Bei den 'Black People.' Revueprobe im Metropol-Theater," *Vossische Zeitung*, July 11, 1926; bur., "Schwarze Revue. 'Black People' im Metropol-Theater," *Berliner Tageblatt*, July 14, 1926; Georg, "'Schwarzes Volk.' Negerrevue im Metropoltheater," *Berliner Volkszeitung*, July 14, 1926; Li, "Black People. Neger-Revue im Metropoltheater," *Neue Berliner Zeitung. Das 12 Uhr Blatt.*, July 14, 1926; Hans Siemsen, "Negerrevue im Metropol," *8 Uhr Abendblatt*, July 14, 1926; Erich Urban, "'Black People.' Neger-Revue im Metropol-Theater," *BZ am Mittag* July 14, 1926; AM, "'Black People,' Neger-Revue im Metropol-Theater," *Vossische Zeitung* July 15, 1926; schr., "Black People," *Deutsche Allgemeine Zeitung*, July 15, 1926; Kurt Groetschel, "Neger-Revue im Metropol-Theater. 'Black People,'" *Das kleine Journal*, July 17, 1926; g., "Metropol-Theater: 'Black People,'" *Welt am Montag*, July 19, 1926.

33. Program for "Die schwarze Revue" at the *Ufa-Palast am Zoo* (ca. June 1928), n.p. My thanks to Hans Pehl for providing me with a copy of the program.

34. In addition to the Berlin sources listed in footnote 26 of chapter 2, see the following notes on Wooding's 1928 revue from the African American press: "Going to Germany," the *Pittsburgh Courier*, June 9, 1928; "Race Entertainers Swoop in on Germany," *Baltimore Afro-American*, June 28, 1928; "Louise Warner Over There," *Chicago Defender*, July 21, 1928; Joel A. Rogers, "Johnny Hudgins Starts Home on the First Boat," *Baltimore Afro-American*, July 28, 1928; Ivan H. Browning, "News of London," *New York Amsterdam News*, August 1, 1928; "So Johnny Came Sailing Home Again," *New York Amsterdam News*, August 8, 1928. Further information is also available in Bernhard Behnke with Mark Berresford, "Sam Wooding and the Chocolate Kiddies at the Ufa-Palast in Berlin in June 1928," *VJM's Jazz and Blues Mart* (Spring 2005): 2–4.

35. For the 1931 show, see ML., "'Louisiana.' Douglas' Revue-Operette im Deutschen Künstlertheater," *Berliner Morgenpost* July 15, 1931. On *Louisiana* and Douglas' work during the late 1920s and early 1930s more generally, see Lotz, *Black People*, 341–377.

36. Eric Prieto, "Alexandre Striello and the Beginnings of the Biguine," *Nottingham French Studies* 43:1 (Spring 2004), 30.

37. "Filmmann eröffnet Neger-Bar," *Film-Kurier*, February 27, 1932, cited in Nagl, *Die unheimliche Maschine*, 733. Though much remains unknown about the *Biguine*, it seems certain that it opened in February 1932, rather than in 1926 as is implied by the dating of an advertisement reprinted elsewhere (see Alonzo and Martin, *Zwischen Charleston und Stechschritt*, 366; Bärbel Schrader and Jürgen Schebera, *Kunst-Metropole Berlin 1918–1933* [Berlin and Weimar: Aufbau Verlag, 1987], 115). An identical advertisement to the one reprinted in these sources appears in the Berlin newspaper *Tempo* on March 3, 1932.

38. Joachim Zeller, *Weisse Blicke—Schwarze Körper: Afrikaner im Spiegel westlicher Alltagskultur: Bilder aus der Sammlung Peter Weiss* (Erfurt: Sutton Verlag, 2010), 201; Klaus Völker and Max Hermann-Neisse, *Max Hermann-Neisse: Künstler, Kneipen, Kabaretts—Schlesien, Berlin, im Exil* (Berlin: Edition Hentrich, 1991), 151; "Verschiedenes," *Zeitschrift für Musik* 99 (1932), 456; R. W. Canem, "Umschau," *Fliegende Blätter* 88 (June 9, 1932): 365.

39. Reviews of Welch's performances can be found in: *Das kleine Journal* (June 24, 1932); *Das 12-Uhr Blatt* (June 22, 1932); *Berliner Wochenschau* (June 24, 1932), and *Berliner Tribüne* (June 28, 1932). My thanks to Stephen Bourne for providing me with copies of these texts.

40. A photograph of Douglas at the *Biguine* alongside the identical Black staff members from *Tempo* is reproduced in Martin and Alonzo, *Zwischen Charleston und Stechschritt*, 366. It is mistakenly dated to 1929 by the *Stiftung Preußischer Kulturbesitz*. While it is clear from this photograph that Douglas was at the *Biguine* sometime in 1932, there is as of yet no further documentation.

41. "Dinah ist da!" *Tempo*, September 2, 1932.

42. Adolf Stein [Rumpelstilzchen], *Nu wenn schon* (Berlin: Brunnen Verlag, 1932), 231.

43. The situation of African migrant workers during Weimar is treated in Robbie Aitken, "Surviving in the Metropole: The Struggle for Work and Belonging amongst African Colonial Migrants in Weimar Germany," *Immigrants & Minorities* 28:2–3 (2010), 213–15.

44. In the 1927 edition of the yearbook, which details performers for the previous year, individual members of the dance company at the *Theater am Admiralspalast* are listed, including African American and Afro-German performers, Ralph Grayson and Louis Brody (*Deutsches Bühnen-Jahrbuch*, vol. 38 [Berlin: Genossenschaft Deutscher Bühnen-Angehöriger, 1927], 245). The very next year, this section of this publication disappears (*Deutsches Bühnen-Jahrbuch*, vol. 39 [Berlin: Verlag Deutscher Bühnen-Angehöriger, 1928], 265) and with it references to African American, Afro-German, and Afro-European performers.

45. Further context to these performers, as well as other examples, can be found in: Robbie Aitken and Eve Rosenhaft, *Black Germany: The Making and Unmaking of a Diaspora Community, 1884–1960* (Cambridge and New York: Cambridge University Press, 2013), 194–230. Individual biographies of some performers also exist, for example, Monika Firla, *Der kameruner Artist Hermann Kessern: ein schwarzer Crailsheimer* (Crailsheim: Baier, 2010); Rea Brändle, *Nayo Bruce: Geschichte einer afrikanischen Familie in Europa* (Zurich: Chronos, 2007).

46. Advertisement for "Die blaue Maus" at the *Atrium-Beba-Palast*, *Berliner Tageblatt* December 2, 1928; AP, "Saxophon-Susi. Alhambra," *Vossische Zeitung*, November 4, 1928. Further discussion of Benga's significance for modernists during the period is given in James Smalls, "Féral Benga's Body," *Africa in Europe: Studies in Transnational Practice in the Long Twentieth Century*, eds. Robbie Aitken, John Macvicar, Eve Rosenhaft (Liverpool: Liverpool University Press, 2013), 99–120.

47. It was reported in the African American press that Bayton earned a total of $200,000 during her almost two years in Germany (Floyd J. Calvin, "Earns $200,000 on German Stage in 19 Months," the *Pittsburgh Courier*, February 11, 1928). Additional examples of such performers as reported in the African American press can be found in the writings of Ivan H. Browning, himself a performer with the Four Harmony Kings. See Ivan H. Browning, "Across the Pond," *Chicago Defender*, May 28, 1927, 6; "European Notes," *New York Amsterdam News*, February 9, 1927, 10; "News of Our Entertainers in Europe," *New York Amsterdam News*, April 18, 1928, 7; "News of London," *New York Amsterdam News*, August 1, 1928, 6.

48. On this development, see Daniel M. Bell, "The Saxophone in Germany, 1924–1935: A Cultural History," *The Saxophone Symposium* 29 (2004): 1–38. More generally, see Stephen Cottrell, *The Saxophone* (New Haven: Yale University Press, 2012).

49. Ernst Krenek, *Jonny spielt auf. Oper in 2 Teilen. Klavierauszug mit Text vom Komponisten* (Vienna: Universal Edition, 1954[1926]), 29, m680.

50. See, for example, Yva's photographs of Louis Brody as saxophone player overlaid alongside images of dancing women (Marion Beckers and Elisabeth Moortgat, eds., *Yva : Photographien 1925–1938* [Tübingen: Wasmuth, 2001]) that originally appeared in *Die Berliner Illustrirte Zeitung* or Frans Masereel's visual work *Jazz* from 1931, which depicts three Black saxophone players standing over a white female dancer (reprinted in Sell Tower, *Envisioning America*, 105).

51. Michael Cowan, *Technology's Pulse: Essays on Rhythm in German Modernism* (London: IGRS Books, 2011), 196–98, here 197.

52. The image of Helm is reprinted in Cowan, *Technology's Pulse*, 205. A photograph of Rosa Valetti with a saxophone can be found in *Uhu* 2: 2 (November 1925), 38; Schroeter can be seen in Beckers and Moortgat, eds., *Yva : Photographien 1925–1938*, 28; Trude Hesterberg's performance was reprinted in the *Berliner Illustrirte Zeitung* 35 (September 5, 1926), 1151; For Knight's painting, see *Berliner Illustrirte Zeitung* 35 (July 11, 1926), 871.

53. My thanks to Konrad Nowakowski and Hans Pehl for their invaluable help in identifying Jones.

54. Lotz, *Black People*, 65–87.

55. Mark Miller, *Some Hustling This! Taking Jazz to the World, 1914–1929* (Toronto: Mercury Press, 2005), 34.

56. For a discussion of examples of female blackface, see Martin and Alonzo, eds., *Zwischen Charleston und Stechschritt*, 352–71.

57. The first documented example of Steiner's parody is in the revue "Wieder Metropol" in September 1926, where she, alongside stars Hans Albers and Max Hansen, performed (potentially in blackface) in a scene dubbed "Negro Revue" (Program "Wieder Metropol," Institut für Theaterwissenschaft der Freien Universität Berlin. Theaterhistorische Sammlungen, ca. 1926). Steiner continued to perform her Baker parody in a 1927 performance at the *Pavillon Mascotte* (Advertisement in *Berliner Tageblatt*, January 16, 1927). In 1929, she again appeared as Baker in Nelsons Künstlerspiele, an illustration of which can be found in "Die Tänzerin Jenny Steiner in einer witzigen Josephine Baker-Parodie (Nelsons Künstlerspiele in Berlin)," *Berliner Illustrirte Zeitung* 38 (January 24, 1929): 159. Steiner's parodies of Baker are discussed in Nenno "Femininity, The Primitive, and Modern Urban Space" (150) as well as in Alan Lareau, *"Bitte einsteigen!* Josephine Baker's 1928 Return to Berlin," *Topography and Literature: Berlin and Modernism*, eds. Rolf Goebel and Sabine Hake (Göttingen: V&R, 2009), 81; Nagl, *Die unheimliche Maschine*, 694–95.

58. Petro, "The Hottentot and the Blonde Venus," 139.

59. Grossmann, *Reforming Sex*, 3.

60. Jelavich, *Berlin Cabaret*, 185–86.

61. Lareau, *"Bitte einsteigen!"* 81.

62. Program for *Madame Pompadour*, Institut für Theaterwissenschaft der Freien Universität Berlin. Theaterhistorische Sammlungen, ca. 1927. On Harris and his stage persona "Snowball," see Don Rayno, *Paul Whiteman: Pioneer in American Music*, vol. 1 (Lanham, MD: Scarecrow Press, 2003), 160–61.

63. *The Great Attraction* premiered three months later than Kortner's *The Good Sinner* and it is unclear whether the two productions had any influence on each other. On *The Good Sinner*, see Nagl, *Die unheimliche Maschine*, 696–99.

64. The document has been reprinted as "Erlaß wider die Negerkultur für deutsches Volkstum," *Quellen zur Geschichte Thüringens*, ed. Jürgen John, vol. 3 (Erfurt: LZT, 1996), 140–41. Numerous, mostly negative reactions to the decree were published, e.g.: "Frick blamiert sich nach Jazz-Noten," *8 Uhr Abendblatt*, April 15, 1930; "Frick zieht gegen den Drachen Jazz," *Vossische Zeitung*, April 15, 1930; "Ehrenrettung des Jazz,"

Berliner Volkszeitung, April 24, 1930; Josef Freudenthal, "Jazzmusik verboten!" *Der Artist* 2315 (May 2, 1930); Eberhard Preußner, "Kultur-Reaktion," *Musik und Gesellschaft* 1 (July 1930): 96–98. On the 1930 ban, see chapter 7 for further discussion.

65. A. Sacher-Woenckhaus, ". . . unsere modernen Tänze sind *keine* Niggertänze mehr . . ." *Uhu,* 8:7 (April 1932): 83–89. Italics in original. See the related discussion of this text in Theodore Rippey, "Rationalization, Race, and the Weimar Response to Jazz," *German Life and Letters* 60:1 (January 2007), 86–88.

66. "Frick blamiert sich nach Jazz-Noten." That this may be Kurt Weill, rather than "Bruno Weil," is hinted at in the text through references to this composer producing "songs" and that he found it unsurprising that this came from Weimar, supposedly the only German city which has yet to produce the *Threepenny Opera.* The article also includes the anonymous opinion of a Black musician. This was possibly Sam Wooding, who was performing in Berlin in April 1930 when the decree was issued (see chapter 2).

67. Ibid., 86.

68. Kitty is shadowed throughout the film by a portly white American named Tommy, who is infatuated with her and eventually orchestrates her release from the contract with Jackson. By the end of the film, however, Tommy gives up his claim on Kitty, thus removing one further impediment to Kitty's own recuperation as white, German woman and wife.

69. "Du warst mir ein Roman" features music by Bronislaw Kaper and lyrics by Fritz Rotter. It was released by the Odeon record company as O-4984a in 1931 as performed by Richard Tauber and the Odeon Künstler-Orchester.

70. James Donald, "Kracauer and the Dancing Girls," *New Formations* 61 (Spring 2007), 61.

71. Hans Pehl, *Afroamerikanische Unterhaltungskünstler in Frankfurt am Main,* 92. Kracauer's original text is "Exzentriktänzer in den Ufa-Lichtspielen," *Frankfurter Zeitung* (Stadt-Blatt), October 16, 1928. Further examples of Kracauer's writing about Black performers and jazz are discussed below.

72. Siegfried Kracauer, "The Mass Ornament," *The Mass Ornament: Weimar Essays,* ed. Thomas Y. Levin (Cambridge, MA: Harvard University Press, 1995), 79.

73. Miriam Hansen, *Cinema and Experience: Siegfried Kracauer, Walter Benjamin, and Theodor W. Adorno* (Berkeley and Los Angeles: University of California Press, 2012), 51

74. Ibid., 50.

75. Kracauer, "Mass Ornament," 81.

76. On Kracauer's position on jazz and Blackness, see Rippey, "Rationalization, Race, and the Weimar Response to Jazz," 89–92.

77. Kracauer, "Mass Ornament," 77.

78. Siegfried Kracauer, *The Salaried Masses: Duty and Distraction in Weimar Germany,* trans. Quintin Hoare (New York: Verso, 1998), 29

79. Ibid.

80. Ibid., 32.

81. Siegfried Kracauer, "Negerball in Paris," *Frankfurter Zeitung,* October 17, 1928. Also available as Siegfried Kracauer, "Negerball in Paris," *Schriften,* ed. Inka Mülder-Bach, vol. 5.2 (Frankfurt am Main: Suhrkamp, 1990), 127–29.

82. Kracauer, "Negerball in Paris," 127.

83. Ibid.

84. Ibid.

85. Ibid., 128.

86. Making the connection between Blackness qua performance even more strongly, Kracauer suggests "that these common Negroes would first have to be translated into American in order to be Negroes" (Ibid.). On this idea, see further, Rippey, "Rationalization, Race, and the Weimar Response to Jazz," 93–94.

87. Ibid., 129.

88. Ibid.

89. Rippey, "Rationalization, Race, and the Weimar Response to Jazz," 95.

90. Siegfried Kracauer, "Haupt- und Staatsaktion im Schumann-Theater," *Frankfurter Turmhäuser: Ausgewählte Feuilletons, 1906–1930*, ed. Andreas Volk (Zurich: Edition epoca, 1997), 120. Originally published August 5, 1928, in the *Stadt-Blatt* of the *Frankfurter Zeitung*.

91. Ibid.

CHAPTER 5

The quotation cited in the epigraph is from Alfred Baresel, quoted in Karl Holl, "Jazz im Konservatorium," *Melos* 7 (1928), 31.

1. "Jazz Bitterly Opposed in Germany," the *New York Times,* March 11, 1928, Amusements section, 8. See also: Alfred Einstein, "Some Berlin Novelties," the *New York Times,* February 19, 1928, X8.

2. Susan C. Cook, *Opera for a New Republic: The Zeitopern of Krenek, Weill, and Hindemith* (Ann Arbor: UMI Research Press, 1988), 84–110.

3. Jacques Attali, *Noise: The Political Economy of Music,* trans. Brian Massumi (Minneapolis: University of Minnesota Press, 1985), 63.

4. Quoted in Peter Cahn, *Das Hoch'sche Konservatorium in Frankfurt am Main (1878–1978)* (Frankfurt am Main: Dr. Waldemar Kramer, 1979), 21.

5. Cahn, *Das Hoch'sche Konservatorium,* Anhang I, 377.

6. Leo Kestenberg, *Musikerziehung und Musikpflege* (Leipzig, 1921), quoted in Ulrich Günther, *Die Schulmusikerziehung von der Kestenberg-Reform bis zum Ende des Dritten Reiches* (Neuwied am Rhein: Luchterhand, 1967), 13.

7. Leo Kestenberg, *Bewegte Zeiten: Musisch-musikantische Lebenserinnerungen* (Wolfenbüttel: Möseler Verlag, 1961), 72.

8. Cahn, *Das Hoch'sche Konservatorium,* 247. See further Peter Cahn, "Zum Frankfurter Musikleben in den zwanziger Jahren," *Ein halbes Jahrhundert: was da ist in Frankfurt,* eds. Gerhard König and Adam Seide (Frankfurt am Main: Eichborn, 1983), 211–17.

9. On Sekles' life as an educator and musician, see Joachim Tschiedel, *Bernhard Sekles, 1872–1934: Leben und Werk des Frankfurter Komponisten und Pädagogen* (Schneverdingen: Verlag für Musikbücher Karl Dieter Wagner, 2005); Karl Holl, "Bernhard Sekles," *Die Musik in Geschichte und Gegenwart,* vol. 12 (Kassel: Bärenreiter, 1965), 480–81.

10. Cahn, *Das Hoch'sche Konservatorium,* 295.

11. Quoted in Peter Cahn, "Eine handschriftlich hinterlassene Formenlehre von Bernhard Sekles," *Neue Musik und Tradition: Festschrift Rudolf Stephan*, eds. C.M. Schmidt and W. Seidel (Laaber: Laaber-Verlag, 1990), 420. The quote is from page 136 of a handwritten manuscript held at the library of the *Hochschule für Musik und darstellende Kunst* in Frankfurt am Main.

12. Bernhard Sekles, "Kleiner Shimmy," *Das neue Klavierbuch* (Mainz: B. Schotts Söhne, 1927), 8.

13. Bernhard Sekles, *Grundzüge der Formenlehre*, unpublished and undated manuscript held at the *Hochschule für Musik und darstellende Kunst* in Frankfurt am Main, 131. Italics in original.

14. Ibid., 133. Italics in original.

15. Sekles also wrote a text on improvisation for children. See Bernhard Sekles, *Elementarschule der Improvisation*, unpublished and undated manuscript held at the *Hochschule für Musik und darstellende Kunst* in Frankfurt am Main, n.d. (likely after 1925).

16. Bernhard Sekles, "Fünfzig Jahre Dr. Hochs Konservatorium," *Frankfurter Zeitung*, Stadtblatt (January 22, 1928).

17. "Kreuz und Quer. Jazz-Klasse an Dr. Hoch's Konservatorium," *Zeitschrift für Musik* 94 (1927), 706. Italics in original.

18. Theodor W. Adorno, "Bernhard Sekles 'Die zehn Küsse' [Review]," *Gesammelte Schriften*, ed. Rolf Tiedemann, vol. 19 (Frankfurt am Main: Suhrkamp, 1997), 73.

19. Seiber's vision of jazz and activities as head of the *Jazzklasse* are discussed in the concluding section of this chapter.

20. "Kreuz und Quer. Jazzklasse an Dr. Hoch's Konservatorium," 706. Italics in original.

21. The *Jazzklasse* debate is treated in the following secondary sources: Cahn, *Das Hoch'sche Konservatorium*, 216–64; Pascale Cohen-Avenal, *Si on a du jazz, pas besoin de schnaps: Jazz, négritude et démocratie sous la République de Weimar* (New York: Peter Lang, 2011), 68–71; Kathryn Smith Bowers, "East Meets West: Contributions of Mátyás Seiber to Jazz in Germany," in *Jazz and the Germans: Essays on the Influence of "Hot" American Idioms on 20th-Century German Music*, ed. Michael J. Budds (Hillsdale, NY: Pendragon Press, 2002), 119–40; Schröder, *Tanz- und Unterhaltungsmusik*, 387–89; and Susan Cook, "Jazz as Deliverance: The Reception and Institution of American Jazz during the Weimar Republic," *American Music* 7 (Spring 1989), 40–42; Theodore Rippey, "Rationalization, Race, and the Weimar Response to Jazz," *German Life and Letters* 60:1 (January 2007), 78–81.

22. The national scope of the announcement was already on display through the two articles published in Berlin's *Vossische Zeitung* ("Du lernst Jazz nach Noten," *Vossische Zeitung*, November 12, 1927; Ernst Klein, "Der Frankfurter Jazzskandal," *Vossische Zeitung*, December 10, 1927) as well as the caricature "Lehrstuhl für Jazz" from *Simplicissimus* 32.38 (December 19, 1927): 527. The announcement was also reprinted in Hamburg in "Ein Konservatoriumsklasse für Jazz," *Hamburgischer Correspondent*, November 11, 1927.

23. Paul Schwers, "Jazz als akademisches Lehrfach!" *Allgemeine Musikzeitung* 54 (1927), 1194–95. Major resistance to the *Jazzklasse* came from the city of Munich and the *Münchner Tonkünstlerverein*. See for example "Jazz im Konservatorium," *Münchner Neueste Nachrichten*, November 29, 1927.

24. Schwers, "Jazz als akademisches Lehrfach!" 1195. Italics in original.

25. Further examples of the conservative critique are: Karl Schaezler, "Jazz," *Hochland* 25 (January 1928): 439–41; "Niggermusik und Frankfurter Konservatorium," *Das Echo* 2322 (January 12, 1928): 82.

26. On the linkage of "Jewishness" and modernism and modernity in German-speaking Central Europe, see also the discussions of this idea in chapters 3 and 6.

27. Schwers, "Jazz als akademisches Lehrfach!" 1195.

28. Ibid.

29. As Schwers writes a bit later, jazz's "white slaves suffer under it" (ibid.).

30. Leon Lencov, "Kreuzzug gegen den Jazz," *Der Artist* 2189 (December 2, 1927).

31. Karl Holl, "Jazz am Konservatorium," *Frankfurter Zeitung,* November 25, 1927. A reading similar to Holl's can be found in Walter Bertens, "Jazz-Konservatorium," *Musik im Leben* 4:1 (1928): 15–16.

32. Ibid.

33. Karl Holl, "Jazz im Konservatorium," *Melos* 7 (1928), 32. Although printed a few months later, this article, appearing in the progressive music journal *Melos*, draws heavily on the original publication from the *Frankfurter Zeitung*. There are only slight modifications, such as the above quote.

34. Holl, "Jazz am Konservatorium."

35. Ibid.

36. Ibid.

37. Bernhard Sekles, quoted in "Kreuz und Quer. Weiteres vom Jazz-Konservatorium," 32–33. It is also partially reprinted in "Zum letzten Mal: 'Jazz im Konservatorium,'" *Frankfurter Zeitung,* December 13, 1927. The later article would make reference to the *Jazzklasse* as a "fresh wind" in the halls of music. This phrase was picked up by Nazi ideologue, Alfred Rosenberg, in his discussion of the *Jazzklasse* in *Der Sumpf: Querschnitte durch das 'Geistes-'Leben der November-Demokratie* (Munich: Zentralverlag der NSDAP, 1939 [1930], 34–35).

38. Sekles, quoted in "Kreuz und Quer. Weiteres vom Jazz-Konservatorium," 32. It is important to make clear that Sekles was not only replying to Schwers and the voices assembled in this article, but also to the *Münchner Tonkünstler Verein* and the protest of Hermann W. v. Waltershausen.

39. Sekles, quoted in "Kreuz und Quer. Weiteres vom Jazz-Konservatorium," 32.

40. It is interesting to note the anonymous poem published just underneath Sekles' second announcement. Replete with anti-Black and anti-Semitic racism, it suggests, for example, that the "Hottentots" will build a memorial to Sekles ("Kreuz und Quer. Weiteres vom Jazz-Konservatorium," 33).

41. Heinrich Strobel, "Unzeitgemäße Proteste," *Musikblätter des Anbruch* 10 (1928), 25.

42. Alfred Baresel, *Das Jazzbuch* (Leipzig: Zimmerman, 1925). Published in late 1925, by the end of 1926, Baresel's work had already gone through four printings.

43. Alfred Baresel, "Kampf um das Frankfurter Jazz-Konservatorium," *Neue Musik-Zeitung* 49 (1927/28), 267. Italics in original.

44. Ibid.

45. Alfred Baresel, "Kunst-Jazz," *Melos* 7 (1928), 354–55.

46. Ibid., 355. Here, he cites Paul Whiteman's 1926 book *Jazz* as proof, remarking that even Whiteman, "King of Jazz," whom Baresel labels one of the greatest "corruptors" (*Verderber*) of a new musical idea, admitted that it was left to the European to discover the artistic possibilities of jazz.

47. Ibid., 356.

48. Seiber's writings on jazz include: "Jazz-Instrumente, Jazz-Klang und neue Musik," *Melos* 9 (1930): 122–26; "Jazz als Erziehungsmittel," *Melos* 7 (1928): 281–86; "Jazz und die musikstudierende Jugend," *Der Artist* 2305 (February 21, 1930); "Jazz-Unterricht," *Frankfurter Zeitung,* September 8, 1928; "Rhythmic Flexibility in Jazz? A Study of Jazz Rhythm," *Music Review* 6 (1945): 30–41, 89–94, 160–71; *Schule für Jazz-Schlagzeug* (Mainz: B. Schott's Söhne, 1929); "Welche Rolle spielt die Synkope in der modernen Jazzmusik?," *Musik-Echo* 1:3 (May/June 1930); "Jugend und Jazz," *Zeitschrift für Schulmusik* 3 (1930): 29–32; "Einiges über meine 'Leichten Tänze,'" *Melos* 12 (1933): 11–12. On Seiber, see Smith Bowers, "East Meets West: Contributions of Mátyás Seiber to Jazz in Germany," 119–40.

49. Seiber arrives in New York on October 3, November 14, and December 26, 1927 (Ancestry.com. *New York, Passenger Lists, 1820–1957* [database online]. Provo, UT, USA: Ancestry.com Operations, Inc., 2010). Seiber was therefore likely hired as director of the *Jazzklasse* in early 1928.

50. On the complex structure of radio, public, jazz, classical, and popular music at *SWR*, see Michael Stapper *Unterhaltungsmusik im Rundfunk der Weimarer Republik* (Tutzing: Hans Schneider, 2001), 30–34, 56–66.

51. Stapper, *Unterhaltungsmusik im Rundfunk der Weimarer Republik*, 60.

52. Joachim-Felix Leonard, ed., *Programmgeschichte des Hörfunks in der Weimarer Republik*, vol. 2 (Munich: dtv, 1997), 960.

53. On the *Jazzklasse* in relation to the question of jazz in Weimar radio, see Bernd Hoffmann, "Jazz im Radio der frühen Jahre," *That's Jazz: Der Sound des Jahrhunderts*, ed. Klaus Wolbert (Frankfurt am Main: Zweitausendeins, 1997), 577–84.

54. Seiber, "Jazz als Erziehungsmittel," *Melos* 7 (1928), 281–86.

55. Ibid., 281.

56. J. Bradford Robinson, "The Jazz Essays of Theodor Adorno: Some Thoughts on Jazz Reception in Weimar Germany," *Popular Music* 13:1 (1994), 12.

57. Seiber, *Schule für Jazz-Schlagzeug*, 29.

58. Seiber, "Jazz als Erziehungsmittel," 284.

59. Ibid., 285.

60. Cook makes the argument that in a 1945 essay, "Rhythmic Freedom in Jazz?" Seiber gave up on jazz and its potential ("Jazz as Deliverance," 42). Smith Bowers, on the other hand, counters that Seiber is more likely referring in this passage to popular tunes with jazz-like effects ("East Meets West," 139).

61. Alban Berg, *Handschriftliche Briefe, Briefentwürfe und Notizen aus den Beständen der Musiksammlung der Österreichischen Nationalbibliothek*, vol. 1, ed. Herwig Knaus (Wilhelmshaven: F. Noetzel, 2004), 98. This was one of a set of comments Berg

made regarding jazz. On these, see Konrad Nowakowski, "Jazz in Wien: Die Anfänge" *Anklaenge 2011/2012*, Special Issue: Jazz Unlimited: *Beiträge zur Jazz-Rezeption in Österreich* (Vienna: Mille Tre Verlag, 2012), 129–31.

62. Seiber, "Jazz-Instrumente, Jazz-Klang und Neue Musik," 126.

63. Kurt Weill, "Notiz zum Jazz," *Musikblätter des Anbruch* 10 (1928), 138.

64. Ibid.

65. Seiber, "Jazz und die musikstudierende Jugend."

66. Ibid. In his 1936 essay, Theodor W. Adorno similarly speaks of the "Negerfabel" (fable of the Negro) regarding the origins of jazz (Thedor W. Adorno, "Über Jazz," *Gesammelte Schriften*, ed. Rolf Tiedemann, vol. 17 [Frankfurt am Main: Suhrkamp, 1997], 87). See chapter 7 for further discussion of Adorno's jazz theory.

67. Ibid. Behind the Singing Sophomores were the very same Revelers, who only used this alternate name when working for Columbia Records.

68. Ibid. Italics in original.

69. Ibid.

70. "Erstes Konzert der Jazz-Klasse," *Südwestdeutsche Rundfunk-Zeitung* 5:9 (March 3, 1929), 9. A reproduction of the program can be found in Leonhard, *Programmgeschichte des Hörfunks in der Weimarer Republik*, 960.

71. Ibid. On Henkel, see Michael Kater, *Different Drummers: Jazz in the Culture of Nazi Germany* (New York: Oxford University Press, 1992), 44.

72. Arthur Hollde, "Jazz im Konservatorium. Eine Matinee im Hochschen Konservatorium," *Frankfurt General-Anzeiger* (Stadtbeilage), March 6, 1929.

73. "Sinfonisches Jazzkonzert der Jazzklasse von Dr. Hoch's Konservatorium," *Südwestdeutsche Rundfunk-Zeitung* (March 9, 1930): 9; "Sinfonisches Jazz-Konzert der Jazz-Klasse von Dr. Hochs Konservatorium," *Funkstunde* 10 (March 11, 1930): 295. The concert program was also reprinted in the US press as well: "Mahler's 'Eighth' in London," *New York Times,* May 4, 1930. A further radio appearance by Seiber and his jazz students took place on November 5, 1929. On Seiber's compositions, from this period and later, see Smith Bowers, "East Meets West," 130–36.

74. "Bunter Abend," *Südwestdeutsche Rundfunk-Zeitung* 7:47 (November 22, 1931), 10.

75. Hans Pehl, "Vom Kaiserreich zur Weimarer Republik," *Der Frankfurt Sound: Eine Stadt und ihre Jazzgeschichte(n)*, ed. Heinrich Schwab (Frankfurt am Main: Societätsverlag, 2004), 25.

76. Recordings of his two *Jazzolettes* further reveal that he drew specific inspiration from Gershwin's *Rhapsody in Blue*, e.g., in instrumentation and tonality (Ebony Band, *Dancing the Jazz Fever of Milhaud, Martinu, Seiber, Burian & Wolpe*, Compact Disc [Channel Classics CCS 30611, 2011]).

77. Theodor W. Adorno, "Frankfurter Opern- und Konzertkritiken [May 1929]," *Gesammelte Schriften*, ed. Rolf Tiedemann, vol. 19 (Frankfurt am Main: Suhrkamp, 1997), 156.

78. The number of students annually enrolled in the jazz program at Hoch's Conservatory between 1928 and 1932 varied between 10 and 19 (Cahn, *Das Hoch'sche Konservatorium*, 378).

79. W. St., "Die Syncopators beim Training. Die Jazzklasse im Hoch'schen Konservatorium," *Stadt-Blatt der Frankfurter Zeitung,* November 18, 1932.

80. In 1938, the conservatory was made public and renamed the *Hochschule für Musik und darstellende Kunst.*

81. On the history of jazz in Frankfurt, see Jürgen Schwab, ed., *Der Frankfurt Sound.*

82. Schulz-Köhn did receive a doctorate in 1940 with the publication of his important study of the recording industry, *Die Schallplatte auf dem Weltmarkt* (Berlin: Reher, 1940).

83. Dietrich Schulz-Köhn to Langston Hughes, January 31, 1958, *Langston Hughes Papers,* James Weldon Johnson Collection. Beinecke Rare Book and Manuscript Library. Yale University.

CHAPTER 6

The quotation cited in the epigraph is from Langston Hughes, *Fine Clothes to the Jew* (New York: Knopf, 1927), xiii.

1. Langston Hughes, *I Wonder as I Wander: An Autobiographical Journey* (New York: Hill and Wang, 1962), 69. On Hughes' life and works, see the biography by Arnold Rampersad, *The Life of Langston Hughes,* 2 vols. (New York: Oxford University Press, 1986–88). On Hughes' role within African American diasporic culture in Europe during the interwar period, see Brent Hayes Edwards, *The Practice of Diaspora: Literature, Culture, Translation, and the Rise of Black Internationalism* (Cambridge, MA: Harvard University Press, 2003), 59–68.

2. Hughes, *I Wonder as I Wander,* 71.

3. Ibid.

4. Ibid., 72. Lenox Avenue was a famous street in 1920s Harlem. Today it is also known as Malcolm X Boulevard.

5. The exchange has primarily been considered from the perspective of the history of the Harlem Renaissance and the individual biographies of figures like Langston Hughes. Recently, however, scholars have begun to explore the connections between the Harlem Renaissance and Weimar modernism. See A. B. Christa Schwarz, "New Negro Renaissance—'Neger-Renaissance': Crossovers between African America and Germany during the Era of the Harlem Renaissance," *From Black to Schwarz: Cultural Crossovers between African America and Germany,* eds. Maria I. Diedrich and Jürgen Heinrichs (Berlin: LIT Verlag, 2010), 49–74; Leroy Hopkins, "Louis Douglas and the Weimar Reception of Harlemania," *Germans and African Americans,* eds. Larry A. Greene and Anke Ortlepp (Jackson: University Press of Mississippi, 2011): 50–69.

6. Langston Hughes, "To a Negro Jazz Band in a Parisian Cabaret," *Collected Poems of Langston Hughes,* eds. Arnold Rampersad and David Roessel (New York: Knopf, 1994), 60. Hereafter abbreviated as CPLH.

7. Edwards, *The Practice of Diaspora,* 66.

8. Charles Harald Nichols, ed., *Arna Bontemps–Langston Hughes Letters, 1925–1962* (New York: Dodd, 1980), 372.

9. Tobias Nagl, *Die unheimliche Maschine: Rasse und Repräsentation im Weimarer Kino* (Munich: edition text+kritik, 2009), 667.

10. On the translation of Hughes in the Spanish-speaking world, see Vera M. Kutzinski, *The Worlds of Langston Hughes: Modernism and Translation in the Americas* (Ithaca: Cornell University Press, 2012).

11. Edwards, *The Practice of Diaspora*, 110. Italics in original.

12. Else Feldmann, "Neger, die Dichter sind," *Arbeiter-Zeitung* (Vienna), December 18, 1928.

13. Hughes, "To a Negro Jazz Band in a Parisian Cabaret," *CLPH*, 60.

14. On the role of the blues in Hughes' work, see Steven C. Tracy, *Langston Hughes and the Blues* (Urbana: University of Illinois Press, 1988).

15. Langston Hughes, "Negro," CPLH, 24. Section headings that appear in quotations all refer to the titles of poems written by Hughes.

16. Rampersad, *The Life of Langston Hughes*, vol. 1, 57.

17. Hans Goslar, *Amerika 1922* (Berlin-Wilmersdorf: Hermann-Paetel, 1922).

18. On travel literature in Weimar, in particular on the role played by African Americans, see Sara Markham, *Workers, Women, and Afro-Americans: Images of the United States in German Travel Literature from 1923–1933* (New York: Peter Lang, 1986).

19. Alfred Kerr, *New York und London: Stätten des Geschicks, Zwanzig Kapitel nach dem Weltkrieg* (Berlin: Fischer, 1923), 85. Ellipses in original.

20. PB, "Farbige Millionäre in New York," *Vossische Zeitung*, March 4, 1922; Kober, "Der schwarze Mann. Aufstieg einer Rasse," *Vossische Zeitung*, August 21, 1922.

21. Harlem is, for example, the focus of Joseph Chapiro, "Die amerikanische Neger-Hauptstadt," *Berliner Tageblatt*, March 31, 1929. For a discussion of further examples of German travelers to Harlem during the 1920s, see Dorothea Löbbermann, "Touristische Begierde. Harlem als New Yorker Attraktion," *Fremdes Begehren: transkulturelle Beziehungen in Literatur, Kunst und Medien*, eds. Eva Lezzi, Monika Ehlers, and Sandra Schramm (Cologne: Böhlau, 2003), 121–31. Additionally, in 1931, a German reporter named Hellmut H. Hellmut visited the Cotton Club in Harlem and captured a rare, live performance of Cab Calloway. See Cab Calloway, Lethia Hill, Eddie Rector, et al., *Live from the Cotton Club* (Hambergen: Bear Family Records, 2003).

22. Hans Goslar, "Der amerikanische Neger," *Vossische Zeitung*, April 1, 1922; Hans Goslar, *Amerika 1922* (Berlin-Wilmersdorf: Hermann-Paetel, 1922), 71.

23. Goslar, *Amerika 1922*, 64.

24. Ibid., 76.

25. Ibid., 68.

26. Nils Roemer, "Jewish Traveling Cultures and the Competing Visions of Modernity," *Central European History* 43:3 (September 2009), 429.

27. Ibid., 430.

28. Goslar, *Amerika 1922*, 71.

29. Langston Hughes, "Negro," CPLH, 26. In CPLH, lines 2 and 3 are rendered as separate lines. However, like Goslar's translation, the original publication in *Crisis* ren-

dered them as one line, which has been maintained here (see Langston Hughes, "Negro," the *Crisis* 23.3 [January 1922]: 113).

30. Goslar, *Amerika 1922*, 71. Again, this layout is identical to that which one finds in Goslar's text, i.e., with the last two words of the second line pushed to the right margin.

31. Lawrence Venuti, *The Translator's Invisibility: A History of Translation* (New York: Routledge, 2004), 20.

32. Ibid., 71.

33. Georg Widenbauer, "Die schwarze Weltgefahr" *Deutschlands Erneuerung* 7:12 (1923), 735.

34. Ibid.

35. Ibid., 736.

36. Ibid., 735.

37. English-language reprintings of Hughes' work can be found in Franz Friedrich Oberhauser, "Black City Haarlem [sic]," *Kölnische Zeitung,* September 4, 1929; also published in *Neue Freie Presse,* September 22, 1929; Marie Leitner, Langston Hughes, and Countee Cullen, "The Weary Blues / She of the Dancing Feet Sings," *Der Querschnitt* 6:7 (1926): 518–19.

38. Alain Locke—Arthur Rundt Correspondence, 1926–28, *Alain Locke Papers*, 164–82, Folder 7, Moorland-Spingarn Research Center, Howard University.

39. In a letter to Alain Locke from 1926 (the exact date is obscured by an ink stain), Rundt sends his regards to Hughes and mentions that he was pleased by the card he received from Hughes. Hughes also appears to have mentioned Rundt in a later letter to Anna Nussbaum. See her response to Hughes on January 28, 1928 (*Langston Hughes Papers,* James Weldon Johnson Collection, Beinecke Rare Book and Manuscript Library, Yale University. Further references to the *Langston Hughes Papers* will be abbreviated hereafter as LHP).

40. "Communism Practised in Palestine Colonies," *New York Times,* March 8, 1925, X15. See further: Arthur Rundt and Richard A. Bermann, *Palästina: Ein Reisebuch* (Leipzig, Vienna, Zurich: P.E.L., 1923).

41. Arthur Rundt, *Der Mensch wird umgebaut. Ein Russlandbuch* (Berlin: Rowohlt, 1932).

42. Paul Huldermann translated two articles by Alain Locke into German and published them in the *Deutsche Allgemeine Zeitung* (Alain Locke, "Der Neger in der amerikanischen Kultur," February 3, 1929; "Negerdichtung der U.S.A.," February 10, 1929). He also attempted to publish a translation of a new work by Locke that would have been similar to *New Negro* as is discussed in his correspondence with Locke (Alain Locke—Paul Huldermann, Correspondence, *Alain Locke Papers*, Box 164–38, Folder 10, Moorland-Spingarn Research Center, Howard University). See further Schwarz "New Negro Renaissance—'Neger-Renaissance,'" 61.

43. Arthur Rundt, *Amerika ist anders* (Berlin: Wegweiser, 1926), 75.

44. Ibid., 76.

45. Löbbermann, "Touristische Begierde. Harlem als New Yorker Attraktion," 123.

46. Rundt translates Angelina Grimke's "The Black Finger"; Joseph Cotters', "And

What Shall You Say?"; Hughes' "Our Land," "Poem (Youth)," and "I, Too." Rundt's translations of the above pieces in the *Frankfurter General-Anzeiger* were published in that paper on March 18 ("New Yorker Brief," translation of Cotter), April 4 ("Harlem, das Negerghetto"), May 2 ("Der schwarze Finger," translation of Grimke), and May 20, 1925 ("Neger-Lyrik. Drei Gedichte von Langston Hughes," translation of the three poems by Langston Hughes). The May 20 publication of "I, Too" was the very first of Rundt's translations of Hughes, followed shortly thereafter by its publication as, "Neger-Lyrik. Zwei Gedichte von Langston Hughes," *Prager Tagblatt,* June 14, 1925.

47. Rundt, *Amerika ist anders,* 71; "Der amerikanische Neger," 211; "Neger-Lyrik. Zwei Gedichte von Langston Hughes," *Prager Tagblatt,* June 14, 1925.

48. Arthur Rundt, "Die schwarze Welle," *Uhu* 1:11 (August 1925), 32. English in original italicized.

49. Rundt, *Amerika ist anders,* 75. English in original italicized.

50. Alfred Rundt, "Der amerikanische Neger," *Velhagen & Klasing Monatshefte* 41:2 (1927), 212. English in original italicized.

51. Langston Hughes, "I, Too," CPLH, 46.

52. Rundt, *Amerika ist anders,* 71. Again, it must be borne in mind that slight variations exist between all four published examples of Rundt's translation, in particular between the opening line and treatment of the last three lines of the poem.

53. That this was no mere misreading is indicated by the fact that Rundt correctly reads the future tense in the more difficulty parsed "Nobody'll" of Hughes' poem and translates it as "Keiner wird." Moreover, Rundt is the only translator out of the seven who translate "I, too" to use "wollen" (to want) rather than "werden" (to become).

54. For example, Henri Barbusse, *Die Kette: Visionärer Roman,* trans. Anna Nussbaum, 2 vols. (Berlin: Neuer Deutscher Verlag, 1926).

55. Nussbaum corresponded with Dreiser from 1926–29, the result of which being the publication of Theodor Dreiser, *Schwester Carrie,* trans. Anna Nussbaum (Berlin: Zsolnay, 1929).

56. Lisa Silverman, "*Zwischenzeit* and *Zwischenort:* Veza Canetti, Else Feldmann, and Jewish Writing in Interwar Vienna," *Prooftexts* 26:1–2 (Winter/Spring 2006), 45.

57. Anna Nussbaum, "Negerromane," *Sozialistische Monatshefte* 28:16/17 (1922), 661.

58. On the *Southern Syncopated Orchestra in Vienna, see Kon*rad Nowakowski, "'30 Negroes (Ladies and Gentlemen)': The Syncopated Orchestra in Vienna," *Black Music Research Journal* 29:2 (Fall 2009): 229–82. Though this essay does not contain a discussion of Nussbaum's comments, Nowakowski's later work does. See his "Jazz in Wien: Die Anfänge," *Anklaenge 2011/2012,* Special Issue: *Jazz unlimited. Beiträge zur Jazz-Rezeption in Österreich* (Wien: Mille Tre Verlag, 2012), 71.

59. I cannot here do justice to the broader cultural, historical determinants at work in 1920s Vienna, a context that in many ways led to the unique creation that was Nussbaum's *Africa Sings.* Rather, and standing in parallel to the absent consideration of the equally rich background of Langston Hughes, a thoroughgoing discussion of Nussbaum's development during the mid-1920s must be bracketed out here. On jazz and the

African diasporic presence in Vienna more generally during these years, see Nowakowski, "Jazz in Wien: Die Anfänge."

60. Anna Nussbaum, "Neger-Musik," *Der Tag,* September 25, 1927. See further discussion of this piece in Nowakowski, "Jazz in Wien," 71.

61. Anna Nussbaum to Langston Hughes, December 7, 1927, *LHP.*

62. Anna Nussbaum, "Afrika singt," *Der Tag,* December 25, 1927. The translations are by Josef Luitpold and Nussbaum. She mentions sending a clipping of the article to Hughes in her second letter to him from January 20, 1928, *LHP.*

63. Anna Nussbaum to Langston Hughes, December 7, 1927, *LHP.*

64. For example, in April 1928, she wrote to Claude McKay to request a copy of his 1922 collection *Harlem Shadows.* Published just over six months later, *Afrika singt* contains 19 poems from this collection (Anna Nussbaum to Claude McKay, March 30, 1928. *Claude McKay Collection.* James Weldon Johnson Collection. Beinecke Rare Book and Manuscript Library. Yale University).

65. George S. Schuyler, "Views and Reviews," the *Pittsburgh Courier,* March 3, 1928, A8.

66. Anna Nussbaum, "Die afro-amerikanische Frau," *Der Tag,* February 12, 1928.

67. Schuyler, "Views and Reviews."

68. Anna Nussbaum, "The Afro-American Woman" (Du Bois, *The Papers of W. E. B. Du Bois*); Anna Nussbaum, "The Afro-American Woman," *Norfolk Journal and Guide,* March 31, 1928.

69. Nussbaum, "Die afro-amerikanische Frau"; Nussbaum, "The Afro-American Woman" (*The Papers of W. E. B. Du Bois*); and Nussbaum, "The Afro-American Woman," *Norfolk Journal and Guide.*

70. Examples of awkward renderings in *Afrika singt* are detailed in Alan Lareau, "Harlem in Vienna: The Anthology Afrika singt (1929)," unpublished conference paper, MLA Convention, New York, December 29, 2002.

71. Hughes, "Negro," CPLH, 24.

72. Nussbaum, *Afrika singt,* 15.

73. Hanna Meuter and Paul Therstappen, eds. and trans. *Amerika singe auch ich. Dichtungen amerikanischer Neger* (Dresden: Jess, 1932), 89. On Meuter and this collection, see footnote 126. At the same time, this is not to suggest that Nussbaum was the only translator who retained these proper names. For example, Austrian translator and poet Josef Kainer did so as well in his 1926 translation of "Negro" (Josef Kainer, "Negerdichtungen," *Arbeiter-Zeitung* [Vienna], August 6, 1926).

74. Nussbaum, *Afrika singt,* 8.

75. Ibid., 9.

76. Ibid., 10.

77. In English: W. E. B. Du Bois, "Afrika singt," the *Crisis* 36 (March 1929): 87, 98; H. L. Mencken, "Afrika singt," *American Mercury* 17 (1929): x, xii. Besides Hesse's review referred to below, see in German: Rudolf Holzer, "Afrika singt . . ." [Review], *Wiener Zeitung,* May 30, 1929, 1–3; Rudolf Kayser, "Afrika singt" [Review], *Neue Rundschau* 40 (1929): 429; Edlef Köppen, "Afrika singt," *Die literarische Welt* 5 (May 31, 1929): 6; Ernst Lissauer, "Gesang des schwarzen Volkes," *Die Literatur* 31

(1928/29): 389–91; Ernst Lothar, "Erschütternde Melodie," *Neue Freie Presse,* December 12, 1928, 1–3; Fritz Rostosky, "Afrika singt" [Review], *Die schöne Literatur* 31 (February 1930), 90; John Sieg, "Americana," *Die Tat* 21 (1929), 67; Kurt Tucholsky, "Afrika singt" [1929], *Gesammelte Werke,* vol. 7, eds. Mary Gerold-Tucholsky and Fritz J. Raddatz (Reinbek bei Hamburg: Rowohlt Verlag, 1975): 235–36; Martha Weltsch. "Afrika singt . . . ," *Jüdische Rundschau* 26 (February 1929): 101.

78. Percy Julian, "The New Interest of Austrian Youth in Negro Prose and Poetry." the *Crisis* 40 (November 1933), 253.

79. Ibid.

80. Hermann Hesse, *Sämtliche Werke,* ed. Volker Michels, vol. 4 (Frankfurt am Main: Suhrkamp, 2001), 119.

81. Langston Hughes, "Auch ich bin Amerika. Negerlieder von Langston Hughes," trans. Anna Nussbaum *Atlantis* 1:9 (1929): 549. This was a selection of three of his poems from *Africa Sings,* including "The Negro Speaks of Rivers" (Der Neger spricht von Strömen), "Cross" (Zwischen schwarz und weiß), and "I, Too" (Auch ich singe Amerika). Other examples include: Langston Hughes, "Ruby Brown," *Die Frau* (Vienna) 38:6 (June 1, 1929): 1; Langston Hughes and Frank Horne, "Afrikanischer Tanz / Der Neger spricht von Strömen / Arabeske," *Die Literatur* 31 (1929): 378, 380; Hermann Kesser and Langston Hughes, "Übler Bursche," *Die Weltbühne* 24 (1929): 614; Langston Hughes, "Ich bin ein Neger," *Arbeiter-Zeitung* (Vienna), December 29, 1929.

82. Alfons Goldschmidt, *Acht Menschen in der Todeszelle* (Berlin: Tribunal, 1932), 16.

83. Anna Siemsen, Langston Hughes, and Paula Kurgass, "Amerikanische Negerlieder," *Urania* IX:8–9 (1929): 218, 252, 281.

84. [Thomas] Otto Brandt, Langston Hughes, and Countee Cullen, "Drei Gedichte junger Neger," *Literarische Monatshefte* 1:6 (May/June 1930): 11.

85. Slovene translations from *Africa Sings* were done by Mile Klopcic and Cvetko Kristan. See Igor Maver, "The Question of Literary Transmission and Mediation: Aesthetic, Linguistic and Social Aspects of Slovene Translations from American Verse until 1945," *Slovene Studies* 13:1 (1992), 96.

86. On the compositions other than those by Bornefeld, Reinitz, and Heymann, see Malcom Cole, "'Afrika singt:' Austro-German Echoes of Harlem Renaissance," *Journal of the American Musicological Society* 30:1 (Spring, 1977): 72–95. See further Helmut Bornefeld, *Afrika singt. Ein Zyklus für tiefere Stimme und Klavier nach Worten schwarzer Dichter* [1931] (Stuttgart: Carus), 2010. Werner Richard Heymann produced "Er oder ich" from Hermann Kesser's translation of Hughes' poem "Suicide," translated as "Selbstmord" for *Africa Sings.* Though the song was never published, I thank Elisabeth Trautwein-Heymann for providing me with a copy.

87. Three songs from *Schatten über Harlem* were published by Universal Edition. These were Béla Reinitz, "Lied aus Dixieland," U.E. 7117 (Vienna: Universal Edition, 1930); "Schatten über Harlem," U.E. 7118 (Vienna: Universal Edition, 1930); "Weißer Bruder, was wirst du sagen?" U.E. 7119 (Vienna: Universal Edition, 1930).

88. Cole, "Austro-German Echoes," 82.

89. Ibid.

90. Joachim-Felix Leonard, ed., *Programmgeschichte des Hörfunks in der Wei-*

marer Republik, vol. 2 (Munich: dtv, 1997), 957. Radio played a role in disseminating the poems in non-musical form as well. In early 1929, Ernst Glaeser produced a presentation using readings of poetry from *Africa Sings* (Ibid., 954). Around the same time, the radio program "Song" included a recitation of Hughes' "Negro" as translated by Nussbaum (Ibid., 955–56).

91. Cora Gary Illidge, "Abbie Mitchell Captivates Hearers," the *New York Amsterdam News*, November 25, 1931, 7; Edward G. Perry, "Abbie Mitchell in N.Y. Concert," *Afro-American*, May 2, 1931, 15; Maude Roberts George, "Abbie Mitchell Wins High Praise in Song Recital," the *Chicago Defender*, November 7, 1931, 10.

92. It is unclear how Abbie Mitchell came to know these works, though one strong possibility is through her daughter, Marion Cook, or her son-in-law, Louis Douglas, who is discussed in chapter 4.

93. M.G., "Skandal im Landestheater," *Deutsches Volksblatt,* October 20, 1930. *Landesarchiv Baden-Württemberg Staatsarchiv Ludwigsburg* E 18 VII Bü 456. Hereafter abbreviated as LBW.

94. Ibid.

95. "Kundgebungen am Theater," *Stuttgarter Neues Tagblatt,* October 20, 1930, LBW.

96. Karl Konrad Düssel, "Uraufführung und Theaterskandal. 'Schatten über Harlem' im Landestheater," *Stuttgarter Neues Tagblatt,* October 20, 1930, LBW.

97. "Vom Landestheater. Unerhörter Theaterskandal bei einer Uraufführung," *Der Beobachter,* October 25, 1930, LBW.

98. "Der Kulturbolschewismus auf der Bühne," *Völkischer Beobachter,* October 24, 1930, LBW.

99. "Um die Freiheit der Kunst," *Berliner Tageblatt,* October 28, 1930, LBW.

100. See for example: Molodet, "Kulturfaschismus gegen Landestheater. Theaterskandal um 'Schatten über Haarlem [sic]," *Beilage zur Süddeutschen Arbeiter-Zeitung,* October 20, 1930, LBW; "Uraufführung: 'Schatten über Harlem,'" *Arbeiter-Tribüne,* October 25, 1930, LBW; "Theaterskandal im Reich," *Die Rote Fahne,* October 22, 1930, LBW.

101. To be sure, the Nazis did not forget, and as Kim Kowalke notes, in 1940, after an initial raid of Universal Edition, the Viennese publisher of modern music, to confiscate music by Weill and Eisler, they returned to collect, amongst other things, 160 copies of music from *Schatten über Harlem* (Kim Kowalke, "Dancing with the Devil: Publishing Modern Music in the Third Reich," *Modernism/Modernity* 8:1 [2001], 27).

102. Martin Ulmer, *Antisemitismus in Stuttgart 1871–1933. Studien zum öffentlichen Alltag* (Berlin: Metropol, 2011), 379.

103. Ossip Dymow (Ossip Dymov) was born Yosef Perelman in Bialystok in 1878. Further biographical information is available in Maxim D. Shrayer, eds., *An Anthology of Jewish-Russian Literature: Two Centuries of Dual Identity in Prose and Poetry,* vol. 1 (Amonk, NY: M.E. Sharpe, 2007), 168–69.

104. "Harlem: 5 Neighborhoods," *Encyclopedia of the Harlem Renaissance,* eds. Cary D. Wintz and Paul Finkelman (New York: Routledge, 2004), 477.

105. Ossip Dymow, *Schatten über Harlem. Komödie in Vier Akten* (Berlin: C. Sommer, 1930), 19. Held at the New York Public Library's Theater Division, this is the only

known copy of the script. After the scandal, however, a brief excerpt was published in *Die Weltbühne* (Ossip Dymow, "Schatten über Harlem." *Weltbühne* 26 [1930]: 788–92).

106. Ibid., 26.

107. News of the lynching reached Germany on May 10, with articles on the case appearing, for example, in *Die Vossische Zeitung* ("Furchtbare Lynchjustiz in Texas") and *Berliner Volkszeitung* ("Lynchmord in Texas"). More pointedly, the pro-democratic weekly *Welt am Montag* published three articles about this single case within one month. First, it highlighted the case in a front-page headline, "Neue Neger-Progrome in Amerika," on May 12, 1930, which was followed later with an article discussing Walter White's work on lynching, highlighting the cases where African Americans were burned and lynched ("Der geröstete Neger," *Die Welt am Montag,* June 2, 1930).

108. For example "Theaterskandale im Reich," *Danziger Neueste Nachrichten,* October 20, 1930, LBW.

109. "Staatliche Verseuchung," *Der Angriff,* October 26, 1930, LBW.

110. F. Sch., "Württ. Landestheater. Uraufführung: 'Schatten über Harlem,'" *Süddeutsche Zeitung,* October 20, 1930, LBW. First italics in original, English "colored people" in original italicized.

111. Gabriele Hayden develops this argument for Dymow and *Shadows over Harlem* in her "Performing Blackness in Weimar Germany," unpublished conference paper, ACLA Convention, Providence, RI, March 29, 2012.

112. Scott Spector, "On Modernism without Jews: A Counter-Historical Argument," *Modernism/Modernity* 13:4 (November 2006), 628.

113. Ibid., 620–21.

114. Dymow, *Schatten über Harlem*, 66.

115. Part of the confusion on the part of the audience can be put at the feet of the director, Friedrich Brandenburg, who, as some critics noted, emphasized the tragic elements of the play at the expense of its comedy (M. G., "Skandal im Landestheater," *Deutsches Volksblatt,* October 20, 1930, LBW; Hermann Wissenharter, "Schatten über Harlem," *Württemberger Zeitung,* October 26, 1930, LBW).

116. Düssel, "Uraufführung und Theaterskandal. 'Schatten über Harlem' im Landestheater."

117. Langston Hughes, "Laughers," CPLH, 27.

118. Langston Hughes, *Fine Clothes to the Jew* (New York: Knopf, 1927), xiii.

119. Langston Hughes, Review of W. C. Handy, *The Blues, Opportunity* (August 1926), 258.

120. Ossip Dymow, "Neger-Getto [sic] Harlem. Die schwarze Stadt im Völkerbabel von Neuyork," *Das kleine Blatt* (Vienna), April 27, 1931.

121. Another leading African American newspaper, the *Chicago Defender*, referred similarly to the fascist objection to "Harlem culture" ("Harlem Play Results in German Uprising," the *Chicago Defender,* October 25, 1930, 8).

122. "Germans Start Riot at Negro Play," *Baltimore Afro-American,* October 25, 1930, 9.

123. "German Fascists in Riot over Negro Play," *New York Times,* October 20, 1930, 9.

124. Nussbaum to Du Bois, Letters from November 7, 1930, and December 29, 1930 (Du Bois, W. E. B. et al. *The Papers of W.E.B. Du Bois*. University of Massachusetts at Amherst).

125. Josef Luitpold "Zwischen Zeiten, Klassen, Kontinenten," *Arbeiter-Zeitung*, June 28, 1931; Anna Siemsen, "Anna Nußbaum. Ein Leben für die Internationale," *Kulturwille* 9:1 (January 1932): 3–4.

126. One more anthology of African American poetry would be published before Weimar's end: Meuter and Therstappen's *Amerika singe auch ich* (*I, too, sing America*). The impetus behind this project was Hannah Meuter, a young sociologist with an interest in African American culture (Hannah Meuter, "Der neue Neger in der amerikanischen Literatur," *Kölner Vierteljahreshefte für Soziologie* 6:3 [1927]: 269–73). The collection was the only volume published of a planned series on "Der neue Neger" (the New Negro) and includes translations side-by-side with the English source text. Still, despite its later date of publication, the collection was much less current than *Africa Sings* as it is based on Robert T. Kerlin's anthology *American Negro Poetry* from 1923. Finally, for a variety of reasons, the work simply did not enjoy the same resonance with the literary public or with composers of the period.

127. On the translation of Hughes after World War II, see Daniel Brown, "'Black Orpheus': Langston Hughes Reception in German Translation (An Overview)," *Langston Hughes Review* IV:2 (Fall 1985): 30–37.

128. Hayes, *The Practice of Diaspora*, 119.

129. Theodor W. Adorno, "Oxforder Nachträge [1937]," *Gesammelte Schriften*, ed. Rolf Tiedemann, vol. 17 (Frankfurt am Main: SuhrKamp, 1997), 101.

CHAPTER 7

The quotation cited in the epigraph is from Theodor Adorno, "Scientific Experiences of a European Scholar in America," *Critical Models: Interventions and Catchwords*, trans. Henry W. Pickford (New York: Columbia University Press, 1998), 241.

1. Bernd Hoffmann shows through quantitative analysis of references to jazz in the music journals *Die Musik* and *Deutsche Tonkünstlerzeitung* that "there is a turn away from the positive reception [of jazz] already before the influence of the cultural-political coordination by the National Socialists" (*Aspekte zur Jazz-Rezeption in Deutschland: Afro-amerikanische Musik im Spiegel der Musikpresse 1900–1945* [Graz: Akademische Druck & Verlagsanstalt, 2003], 46). At the same time, it must be borne in mind that Hoffmann's analysis also shows that modernist journals like *Der Querschnitt* and *Melos* continued to contain positive references to jazz into the early 1930s. See figures B4 and B5 in his *Aspekte zur Jazz-Rezeption in Deutschland*, 218–19.

2. Wilhelm Frick, "Erlaß wider die Negerkultur für deutsches Volkstum," *Quellen zur Geschichte Thüringens*, ed. Jürgen John, vol. 3 (Erfurt: LZT, 1996), 140–41. Further, Alan E. Steinweis, "Weimar Culture and the Rise of National Socialism: The *Kampfbund für deutsche Kultur*," *Central European History* 24 (January 1991), esp. 414. In connection with later Nazi actions against jazz, see Heribert Schröder, "Zur

Kontinuität nationalsozialistischer Maßnahmen gegen Jazz und Swing in der Weimarer Republik und im Dritten Reich," *Colloquium: Festschrift Martin Vogel zum 65. Geburtstag,* ed. Heribert Schröder (Bad Honnef: Gudrun Schröder, 1988), 175–82.

3. All told, Adorno authored some seven pieces on jazz: "Abschied vom Jazz [1933]," *Gesammelte Schriften,* ed. Rolf Tiedemann, vol. 18 (Frankfurt am Main: Suhrkamp, 1997), 795–99; [Hektor Rottweiler], "Über Jazz [1936]," *Gesammelte Schriften,* vol. 17, 74–100; "Oxforder Nachträge [1937]," *Gesammelte Schriften,* vol. 17, 100–8; Wilder Hobson, *American Jazz Music,* New York: Norton & Company 1939. Winthrop Sargeant, *Jazz Hot and Hybrid,* New York: Arrow Editions 1938 [1941], *Gesammelte Schriften,* vol. 19, 382–99; "Jazz," *Dictionary of Arts,* eds. Dagobert D. Runes and Harry G. Schrickel (New York: Philosophical Library, 1946), 511–13; "Zeitlose Mode. Zum Jazz [1953]," *Gesammelte Schriften,* vol. 10, 123–37; Theodor Adorno and Joachim Ernst-Berendt, "Für und Wider den Jazz," *Merkur* 7:9 (1953): 887–93.

4. Responses to Adorno's jazz theory are quite numerous and run the gamut from serious engagement to offhand comment: Theodore Gracyk, "Adorno, Jazz, and the Aesthetics of Popular Music," *The Musical Quarterly* 76 (Winter 1992): 526–42; Ulrich Schönherr, "Adorno and Jazz: Reflections on a Failed Encounter," *Telos* 87 (Spring 1991): 85–96; Harry Cooper, "On Über Jazz: Replaying Adorno with the Grain," *October* 75 (Winter 1996): 99–133; James M. Harding, "Adorno, Ellison, and the Critique of Jazz," *Cultural Critique* 31 (Autumn 1995): 129–58; James Buhler, "Frankfurt School Blues: Rethinking Adorno's Critique of Jazz," *Apparitions: Essays on Adorno and Twentieth-Century Music,* ed. Berthold Hoeckner (New York: Routledge, 2006): 103–30; Cornelius Partsch, *Schräge Töne: Jazz und Unterhaltungsmusik in der Kultur der Weimarer Republik* (Stuttgart: J. B. Metzler, 2000), 256–68. See also in this regard, Richard Leppert's comments in *Essays on Music,* trans. Susan Gillespie, ed. Richard Leppert (Los Angeles and Berkeley: University of California Press, 2002), 330–58.

5. J. Bradford Robinson, "The Jazz Essays of Theodor Adorno: Some Thoughts on Jazz Reception in Weimar Germany," *Popular Music* 13:1 (1994), 1.

6. Recently, Konrad Nowakowski has detailed a number of problems with Robinson's argument in his "Jazz in Wien: Die Anfänge," *Anklaenge 2011/2012,* Special Issue: Jazz unlimited. Beiträge zur Jazz-Rezeption in Österreich (Wien: Mille Tre Verlag, 2012), 127–28.

7. Adorno's discussion of the *Jazzklasse* is referenced in chapter 5. Adorno refers to Whiteman in "Ad vocem Hindemith. Eine Dokumentation," *Gesammelte Schriften,* ed. Rolf Tiedemann, vol. 17 (Frankfurt am Main: Suhrkamp, 1997), 223. He mentions The Revelers in "Musikalische Aphorismen," *Gesammelte Schriften,* vol. 18 (Frankfurt am Main: Suhrkamp, 1991), 34–35. Finally, he references Baker in his negative review of Louis Douglas' *Black People* (at which, not Baker but Maud de Forest performed) at the *Frankfurter Schauspielhaus* ("August 1927," *Gesammelte Schriften,* vol. 19 [Frankfurt am Main: Suhrkamp, 1997], 99). On the appearance of Bechet and the jazz band Mississippi Jazzers, as well as *Black People* in Frankfurt am Main in 1927, see Hans Pehl, *Afroamerikanische Unterhaltungskünstler in Frankfurt am Main. Eine Chronik von 1844 bis 1945* (Frankfurt am Main: n.p., 2010), 74–79.

8. On Adorno's contact with jazz in Vienna, see Konrad Nowakowski, "Jazz in Wien," 130–31.

9. Theodor W. Adorno, *Der Schatz des Indianer Joe. Singspiel nach Mark Twain* (Frankfurt am Main: Suhrkamp, 1979). Hereafter cited in the body text with the abbreviation *S*.

10. Theodor Adorno, *Kompositionen*, eds. Heinz-Klaus Metzger and Reiner Riehn (Munich: Musik-Konzepte, 1980).

11. Rolf Tiedemann, "Adorno's *Tom Sawyer* Opera Singspiel," *The Cambridge Companion to Adorno*, ed. Tom Huhn (New York: Cambridge University Press, 2004), 392–93. Though slightly different, this text is largely an English translation of Tiedemann's original German afterword.

12. Karla Schultz "Utopias from Hell: Brecht's 'Mahagonny' and Adorno's 'Treasure of Indian Joe," *Monatshefte* 90:3 (1998): 307–16; Peter-Ulrich Philipson, "Kindermodell der Moderne. Adornos Schatz des Indianer Joe," *Geschichte, Kultur, Bildung: Philosophische Denkrichtungen. Johannes Rohbeck zum 60. Geburtstag*, eds. Peggy H. Breitenstein and Johannes Rohbeck (Hannover: Siebert, 2007), 103–16; Christopher D. Morris, "Impossible Alternatives to Tom Sawyer's Delusions in Twain and Adorno," *University of Toronto Quarterly* 81:2 (Spring 2012): 219–45.

13. Susan C. Cook, *Opera for a New Republic: The* Zeitopern *of Krenek, Weill, and Hindemith* (Ann Arbor: UMI Research Press, 1988), 4.

14. Theodor W. Adorno and Alban Berg, *Briefwechsel 1925–1935* (Frankfurt am Main: Suhrkamp, 1997), 276.

15. Martin Hufner, *Adorno und die Zwölftontechnik* (Regensburg: ConBrio Verlagsgesellschaft, 1996), 93.

16. On Adorno's activities during the first months of the Nazi regime, see Stefan Müller-Doohm, *Adorno: Eine Biographie* (Frankfurt am Main: Suhrkamp, 2003), 262–76.

17. Ibid.

18. Ibid.

19. Adorno and Berg, *Briefwechsel 1925–1935*, 279–80.

20. In addition to the differences discussed below, Adorno excises one of the major figures of the plot, Becky Thatcher, who is Tom's love interest and subject of much of the novel. Becky's femininity and Tom's relationship with her is, in part, substituted through the figure of Huck.

21. Sigmund Freud, *The Interpretation of Dreams*, trans. James Strachey, *The Standard Edition of the Complete Psychological Works of Sigmund Freud*, ed. James Strachey, vols. IV-V (London: Hogarth Press, 1953), 196.

22. Edgar H. Hemminghaus, *Mark Twain in Germany* (New York: AMS Press, 1966 [1939]), 144n4.

23. In both German translations and the English original of Twain's *The Adventures of Tom Sawyer*, a forward by the author specifies that the story takes place some thirty or forty years in the past, that is to say in the period between 1836 and 1846.

24. Hemminghaus, *Mark Twain in Germany*, 130–31.

25. Mark Twain, *Tom Sawyers Abenteuer und Streiche*, trans. Margarete Jacobi (Stuttgart: Lutz, 1892). On the various editions produced of Twain's works before and during the 1930s, see Hemminghaus, *Mark Twain in Germany*, 83–96, 123–31.

26. Though not all passages display this level of similarity, the montage quality of

Adorno's work is obviously intentional, as can be seen in the following comparison of Jacobi's translation and Adorno's *Treasure*.

First, Jacobi's text:

> "Heut' Nacht. Ich denk', da werden sie den alten Williams holen kommen."
>
> "Der ist aber schon am Sonnabend begraben worden, warum haben sie ihn da nicht schon in der Nacht geholt?"
>
> "Na, du redst auch, wie du's verstehst! Sonnabend Mitternacht ist doch schon Sonntag und da hat kein Teufel mehr was zu suchen hier oben. Der wird sich schwer hüten, sich am Sonntag blicken zu lassen (Twain, *Tom Sawyers Abenteuer und Streiche*, 59–60)

Next, Adorno's version of the same scene:

> HUCK: Da werden sie den alten Williams holen kommen, der war schon schlecht genug.
>
> TOM: Der ist aber schon am Sonnabend beerdigt worden, warum haben sie ihn da nicht in der Nacht geholt?
>
> HUCK: Können vor Lachen. Sonnabend Mitternacht ist schon Sonntag. Da hat kein Teufel mehr was zu suchen hier oben. Der wird sich schwer hüten, sich am Sonntag blicken zu lassen. (*S* 20)

27. Theodor W. Adorno and Walter Benjamin, *The Complete Correspondence, 1928–1940*, ed. Henri Lonitz, trans. Nicholas Walker (Cambridge, MA: Harvard University Press, 1999), 24.

28. Ibid., 26

29. Ibid., 24.

30. Ibid., 25.

31. Theodor Adorno, "The Idea of Natural History," *Telos* 60 (June 1984), 111.

32. Ibid., 118.

33. Walter Benjamin, *The Origin of the German Tragic Drama*, trans. John Osborne (London: Verso, 1993), 177–78.

34. Susan Buck-Morss, *The Dialectics of Seeing: Walter Benjamin and the Arcades Project* (Cambridge, MA: MIT Press), 170.

35. *Mark Twain's Book of Animals*, ed. Shelley Fisher Fishkin (Berkeley and Los Angeles: University of California Press, 2010), 1–33.

36. Christina Gerhardt, "The Ethics of Animals in Adorno and Kafka," *New German Critique* 97 (January 2006), 162.

37. Theodor W. Adorno and Ernst Krenek, *Briefwechsel* (Frankfurt am Main: Suhrkamp, 1974), 57.

38. Gerhardt, "The Ethics of Animals in Adorno and Kafka," 166.

39. On the significance of such unnamed animals in *Schatz*, see Morris, "Impossible Alternatives to Tom Sawyer's Delusion in Twain and Adorno," 240–41.

40. Peter von Haselberg, quoted in Steinert, *Entdeckung der Kulturindustrie oder: Warum Professor Adorno Jazz-Musik nicht ausstehen konnte* (Vienna: Verlag für Gesellschaftskritik, 1992), 228n14.

41. Anthony Krupp, *Reason's Children: Childhood in Early Modern Philosophy* (Lewisburg: Bucknell University Press, 2009), 14–15.

42. Morris, "Impossible Alternatives to Tom Sawyer's Delusions in Twain and Adorno," 238.

43. Adorno and Krenek, *Briefwechsel*, 57.

44. Ibid., 56.

45. Tiedemann, "Adorno's *Tom Sawyer* Opera Singspiel," 386–389.

46. Morris, "Impossible Alternatives to Tom Sawyer's Delusion in Twain and Adorno," 241.

47. On the history of the case and its position in twentieth-century American history, see James Goodman, *Stories of Scottsboro* (New York: Pantheon Books, 1994) and Dan T. Carter, *Scottsboro: A Tragedy of the American South* (Baton Rouge: Louisiana State University Press, 2007). More recently, Susan D. Pennybacker has analyzed the case from a transnational perspective in order to shed new light on British history in the 1930s, see *From Scottsboro to Munich: Race and Political Culture in 1930s Britain* (Princeton: Princeton University Press, 2009).

48. Quoted in Goodman, *Stories of Scottsboro*, 5.

49. James A. Miller, Susan D. Pennybacker, and Eve Rosenhaft, "Mother Ada Wright and the International Campaign to Free the Scottsboro Boys, 1931–1934," *American Historical Review* 106:2 (2001), 388.

50. On the *Rote Hilfe*, see Sabine Hering and Kurt Schilde, eds., *Die Rote Hilfe: die Geschichte der internationalen kommunistischen "Wohlfahrtsorganisation" und ihrer sozialen Aktivitäten in Deutschland (1921–1941)* (Opladen: Leske+Budrich, 2003). On Münzenberg and the *League Against Imperialism* in this context, see Miller, Pennybacker and Rosenhaft, "Mother Ada Wright," 397–98.

51. Cited in Miller, Pennybacker and Rosenhaft, "Mother Ada Wright," 403.

52. Godo Remszhardt to William Pickens, Field Secretary of NAACP, June 4, 1930, *W. E. B. Du Bois Papers*, Special Collections and University Archives, University of Massachusetts Amherst Libraries MS 312.

53. Godo Remszhardt to Langston Hughes, July 15, 1930, *Langston Hughes Papers,* James Weldon Johnson Collection, Beinecke Rare Book and Manuscript Library, Yale University.

54. Susan Buck-Morss, *Hegel and Haiti and Universal History* (Pittsburgh: University of Pittsburgh Press, 2009), 19–20.

55. Buck-Morss, *Hegel and Haiti,* 80.

56. Roy Wright, thirteen years old in 1931, would later state that before his testimony, he was taken into a separate room and beaten by the deputy sheriff until he agreed to implicate the other African American riders (Goodman, *Stories of Scottsboro*, 94).

57. Goodman, *Stories of Scottsboro*, 21.

58. Goodman, *Stories of Scottsboro*, 21–22. That this idea was present in Germany is partially confirmed by the following statement from Alfons Goldschmidt: "At first both girls vigorously denied having been attacked by the boys. But they are prostitutes, entirely in the hands of the police, who can convict them for perjury or other crimes punishable with years of imprisonment" ("Aus dem Lande der 'Freiheit,'" *Der Funke,* May 10, 1932).

59. Jim's mangled English in Adorno is present in Jacobi's translation as well. Compare Twain, *Tom Sawyers Abenteuer und Streiche*, 23.

60. Theodor W. Adorno, "Abschied von Jazz," *Europäische Revue* 9 (1933): 313–16.

61. In a short paragraph written for the journal *Die Musik*, Adorno states that: "The end of jazz, long prophesied, has come" (Theodor Adorno, "Musikalische Aphorismen [1932]," *Gesammelte Schriften*, ed. Rolf Tiedemann, vol. 18 [Frankfurt am Main: Suhrkamp, 1997], 22).

62. Hans Th. David, "Abschied vom Jazz," *Melos* 9 (1930): 413–17. Indeed, between 1926 and 1933 no less than four separate articles bore the title "Twilight of Jazz" (Jazz-Dämmerung) and two the title "Farewell to Jazz."

63. A discussion of the multiple and uneven legal measures taken against jazz by the Nazis can be found in Schröder, "Zur Kontinuität nationalsozialistischer Maßnahmen gegen Jazz und Swing in der Weimarer Republik und im Dritten Reich." On the history of jazz and entertainment music in Weimar radio, see Michael Stapper, *Unterhaltungsmusik im Rundfunk der Weimarer Republik* (Tutzing: Hans Schneider, 2001). For jazz in Weimar and Nazi radio, see Joachim Ernst Berendt, "Jazz als Indiz: Beiträge zu einer Geschichte des Jazz am deutschen Rundfunk (1924–1975)," *Ein Fenster aus Jazz: Essays, Portraits, Reflexionen* (Frankfurt am Main: Fischer, 1977), 290–309.

64. Kolb had been made director of the *Funkstunde* in February, yet his tenure there was short-lived. Already in April, he was replaced by the writer Friedrich Arenhövel, who had been handpicked by Goebbels. On Kolb's position within the Nazi hierarchy, see Ansgar Diller, *Rundfunkpolitik im Dritten Reich* (Munich: dtv, 1980), 56–59, 114. On Kolb and the *Funkstunde* ban, see Axel Jockwer, *Unterhaltungsmusik im Dritten Reich* (University of Constance, PhD diss., 2005), 287–88.

65. Press release of the *Berliner Funk-Stunde*, March 8, 1933. Reprinted in Albrecht Dümling and Peter Girth, eds., *Entartete Musik. Dokumentation und Kommentar* (Düsseldorf: Der kleine Verlag, 1993), 120. The ban is further referenced in "Keine Jazzmusik mehr!" *NS Funk* 1 (March 19, 1933), 27; "Haben Sie schon gehört, dass . . . ?" *Der Artist* 2466 (March 24, 1933).

66. Ibid.

67. Ibid.

68. Theodor Adorno, "Farewell to Jazz," 496. Translation slightly modified.

69. Adorno, "Farewell to Jazz," 497. Translation slightly modified.

70. Ibid.

71. Ibid., 497–98. Translation slightly modified.

72. Thus in the 1953 "Perennial Fashion—Jazz," he writes: "The fact is that what jazz has to offer rhythmically is extremely limited. The most striking traits in jazz were all independently produced, developed and surpassed by serious music since Brahms" (Adorno, "Perennial Fashion—Jazz," *Prisms*, trans. Samuel and Shierry Weber [Cambridge, MA: MIT Press, 1983], 123).

73. Adorno, "Farewell to Jazz," 499.

74. Adorno and Berg, *Briefwechsel 1925–1935*, 280.

75. Lydia Goehr, *Elective Affinities: Musical Essays on the History of Aesthetic Theory* (New York: Columbia University Press, 2008), 400.

76. On Seiber's role in "On Jazz," see Nick Chadwick, "Mátyás Seiber's Collaboration in Adorno's Jazz Project, 1936," *British Library Journal* 21 (Autumn 1995): 259–88.

77. On Adorno's experience of jazz in Britain during the mid-1930s, see Evelyn Wilcock, "Adorno, Jazz, and Racism: 'Über Jazz' and the 1934–7 British Jazz Debate," *Telos* 107 (Spring 1996), 65–67; Catherine Parsonage, *The Evolution of Jazz in Britain, 1880–1935* (London: Ashgate, 2005), 61–77.

78. The three songs remain unpublished and are located in the Theodor W. Adorno Archiv at the *Akademie der Künste* in Berlin.

CONCLUSION

The quotation cited in the epigraph is from "Good Bye Jonny" (1939), music by Peter Kreuder, text by Hans-Fritz Beckmann.

1. A powerful example of the synthesis of anti-Black and anti-Semitic racism that took place during the final years of the Weimar Republic is Alfred Rosenberg, *Der Sumpf: Querschnitte durch das 'Geistes-'Leben der November-Demokratie* (Munich: Zentralverlag der NSDAP, 1939 [1930]), 26–43.

2. Goebbels quoted in Heribert Schröder, "Zur Kontinuität nationalsozialistischer Maßnahmen gegen Jazz und Swing in der Weimarer Republik und im Dritten Reich," *Colloquium: Festschrift Martin Vogel zum 65. Geburtstag*, ed. Heribert Schröder (Bad Honnef: Gudrun Schröder, 1988), 179.

3. On the history of jazz in the Third Reich, see Michael Kater, *Different Drummers: Jazz in the Culture of Nazi Germany* (New York: Oxford University Press, 1992); Michael Kater, "Forbidden Fruit? Jazz in the Third Reich," *The American Historical Review* 94:1 (1989): 11–43; Horst J. P. Bergmeier and Rainer E. Lotz, *Hitler's Airwaves: The Inside Story of Nazi Radio Broadcasting and Propaganda Swing* (New Haven: Yale University Press, 1997); Bernd Polster, ed., *Swing Heil. Jazz im Nationalsozialismus* (Berlin: Transit, 1989); Mike Zwerin, *Swing under the Nazis: Jazz as a Metaphor for Freedom* (New York: Cooper Square Press, 2000); Christian Kellersmann, *Jazz in Deutschland von 1933–1945* (Menden: Der Jazzfreund, 1990).

4. Erica Carter, *Dietrich's Ghosts: The Sublime and the Beautiful in Third Reich Film* (London: BFI Publishing, 2004), 214.

5. Ibid., 215.

6. Ibid., 175.

7. Guido Fackler, "Zwischen (musikalischem) Widerstand und Propaganda—Jazz im 'Dritten Reich,'" *Musikalische Volkskultur und die politische Macht*, ed. Günther Noll (Essen: Verlag Die Blaue Eule, 1994), 439–41.

8. Marita Gründgens, "Ich wünsche dir Glück, Jonny" (Electrola 3161). See also the recordings by Nina Buser (Brilliant 319, DeBeGe 2116) and Carla Carlsen (Telefunken A 1700). Further details on these recordings are included in Rainer Lotz ed., *Die deutsche National-Discographie*, Series 1 "Discographie der deutschen Kleinkunst," eds. Klaus Krüger and Rainer Lotz, vols. 4 and 5 (Bonn: Birgit Lotz Verlag, 1996 and 1998).

9. Kurt Herbst, "Zwei Punkte im Kapitel: Rundfunk und Unterhaltungsmusik," *Die Musik* 27 (December 1934), 220. See below for further discussion of Herbst.

10. Gründgens' career is discussed in Evelin Förster, "Die grosse Kunst der kleinen Schwester. Marita Gründgens—Ein Multitalent," *Fox auf 78* 27 (Winter 2013): 16–18.

11. Marita Gründgens, "Ich wünsch' mir eine kleine Ursula" (Electrola EG 3771).

12. Her performances of Jolson took place as part of early appearances on *Westdeutscher Rundfunk* in Düsseldorf in 1929 ("Gründgens, Marita," *Tondokumente der Kleinkunst und ihre Interpreten 1898–1945*, ed. Berthold Leimbach [Göttingen: Leimbach, 1991], n.p.).

13. Marita Gründgens, "Filmsucht" (Telefunken A 1567).

14. See the entry for the Nina Buser recording in Lotz, ed., *Die deutsche National-Discographie*, Series 1 "Discographie der deutschen Kleinkunst," vol. 5, 1143. Though here "blues" indicates tempo rather than genre, the association "blues" had with African American popular music remained.

15. Kater, *Different Drummers*, 37.

16. Herbst, "Zwei Punkte im Kapitel: Rundfunk und Unterhaltungsmusik," 220.

17. See the entry in *Hofmeisters Musikalisch-literarischer Monatsbericht* 107 (January 1935), 4.

18. Hans Bund mit seinem Streichorchester with vocals by Eric Helgar, "Jonny hat Sehnsucht nach Hawaii" (Telefunken A 1716); Quartettgesang, "Johnny hat Sehnsucht nach Hawaii" (Woolco 10706); Fritz Domina with vocals by Paul Dorn, "Johnny hat Sehnsucht nach Hawaii" (Kristall 3103).

19. Alan Lareau, "Undermining Gender in Weimar Cabaret and Beyond," *Popular Music and Society* 28 (February 2005), 27.

20. It is present, for example, on the Austrian *Schlager* singer Freddy Quinn's album *Überall ist es schön* (Polydor 1973) as well as the German *Schlager* singer Lolita on *Ihre größten Erfolge* (Bear Family Records 2004).

21. Dishwashing is referenced directly within the "interview" with Jonny in *Der Deutsche Rundfunk* (see below). The title *Jonny spült ab*, nonetheless, has an older history and possibly originated from the caricature "Daitsche Kunst" in the Nazi periodical *Die Brennessel* (5:5 [January 30, 1934], 69) by an illustrator with the initials T. E. S. See the reproduction in Eckhard John, *Musikbolschewismus: Die Politisierung der Musik in Deutschland 1918–1938* (Stuttgart: Metzler, 1994), 364.

22. On Eichborn's later career as a composer for film, see the brief discussion in Robert C. Reimer, "Turning Inward: An Analysis of Helmut Käutner's *Auf Wiedersehen, Franziska; Romanze in Moll; Unter den Brücken*," *Cultural History through a National Socialist Lens: Essays on the Cinema of the Third Reich*, ed. Robert C. Reimer (Rochester: Camden House, 2000), 231–32.

23. Hugo Hartung, *Wir Wunderkinder: Der dennoch heitere Roman unseres Lebens* (Düsseldorf, Droste-Verlag, 1957). On Hartung, see Helga Schreckenberger, "'Es war vielleicht ein neues Exil und vielleicht das schmerzlichste.' Das Thema der Rückkehr in Oskar Maria Grafs Briefen an Hugo Hartung," *Erste Briefe/First Letters aus dem Exil 1945–1950. (Un)mögliche Gespräche. Fallbeispiele des literarischen und künstlerischen Exils*, eds. Primus-Heinz Kucher, Johannes F. Evelein, and Helga Schreckenberger (Munich: edition text + kritik, 2012), 128–42.

24. Listing for programs originating from Munich on Monday, February 25, *Der Deutsche Rundfunk* 13:9 (1935), 26.

25. Patrick Merziger, "Humour in the *Volksgemeinschaft*: The Disappearance of Destructive Satire in National Socialist Germany," *The Politics of Humour: Laughter,*

Inclusion, and Exclusion in the Twentieth Century, eds. Martina Kessel and Patrick Merziger (Toronto: University of Toronto Press, 2012), 141.

26. Ibid., 131–32.

27. "'Jonny spült ab.' Hörspiel von H. Hartung und B. Eichhorn," *Der Deutsche Rundfunk* 13:9 (1935), 66.

28. Hugo Hartung, "Zwiegespräch mit Jonny," *Der Deutsche Rundfunk* 13:9 (1935), 6.

29. Ibid. Ellipsis in original.

30. Ibid.

31. Merziger, "Humour in the *Volksgemeinschaft*: The Disappearance of Destructive Satire in National Socialist Germany," 141.

32. Ibid.

33. W. G., "'Jonny spült ab,' Der Schwabensender," *Der Deutsche Rundfunk* 13:11 (1935): 67.

34. Ibid.

35. Wolfgang von Bartels, "Rundfunk-Kritik," *Zeitschrift für Musik* 102 (April 1935), 459.

36. Kurt Herbst, "Die Grenzen zwischen Kitsch und Parodie in der Musik," *Die Musik* 27 (April 1935), 505.

37. Will Reichartz, quoted in Merziger, "Humour in the *Volksgemeinschaft*: The Disappearance of Destructive Satire in National Socialist Germany," 141.

38. Ibid.

39. This claim is based upon known discographical records as well as the listings in the volumes of *Hofmeisters Musikalisch-literarischer Monatsbericht* from 1935 to 1941.

40. On this exhibition, see above all the two slightly different editions of *Entartete Musik: Dokumentation zur Düsseldorfer Ausstellung von 1938*, eds. Albrecht Dümling and Peter Girth (Düsseldorf: DKV, 1988 and 1993).

41. For example, Alan Lareau, "Jonny's Jazz: From Kabarett to Krenek," *Jazz and the Germans: Essays on the Influence of "Hot" American Idioms on 20th-Century German Music*, ed. Michael Budds (Hillsdale, NY: Pendragon Press, 2002), 23.

42. Lutz Koepnick, *The Dark Mirror: German Cinema between Hitler and Hollywood* (Berkeley and Los Angeles: University of California Press, 2002), 129.

43. Hans Albers, "Good Bye, Jonny!" (Odeon O-4650).

44. A more clearly jazzy example is Franz Thon's recording featuring vocalist Rudi Schuricke (Franz Thon mit seinen Tanzrhythmikern, "Good-Bye Jonny" [Imperial 17244]).

45. For cases of Nazi persecution and intimidation of jazz musicians as well as jazz musicians' often successful attempts at evasion, see Kater, *Different Drummers*, 38–56.

46. Carter, *Dietrich's Ghosts*, 214. Carter's reading here is based on Sabine Hake's discussion of the Douglas Sirk film *Schlußakkord* (1937) in her *Popular Cinema of the Third Reich* (Austin: University of Texas Press, 2001), 107–27.

47. The two instrumental versions are both by bandleader Will Glahé (Electrola E.G. 6722 and Columbia DW 4823). Recordings with vocals include Peter Kreuder, vocals by Kurt Mühlhardt (Telefunken A 2855); Egon Wolff with unnamed vocalist (Odeon O-31 483a); Otto Stenzel, vocals by Paul Erdtmann (Gloria GO 41 293 a); Franz Thon mit seinen Tanz-Rhythmikern, vocals by Rudi Schuricke (Imperial 17244);

Iska Geri und die Neun Casaleons (Imperial 19119); Jan Behrens featuring vocals by the Heyn Quartett (Polydor and Grammophon 11074A).

48. Ernst Krenek, *Jonny spielt auf. Oper in 2 Teilen. Klavierauszug* (Vienna: Universal Edition, 1954), 2. Alfred Baresel's jazz handbook lists the "Swanee whistle" as a secondary percussion instrument of a typical jazz formation (*Das Jazzbuch* [Berlin: Zimmermann, 1925], 34).

49. Geri, "Good bye, Jonny!"

50. Iska Geri, "Känguruh" (Deutsche Grammophon Gr 47 532).

51. Peter Kreuder cites the identical section from "Old Folks at Home" in his "Piano-Medley aus dem Tonfilm Wasser für Canitoga" (Telefunken A 2854).

52. The singer Lottie Gee performed it as the fourth song in the program ("Program of Chocolate Kiddies Revue," Institut für Theaterwissenschaft der Freien Universität Berlin, ca. May 1925).

53. On Krenek's use of this motif in *Jonny spielt auf* as well as the possible connection to the *Chocolate Kiddies*, see Jonathan Wipplinger, "Performing Race in Ernst Krenek's *Jonny spielt auf*," *Blackness and Opera*, eds. Naomi André, Karen M. Bryan, and Eric Saylor (Urbana: University of Illinois Press, 2012), 243–45; Konrad Nowakowski, "Krenek, Baker—und Briggs? Der Aufstand gegen die 'Vernegerung Wiens' Anfang 1928," *Anklaenge 2011/2012*, Special Issue: Jazz Unlimited: *Beiträge zur Jazz-Rezeption in Österreich* (Vienna: Mille Tre Verlag, 2012), 196–97.

54. Marita Gründgens does parody "Good Bye, Jonny!" and Albers' performance of it in her "Filmrückblick 1940" ("Film Review 1940") (Electrola 7068), in a sense closing the Nazi-era Jonny cycle that had begun with her.

55. "Good bye, Jonny!" is included as "Leb' wohl, Peter!" in the collection Peter Kreuder, *Melodien: 20 der schönsten Tanz- und Lied-Kompositionen für Gesang und Klavier* (Leipzig: Sikorski, ca. 1940), 34–35. Though issued without a date of publication, the collection includes "Die drei Codonas" from the 1940 film of the same name. See further Axel Jockwer, *Unterhaltungsmusik im Dritten Reich* (University of Constance, PhD diss., 2005), 246–47; Kellersmann, *Jazz in Deutschland von 1933–1945*, 46–47.

Index

807th Pioneer Infantry Band, 53

Adorno, Theodor W., 17, 146, 226, 264n81, 294nn3–4, 294n8, 295n16, 299n77; "Abschied vom Jazz" ("Farewell to Jazz"), 197–98, 220–25, 298n61; aesthetic theory, 16, 68, 70; animals, 208–9; critique of Sekles, 148, 162; *Der Schatz des Indianer Joe* (*The Treasure of Indian Joe*), 19–20, 199, 200–203, 205, 206, 207, 208, 209, 210, 212, 216, 217, 219–20, 224, 225, 295n25; *The Dialectic of Enlightenment*, 196, 206, 211; *Jazzklasse* debate, 162, 294n7; "Music in the Background," 70–71, 72; "On the Social Situation of Music," 72; rejection of jazz, 19, 196, 197–98, 284n66; Scottsboro Boys, 213–17, 239; shock, 73–74, 79; Twain as source material, 204–20, 239, 295n20, 295n26, 297n59; "Über Jazz" ("On Jazz"), 159, 197; "Zeitlose Mode: Zum Jazz" ("Perennial Fashion–Jazz")," 197

Aeolian Hall, 87, 93, 95

Alabam Fantasies, 58, 59, 60. See also *Chocolate Kiddies*

Albers, Hans, 233, 235–37, 278n57

Alhambra, 52, 126

Ammons, Albert, 2

Ansermet, Ernest, 27

Antheil, George, 43, 142; *Transatlantic*, 200

Apollo-Theater, 34, 37, 124, 252n107

Armstrong, Louis, 11, 12, 85, 164, 165, 201, 220, 244n41

Attali, Jacques, 79, 143–44

Baker, Josephine, 16, 45, 51, 81, 82, 103, 114, 124, 125, 126, 128, 131, 135, 138, 180, 199, 271n72, 273n22, 278n57; *Bitte einsteigen!* (*All Aboard!*), 130; *Memoiren*, 274n22; *Shuffle Along*, 170

Balieff, Nikita, 57

Balz, Bruno, 230, 235

Barbusse, Henri, 177

Baresel, Alfred, 18, 106, 141, 155, 156–57, 272n77280, 282n42, 283n46, 302n48

Barka, Myriam, 34

Barthelme, George, 25–26, 39, 111, 246nn16–17

Bates, Ruby, 213, 216–17, 219

Baudelaire, Charles, 70, 73

Baum, Vicki, 98, 127

Bayton, Ruth, 126, 277n47

Beasley, Shakey (Clarence), 59, 263n66

Bechet, Sidney, 2, 27, 179; *Black People*, 199, 294n7

Beckmann, Hans-Fritz, 233, 299

Beethoven, Ludwig van, 90, 100, 142

Beethovensaal, 52

Bekker, Paul, 75–76

Béla, Dajos, 61, 88

Benga, François (Féral), 126, 277n46

Benjamin, Walter, 17, 68–69, 70, 71, 72, 74, 77, 79, 196, 206, 207, 264n81

Bennett, Gwendolyn, 189

Berg, Alban, 160, 202, 203, 224, 244n40, 283n61

Berlin, Irving, 237

Berliner Funkstunde, 80, 162, 198, 221–22, 227, 267n125, 298n64

Bie, Oscar, 45, 51, 52, 76, 78–79, 80, 97